Identities in Motion

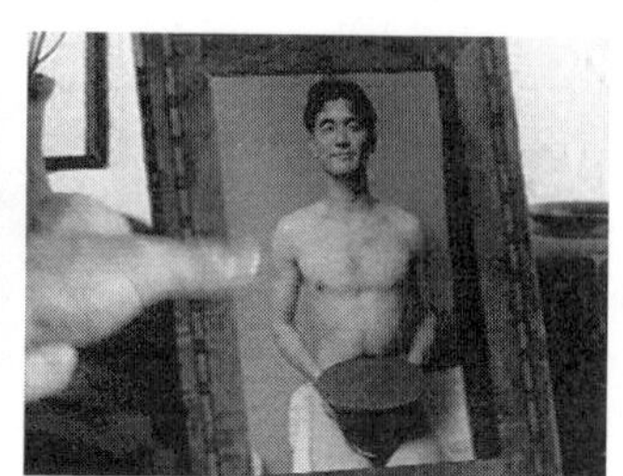

IDENTITIES IN MOTION

Asian American Film and Video

Peter X Feng

Duke University Press *Durham & London* 2002

Printed in the United States
of American on acid-free paper ♾
Designed by C. H. Westmoreland
Typeset in Bembo with Frutiger
display by Tseng Information
Systems, Inc.
Library of Congress Cataloging-
in-Publication Data appear on
the last printed page of this book.

for my family

CONTENTS

ACKNOWLEDGMENTS

For obvious reasons, my greatest debt is to all Asian American filmmakers and videomakers; I cannot list them all, but I can acknowledge those who lent or gave me material that I drew on for this book (some even read chapters): Marlon Fuentes, Richard Fung, Kayo Hatta, Michael Idemoto, Nancy Kelly, Felicia Lowe, Chris Chan Lee, Quentin Lee, Justin Lin, Ming-Yuen S. Ma, Eric Nakamura, Spencer Nakasako, Steven Okazaki, Fatimah Tobing Rony, Renee Tajima-Peña, Rea Tajiri, Janice Tanaka, Kenji Yamamoto, and Lise Yasui.

I would not be where I am today without several people; thanking them seems feeble. By the time I saw the light at the end of the dissertation tunnel, my advisor Lauren Rabinovitz was already thinking about this book. Marina Heung, Sumiko Higashi, and Esther Yau may think I didn't notice how they stepped in at crucial moments, gave me a push, and quietly slipped away. Gina Marchetti read chapters, edited and/or published some of them, and generally pushed me to put my work out there. Kent Ono at one point or another did all of the above, often at the drop of a hat, and fed me from time to time as well.

This project began at the University of Iowa, where I was supported by a Seashore Fellowship; in addition to Lauren Rabinovitz, I was mentored by Charles F. "Rick" Altman, Samuel Becker, Barbara Eckstein, Kathleen Newman, Bruce Gronbeck, John Peters, Eric Rothenbuhler, and many others. Carol Schrage and Chris Brenneman helped me get my first Asian American Film class off the ground. Dudley Andrew and the Institute for Cinema and Culture provided me with a grant to program films and videos; Becky Albitz and The University of Iowa Libraries matched it.

Phase two of this project was enabled by the University of Delaware; a General University Research grant got me on my way. Linda Russell helped me acquire videos and other research materials. Francis Poole of the UD Libraries tracked down videos for me. My research has been focused by conversations with my colleagues in Film Studies and Ethnic and Cultural Studies: Ed Guerrero, Kevin Kerrane, Tom Leitch, Alvina Quintana, Carol Robinson, and Harris Ross. I owe a tremendous debt to George Miller for encouraging me to accept an invitation to teach at UC-Irvine, despite the fact that I had only just arrived in Delaware. Jerry Beasley has been unfailingly supportive in the final stages of this project.

Rhona Berenstein arranged for me to come to Irvine as Chancellor's Visiting Assistant Professor of Film Studies; in California, my research took off and I merely held the reins. Vikki Duncan and Allison Spencer kept things running smoothly. Ellen Broidy and the UCI Libraries acquired still more videos for me. Anne Friedberg and Patricia Levin created space in the Film and Video Center for Asian American cinema.

Helen Lee and Wm. Satake Blauvelt provided my first introductions into the circle of independent filmmakers, a debt that can never be repaid.

My research was assisted by the staffs who maintained very diverse collections: Marjorie Lee and Raul Ebio of the UCLA Asian American Studies Center Research Room; Priscilla Wegars of the University of Idaho's Alfred W. Bowers Laboratory of Anthropology; Marva Felchlin of the Autry Museum of Western Heritage; and the people at the Pacific Film Archive, Video Data Bank, and Women Make Movies. Judi Nihei and Pamela Wu of Farallon Films dug into the files for me. I cannot imagine a world without Pam Matsuoka at National Asian American Telecommunications Association and Linda Mabalot and Abe Ferrer at Visual Communications.

Juliana Chang, Rachel Lee, and Kent Ono arranged for me to visit their campuses to present work in progress. Portions of the manuscript also benefited from feedback at the following annual conferences: Association for Asian American Studies (Ann Arbor 1994, Seattle 1997, Honolulu 1998), Console-ing Passions (Seattle 1995), Ohio University Film Conference (1994), and Society for Cinema Studies (New York 1995, San Diego 1998). Chapter 2 benefited from the input of the UC-Davis Asian Pacific American Cultural Politics Colloquium.

I have no doubt learned more than I realize (but less than I could) from my students at UI, UCI, and UD, particularly from graduate seminars that I convened at UCI and UD.

I am indebted to many people for discussing concepts, sharing works in progress, and proferring bibliographic help: Poonam Arora, Mariam Beevi, Monica Chiu, Timothy Corrigan, Sharon Fong, Karen Gaffney, Marti Lahtti, Sean Metzger, Melanie Nash, Kathleen Newman, Shari Roberts, Hank Sartin, and Michael Zryd.

Individual chapters have benefited tremendously from the careful readings (always more attentive than I would have thought possible) of my colleagues and friends: Martin Brückner, Mark Chiang, Lynda Goldstein, Gayatri Gopinath, Julia Lesage, Sandra Liu, Susan Matsen, Viet Nguyen,

Sarah Projansky, Jeanette Roan, Karen Shimakawa, A. Timothy Spaulding, and Julian Yates.

Chapters and portions of chapters were previously published in different form; my thanks to the editors and readers for feedback. Permission to republish material is gratefully acknowledged. "Lost in the Media Jungle: Tiana Thi Thanh Nga's Hollywood Mimicry," *Amerasia Journal* 23, no. 2 (1997), the Regents of the University of California. "Decentering the Middle Kingdom," *Jump Cut* 42 (1998). Chapter 6 and portions of Chapter 8 were drawn from "Being Chinese American, Becoming Asian American: *Chan Is Missing,*" *Cinema Journal* 35, no. 4 (1996), University of Texas Press.

To the colleagues and makers who mentor and inspire me, I see traces of your example on every page: Roddy Bogawa, Jachinson Chan, Wilson Chen, John Cheng, Soo-Young Chin, Chungmoo Choi, Curtis Choy, Elena Tajima Creef, Marisa De Los Santos, Fernando Delgado, Allan deSouza, Cindy Fuchs, Kip Fulbeck, Neil Gotanda, Darrell Hamamoto, Karin Higa, Stewart David Ikeda, Laura Hyun-Yi Kang, Daniel Kim, Kyung Hyun Kim, L. S. Kim, Dorinne Kondo, Josephine Lee, Walter Lew, Jupong Lin, John Liu, Lisa Lowe, Aaron Han-Joon Magnan-Park, Yong Soon Min, Ken Narasaki, Gary Okihiro, John Streamas, Radha Subramanyam, Kimi Takesue, David Teague, Tran T. Kim-trang, John Kuo Wei Tchen, Daniel Tirtawinata, Markha Valenta, Leti Volpp, and Paul Yi.

Thanks for community to Asian American Studies East of California, the Asian/Pacific/American Caucus of the Society for Cinema Studies, and to AAGPSO for showing the way to go.

Ken Wissoker and the staff at Duke University Press have been instrumental, as one would expect, and wonderful, as one would hope.

For friendship and support, I thank Nancy, Becky, and Jay.

This book is dedicated to Mom and Dad, and also to the third generation of Fengs and Wongs.

Introduction

Locating Asian American Cinema in Discontinuity

But then to shape one's work and so become a creative artist implies the need to distance oneself from one's subject, and this is a wanton betrayal of one's real feelings.

In short, art is both necessary and inadequate for a true rendering of life. —D. C. Muecke, *Irony and the Ironic*

Unable to penetrate the wall of amnesia, I constructed images from the elements of my craft—actors, spaces, and light—and projected them onto a wall, *the* wall, to hint at what it obscured. And slowly the beam of light burned peepholes through that wall, revealing some of what lurked behind it, although I sometimes suspect that the secrets were merely the motivation, while the films, themselves, the real thing revealed. —Michelle Citron, *Home Movies and Other Necessary Fictions*

As markers of the discontinuous representation of the past, movies are analogous to the processes of memory, papering over gaps in history and producing radical disjunctures in our sense of the past.[1] Movies are always inadequate renderings of identity, renderings whose artificiality may be revealed if we turn our attention to the process of projection, which provides a vantage point (akin to Citron's peepholes) from which we can illuminate identity. By employing the cinematic apparatus to conduct this investigation, Asian American filmmakers and videomakers attempt to seize control of a discourse that historically has projected stereotypical representations of Asian Americans, reminding us that the wall of representation that obscures Asian American identity is constructed not just by filmmakers but by the cinematic apparatus itself. Asian American filmmakers must contend not just with previous representations (specific movies) but with the cultural apparatus of cinema, the industry that produces and distributes movies and the audiences that consume them—in short, the social formations that channel cinematic texts. This book traces the ways that Asian American filmmakers and videomakers frame and are framed by history. Asian American makers[2] construct Asian American cinematic identity by locating their subjectivities in relation to dominant cinematic discourses, signifying on cinematic conventions by repeating them ironically or "splitting" them. The central theme of this volume is that cinema has defined what it means to be American, including the conditions that Asian Americans must meet to be considered American. Cinema is thus a technology not of reality but of fantasy: rather than depict the way things are, it shows us the way things could be. The first three chapters, which together I have labeled "Myths of Origin," examine movies about three crucial moments that defined the American nation and the roles that Asian Americans would play in it: the settlement of the American West, the incorporation of the Philippines into the U.S. empire, and the United States' entry into World War II. The second section, "Travelogues," examines movies made by Asian American filmmakers who visit their families in China and Vietnam. The last part, "Performing Transformation," examines how attempts to redefine Asian American subjectivity are at times rendered incomprehensible due to the shared investment by Asian American makers and audiences in the categories to which we have grown accustomed. In a brief afterword, I consider how a series of recent movies about Asian American adoptees alternately challenge and confirm essentialist conceptions of subjectivity.

The title of this volume, *Identities in Motion,* is inspired by Michele Wallace's observation that the process of identification is "constantly in motion" (1993, 265). Describing an identificatory process "in motion" is intuitive: What does it mean to describe "identities" themselves in motion? If identity is the endpoint of a subjectivity's coming into consciousness, are not identities in motion identities that have not fully formed? If there is no such thing as fixed identity, then isn't the formulation identities in motion redundant? This paradoxical phrase is meant to highlight the complex relationship of identity to the cinematic apparatus. The term identities in motion is structured by the absence of an anticipated word ("pictures"); but the formulation "identities in motion pictures" attributes the motion to the medium, to cinema, and not to the identities themselves. As it is my contention that identities are formed in part *by* cinema, I emphasize that I do not see identities as already constituted categories that are depicted, reproduced, or represented in motion pictures. If cinema is understood as simply depicting already constituted identities, then, ironically, cinema *arrests the motion* of identity.

Movies do not merely reflect social formations, nor is identity produced by movies (and injected into society). Where, then, are the identities in motion? Of course, identities are not located in movies themselves, but in the cinematic apparatus—which is to say, identities are ultimately mobilized within the spectator. It is after all the human mind that receives twenty-four still images per second (thirty in the case of video) and perceives motion where there is none. Cognitive film theorist Joseph Anderson has described films as programs that run on computers (the viewer's perceptual systems) "whose operating systems were designed for another purpose" (1996, 12). Just as the human mind animates still images, so does the spectator receive cinematic discourse on identity and put it into motion. If the discourse seems to reside in movies themselves and not in the spectator, that is because cinema is not a neutral medium but a system that implicates maker and audience in a network of power. Craig Owens, refering to Michel Foucault and Louis Marin, affirms, "Both work to expose the ways in which domination and subjugation are *inscribed within* the representational systems of the West. Representation, then, is not—nor can it be—neutral; it is an act—indeed, the founding act—of power and culture" (1992, 91). Cinema is an expression of culture and, as such, an expression of power, and although cinema is powerless without an audience, the audience attributes the power not to itself but to the cinema: the cultural apparatus.

The unspoken phrase "identities in motion pictures" also evokes the identity of movies themselves. In philosophy, the term identity refers to the perceived correspondence of concepts, as when Hegel proposes an identity of truth with the totality of reality. Motion pictures are often identified with history, which is to say, movies are often perceived as historical representations. But because there is no identity between movies and reality—that is, movies only refer to reality, they do not correspond to it—it follows that there is no identity between movies and history. That said, cinema is like history in that it is a discontinuous representation of reality, history being a discontinuous representation of the past. Just as the material of film is itself a narrative of discontinuity (still photos animated to create the illusion of a continuous flow of time), so is history a narrative whose very existence reveals that our connection to the past is an illusion. If we were truly connected to the past we would have no need for historical narratives; history, like all stories, is repeated because its truths are not self-evident.[3]

The continual repetition of history by cinema reveals anxiety about historical truth; that is, history must continually be repeated so as to persuade us of the legitimacy of the status quo, but the continued repetition suggests that history is actually a construction that can be contested.[4] If history were not repeated, if our connection to the past were self-evident, then identity would be fixed; history's motion implies identities in motion. Indeed, it is precisely history's movement, its repetition, that allows Asian American makers to propose alternative explanations of our present, alternative connections to the past: Asian American makers remobilize historical texts. Homi Bhabha has argued that the maintenance of rule requires the repetition of colonial discourse: repetition permits colonial discourse to be separated from its context in the maintenance of power, allowing its redeployment in the service of resistance. Bhabha calls this phenomenon "splitting,"[5] providing a metaphor for the reception of traditional discourses and the production of resistance to those discourses, a metaphor that describes the framework for Asian American cinema as a whole.

Because splitting turns on the redeployment of texts, Asian American movies are engaged in a process of citation that suggests that Asian American cinema is more akin to literary criticism than to literature, more metafiction than fiction. Asian American cinematic identity emerges from the citation of cinematic texts in Asian American movies. Identities are not to be found "in motion pictures"; rather, identities move *away from* cited movies: identities are put "in motion" by movies. Identity emerges from the friction between cited cinematic texts and the Asian American movies that incorporate them, which is to say that identity is produced by the friction between movies that arrest identity (essentialism) and Asian American movies that construct identity. Like José Esteban Muñoz, I understand identity to emerge from the friction between essentialist and constructivist perspectives of subjectivity at "precisely the moment of negotiation when hybrid, racially predicated, and deviantly gendered identities arrive at representation" (1999, 6). Muñoz employs the term "identities-in-difference"

(6) to signal his focus on identities that neither conform to dominant ideology nor resist it, but rather "[work] on and against dominant ideology" (11).[6] This friction provides the evidence that identities are indeed in motion.

This study does not foreground "deviantly gendered identities," as Muñoz's *Disidentifications* does; nonetheless, discourses of race and gender are mutually implicated throughout this volume. It might also be argued that all Asian American gendered identities are deviant, following David Eng's "Out Here and Over There": "Legal and cultural discourses on 'deviant' sexuality affect not merely those contemporary Asian American subjects who readily self-identify as gay or lesbian (a strict form of identity politics); rather, queerness comes to describe, affect, and encompass a much larger Asian American constituency—whatever their sexual identities or practices—whose historical disavowed status as U.S. citizen-subjects under punitive immigration and exclusion laws renders them 'queer' as such" (1997, 40–41). Asian American gendered identities that "[work] on and against dominant ideology" are deviant in this sense, and the friction between "queer" and Eng's " 'queer' as such" accords with the friction between essentialist and constructivist notions of identity from which Asian American cinematic identity emerges.

If Asian American cinematic identity neither conforms to nor merely resists dominant ideology, that emergence follows the pattern set by the term Asian American itself, which yokes together groups of diverse ethnic, cultural, and national origins.[7] Asian American identity always exists in tension with ethnic identities such as Korean American and Vietnamese American; Asian American identity is instrumental and contingent even when these ethnic identities are conceived of as primordial and "timeless" (essential). Pan-ethnic Asian American identification results from a discursive history that aligns interpretations of ethnic experiences, such that Asian Americans attempt to identify across the discontinuity of ethnic differences.[8] In other words, Asian American identity exists due to a particular interpretation of historical discontinuity, an interpretation that is itself subject to revision. It is only with this contingency in mind that I can use a potentially monolithic term like Asian American identity in the singular, a formulation that I contend nonetheless is more appropriate than Asian American identities in the plural, which reduces Asian American to an umbrella grouping diverse ethnic identities. In other words, Asian American identity is meant to express the same inner contradictions that the term

Asian American does.[9] Those contradictions must be continually interrogated, or else Asian American elides its discontinuity. Susan Koshy notes, "There is no literal referent for the rubric 'Asian American,' and, as such, the name is marked by the limits of its signifying power. It then becomes our responsibility to articulate the inner contradictions of the term and to enunciate its representational inconsistencies and dilemmas" (1996, 342).

One representational dilemma of the term Asian American is its interchangeability with the terms Asian/Pacific Islander and Asian (North) American, terms that attempt to include (but often elide) the Asian diaspora in the Pacific, Pacific Islanders, and the Asian diaspora in Canada. In some cases, inclusion may be merely rhetorical; in other cases, inclusion may be assumed at the cost of specificity (as when Canadian author Joy Kogawa is discussed as an Asian American author). These problematics of inclusion and elision reveal traces of imperialism: the United States' military interests in the Pacific and Canada as the "weak neighbor" whose unguarded border allows the United States to focus its attention elsewhere on the globe. Diverse histories of colonization and migration have produced different mixes of ethnic and national origin on both sides of the border. The legacy of British colonialism accounts in part for the significant numbers of Indians in Canada, as well as immigrants from the Caribbean. In this book, I have justified inclusion of Canadian makers in the context of discussions of the circulation of bodies and capital in the Chinese and Indian diasporas, such as Chapter 4's discussion of Trinidad-born Canadian videomaker Richard Fung's journey to China in *The Way to My Father's Village,* and Chapter 7's analysis of the transnational character of Canadian filmmaker Deepa Mehta's *Fire,* set in India. In these cases, the representational dilemma posed by the relation between Asian American and Asian Canadian cinematic production returns our attention to identities in motion, the process by which Asian bodies circulate between East and West, as well as the attendant negotiation of Americanness.

The study of Asian American cinema requires a methodology that can deal with identities in motion, that can explore the multiple gaps that constitute Asian American cinematic identity. These gaps include the gaps of history (the absence of narratives that would connect Asian Americans to the United States), gaps in representation (the anxious repetition that permits splitting results from an awareness that dominant discourse does not correspond with reality), gaps between essentialist and constructivist identity formations, and finally, gaps between the fields of Asian American studies and film studies. Asian American studies has historically been concerned with articulating the context from which Asian American experiences can be interpreted; such work redresses the exclusion of Asian Americans from mainstream discourses without offering a theory of representation. In the field of film studies, culture was initially understood in terms of national cinema paradigms, establishing a discursive terrain in which minority film production is understood as cultural nationalism (whereas Asian American studies has historicized cultural nationalism as an aspect of racial formation). This book therefore develops a theory of representation for Asian American studies (work initiated by Lisa Lowe and David Palumbo-Liu, among others) and extends a racial formation approach to film studies (following Manthia Diawara, Rosa Linda Fregoso, Ed Guerrero, Hamid Naficy, Chon Noriega, and others).

Asian American cinema's ambivalence toward representation is expressed though significations on cinematic tradition.[10] Just as Asian American cinematic identity exists in tension with discourses of Americanness, so do Asian American makers define their own subjectivity in relation to cinema. Attracted and repelled by the power it offers, they do not fully identify with cinema as a representational system. Muñoz terms this ambivalent relation "disidentification," describing identifications that work on and against dominant ideology (as opposed to "counteridentification," which reproduces the logic of the dominant ideology). The Asian American cinematic identities that interest me are defined by a difference from cinematic tradition that is not merely oppositional. Instead, Asian American makers engage in an ambivalent critique of cinematic convention (as one would expect from makers who construct movies that criticize cinema). This ambivalent critique contributes to a disidentification with Americanness: more specifically, a disidentification with narratives of bourgeois assimilation. Asian American cinema interrogates the mutual implication of assimilation narratives and conventional cinematic forms.

The ambivalence of Asian American cinema's critique of bourgeois American identity and conventional cinematic storytelling can be charted by measuring the extent to which any given movie is implicated in the motion picture industry's standardized modes of production. Even an independently funded movie must be aware of the requirements of distributors and exhibitors for products that conform to established parameters, such as the thirty-minute and sixty-minute blocks that govern broadcast television. The story of a movie's production thus traces the complex process of cinematic disidentification; throughout this book, I preface my analyses with detailed production histories outlining the material constraints on Asian American media production.[11] In a time when television specials on "the making of" Hollywood's latest blockbuster and movie stars' salaries are leaked to promote movies and careers, it is important to remember the limited resources available to independent makers. Independent film and video is funded by cobbling together grants, running up balances on credit cards, and taking advantage of actors and technicians willing to work for little or no pay. Throughout this book, production histories attest to the tremendous effort it takes to conceive, produce, and distribute these cinematic texts. In a sense, these accounts serve as a how-to for aspiring independent makers, emphasizing the "motion" involved in conveying cinematic identity.

To illustrate the complicated processes of cinematic disidentification as it is implicated in a critique of bourgeois Americanization, I want to turn to the video *a.k.a. Don Bonus,* a diary of a year in the life of a Cambodian American teenager. Simply describing *a.k.a. Don Bonus* as a diary implies modes of address and narrative structure that attend the first-person genre, yet the title of the video evokes the multiple subjectivities involved in collaborative authorship. The video's split subjectivity produces an ironic discourse that calls systems of representation into question, thereby critiquing the documentary and diary formats as well as the U.S. government's characterization of Cambodian immigrants.

Irony and *a.k.a. Don Bonus*

In the summer of 1991, Spencer Nakasako taught an eight-week course in San Francisco's Tenderloin at the Vietnamese Youth Development Center. Using camcorders, the kids developed their own projects, ranging from short narrative movies to documentaries (J. White, 1995).[12] Meanwhile, Nakasako and Wayne Wang were discussing the possibility of getting people to document their personal lives in "video diaries," perhaps to produce a series of short pieces for PBS. In 1992, Nakasako secured $25,000 in seed money from National Asian American Telecommunications Association (NAATA) and tapped one of his former students, Sokly Ny, to document his senior year. Ny and Nakasako would meet once or twice a week for dinner, screen rushes, and discuss the upcoming week. At the end of his senior year, the two trimmed the approximately eighty hours of footage to forty hours; during the summer they edited the footage into fourteen one-hour segments, working on outmoded (and therefore available) linear editing equipment at a video production house owned by a friend of Nakasako's. Over the next year, working with three different editors in succession, Ny and Nakasako edited the footage down to a sixty-minute movie (Nakasako, telephone interview, 23 Nov. 1997). The video made the circuit of Asian American film festivals and community events, eventually airing on PBS as part of their *P.O.V.* series in 1996; the program won an Emmy for Cultural and International Programming.[13]

a.k.a. Don Bonus relates the events of Sokly Ny's senior year, highlighted by the family's relocation from Sunnydale to the Tenderloin to the Sunset District, Ny's struggle to pass a proficiency examination (he fails once and apparently gets away with cheating the second time), and his brother Touch's arrest for attempted murder. These three plotlines are interwoven throughout the film, most notably in the simultaneous scheduling of Touch's sentencing hearing and Ny's graduation (a coincidence that prevents Ny's family from attending his graduation). The family's continual relocation (due to the short-sighted and slow-moving Housing Authority) is compared directly with the U.S. government's foreign policy in Southeast Asia, so that the continual uprooting of the family in the United States is equated with the turmoil that brought them to the United States in the first place.[14] These relocations are explicitly tied to Touch's story when he returns to the family on the occasion of their arrival in the Tenderloin.

The video's structure cycles among these three plotlines; while the scenes are arranged chronologically, a series of fades-to-black punctuate the video and divide it into eight segments. The first two segments set the stage: a brief segment introduces us to Ny's school (where even his teachers call him "Bonus") and deftly establishes his precarious academic standing (the entire segment lasting less than two minutes), followed by a lengthier "afterschool" segment depicting Ny's homelife and the crew he hangs with. This second segment centers on an act of vandalism, a theme picked up in the third segment, which details the aftermath of a break-in. In the next segment, the family moves to the Tenderloin, Touch returns, and they are invited to spend Thanksgiving with their older brother Chandara's in-laws; this and the following segment, precisely in the middle of the video's development, depict Ny's desire to reestablish the extended family. Ny sees Chandara twice, once at Thanksgiving and once at Lunar New Year, and both times he expresses his longing for his older brother, who seems to have attained a somewhat rarefied middle-class standing. The sixth segment details Touch's arrest, and in the seventh segment Ny prods his family to talk about the meaning of recent events; after much evasion, one relative is finally irritated enough by Ny's insistent questioning that he spins a rap linking Nixon, the bombing of Southeast Asia, and the poverty from which juvenile delinquency emerges. "This is reality," he asserts, where problems can't be solved in two hours, alluding to the running time of a feature film, all but explicitly stating that movies oversimplify complex problems, and implicitly putting down Ny's attempt to capture a succinct explanation of their situation on tape. As the final segment begins, the family arrives in their new home in the Sunset District and Ny explains the proficiency test that he must pass to graduate. Touch is sentenced to reform school, and Ny's voice-over states that his family has come together in the wake of Touch's arrest. At a family picnic sometime later, Ny expresses his contentment; as the image fades out, his voice-over states, "The only thing missing is Touch. If he could be with us, everything would be fine."

a.k.a. Don Bonus is first and foremost an indictment of the American Dream. The failure of social service programs is continually linked to the government's foreign policy in Southeast Asia, explicitly through references to Nixon and U.S. bombs, implicitly through a narrative structure that connects the continual relocation of Ny's family with efforts to protect, rehabilitate, and reconstitute the family. This structure is initiated when Ny tells how his father sacrificed himself to the Khmer Rouge to allow his family to escape, and is developed when Ny almost nonchalantly describes the escape itself and how his older brother temporarily abandoned him in the jungle when he became too heavy to carry.[15] This narrative of perpetual abandonment and reunion with the family recurs throughout the video and is also directly tied to their living arrangements in the United States. Early in the video, Ny reveals that he lives in Sunnydale because his mother has rented a separate apartment so that her children will not have to live with their stepfather, whom they detest. Throughout the first half of the video, Ny complains that his mother is never at home; when she visits Cambodia for several weeks, he trashes the apartment in frustration and loneliness. He also tells us that Touch does not live in Sunnydale because he is afraid of the neighborhood; it is intimated that he became involved with a gang during this period, perhaps leading indirectly or directly to his arrest for attempted murder, the event Ny credits with reconstituting the family (Touch's reform school working simultaneously to re-form the family). The family is temporarily and problematically unified in the middle of the film at the Tenderloin apartment: Touch returns, Mom is back from Cambodia, and the family celebrates an American and a Cambodian holiday with Chandara. Ny bursts into tears in Chandara's presence because he knows it is only temporary, and he leaves the party to sit in the car, reenacting his childhood abandonment and reunion with Chandara, who eventually returns and tells Ny to come inside and eat. The scene immediately fades out and the next segment begins with Touch already detained at the Juvenile Center. Through a process of narration and editing, Ny links the family's forced migration from Asia with the dissolution of family bonds, indicting the government's foreign and domestic policies.

a.k.a. Don Bonus reveals an exceptionally dense structure within a transparent chronological organization. In this manner, it seems simultaneously sophisticated and straightforward. If the audience assigns too much faith to the "video diary" as an organizational conceit—as a concept guiding the production of the video—they will fail to consider how the video is actually a sophisticated documentary structured *as if* it were a diary. The controlled structure veiled under the conceit of externally imposed organizational logic has its formal corollary at the level of technique: the video's departures from documentary convention are not merely creative solutions to limited resources, but sly significations on cinematic convention. Home video, cinema verité, and talking heads documentary are just a few of the cinematic traditions *a.k.a. Don Bonus* invokes: most of Ny's high school friends interact with the camera operator, as in home video; Ny narrates events as they happen in front of the camera, combining the role of field reporter with the function of cameraman; and he also sets up his camera for talking heads sequences, shooting through a bathroom mirror or using a window sill as a tripod.

I would argue that the video's various talking heads sequences ironically enact two criticisms frequently leveled at interview-based documentaries: that these sequences stand in for action that could not be captured on camera, and that they rely on mise-en-scène to establish the authority of the expert providing the testimony. When Ny relaxes in the bathtub waiting for his mother to come home so they can talk, the existential angst that attends waiting is conveyed by the framing: Ny's talking head is isolated in the corner of the frame, and the wide expanse of blank bathroom tile conveys the

a.k.a. Don Bonus. "Talking head" in domestic space.

"Talking head" in the library. Note Don's eyes, which are neither fixed on the camera nor on an off-screen interviewer.

quotidian reality of apartment living. In another sequence, Ny repairs to what appears to be the school library, thereby parodying the bookshelves commonly used as a backdrop to establish the speaker's erudition.

In this sequence, Ny describes the rage that causes him to trash the apartment where he lives, an inarticulate expression of his frustration. And yet, he describes this confused act in a highly articulate, sensitive fashion. The way we interpret this irony depends greatly on how we attribute authorship to the video. D. C. Muecke draws a distinction between *observable irony,* when an observer chances upon a contrast that exists before him or her and labels it ironic (1982, 43), and *instrumental irony,* wherein an ironist fashions an irony. In the case of documentary, if we conceive of the documentarian as a mere observer who does not interact with the profilmic (the space before the camera that can potentially be photographed) but simply records it, later preserving or even creating a contrast through the principle of juxtaposition, then the documentarian is trafficking in observable irony.

But to the extent that a documentarian arranges and interacts with the profilmic, arranging the scene before photographing it, the documentarian is engaging in instrumental irony. This distinction is important because it determines whether we understand Ny to be the naïve espouser of an existing (observable) irony (what philosophers call an *alazon*), or a dissembler who feigns unawareness of the ironic contrast that he or she is articulating (called an *eiron*), like the fool in *King Lear* (see Muecke, 1982, 35–37). We can read Ny as the sophisticated agent of his own representation, or as the unwitting naïf who illuminates an ethnographic study.[16]

Both autoethnography and autobiography are structured by a division of the self-as-subject from the self-as-observer, Don Bonus the "character" versus Sokly Ny the videomaker.[17] This divide is akin to (but not precisely the same as) the makers' multiple roles as camera operator and editor, the one recording and the other shaping. The divided authoring subject is especially complex in *a.k.a. Don Bonus,* because the film was coedited by Spencer Nakasako and Sokly Ny, shot by Ny, and stars Ny. The video thus turns on disjunctions between Nakasako as filmmaker and Ny as subject, Nakasako as editor and Ny as director, and Ny as narrator and Ny as protagonist. Our interpretations of the video are shaped by the way its authors are framed, by the manner in which we interpret the collaborative process. When *a.k.a. Don Bonus* aired on PBS, it was preceded by a brief interview with Nakasako followed by another interview with Ny; in the version distributed by NAATA, Ny's interview remains but Nakasako's interview has been excised. This troubling omission de-emphasizes Nakasako as a mediating collaborator, romanticizing Ny as gifted neophyte and drawing attention away from the divided authoring subject of the video.[18] In this manner, the video is shaped by the cinematic apparatus and its tendencies even as it attempts to expose cinema's functioning.

a.k.a. Don Bonus employs talking heads sequences to signify on documentary convention, employing cinema to critique cinematic discourse, "[using] representation against itself to destroy the binding or absolute status of any representation."[19] Homi Bhabha's theory of "splitting" provides a theoretical framework for understanding the ways that *a.k.a Don Bonus* is able to critique certain cinematic modes of representation while simultaneously recognizing that it is implicated in those modes.[20] The video's talking heads sequences engage in the practice of splitting, of doubling the signifier; but in that act of repetition, the video risks reinscribing the logic of cinematic convention, replicating its own marginality by reaffirming the normativity of the discursive patterns it critiques.[21] In investigating cinematic tradition, *a.k.a. Don Bonus* is inevitably interpreted via the categories and critical traditions associated with cinema history; in short, the video is framed by cinematic tradition that denies marginal makers the ability to speak to the culture at large, limiting them to illuminating underrepresented communities. In other words, Asian Americans are not filmmakers: we produce guerrilla video, autoethnography, and autobiographical essay.[22] Each of these labels inserts a movie into a different historical tradition: guerrilla video posits community-based activism; autoethnography suggests efforts to put cameras in the hands of representative minorities; and autobiographical essay evokes a history of video art and avant-garde filmmaking (artistic media that have traditionally accepted women, queers, and other cultural exiles, especially if their work is first and foremost about life on the margins). These different historical traditions are in a sense different notions of reality, or rather, different notions of the relationship of art to reality. Each cinematic tradition implies a different politics: the guerrilla videomaker seeks to change the world; the autoethnographer to explicate his or her world; and the autobiographer shares his or her perspective of the world. These distinctions are meant to be suggestive only—it is a fine line between sharing one's perspective of the world and seeking to change it.[23]

For this reason, I insist that *a.k.a. Don Bonus* is not merely intervening in the representation of Asian Americans, but signifying on cinematic discourses generally; the video does not simply depict the world but *interprets* the ways the world has been represented, thereby seeking to transform the world by transforming cinema. Whereas the conventions of talking heads documentaries are intended to establish the authority of the speaker and the objectivity of the maker, *a.k.a. Don Bonus*'s splitting of documentary discourse suggests that these conventions actually mark the maker's submission to the authority of cinema. The two-pronged strategy of rewriting cinematic history while simultaneously challenging cinema's legitimation of truth claims is akin to Judith Butler's description of (dis)identification as the "uneasy sense of standing under a sign to which one does and does not belong."[24] To identify as an Asian American maker is to stand under the sign of cinema, where Asian American makers belong insofar as they construct a discontinuous history of cinema that includes Asian American makers, and do not belong insofar as continuous cinematic histories exclude Asian Americans. Asian American makers are thus engaged in a project of signifying on cinematic convention, using cinema to critique cinema, using a mode of communication to convey messages that subvert that mode: "Nor do contemporary artists oppose their own representations to existing ones; they do not subscribe to the phallacy of the positive image. (To do so would be to oppose some 'true' representivity to a 'false' one.) Rather, these artists challenge the activity of representation itself which, by denying them speech, consciousness, the ability to represent themselves, stands indicted as the primary agent of their domination" (Owens, 1992, 262).

The critique of representation is an attack not on distorted images, for all cinematic images are distortions. It is not a matter of putting forth the "correct" view of reality, but of interrogating the relation between appearance and reality. That relation has been explored by theorists interested in irony, to which "opposition, contradiction, contrariety, incongruity or incompatibility" between appearance and reality is fundamental (Muecke, 1982, 35); irony is the phenomenon of saying one thing and meaning another. Marginal speakers, whose lives are shaped by contradictions between their lived reality and the ways that reality is perceived from the center, are well acquainted with irony. For example, Linda Hutcheon notes that Claudia Mitchell-Kernan's analysis of African American "signifyin'" illuminates our understanding of irony, insofar as signifyin' involves the encoding and decoding of implicit messages (1994, 31). Although not all marginalized people "signify," people on the margins are all characterized by modes of perception that account for the coexistence of multiple perspectives: "double consciousness" (Du Bois), "the spectre of comparisons" (Benedict Anderson, after José Rizal),[25] "intellectual Eurasianism" (Han Suyin), and the "closet"[26] are distinctly different ways of seeing that share this sense of doubled perception, and *a.k.a. Don Bonus* reveals a similarly ironic perspective when it signifies on cinematic convention.[27]

Cinema's appeal can be traced to the apparent referentiality of the cinematic medium (the verisimilitude of the cinematic illusion and the attribution of objectivity that follows thereafter), a referentiality that tends toward a unified (not a doubled) perception. Rather than deny the referential appeal of cinema, the movies discussed in these pages seek to illuminate that appeal, the heart of cinema's ability to deceive us. By contrast, literature is unable to deceive because a literary text cannot present itself as referent, only as account: in *Camera Lucida,* Roland Barthes says, "It is the misfortune (but also perhaps the voluptuous pleasure) of language not to be able to authenticate itself" (1981, 85). Writing is so evidently a representation of reality, a translation of reality into language, that it is clearly never truthful: writing cannot deceive me as to its authenticity—for that we need cinema.

The interrogation of deception implies a marshaling of mutually contradicting stories that contend with each other to produce meaning. The complex interplay of narratives in these movies requires a theoretical approach that accounts for the dynamic interplay among a variety of discourses, an interpretive methodology that enables us to account for the discursive recontextualization of narratives. In other words, we need to understand how narratives are deployed in these films/videos in such a way that they speak in multiple discursive contexts, how voices speak both for themselves and for the makers. When Asian American makers critique cinematic representation, they construct their identities with respect to surrounding alien discourses such as newsreel footage, government documents, Hollywood feature films, and so on. The various discourses are analogous to "the social diversity of speech types" that Bakhtin labels *heteroglossia* (1981, 263); one's own voice is defined in relation to these surrounding discourses.[28] Asian American cinema seeks to preserve its own distinctiveness while transforming the consensual cinematic language. Asian American cinematic texts speak in a language that validates Asian Americans (by promoting a sense of inclusion in a select group that figuratively speaks the same language), but seek also to redefine Bakhtin's "unitary" language so that Asian American voices can be better heard, working the borders of cinematic discourse.[29] Bakhtin's emphasis on language "on the borderline" points up the active process of self-constitution expressed by utterances in heteroglossic context: "All languages of heteroglossia, whatever the principle underlying them and making each unique, are specific points of view on the world" (291).

Into the Gap

All of the movies discussed in this book deal, in one way or another, with *gaps* in the cinematic representation of Asian Americans, with the discontinuity of history as represented by both dominant and marginal cinemas. These films and videos do not attempt to plug gaps in memory and history by reconstructing what is missing, for such a strategy denies the historical process that produced those gaps: these films and videos create imagery that fills the gap while constantly speaking its own inadequate referentiality. Similarly, by implicitly or explicitly thematizing their location in relation to mainstream cinema, these movies call attention to the forces that marginalize Asian American makers; by signifying on cinematic conventions, Asian American makers call attention to the ways those conventions participate in constructing a cinematic tradition that excludes Asian American voices.

Asian American identity is defined not by history, but by gaps in history: the absence of information bespeaks a historical trauma that defines Asian Americans. It is not just that these gaps correspond with founding moments in Asian American history, but that the investigation of these gaps returns us continually to those moments of crisis, renewing the traumas and thereby renewing (mis)identity. As multimedia artist Theresa Hak Kyung Cha famously wrote, "Our destination is fixed on the perpetual motion of search" (1995, 81). In the act of examining historical trauma, of theorizing why certain things are forgotten, these movies seek identity in the interplay between memory and history; in so doing, they further theorize the relation between family stories and the histories of ethnicity. For example, the movies made by Sansei women that I discuss in Chapter 3 attempt to understand the legacy of the Internment by examining the effects of the Internment on the makers' families, specifically on their parents. In so doing, the movies attempt to understand a "generation" of Japanese Americans, the word generation itself a metaphor that implies that "the people" (a historically constituted aggregate) are structured like a family. The stuff of these histories is not (merely) names, dates, and numbers, but stories, recipes, snapshots. This intimate ephemera informs not just Asian American history (as in the collective history of all Asian Americans) and the histories of Asian Americans (as in individual biographies of each and every Asian American) but Asian American histories, a constellation of different versions of the history of (an) ethnicity. Therefore, the history and identity, the very existence of Asian Americans is at stake. By this I do not mean to suggest that people of Asian descent will cease to exist, but that their existence *as* Asian Americans is threatened. In other words, the term Asian American is a discursive construction that implies a series of identifications that are not so much primordial (with ties to a mythic past of continuity) as instrumental (that is, political: dependent on a particular construction of the historical past)—a past predicated on *dis*continuity.[30]

By discontinuous representations of the past, I mean to describe the relationship of Asian Americans to a historical record that was not written with us in mind. Investigating the historical record with Asian Americans in mind calls attention to the ways ideology has shaped the telling of history, investigating the terms under which Asian Americans are included in the telling of history and the terms by which Asian Americans narrate their own history (itself marked by ideological contradictions and by the exclusions of certain identity formations). In short, the term Asian American is an inherently political term, not a cultural one. Yen Le Espiritu (1992) argues that people of Asian descent had to see themselves as Americans first—sharing the English language, abandoning the conflicts that had historically divided the nations of Asia—before they could come together as "Asian Americans": thus "Asian American" without a hyphen, rendering "Asian" into an adjective, rather than "Asian-American," rendering both Asian and American into nouns. The hyphen implies that Asia and America are discrete spaces that require bridging, obscuring the discursive construction of boundaries that defines Asian and American as different and mutually exclusive. Asia and America detach themselves from history, insisting through the hyphen that there was a "time" when "space" was clearly bound. Asian-hyphen-Americans are thus located outside of history, in a world where Asia and America are separable entities without discernible mutual influence. Asian Americans (no hyphen), on the other hand, situate ourselves in history by calling attention to the temporal and spatial migrations that brought us here as well as the discursive power of concepts such as "nation" to define who, where, and when we all are.[31]

By organizing this book around an investigation of the construction of America and Asian American identity in movies, I have undertaken to illuminate how Asian American cinematic identity is constituted through discontinuous representations of the past. As such, the chapters that follow are not arranged to narrate the historical growth *of* Asian American cinema, but rather to examine different relationships of Asian American film and video *to* history. I have sought to emphasize how each movie articulates its own discontinuous relation to the past, a project in opposition to the construction of a history of Asian American cinema, which would necessarily stress continuity. At the same time, Asian American cinema's investment in interrogating cinematic discourse reveals a profound awareness of diverse cinematic traditions ("tradition" signaling a discourse of "continuity"). By intervening in those traditions, Asian American cinema critiques the construction of a monolithic cinematic apparatus and a unified cinema audience; the articulation of diversity suggests many possible histories of Asian American cinema yet to be written.

Part 1, "Myths of Origin," examines the construction of Asian American ancestors by cinema, arguing that these films tell us more about contemporary Asian American politics than about the historical periods they purport to represent. Furthermore, each chapter deals with a different cinematic tradition: ethnographic film, the romance narrative, and home movies, respectively. Chapter 1 examines *Bontoc Eulogy* and *On Cannibalism* as interrogations of the role of the motion picture camera in early twentieth-century ethnography, when the nascent medium of cinema participated in discourses of scientific racism and U.S. imperialism. Chapter 2 looks at feature films, focusing on the first generation of women to settle the frontiers of the Northwest and Hawai'i: *Thousand Pieces of Gold* and *Picture Bride* are briefly contrasted with the contemporary green card comedy, *Living on Tokyo Time,* underlining shifts in sexual politics in the 1980s. Chapter 3 discusses three Sansei women makers and their essays on the legacy of the Internment for their families (*A Family Gathering, History and Memory, Who's Going to Pay for These Donuts, Anyway?*). The makers in this section examine cinema's role in distinguishing between Americans and foreigners ("others"), telling three different tales about encounters between the West and the East: the time when the West began to photograph the East, the time when Asians first contemplated becoming Americans, and the time when the United States segregated Asian Americans from the body politic.

Part 2, "Travelogues," features two chapters about Asian American makers documenting their visits to Asia. These movies grapple with the vocabulary of the travelogue, the cinematic equivalent of tourism, wherein the desire to see something new is balanced by the need to discover anew that which has been seen before by a previous visitor. The legacy of war and political upheaval colors expectations about what will be found, as do family stories relaying mythologies of the homeland. Chapter 4 deals with three visits to China (*China: Land of My Father, The Way to My Father's Village,* and *Made in China*); in Chapter 5, *From Hollywood to Hanoi* journeys to North and South Vietnam. The historical differences between the United States' relationships with China and Vietnam have produced different Asian American experiences, to say nothing of the disparity in the coverage by the U.S. media of the war in Vietnam and political developments in China. These chapters contest existing representations of Asia even while they admit that their subjectivities cannot be easily separated from those representations. Like Part 1, this section examines how our personal history is shaped by the political histories of the formation of nations, but if Part 1 emphasized journeys back in time (to key historical moments), Part 2 emphasizes journeys across space (to see what things look like now).

Part 3, "Performing Transformation," examines the articulation of liminality. In these chapters, the inadequacy of labels such as Chinaman, lesbian, and refugee is demonstrated through consideration of the complex ways identity is continually negotiated. Chapter 6 takes up *Chan Is Missing,* a breakthrough Asian American feature film that deconstructs the notion of unitary Chinese American identity. Chapter 7 describes two feature films that thematize the clash of contemporary queer politics with conservative family structures (*Fire* and *The Wedding Banquet*); the exploration of transgressive sexuality in the context of transnational film production reveals the investment of nationalist movements in heteronormativity. Chapter 8 focuses on issues of performance and literary adaptation in a feature-length experimental film and a Hollywood production; both *Surname Viet Given Name Nam* and *The Joy Luck Club* orchestrate a number of women's voices to speak to the adaptation of traditions to new cultural contexts. Each of these chapters describes how our external behavior is related to our inner subjectivity; that is, these movies explore the ways we *perform* who we are, always remembering that history compels us to perform in certain ways.

This book attempts to imitate the activity of the movies it discusses. In linking these movies together while emphasizing their uniqueness, I construct a discontinuous understanding of the relationship of individual movies. Citing and remobilizing cinematic texts, my own argument about Asian American identity is constructed in relation to surrounding discourses. I engage in a practice of "splitting" these movies, translating them into another medium and thereby resisting the discursive power of cinema (thereby extending the resistance that I argue is already expressed in Asian American movies). By imitating Asian American movies, I hope that a degree of their political efficacy will rub off on this book, a degree of the performative dimension that I argue makes cinema more effective than prose in articulating identity. After all, the aim of this book, inspired by Asian American cinema, is to put identities in motion.

I *Myths of Origin*

ETHNOGRAPHY, ROMANCE, HOME MOVIES

CHAPTER 1

The Camera as Microscope

Cinema and Ethnographic Discourse

> I once read that in a certain South American tribe, the medicine man would take his apprentices to a local cinema on their final leg of training. Movies, he tells them, are not unlike the visions the sick see just before they die. For me, movies are not unlike the visions the homesick see when their hearts are bearing the weight of the realization that they're homeless, exiled, or caught in a limbo between native and tourist.—Justin Chin, "The Endless Possibility of a Kiss in a Fevered Faraway Home"

> Not only, in Said's "Orientalist" sense, were we constructed as different and other within the categories of knowledge of the West by those regimes. They had the power to make us see and experience *ourselves* as "Other."—Stuart Hall, "Cultural Identity and Diaspora"

The Louisiana Purchase Exposition, held in St. Louis in 1904, celebrated U.S. economic power at the dawn of the twentieth century. As at most World's Fairs, the latest in technological innovations were displayed, and the history of U.S. westward expansion was commemorated. The fair was also a museum and laboratory for the study of anthropology, with many "primitive" peoples on display, including the Ainu of Japan and American Indians. By far the largest exhibit was the Philippine Reservation, forty-seven acres set off from the rest of the fairgrounds by a small stream; visitors crossed the Bridge of Spain to enter the compound. More than eleven hundred Filipinos representing a variety of ethnicities lived in dwellings they had built using materials imported from home. They performed their rituals for the fair's visitors, sometimes charging fairgoers for the privilege of using their cameras. It is reported that some visitors sold dogs to the Igorrotes, tribal Filipinos from the northern Cordillera mountains, who then killed, cooked, and feasted on the dogmeat.[1] Tribes who had never seen each other lived in close proximity;[2] their juxtaposition was intended in part to prove that more evolved Filipinos were worthy of the White Man's Burden—a contention supported by the loyal Philippine Scouts (veterans of the U.S. war in the Philippines) who guarded the reservation.[3]

Movies were some ten years old at the time of the World's Fair. Film exhibition had been boosted greatly by the Spanish-American War; the demand for images of the war was met with genuine news footage (or "actualities") as well as scenes staged for the camera ("reenactments").[4] One extremely popular film consisted of a Spanish flag flying in front of a painting of a castle; the flag was lowered and the Stars and Stripes hoisted in its place (the whole film lasting approximately forty-one seconds).[5] Cinema participated in creating popular support for U.S. imperialism, which was justified scientifically by the inferiority of America's "little brown brothers," itself documented on film by ethnographers. From its conception, cinema has been thoroughly implicated in discourses of science and U.S. imperialism; these various discourses intersected in the Philippines, and later in St. Louis.

One hundred years after the birth of cinema, how far have we come? *Bontoc Eulogy* (Marlon Fuentes, 1995) and *On Cannibalism* (Fatimah Tobing Rony, 1994) each interrogate cinema's role in shaping the "science" of racial difference. Fuentes's film tells the story of a contemporary Filipino American's search to find out what happened to his grandfather, a Bontoc Igorrote who disappeared after the World's Fair. Rony's video interrogates ethnographic research films—and Hollywood's *King Kong*—from the perspective of a second-generation Sumatran American. Both movies deal with people of color who were brought to the West—not as laborers in support of Western economies, but as "others" who helped define Western superiority through scientific discourses which themselves legitimated Western imperialism. By deconstructing cinema's role in Western ethnographic practices, both films turn the camera's gaze back on the West. More than that, both movies are about our cinematic forebears, that is the way the cinema's racial discourses have shaped the way we are seen and the way we see ourselves—indeed, the way cinema has *created* us, representationally speaking. It is appropriate, then, that an elusive ancestor occupies the center of both movies: the narrator's imagined grandfather Markod in *Bontoc Eulogy,* the Ompung of my Ompung (grandparent of my grandparent) invoked in *On Cannibalism.*

Both movies signify on ethnographic film conventions. All of the ethnographic footage quoted in *Bontoc Eulogy* is shot with a stationary camera, whose stability supposedly guaranteed the scientific objectivity of the Western camera operators documenting the primitive movements of the Filipinos. Fuentes's staged 16mm footage is likewise shot from a stationary camera, and its evident artifice is an implicit critique of the supposedly unstaged ethnographic film. For if *Bontoc Eulogy* is itself a re-creation inspired by the filmmaker's imagination, isn't ethnographic footage ultimately indicative of similar falsehoods? The ethnographer does not chance upon customs and rituals, but indeed compels them to be performed for his or her (typically his) camera. *On Cannibalism* features extreme close-ups of Rony's mouth as she narrates; this emphasis on the physicality of the production of speech recalls the precise documentation of movement by ethnographers like Félix-Louis Regnault.[6] The early commercial cinema was likewise fascinated with the motion picture's ability to focus attention on mundane physical actions such as sneezes. If early cinema audiences were fascinated by the way cinema made their everyday actions seem strange, Asian American filmmakers a century later are equally fascinated by the ways cinema transformed our everyday actions into ethnographic spectacle.

Bontoc Eulogy

Marlon Fuentes was born in Manila in 1954. A self-taught photographer, he studied behavioral science and anthropology at De La Salle University in Manila, graduating summa cum laude in 1974. His employer sent him to the Wharton School, where he received his MBA in 1977. In 1981 he enrolled in Mark Power's photography course at the Corcoran School of Art in Washington, D.C.; soon thereafter, he began the *Circle of Fear* series.[7] Fuentes may be best known for his *Face Fusion* series (1986–1989), which are assembled from photographs of himself and his then-wife (who is white).[8] According to curator Margo Machida, Fuentes uses photography as "a ritual to relive . . . memories," transforming himself into a shaman (1994, 105); Fuentes comments that his "photography was being generated by an increasingly narrative subtext," leading him naturally to filmmaking (Blumentritt, 1998, 76). In 1991 he was awarded a Presidential Fellowship by Temple University so that he could pursue an MFA in the Film and Video Program. Fuentes's other films include *Sleep with Open Eyes, Tantalus, Arm,* and *Crikee.*

Starting in 1992, Fuentes conducted research on the Louisiana Purchase Exposition of 1904 (also known as the St. Louis World's Fair) and on ethnographic footage of Bontocs and other Filipino groups; the vast majority of still photos used in *Bontoc Eulogy* (1995) came from the Library of Congress, but additional photos and film footage were held by the National Archives, the Human Studies Film Archives at the Smithsonian, and the Museum of the University of Pennsylvania. (Fuentes received a grant from the Independent Television Service (ITVS) in 1993 or 1994; the project was also funded by NAATA. These grants permitted him to hire a research assistant.) He drew music from the Grafias recordings held at the University of Washington's ethnomusicological collection and from musical re-creations performed by the Ramon Obuson Folkloric Group (Obuson's brother Enrico portrays Markod in the film); additional musical material, including adaptations of ethnographic transcriptions, was created by Douglas Quin. Fuentes shot 16mm footage in San Diego's Balboa Park, the site of the 1915–1916 Panama-California Exposition, and in the Mütter Museum of the College of Physicians and Surgeons in Philadelphia.[9] He completed *Bontoc Eulogy* in 1995; the following year, it screened at Asian American film festivals in New York, Seattle, and Washington, D.C., and also at the American Museum of Natural History's Margaret Mead Film and Video Festival and the Film Society of Lincoln Center's New America/New Americans series.

Bontoc Eulogy is premised as a search for ancestors; the central conceit of the film is that the narrator is able to trace his ancestry back to a grandfather who was a Bontoc Igorrote who disappeared soon after being exhibited at the St. Louis World's Fair. The film's narrator is ultimately unreliable, however: there are times when he tells us what Markod thought without telling us if his speculations have any basis. It seems that every event the narrator describes is documented on film, suggesting that the narrator's musings are inspired by screening this footage.

Bontoc Eulogy's opening scenes, seemingly straightforward yet highly contrived, set the tone for the rest of the film. A crank phonograph (commonly known as a Victrola, after one of the most popular brand names)

Bontoc Eulogy. "Marlon" and the crank phonograph; the first shot of the film.

sits on a mat on an uneven brick floor. A figure who we assume is also the narrator—although we only hear him in voice-over and never see him speak—enters the frame and sits before the Victrola. Although we hear some ambient sound, we do not hear any footfalls or the sound of the Victrola being cranked; the cinematography is an arty, high-contrast black-and-white. This footage is clearly stylized; the room does not evoke any associations with work or domestic space. When the figure (for simplicity's sake, I will refer to him as Marlon)[10] puts the needle on the disk, we hear a few seconds of surface noise—hisses and pops—and then what sounds like an ethnographic field recording of a dance and percussion performance. We do not hear these sounds from the cone of the Victrola, with the reverberation and narrow frequency range that we would expect to hear in that space; rather, the sound has a presence that suggests it was added in the editing room. After a few moments, the image fades to black while the sound fades out. Twice more we see Marlon put the needle down: the second time we hear more music, the third time we hear a man's voice speaking Bontoc.

What are we to make of this opening? Marlon does not present himself as an ethnographic researcher—we might expect to see him wearing headphones, seated at a desk, taking notes—nor as a man sorting through a collection of family artifacts (compare this scene with the beginning of *The Way to My Father's Village,* where Richard Fung sorts through a box of his father's papers in what appears to be the dining room of his parents' house). The film does not establish a premise for the investigation (as does Felicia Lowe at the beginning of *China: Land of My Father*). In this opening, if Fuentes does not explain the artificiality of what is to follow, neither does he deliberately mislead us. Instead, he relies on our habit of

Bontoc Eulogy. The narrator's children perform a Méliès-inspired magic trick.

associating sound and image to create meaning, as he does when he shows us images of Marlon looking at medical displays in a museum while the soundtrack describes research conducted at the Smithsonian: we may jump to the conclusion that we are looking at Marlon in the Smithsonian, but the voice-over nowhere implies this is the case. Indeed, certain disjunctions between the voice-over and the image-track, combined with a brooding quality to Marlon's on-screen behavior that bespeaks a performance for the camera (rather than a candidly captured image), lead us to the conclusion that the narrator is unreliable. Early in the film, a girl and a boy, whom the narrator has identified as "my children," conjure a rabbit out of a hat: an obvious jumpcut precedes a puff of smoke. With this brief sequence, Fuentes reminds us of the ways cinema exploits our cognitive processes; by refusing to disguise the manipulation that produces the trick, he puts us on guard. (He also alludes to the trick photography tradition of George Méliès, whose earliest films date from the same era as many of the pseudo-documentary films excerpted in *Bontoc Eulogy;* Méliès himself called some of his films *actualités reconstituées,* or "reconstructed news films.")

The narrator goes on to tell us that he has not been back to the Philippines since arriving in the United States, and that his children were born here: "In the beginning I lived in two worlds: the sights and sounds of my new life, and then the flickering afterimages of the place I once called home." The narration is deliberately ambiguous: Is it describing memories or movies? The narrator eventually tells us of his two grandfathers: Emiliano, who fought the Spaniards in 1896, and Markod, a Bontoc warrior who traveled to St. Louis, leaving his pregnant wife behind. The story of Emiliano is illustrated with representations of U.S. soldiers putting down the Philippine insurrection (an 1899 reenactment entitled *Filipinos Retreat from Trenches*) and a sequence depicting the Battle of Manila Bay (constructed by intercutting footage of a toy boat re-creation at the St. Louis Fair with "actuality" footage of ships firing their cannons). As for Markod, we are told that he was a Bontoc chieftain, and we hear what sounds like a period recording of a man speaking Bontoc, which the narrator translates for us; this is the same recording we heard in the film's opening sequence. In truth, this soundtrack is a fabrication: the source of the text is an account of Chief Fomoaley, the leader of Bontoc Igorrotes who performed at Coney Island a few years after the St. Louis World's Fair.[11] Fomoaley spoke via an interpreter to *The Independent* in 1905; originally an abolitionist magazine (edited for many years by Henry Ward Beecher), *The Independent* began publishing first-person accounts of "undistinguished American men and women" (Holt, 1990, xxix) in 1902, collecting sixteen of them in a book entitled *The Life Stories of Undistinguished Americans As Told by Themselves.* Fomoaley's account was published in *The Independent* in October 1905, then reprinted in the 1906 collection (*Life Stories* was reprinted by Routledge in 1990). Fuentes commissioned Fermina Bagwan, a retired teacher from the Cordilleras, to translate the English-language text into idiomatic Bontoc; she also recited the account for Fuentes's microphone. Fuentes then took the recordings, altered the pitch "to make it more androgenous sounding," and added a "synthetic patina" of digital noise (Fuentes, telephone interview, 15 July 1999).

Who, then, is Markod? Fuentes derived the name from a narrator invoked by Bontoc storytellers. *The First Grammar of the Language Spoken by the Bontoc Igorot,* developed by C. W. Seidenadel (1909) with the assistance of several Bontoc men and women who resided in Chicago in 1906–1907, includes an appendix with a dozen tales related to Seidenadel in 1907. Some of the tales conclude with the narrator identifying himself or herself, but several of them end with words to the effect: "Thus ends the tale told by Malkod." Seidenadel explains: "The narrator must be named; if he is unknown, 'Malkod' must be named as the imaginary inventor of the tale; for . . . 'if "Malkod" is the narrator, you do not dream (of the story)' " (561). Fuentes has interpeted this to mean that the tellers of fictions will be haunted in their dreams unless they attribute the story to Malkod.[12] The name Markod, then, is an obscure clue that reveals that the film's narrator has invented the stories attributed to Markod.[13]

In the second half of *Bontoc Eulogy,* we see Markod (played by Enrico

Bontoc Eulogy. Markod records on a wax cylinder.

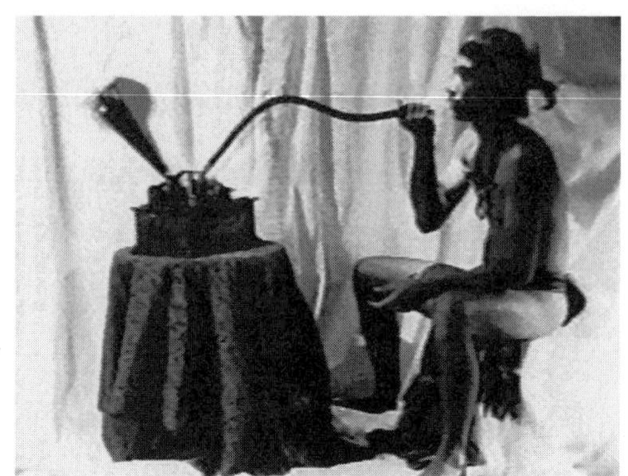

Obuson) in the act of recording his voice on a wax cylinder. Before and after this sequence, we see him slowly rotating on a turntable, standing proudly with his head thrown back. These images are intercut with ethnographic "mugshots" (front and profile), suggesting that Markod's posture is attributable perhaps not to pride but to an ethnographer's instruction to stand so that his features are clearly visible.[14] The rotation also evokes the Victrola: Markod is metaphorically spinning on a platter (later, we see him playing the flute while rotating on the turntable). This circular movement is also a metaphor for the narrator's investigation: turning in circles, never advancing. Whereas Fatimah Rony has argued that all ethnographic film tells an implicit narrative of evolution (1996, 25), of forward progress, Fuentes's film makes no headway in understanding Markod, the Bontoc, or the narrator's own estrangement from the Philippines.

Bontoc Eulogy, then, does not relate a story that the narrator has successfully reconstructed; rather, the film's narrative is of the investigator's journey from supposedly objective primary documents into increasingly subjective understandings of what those documents signify. This progression is neatly encapsulated by the film's use of music. In the opening sequence, when we see the figure of Marlon operating a crank phonograph, we hear two recordings of Bontoc percussion taken from the University of Washington ethnomusicological collection (the Grafias Recordings), recorded in the 1960s. The film's opening credits follow, accompanied by mouth harp music performed by the Ramon Obuson group (professional dancers who perform choreography that attempts to replicate Cordilleran folk dances). After this brief sequence, we hear the narrator's voice for the first time; the music that undergirds his words was composed by Douglas Quin, who

Bontoc Eulogy. In a freeze frame from U.S. Army footage, a Cordilleran boy returns the camera's gaze.

sampled the sounds of Cordilleran instruments and used those samples as raw materials for his score. *Bontoc Eulogy*'s music progresses from authentic to increasingly mediated musical forms, or, more precisely, the soundtrack increasingly foregrounds the mediation of its materials, for even the Grafias Recordings are mediated by technology and ethnographic convention. The film as a whole depicts a similar progression: it could be described as a journey from primary documents to increasingly fanciful stories inspired by them, but it is more meaningfully understood as a movement from narratives that avow their accuracy to narratives that increasingly reveal their unreliability. These gradual revelations critique the faith that we place in the initial accounts.

The final image of *Bontoc Eulogy* depicts Marlon in long shot as he walks up the aisle of an outdoor amphitheater in Balboa Park. Walking from frame left, he pauses in the center of the frame and turns his head to return the gaze of the camera; he then resumes walking and exits frame right. This final image reminds me of two of the period films that Fuentes quotes in the first quarter of the movie. As the narrator finishes telling us of his childhood interest in Philippine tribal life and begins to tell Markod's story, there is a fleeting glimpse of a boy (possibly Bontoc) breaking the fourth wall to gaze into the camera. Shot by the U.S. Army in the Cordilleras in the 1920s, the footage shows a white man operating a handcranked camera; presumably he is filming an activity on the stream or on the opposite bank that we cannot see. The man with the camera pays no attention to the boy, who walks between him and our vantage point; just before leaving the frame, the boy looks over his shoulder, returning our gaze. Fuentes freezes this image, and then inserts a still frame emphasizing this detail. The

Bontoc Eulogy. Actors portraying Filipino rebels retreat frame right . . .

. . . and the U.S. Army enters frame left in the short film *Filipinos Retreat from Trenches* (quoted in *Bontoc Eulogy*).

ethnographic "other" violates the diegetic illusion by returning the camera's gaze. He does not interfere with the camera operator on the riverbank, suggesting that he respects—or is at least indifferent to—the activity. But he glances back at the second camera operator; perhaps he is wondering (as I am) why the white men are filming themselves. The self-reflexive act of filming a camera operator is trumped by this boy, and Fuentes pauses for a moment to make sure we don't miss it. At the end of the film, when Marlon looks into the camera, he reminds us of the artificiality not just of *Bontoc Eulogy,* but of ethnographic and cinematic conventions themselves.

The other film that *Bontoc Eulogy* recalls for me in its closing moments is *Filipinos Retreat from Trenches.* In that film, the story of U.S. military superiority is conveyed in the simplest of narratives: brown men retreat frame right, white men (with the Stars and Stripes waving) enter frame left. The Americans force the Filipinos out of the frame; the shot ends with the American soldiers centered in the image. Merely moving from the margin to the center tells the story of American Manifest Destiny, as the soldiers take command not only of the land, but of the cinematic apparatus. (This simple movement from left to right is of course only possible in a reenactment; guerrilla warfare is hardly so linear and photogenic.)[15] In the final image of his film, Marlon momentarily pauses at the center, but then departs frame right. Although he may have some control of the cinematic apparatus—which is to say, his film puts a marginalized story on center stage—at the end he casts his lot with his cinematic Filipino forebears by leaving frame right. It is important to note that these imagined forebears were African American actors;[16] by echoing them, Marlon is identifying not with real Filipinos, but with cinematic Filipinos. That identification is at least as real as his identification with the figure of Markod.

In paying such careful attention to nuances of movement—in overreading movement—I am in a sense responding to the spirit of ethnographic cinema. At one point in *Bontoc Eulogy,* footage of a dancing child is slowed down and sped up, evoking the researcher's meticulous examination of ethnographic footage. After all, these movies were research tools to provide the most minute information about the appearance and movement of the "others" captured on film.[17] Speaking of the time-motion studies of Regnault, Rony notes, "Detail must be ordered and rationalized, and the sense that one gets is of meticulous management of detail: performers enter the frame at right and exit at left" (1996, 49).

I now want to turn from pre-Hollywood films[18] like *Filipinos Retreat from Trenches* (moving from left to right) to Regnault's ethnographic studies (moving from right to left) and Hollywood movies like *King Kong,* movies that purport to tell a more sophisticated story but that ultimately return to the basic narrative of evolution and racial difference. This is the source material that Rony examines in *On Cannibalism.*

On Cannibalism

Fatimah Tobing Rony was born and raised in Washington, D.C., and Bethesda, Maryland. Her parents were from Indonesia, her mother a Batak from North Sumatra and her father from Palembang in South Sumatra. She earned her Ph.D. in art history at Yale in 1993 (a revised version of her dissertation was published as *The Third Eye* in 1996). Rony produced *On Cannibalism* (1994) at UCLA, while completing an MFA in film and video.

She has also completed three 16mm narrative shorts, *Concrete River* (1997), *Demon Lover* (1998), and *Everything in Between* (2000). At present, she sits on the Film Studies faculty at the University of California, Irvine.

The cannibalism referred to in the title of Rony's video is, first of all, a label applied to the Batak and thereby signals the narrator's attempt to understand if she is herself a cannibal.[19] However, the title does not refer to cannibals but to the act of cannibalism; the video is thus a meditation on the topic of consumption of humans. In *The Third Eye,* Rony employs the phrase "fascinating cannibalism" to describe the consumers of ethnographic cinema: "By 'fascinating cannibalism' I mean to draw attention to the mixture of fascination and horror that the 'ethnographic' occasions: the 'cannibalism' is not that of the people who are labeled Savages, but that of the consumers of the images of the bodies—as well as actual bodies on display—of native peoples offered up by popular media and science" (1996, 10). Rony's video is thus an examination of the discourses of ethnography that offer up savages for public consumption; whereas Fuentes takes his camera to the Mütter Museum in Philadelphia, Rony visits the American Museum of Natural History in New York.

The video opens with footage Rony shot in Paris in 1994 when giving a paper on ethnographic cinema at a colloquium on colonial cinema hosted by the Institut du Monde Arabe (Rony, letter to author, 10 July 1999). A handheld camera explores the perimeter of a fence that seems to encircle the Eiffel Tower; on the soundtrack, we hear the character of Carl Denham from *King Kong.* The mastermind behind the expedition to photograph Kong describes a wall on Skull Island off the coast of Sumatra; behind that wall are things no white man has ever seen. The wall thus separates the civilized and prehistoric worlds. The Eiffel Tower was built to demonstrate that France stood at the pinnacle of Western achievements in science and engineering; it towered over the 1895 Exposition Ethnographique de l'Afrique Occidentale where Regnault recorded his time-motion studies using Marey's *chronophotographe.* Rony's camera does not execute a technically proficient panning shot, nor does it occupy the fixed position necessary to ensure the proper collection of scientific data. Instead, the camera peers through the fence at the Eiffel Tower; if, as on Skull Island, civilization is on the other side of the fence, then the camera is located on the savage side, so we can conclude that the camera is held in the hands of someone who is usually the object of the camera's gaze. At the end of this prologue, the image fades to black.

Next we see a series of video stills of words cut into the stone outside the American Museum of Natural History ("explorer, conservationist, scientist") as a recording of Batak music begins.[20] The stills are followed by a close-up of a pair of lips that narrate the remainder of the video. The narrator tells us that while watching television late one night, she realized that she understood the language spoken by the savages in *King Kong;* according to *The Third Eye,* they speak the dialect of the Nias Islanders with heavy American accents (1996, 177). Just as the opening images tell us that the videomaker aligns herself with the savages, looking back over the fence at the Westerners, here the narrator reveals that a Hollywood film told her that she was a Primitive. The narrator states, "We were star attractions . . . you devoured us," thereby accepting being interpellated as the "other." On the image-track, we see processed images from *King Kong,* footage of the exhibits at the American Museum of Natural History, and ethnographic photographs. The narrator details a history of ethnographic consumption, including an anecdote about an entrepreneur who sold frankfurters as "hot dogs" near the Philippine Reservation at the St. Louis Fair, where dog eating was performed for the fair's visitors.[21] The consumption of the racial "other" is tied to the all-American act of eating a hot dog: "fascinating cannibalism" is undeniably American.

Throughout the video, footage from *King Kong* has been intercut with the ethnographic images. In *The Third Eye,* Rony offers a fascinating reading of *King Kong,* organizing the film's representations of race and gender as an evolutionary taxonomy. At the conclusion of her typology, she reads Kong's climb up the Empire State Building as a conflict between the prehistory that Kong represents and the engineering feat symbolized by the New York skyscraper. *On Cannibalism* amplifies this argument by juxtaposing RKO's logo—an Eiffel-esque radio tower astride the globe—with Kong on the Empire State Building. While the Eiffel Tower and the Empire State Building symbolized scientific progress, technological know-how, and commercial savvy generally, the RKO logo yokes those discourses to the celebration of Hollywood as modern art form par excellence.

Rony also reads the contest between prehistoric and modern in a brief scene in *King Kong* portraying Ann Darrow and Jack Driscoll fleeing Kong through the jungle: "Their running is a literal embodiment of the race of history, a race which is the locus of ethnographic cinema" (1996, 170). The metaphor of history's race is introduced via a quotation from anthropologist Charles Letourneau: "The white race, semitic and indo-european holds, certainly for the present the head in the 'steeplechase' (sic) of human groups."[22] In *The Third Eye,* Rony notes that this scene appears "about two-

On Cannibalism. The RKO logo, excerpted from *King Kong.*

thirds of the way through *King Kong*" (170), and it likewise appears at two-thirds of the way through *On Cannibalism.*

Shortly after this scene, the narrator departs from the stable position of "other" vis-à-vis the West ("we were star attractions . . . you devoured us"). Showing us an image from Regnault's chronophotographic series, "Negress walking with a light weight on her head," the narrator states, "I am a Wolof woman: I come from Dakar, Senegal. I am the Doctor Regnault: I am filming you using the *chronophotographe,* for time motion studies. I am a little girl: I haven't yet learned to see." The narrator has signaled that the cinematic apparatus allows for shifting identification: the spectator no longer occupies simply one position, but takes on a variety of different perspectives made possible by the narrative offered by Regnault's protocinematic photography.[23] She becomes at one moment the object and at the next the subject of ethnographic study; then she becomes a little girl, perhaps recalling the narrator's story of encountering *King Kong* and being told that her mother came from a race of cannibals.

On Cannibalism ends with a variation on the little girl's statement: "I haven't yet learned how to see. I haven't yet begun to believe." Does this statement refer to the narrator's resistance to being told she is a descendent of cannibals? For assistance in interpreting this statement, let's turn again to *The Third Eye,* specifically to Rony's reading of "Negress walking with a light weight on her head":

> The exchange of looks in the chronophotography produced by Regnault . . . belies any simple polarity of subject and object. . . . A Frenchman, dressed in a city suit and hat . . . accompanies the woman as she walks,

> never taking his eyes off her. His walk, meant to represent the urban walk, is there as comparative point of reference to what Regnault terms the woman's "savage locomotion." In addition, he acts as an in-frame surrogate for the Western male gaze of the scientist. There are also two other performers visible at frame left, watching the Frenchman watch the woman. Finally, a little girl, also West African, stares alternately at the group being filmed and the scientist and his camera. She appears to break a cinematic code already established in fin-de-siècle time motion studies: she looks at the camera. In this scenario of comparative racial physiology, the little girl has not learned how properly to see or be seen. (1996, 23)

Like the boy in the U.S. Army footage excerpted in *Bontoc Eulogy,* this West African girl returns the camera's gaze. I would argue that these transgressions mark the resistance of people of color to the cinema's process of "othering." It is important to note, as *On Cannibalism* suggests, that this argument results from my ability to shift identification to different positions within the frame: I do not simply align my subjectivity with the gaze of the camera.[24] Similarly, one of Rony's objectives in *The Third Eye* is to address the dilemma of the spectator of color, whose identification shifts between the white hero and the savage. Rony's concept of "the third eye" derives from W. E. B. Du Bois's double consciousness, which she glosses as "the experience of viewing one's self as an object" (4).

Bontoc Eulogy, On Cannibalism, and other Asian American movies that excerpt films that have regarded us as "other" are all structured around this experience of seeing one self at a remove. I continue this discussion in Chapter 3, focusing on the construction of Japanese Americans as enemies of the United States; if we are grandchildren of the St. Louis World's Fair and the Exposition Ethnographique de l'Afrique Occidentale, we are also "Children of the Camps."[25] But before we turn to the topic of biological ancestors (the movies about the camps all deal with parents and grandparents), I want to turn to feature films that, like *Bontoc Eulogy,* create fictional narratives based on historical accounts of the first generation of Asians to arrive in North America. Unlike the Asians discussed in this chapter, the women who migrated to North America in the nineteenth century served not as objects of scientific study, but as laborers exploited by a rapidly developing economy.

CHAPTER 2

Pioneering Romance

Immigration, Americanization, and Asian Women

> The conviction that a married woman's proper place is in the conjugal home as a servant to her husband and mother to her children is now so widespread and well established that this arrangement appears as a natural feature of human existence rather than historically and culturally specific. The history of the development of the capitalist organization of production is also the history of the development of a particular form of the sexual division of labor. — Carole Pateman *The Disorder of Women*[1]

> Marriage was a foreign country.
> —Mitsuye Yamada, *Camp Notes and Other Poems*

It has been argued that all U.S. film genres are about the formation of community.[2] Given the predominance of romance plots in mainstream U.S. movies, doesn't it also follow that movie romances tell us myths about the formation of American communities?[3] The Western genre, for example, seems at first glance to concern itself with lone male protagonists, and yet, insofar as the genre depicts the taming of the frontier and the establishment of new communities, heterosexual romance is also a central concern, with (white) women representing civilization, education, and rootedness (as opposed to the values of individuality, nature, folk wisdom, and wanderlust personified by the cowboy). Of course, the narrative remains focused on the Western hero who must settle down, rather than on the heroine who needs to adapt to the West.[4] But what if the films were directed not at mythifying the West, but at the avowed demythification of the West? What if the protagonist of these films were not the cowboy, but the Asian female settler?

The movies I examine in this chapter are all tales of migration, romance, and community formation. Set in the early years of Asian migration to the United States, both *Thousand Pieces of Gold* and *Picture Bride* depict the arrival of women into male-dominated Asian workers communities. Insofar as these films are historically accurate, they document the struggles of women not just to adapt to America, but to redefine their role as women within Asian diasporic communities. However, to the extent that these movies depart from historical fact, they reveal the discursive construction of proto–Asian American communities, projections of contemporary desires to cast Asian migrants in our own image.[5] The reasons these women characters have for "choosing" America reflect contemporary Asian American frustrations with being cast as eternal foreigners. American-born Asians counter the perception that we are foreign-born by telling the stories of the first migrants to the United States, both to establish how long we've been here and also to claim immigrants as ultra-American.

But of these movies are historical romances: the turning point for the female protagonists, the moment they decide to devote their lives to America (to becoming American) rather than to Asia (to being Asian) is also the moment when they accept American men as their romantic partners.[6] The desire to become American is inseparable from the narrative of heterosexual romance. Given the uneven forces driving the migration of Asian women and men to America, and the avowedly feminist perspective of contemporary filmmakers, it is ironic and paradoxical that these women would seize American identities by entering into heterosexual marriage. To cast these two films into relief, then, I conclude by examining *Living on Tokyo Time,* a contemporary retelling of an Asian woman's migration and the problems she encounters when marriage is equated with American citizenship.

Because the narratives of acculturation and assimilation in these movies are inseparable from their romance narratives, my argument extends the thesis developed by Gina Marchetti in *Romance and the "Yellow Peril"* (1994) and Laura Kang's "The Desiring of Asian Female Bodies: Interracial Romance and Cinematic Subjection" (1993). Both authors focus on interracial romance in American films, and both draw from Edward Said's *Orientalism* (1979). In Marchetti's words, Hollywood interracial romance narratives "create a mythic image of Asia that empowers the West and rationalizes Euro-American authority over the Asian other. Romance and sexuality provide the metaphoric justification for this domination" (6). Marchetti breaks these narratives down into eight mythic patterns, the most relevant for our purposes being "transcendent romances [that] allow the lovers to 'spiritually' overcome social barriers through their love . . . [and] assimilation narratives, [wherein] the nonwhite lover completely relinquishes his or her own culture in order to be accepted into the American bourgeois mainstream" (8). Only one of the films discussed in this chapter involves an interracial romance, but all three stories describe a romance between a male character who was born in the United States or has otherwise committed himself to become an American, and a female character who migrates from Asia and must decide whether she will become an American. I generally use the term "acculturation" and not "assimilation," as these women do not necessarily assimilate into the American mainstream; indeed, in *Picture Bride* her entry into the community of plantation laborers does not constitute assimilation but her commitment to an oppositional politics.

More generally, by situating these films in the context of American film genres, I am situating narratives about Asian American acculturation in relation to conventionalized modes of cinematic storytelling. Whereas ethnographic film provides a vocabulary of discursive conventions designed to ensure the scientific objectivity of the film as document, romance narratives draw on narrative structures that animate the conflict between individual desires and the sweep of historical change on a global scale. *Bontoc Eulogy* and *On Cannibalism* affirmed their own subjectivity over the purported objectivity of ethnographic convention; *Picture Bride* and *Thousand Pieces of Gold* are implicated in the romance genre even as they attempt to center the subjectivity of Asian women as protagonists.

Any account of movies centering on Asian American women must also account for the paradoxes of Asian American visibility. In the contemporary entertainment marketplace, Asian American women have achieved greater visibility on television (in fiction programming as well as broadcast news) and in mainstream American movies (although, arguably, on the rare occasions when they do appear, Asian American men are more likely to be driving the narrative, whereas Asian American women are more likely to be window-dressing supporting players).[7] Drawing on Rana Kabanni's discussion of Orientalism in European painting, Laura Kang notes that rescuing Oriental women from Oriental men who would prostitute them is one aspect of the white man's burden. In the aesthetics of European painting, the Oriental female was elevated, reversing the Western gender hierarchy (Kang, 1993, 7). The legacy of this hierarchy is evident in U.S. popular culture: whereas (white) women's experiences are typically displaced by men's stories in mainstream film, Asian American women seem to be more visible than Asian American men.

I do not mean to suggest that the popularity of Asian female-centered narratives in U.S. popular culture is due solely to Western cultural fascination with Asian female sexuality. As an Asian American man, my own positioning toward these texts is particularly complex. Insofar as these narratives are structured around providing visual and narrative pleasure to a straight male spectatorial position,[8] they appeal to a straight Asian American male spectatorial position as well. However, to the extent that such positioning comes into conflict with the male spectator's position as an Asian American man—particularly in interracial romance narratives that marginalize Asian American male sexuality—the Asian American male spectator is confronted with the knowledge that this text has not been constructed with him in mind. Nevertheless, such spectators can relate to these narrative texts in a complex fashion, alternately subversive and complicitous.

In my essay "Recuperating Suzie Wong: A Fan's Nancy Kwan-dary" (2000), I attempt to account for the spectatorial pleasure of people of color viewing racist, sexist cinematic texts. Such pleasure is often described as subversive insofar as it involves a remobilization of a mainstream text toward subcultural desires; at the opposite extreme, such pleasure is dismissed as complicitous with dominant cinema, which interpellates spectators of color by recuperating their resistant readings. In accounting for the pleasure that a spectator of color experiences, I argue that such pleasures are fleeting and contingent but nonetheless significant, and that they are driven by a selective memory that recontextualizes key moments in an alternative narrative. Although this spectatorial strategy can account in a limited fashion for the appeal of specific movies, I believe it is particularly oriented toward an understanding of fandom and star discourse, because star discourses are "structured polysemy" (Dyer, 1979, 3), incoherent texts formed out of a multiplicity of competing components.

As a male Asian American spectator, my response to cinematic representations of Asian American women is driven both by identification with the Asian American subjectivity that these characters represent and by disidentification with the gender hierarchy that Kang describes. This contradiction is wholly consistent with these representations, insofar as these representations are themselves contradictory depictions of Asian American women as agents of their own desire and as objects of straight male desires that would deny that agency. The paradox of Asian American female visibility rests on this contradiction; the agency of Asian female characters is often constructed around a critique of Asian patriarchies, yet that critique is frequently contained by the text before it expands to encompass a critique of American patriarchy. We might name that process of textual containment with a generic label: the romance.

Thousand Pieces of Gold

First published in 1981, Ruthanne Lum McCunn's *Thousand Pieces of Gold* (1988) tells the story of a woman named Lalu Nathoy, born in China in 1853 and a resident of Idaho (where she was known as Polly Bemis) from 1872 until her death in 1933.[9] McCunn's "biographical novel" was based on research conducted at the Idaho State Historical Society and elsewhere in Idaho, and she credits Sister Mary Alfreda Elsensohn with providing her with much material, including introducing her to people who had known Polly Bemis (7). (Elsensohn had herself published a book describing Bemis as "Idaho County's Most Romantic Character" in 1979.) McCunn's novel offers fictional invention insofar as it speculates about Nathoy's motivations; for example, to explain the historical fact that Nathoy did not bear children in the United States, McCunn's character states that she does not want to produce biracial children with her white husband, citing the treatment of mixed-race American Indian children (205). McCunn also describes Nathoy's childhood and youth in China, years for which documentation was not available. Finally, McCunn also invented some characters for her narrative, most notably the packer Jim. According to Walter Hesford, however, McCunn always grounded such inventions in historical plausibility; for example, census records do list a Chinese packer in the town of Warren.[10] McCunn also dramatized certain Idaho legends about Polly Bemis, the most popular being the notion that she was won in a poker game. Historian Priscilla Wegars (Titone, 1996) notes that there is no evidence that this ever happened, and further cites evidence that Bemis herself took steps to debunk this legend before her death. Bemis is a popular historical figure; she was inducted into the Idaho Hall of Fame in 1996, and her cabin has been named on the National Registry of Historic Places.[11]

Filmmaker Nancy Kelly first encountered McCunn's book at a conference called "The Women's West" in Idaho; at the time she was best known as a documentary filmmaker, coproducer and codirector (with Gwen Clancy) of the award-winning *A Cowhand's Song* (1981). During the editing of the film, Kelly met Kenji Yamamoto, a Sansei who had studied photography at the San Francisco Art Institute and subsequently founded a film editing company. (The year before they met, Yamamoto had edited Felicia Lowe's *China: Land of My Father.*) Kelly and Yamamoto collaborated on a number of projects, notably another film about modern ranchers, *Cowgirls: Portraits of American Ranch Women* (1985). During the early 1980s, Yamamoto acquired experience editing dramatic movies with Emiko Omori's short *The Departure,* and Susan Shadburne's feature *Shadow Play.* During this time, Kelly and Yamamoto were married; they founded Mother Lode Productions in 1985 to produce *Thousand Pieces of Gold* (1991).

Kelly acquired the rights to McCunn's book after another publisher failed to exercise his option.[12] She and Yamamoto developed the script with writer Anne Makepeace at Robert Redford's Sundance Institute, and cast Rosalind Chao (probably best known at the time for a recurring role on the television series *M*A*S*H*) and Chris Cooper (who had appeared in the television miniseries *Lonesome Dove* and John Sayles's *Matewan*) as their leads. Funding was provided by a few limited partners, American Playhouse Theatrical Films (which secured rights for four broadcasts between 1992 and 1995 one year after the theatrical release), Hong Kong's Maverick Films International, and Britain's Film Four (which secured the rights for British broadcast); according to one reviewer, the film's total budget was less than $2 million (Wilmington, 1991).

Thousand Pieces of Gold was shot on a thirty-five-day schedule on location in Montana. An extensive search for a restored or intact Gold Rush town finally turned up Nevada City (which had also been used in *Little Big Man*). Butte's Chinatown stood in for nineteenth-century San Francisco, and the scenes of rural China were shot in the fields near the crew's hotel (these scenes were desaturated in the lab so that the color would imply drought conditions).[13]

Kelly's film compresses the events of 1872 through 1897 into an eighteen-month period; it omits Polly's youth in China (part 1 of McCunn's book), her life with Charlie Bemis on the River of No Return (part 5), and her subsequent years living in Warren (part 6) and then in a rebuilt cabin on the Salmon River (part 7). The film's narrative begins in China in 1880, where Polly/Lalu's family belongs to a small community of nomadic shepherds (in McCunn's novel, the family are farmers; according to Kelly, because McCunn did not know for certain where Polly had been raised, and because the filmmakers were planning on shooting in Montana, they decided to make her a shepherd from Northern China). Suffering through a bad drought, Polly's father sells her to a marriage broker; Polly ends up in the hold of a ship bound for San Francisco. She is purchased by a packer named Jim, acting as an agent for saloonkeeper Hong King.

Soon after arriving in Warren, Hong King attempts to prostitute Polly to the customers of the saloon. She fends off one "white devil" with a knife, then tells Hong King she will kill herself before she becomes "a hundred men's wife." Hong King's partner, Charlie Bemis, suggests that he allow Polly to work in the saloon. A few months pass and Jim returns; after spending the night with Polly, he leaves town, promising to return with enough money to buy her from Hong King. Soon after, Charlie wins Polly from Hong King in a poker game. She tells Charlie that she is no better off with her new owner; the next morning he tells her that she is free but allows her to stay with him.

Jim returns to town with the money to purchase Polly, but before she can explain that she is living with Charlie platonically, Jim leaves without looking back. When Polly decides she cannot continue to live with Charlie, she leases a boarding house. That winter, resentment against Chinese laborers leads to a movement to expel Chinese from Warren. While attending a celebration of Chinese New Year (Charlie identifies it as the Year of the Horse, which would make it 1882), Charlie is accidentally hit by a bullet fired into the crowd by white miners. Polly nurses him back to health and realizes that she loves him. But come spring, the Chinese are driven out of Warren; Charlie pleads with Polly to move with him to an isolated homestead where they won't be bothered, but she is determined to return to China. Leaving town, she encounters the herbalist Li Ping, who points out that her letters to China have never been answered; he implies that it would be better to make a new life in America. Polly returns to Charlie, and an end-title reports that they lived out their natural lives together on their homestead on the River of No Return.

Thousand Pieces of Gold premiered at the San Francisco International Film Festival in May 1990, then made the festival circuit, eventually securing distribution with Greycat Films, a Las Vegas–based company that had achieved some success in 1990 with John McNaughton's *Henry: Portrait of a Serial Killer.* The film was released nationwide in the summer and fall of 1991 and aired on PBS's *American Playhouse* in 1992. In 1995, the Autry Museum of Western Heritage in Los Angeles took deposit on production materials and props from the film.

A comparison of differences between the plot of McCunn's novel and Kelly's film is instructive, as are moments when both depart from the historical record. (My aim is to discuss the rationales behind and the effects resulting from these revisions, and indeed to contextualize charges of historical inaccuracy, but faithfulness to the historical record is not in and of itself a criterion for evaluation.) For example, parts 2, 3, and 4 of McCunn's book take place in 1872–1894; the movie compresses these events into an eighteen-month period from 1880 to 1882.[14] The film's status as an adaptation of a "biographical novel" means that it is ambiguously positioned as a fiction based on historical truth. Given that Asian American cinema labors under the demands of historical representation, *Thousand Pieces of Gold* is no more or less responsible to historical truth than any other dramatic film representing a historical period—which is not to say that the film has not provoked controversy over its depiction of the past.

One alteration in particular seems to have upset many of the residents of Warren, Idaho: the interpolation of the "driving out" at the conclusion of the film. Chinese Americans were in fact never expelled from Warren, and that fact is a point of pride for the residents (however, the film's depiction of the expulsion is based on historical accounts of another Idaho town, Haley). Walter Hesford notes, "Many Chinese Americans were massacred and lynched in the Idaho territory and, in the 1880s and '90s, were driven out and then excluded from much of the inland West. Thus the film is true to the larger picture and is perhaps to be praised for vividly depicting the racism experienced by the Chinese in America."[15] As it happens, by restricting the film's chronology to the years 1880–1882, the film depicts the peak years of Chinese immigration (Wynne, 1978, 284), which might also imply that the filmmakers sought to rewrite Polly's story so that she stands in for Chinese immigrants generally. In dramatic terms, the "driving out" functions to compel Polly to decide where (and with whom) she will live.

Another alteration: in the film, the character of Jim rejects Polly, believing that she has given herself to Charlie, but in McCunn's novel Jim dies in an accident (1988, 133); once again, the film's revision emphasizes dramatic conflict. Of course, Jim was an invention of McCunn's in the first place, so the filmmakers cannot be faulted (on the grounds of historical accuracy) for taking liberties with his character. McCunn, however, objected to this plot point, because one of her motivations for creating Jim was to counter racist gender stereotypes (Hesford, 1996, 50); in McCunn's view, the movie's Jim is (in Hesford's words) "yet another Chinese male acting unfeelingly and, moreover, losing out sexually to the white male" (55).

The relative status of Chinese and white men in narratives is a particularly thorny issue in Asian American storytelling. When Frank Chin accuses Maxine Hong Kingston of faking Chinese mythology, his avowed concern is that the heroic aspects of the "real" stories are distorted in service of an assimilationist narrative.[16] Whether or not Chinese culture is patriarchal (and much of the controversy arises from commentators who perceive Chin as an apologist for Chinese patriarchy), Chin argues that Kingston's critique of Chinese patriarchy functions to shore up U.S. culture as an apparently nonpatriarchal society that allows and enables feminism to flourish. The connection that Hesford draws between the negative portrayal of Chinese masculinity and sexual competition is implicit in Chin's argument that Kingston's narrative is assimilative: in his view, Kingston is a self-hating Chinese American who reciprocates U.S. society's "racist love" (F. Chin and Chan, 1972). Lisa Lowe (1991b) convincingly argues that Chin's "cultural nationalist" position is driven by the same binarist logic that provides the foundation for essentialist notions of cultural difference. But although Chin's denigration of Kingston as a fake is rhetorically excessive, his argument about the negative evaluation of Chinese masculinity is wholly consistent with the critique of Orientalism formulated by Said, elaborated and modified by Lowe, and cogently summarized by Kang.

One influential reviewer of *Thousand Pieces of Gold* draws attention to the film's depiction of Chinese masculinity even as he reveals an incomplete understanding of Chinese American history. Roger Ebert's review for the *Chicago Sun-Times* gets many details wrong: he identifies Jim as a "wife-trader" who transports Polly from China and sells her to Hong King, and credits Charlie with informing Polly that slavery has been outlawed. Ebert also speaks from precisely the ideological position that Chin decries, implicitly praising the United States as a progressive, pro-feminist society. The opening lines of Ebert's review read: "For some measure of the *progress of women,* consider '1000 Pieces of Gold,' set in the 19th century and telling the story of a Chinese woman sold from man to man as if she were property. The film is based on the little-known fact that *years after slavery was abolished in America,* Asians were still held in involuntary servitude—sometimes by their own people" (1991, n.p.; emphasis added). Ebert's review does not balance this account of Asian tyranny (note the slippage from "Chinese" to "Asian") in the progressive West with mention of the many acts of racism perpetrated by white Americans in the film; he does not describe the driving out, only a "race riot," and only then because it occasions Charlie's shooting and thereby precipitates Polly's love for him.

Ebert's review notwithstanding, the majority of reviewers in mainstream newspapers do not remark on the film's racialized sexual politics except to comment on the film's sensitivity to precisely these issues. In an otherwise feisty critique, the *Village Voice*'s David D. Kim comments that "Kelly and Yamamoto, clearly aware that Asian men are too often portrayed onscreen as emasculated cutouts, breathe some life into Jim (good cop) and Hong King (bad cop)," and remarks, "Kelly and Yamamoto are especially careful about the sexual politics of this interracial coupling" (1991, 70–71). Consistently attributing the film's authorship to the coproducers (and not just to director Kelly), Kim's reading is driven by the politics that he attributes to Yamamoto as an Asian American man.[17] The *Los Angeles Times*'s Michael Wilmington muses: "It's a film with real feeling, a warmth surging up naturally from the performances. And, at the core of 'Thousand Pieces,' fittingly for a film made by an interracial couple (Kelly and her producer-editor husband, Kenji Yamamoto), is an interracial love story of poignancy and conviction. The usual heart of a Western is conflict. Here, love is the core, perhaps a welcome antidote for anyone disturbed by the raw, undiluted ferocity of Spike Lee's powerful 'Jungle Fever' (1991, F8).

Wilmington's comments are curious: virtually *all* narratives are driven by conflict, love stories as well. By claiming that the interracial love in *Thousand Pieces of Gold* is nonconflictual, Wilmington seems to be suggesting that the film depicts a transcendent love, a love that triumphs over social barriers and internalized prejudices, especially when compared with Spike Lee's *Jungle Fever.* Wilmington may be correct to put the two movies in separate categories; after all, as the title of Lee's film would indicate, *Jungle Fever* is less about love than about sexual attraction. But in making the comparison, Wilmington flattens the differences between the historical periods depicted by the two films, not to mention the vastly different positions of Lee and the team of Kelly and Yamamoto: *She's Gotta Have It, School Daze,*

Do the Right Thing, and *Mo' Better Blues* had all established Lee as a commentator on contemporary racialized sexual politics, whereas *Thousand Pieces of Gold* was the first dramatic feature from Kelly and Yamamoto.[18]

Kelly's and Yamamoto's biographies were not the only sources cited to authenticate the production. In a feature article on actor Rosalind Chao on the occasion of the airing of *Thousand Pieces of Gold* on *American Playhouse,* Ron Miller notes:

> Like Lalu/Polly, Chao's lineage stretches back to northern China. Chao's own mother also came to the United States as an immigrant at about the same age as Lalu/Polly, speaking no English. The Chinese dialect spoken by Lalu is Mandarin, the same dialect Chao grew up speaking. Chao's mother also arrived in America at a time of intense racial prejudice against Asians, immediately after World War II. . . .
>
> Like Lalu/Polly, Chao also is married to a white man. (1992a, 4D)

Constructing a narrative in which an actor breaks through in the role she was born to play, Miller lists coincidences across widely divergent historical moments: Is Polly's marriage to a white man in late nineteenth-century Idaho illuminated by Chao's marriage in late twentieth-century California? Is the context of postwar anti-Asian sentiment that Chao's mother faced comparable to the "driving out"?

Polly's Choice

Despite the fact that many of the film's key dramatic points were formulated to emphasize Polly's decision to remain in Idaho with Charlie, returning to China is never a viable option. McCunn's novel describes a series of events in which Polly/Lalu is kidnapped by bandits (her father is coerced into accepting token payment to save the rest of the family) and eventually sold to a house of prostitution, which has an arrangement to send her to San Francisco along with other women, some of whom are destined to be prostitutes and others to be auctioned as wives. Once in Warren, Polly sends letters to China hoping to inform her family of her fate; she thus holds onto hope that if her family has survived they will take her back. In the movie, however, Polly's father sells her to a marriage broker outright; it is not clear whether he realizes she will be sent to "Gold Mountain," but his action is less equivocal than in the novel. As in the book, the movie's Polly sends letters to China, but given her father's deliberate act, the letter-writing seems to indicate Polly's state of denial rather than an attitude of

Thousand Pieces of Gold. Jim abandons Polly . . .

. . . just as her father had abandoned her before.

hope. Furthermore, at the key moment when Jim rejects Polly, the movie presents an insert shot of Polly's father walking away (a representation of Polly's memory, insofar as the shot is preceded and followed by a medium shot of Polly gazing ahead). This insert shot does not simply compare Jim's and her father's actions: it suggests that her rejection by a Chinese suitor is equivalent to being expelled from China.

The movie's incorporation of the "driving out," intended by Kelly to add import to Polly's decision to remain with Charlie, also provides the movie's strongest indictment of white racism. Because Polly is apparently able to remain, however, some measure of credence is given to the white miner's claims that he objects to competition from Chinese laborers specifically, and not to Chinese people generally:

> JONAS: Ain't nobody going home rich what with them Chinks taking it all.
>
> TOBY: Please Jonas. Spare us.[19]

Thousand Pieces of Gold. Polly returns to Charlie as the Chinese laborers are driven out.

> JONAS: I am not talking about Polly now, I'm talking about them yeller miners. Working for nothing so's we can't even get a job no more.

Jonas presumably means that Polly is not one of "*them* Chinks"—those Chinks who offer economic competition—but he might also be saying that Polly isn't a "Chink" at all, because she's "assimilable." (Admittedly, he calls Charlie a "Chink lover," and presumably he is referring to Charlie's romantic love for Polly as well as his friendship with Hong King.) In the movie's striking final images, a river of Chinese men parts for Polly, who rides in the opposite direction. The very fact that she rides a horse suggests that she has achieved a modicum of economic success that has eluded most of the Chinese men, and no one questions her ability to remain. The film's mise-en-scène, with the men walking away from he camera, also draws attention to the queues (the long ponytails) the men wear, and without which the Chinese government would not allow them to return. The film's end title, and Charlie's earlier dialogue, make it clear that the couple will remove themselves from the town to an isolated homestead on the River of No Return; hence it is implied that only by "lying low" can Polly remain. Nevertheless, Polly is clearly marked as exceptional—keep in mind Jonas's acceptance of her. The narrative emphasis on Jonas also might suggest that the "driving out" is a local problem, as opposed to a widespread regional phenomenon encouraged by federal anti-immigrant legislation.[20] (The movie's press kit details the context of anti-Chinese sentiment and congressional legislation, but these larger realities are not elaborated in the film itself.) In the film, Hong King acquires citizenship papers, when in fact, no Chinese could become a naturalized U.S. citizen at the time; the film thus denies federally-sanctioned discrimination against Chinese and implies that anti-Chinese sentiment is a local phenomenon.[21]

Speaking with Polly as he leaves town, the herbalist Li Ping advises her to forget about her family and "cross the river to be reborn on the other side." His words evoke the folktale that Jim and Polly share, in which two lovers could be united for only one night of the year by a bridge of magpies; here, Li Ping suggests that Polly can cross that river permanently—to join Charlie, not Jim. Polly's choice of a romantic partner is thus inseparable from her choice of where to live: Jim on one side of the ocean/river, Charlie on the other. She is given a third option by Hong King, who proposes that they join forces and make money in San Francisco—as partners, he clarifies, presumably aware of Polly's abilities, evidenced by her success running a boarding house. By rejecting his offer, Polly symbolically gives up a life as an entrepreneur in a thriving Chinese American urban enclave.[22] That is, she not only rejects Hong King's proposal, but she does not pursue the option of going into business herself. It is hard to imagine how Polly "helped in the building of a new nation," as critic Ron Miller contends (1992a, 4D), unless it is through the act of falling in love with Charlie. In *Idaho County's Most Romantic Character,* Elsensohn describes Polly's actions in nursing Charlie back to health (an event that precipitates Polly's realization that she loves him) as the moment when the community accepts her assertion of her Americanness: "In the beginning this battle for the life of Bemis won for Polly the respect and admiration of the community in which she lived. In her own right she stood out challenging American womanhood for a place in Western Civilization. Like a butterfly emerging from a cocoon Polly was now free from the chains of slavery. She had brought warmth and humaness [*sic*] to a time and place that was often bleak and brutal" (1979, 22).

On the one hand, then, Polly's choice is not really a choice at all, because the deck is stacked against returning to China. She will become an American; the only question is what kind. As a woman, Polly is not a full-fledged "Chink": Hong King's assertion that Warren is his home is refuted,[23] but when Polly announces that she is going "home" to Charlie, no one challenges her. She even gives up her life as an independent entrepreneur. What is stopping Charlie from moving to San Francisco, where she can run a Chinese American business? Nancy Kelly's film may emphasize Polly's independence, abilities, and decisions, but it also describes specific circumstances whereby Chinese women can become Americans.

Picture Bride

The film *Picture Bride* (1995), by contrast, depicts the formation of an Asian American community. In doing so, it dramatizes a life in which Asian American women give up one set of desires and responsibilities for a new set of duties: to their husbands and children. The film's troubled production history, in which competing desires for the film to represent various experiences and address varied audiences (Japanese, Hawai'ian, and "mainstream" white Americans), offers a counterpoint to the competing identifications that Riyo, *Picture Bride*'s protagonist, must negotiate. *Picture Bride*'s marketing campaign, which drew heavily on stories of the film's production, reveals claims of authenticity (based variously on ethnicity, the personal histories of the filmmakers, and thorough research) in tension with efforts to increase the commercial appeal of the film.

Sansei Kayo Hatta was born in Hawai'i, but relocated to New York with her family at age six.[24] After graduating from Stanford University, she remained in the Bay Area, working with documentary filmmakers Felicia Lowe, Pat Ferrero, and Emiko Omori (Rich, 1995). She earned her MFA in film production at UCLA in the late 1980s; it was at UCLA that she got to know fellow student Lisa Onodera, who had grown up in Berkeley, but also had a Hawai'ian connection: her great-grandmothers had been picture brides.[25] In 1989, Hatta began researching Hawai'ian picture brides, contacting twenty women, most of them in their nineties, with the assistance of historian Barbara Kawakami. Of course, most of the women she interviewed had committed to their marriage; it was more difficult to research runaway picture brides (Rich, 1995). Hatta enlisted her sister, Mari Hatta, who holds an MFA in creative writing from the University of Virginia, to collaborate on a screenplay. While at UCLA, Hatta made short films based on drafts of scenes from the *Picture Bride* script and used the short films in her grant applications (Rony, 1995). Meanwhile, Onodera had associate-produced Arthur Dong's *Forbidden City, USA;* she joined the team as producer. The Hattas and Onodera also recruited Diane Mei Lin Mark, a writer and UH-Manoa professor whose involvement in film includes a stint with Asian CineVision in New York; Mark was also raised in Hawai'i.

Over a four-year period, the producers raised half of their $1 million budget from the National Endowment of the Humanities, the American Film Institute, and the National Endowment for the Arts, as well as NAATA and a variety of foundations, with the lion's share ($300,000) coming from Hawai'i's State Foundation of Culture and the Arts (Rich, 1995), completing a seven-and-a-half-week shoot in July and August 1993 thanks to financial support from local businesses and individuals (listed in the film's credits; Rony, 1996). The remainder of the film's postproduction budget was covered by the Cécile Co., who were persuaded by lead actor Youki Kudoh, who had just modeled for the Japanese lingerie manufacturer in a major ad campaign, to commit the remaining $500,000 (after inspecting the rushes and the script; Rich, 1995).

On the basis of a rough cut, *Picture Bride* was accepted by the 1994 Sundance Film Festival, but the film was pulled when the filmmakers failed to arrive at a satisfactory final edit (Brodie, 1994). During this period, Miramax Films acquired worldwide rights for the film, financed reshoots, and brought in veteran film editor Lynzee Klingman. Following its premiere at the 1994 Cannes Film Festival, the film underwent additional editing and sound design, and a new score was commissioned (Rony, 1996).[26] Returning to Sundance a year after they had withdrawn, *Picture Bride* won the Audience Award for Best Dramatic Feature. The film was released nationwide that summer, opening in New York in late April.

In the period between the screenings at Cannes and Sundance, "artistic differences" between Miramax and the filmmakers were widely rumored. If Cannes symbolizes the ballyhoo of commercial film promotion, Sundance is positioned as the bastion of independent filmmaking; between these two festivals, the phrase "artistic differences" connotes struggles pitting *Picture Bride*'s authenticity against its marketability. (I have been able to substantiate only one account: actor Tamlyn Tomita reports that Miramax pressured her to soften her pidgin accent during Automatic Dialogue Replacement.) Similar struggles are thematized in the film's narrative, as in the use of English-language voice-over and Japanese, pidgin, and standard English on the diegetic soundtrack. Conflicts between accommodation of and resistance to the cinematic marketplace, thematized in the film and circulating in the contextualizing discourses, animate the reception and alternative interpretations of the film along assimilationist and cultural nationalist lines.

Picture Bride opens with two title cards that briefly contextualize the practice of matchmaking in Japan, noting that the introduction of photography enabled matches to be made across greater distances, and informing us that more than 20,000 picture brides from Japan, Okinawa, and Korea emigrated to Hawai'i between 1907 and 1924. The film's prologue, set in Yokohama, is in black and white.[27] In voice-over, an English-speaking narrator (veteran Japanese American actor Nobu McCarthy) tells us that her aunt contacted a matchmaker on her behalf after her parents died. Subtitled Japanese dialogue between Riyo and her aunt reveals that they have concealed her parents' tuberculosis from the matchmaker, so that she can make a fresh start without stigma.

Arriving in Hawai'i, Riyo is dismayed to discover that she was misled about her husband's age (Matsuji is forty-three); they are married in a mass ceremony and then travel by cart to Matsuji's shack, apart from the worker's camp. Riyo refuses to consummate the marriage; her new husband complains that he wasn't told his wife was a frail city girl. The next morning, Riyo joins a group of women working the cane fields, led by Yayoi (who sings work songs, *hole hole bushi*) and Kana. Riyo asks Kana how long it will take to earn enough money for passage back to Japan; Kana earns extra money doing laundry for the bachelor laborers and invites Riyo to join her.

At harvest time, Kana's baby boy wanders into the cane fields after the fires have been lit; both Kana and the boy perish.[28] In the aftermath of this tragedy, the Japanese men meet to discuss a strike; Matsuji notes that they must enlist the Filipinos and the other workers as well. He begins to collect a strike fund, but Riyo refuses to make more than a token contribution. The next day she gathers all her money[29] and makes her way to the ocean on foot, where she is visited by Kana's ghost, who tells her to give up her dream of returning to Japan; Kana's ghost also passes on responsibility for leading the women to Riyo. Riyo returns to the shack and makes peace with Matsuji. The voice-over narrator returns to report that Hawai'i is home to Riyo, her daughter, and her granddaughter.

Choosing Resistance

Picture Bride's press kit provides a wealth of approaches to contextualize the film, including a detailed production history emphasizing community support for the production. (However, the press kit did not report details about the film's troubled postproduction.) In addition to guiding interpretation of the film, the kit skillfully provides "angles" for journalists to pursue; for example, references to members of Hatta's family that inspired different characters are scattered throughout the notes. The kit also includes a quick historical sketch of the economic conditions in Japan that compelled labor migration and of the conditions that Japanese labored under on the plantations. A section labeled "The Phenomenon of the Picture Bride" puts the practice in the context of Japan's tradition of arranged marriages and discusses the social and economic factors that account for the age difference between many of the husbands and wives.

The "human interest" angle predominates in an article written by a Honolulu-based writer for the *New York Times* Sunday Arts section preceding the film's New York opening. Sheryl Dare's article focuses on the women who inspired the film, quoting a surviving picture bride, Ayako Kikugawa, at length, and reproducing her wedding portrait (1995, H16; because the photograph is credited to Miramax, it seems likely that the film's producers arranged for Dare to meet with Kikugawa). Kayo Hatta is also quoted in this article, and although she briefly discusses the production and postproduction phases of her film, most of her comments focus on her interviews with and impressions of the picture brides that inspired her story. Hatta is also quoted defining three central Japanese values that account for the success and stability of these marriages, which the *Times* article misspells: "Gaman, which means perseverance; enryo, which is holding in your emotions; and shigata ganai, which is a sense that 'this is fate, it can't be helped, so just make the best of the situation' " (H16). Dare's article emphasizes Japanese fatalism.

By contrast, articles in periodicals specializing in independent film emphasize these women's *resistance.* Writing in *The Independent,* Fatimah Tobing Rony emphasizes the importance of *hole hole bushi* songs as an inspiration for Hatta's narrative: "the raunchiness of the songs and the hardship and abuse they described flew in the face of the stereotype of Japanese women as docile geisha girls" (1995, 15). Beyond the attitudes of defiance expressed in the songs themselves, Rony's article implies that Hatta's inclusion of the songs in her film serves to challenge stereotypes of submissive Japanese femininity. Rony's article also highlights Hatta's decision to employ as many women as possible and her regret at not being able to develop more fully her depiction of the racial stratification of the plantations and the role the *haole*s played in fostering that divisiveness.

These subtexts of resistance and interethnic cooperation are crucial to a deeper understanding of the structure of *Picture Bride*'s narrative. By returning to Matsuji and (presumably) investing her money in the strike fund, Riyo participates in what the press kit describes as "the first multinational workers strike." Ron Takaki notes that the Japanese laborers had based their solidarity in the Great Strike of 1909 on Japanese nationalism, thereby "open[ing] the way for planters to pit workers from other countries against the Japanese strikers" (1983, 164). Gary Okihiro argues that the 1920 strike differed from earlier strikes in that it "indicated an Americanized settler community as opposed to an alien migrant one" (1991, 66). The 1920 strike thus represents a signal shift away from an identity based on ties of culture and blood, toward an identity based on class and race rather than ethnicity. So while Riyo, like Polly in *Thousand Pieces of Gold,* realizes that there is no one back "home" waiting for her, her decision to stay is based on more than romantic love. Riyo takes an active role in the Japanese American (and budding Asian American) workers community, and when next we see her working the fields, she is leading the singing of *hole hole bushi.* Her song, which asserts that only mothers can protect their children from the brutal indifference of the field bosses (*lunas*), might be a tribute to Kana, but could also be taken as her statement that she intends to raise a family in Hawai'i.[30] It is these commitments to the community of workers that make Riyo's decision to stay in Hawai'i much more than a romance. (By comparison, Polly's decision in *Thousand Pieces of Gold* is primarily romantic; the historical context of the stories is important here, for the driving out depicted in *Thousand Pieces of Gold* comes at a time when cheap Chinese labor was no longer needed, whereas the Asian American workers in *Picture Bride* were crucial to the territory's economy, as Okihiro argues in the second section of *Cane Fires* [1991]). After all, when Kana's ghost instructs Riyo to return to the fields, she tells her to "take care of the girls"—she doesn't mention Matsuji.

The construction of an activist, resistant Asian American community accounts for much of the appeal of *Picture Bride* to contemporary Asian Americans, and indeed my earlier discussion of *Thousand Pieces of Gold* lamented the narrative resolution wherein Polly removes herself from the Chinese American community. However, if community is possible in *Picture Bride,* it is due not to the politics of its narrative, but to its historical setting: prestatehood Hawai'i can sustain an Asian American community in part because of its isolation from the mainland. (Is Polly and Charlie's home on the River of No Return all that different from Riyo and Matsuji's shack set away from the workers camp?) On Hawai'i, the Japanese immigrants can celebrate Obon, but in Warren, the whites regard Chinese New Year's celebrations with unease. It is surely possible for audiences disinclined to pick up on *Picture Bride*'s critique of capitalism and white racism

Nakayama Yasubei is here.

Picture Bride. Riyo plays samurai among the laundry.

to interpret the film's concluding images celebrating the preservation of Japanese culture as a feel-good ending depicting multicultural diversity; just as it is possible for a politicized, Asian American audience to celebrate the preservation of cultural difference without fully considering the ways that Hawai'i's economy is isolated from the mainland.

With these differences in setting in mind, *Picture Bride*'s and *Thousand Pieces of Gold*'s narrative resolutions also differ insofar as they conceive romance differently. For example, in *Picture Bride* romance is emphasized as a performative act: Kana counsels Matsuji to act like Valentino to win Riyo's heart; this advice comes as they are walking home after taking in a samurai movie projected by a traveling *benshi* (silent film narrator) played by Toshiro Mifune. A few scenes later, when Matsuji shows up with a cart to take Riyo on a tour of the island, he interrupts her as she acts out the role of the samurai in the film they have just seen. Kana and Riyo are hanging out the laundry to dry, and the white sheets offer a visual echo of the movie screen erected in the middle of a cane field. The cinema may be the reference point for these women's notions of romance, but it also provides an opportunity for identification across gender lines.

The other great romance depicted in *Picture Bride* is that between Riyo and Hawai'i itself. Matsuji attempts to seduce Riyo with a day exploring the island's beauty, just as he enticed her to marry him by describing the island paradise in his letter. Of course, Hawai'i is no fantasy land: when *Picture Bride* shifts from black and white to color as the film's prologue concludes, it does not represent Riyo's arrival in Oz, but her rude awakening from her illusions about her husband. But Hawai'i is also the land of ghosts, and as such it revises the Japanese tradition of the ghost story, because Matsuji and Riyo agree that it was hard to believe in ghosts in Japan, but in Hawai'i ghosts exist. These Hawai'ian ghosts are benevolent, covering Riyo with leaves when she falls asleep in the fields, and if they are all like Kana, they represent the spirit of perseverance and offer a link to the history of Asian workers on the island.

It is the layering of these different narratives of seduction and integration that I wish to sort out here. In *Thousand Pieces of Gold,* Polly's decision to make her home in Idaho is inseparable from her romance with Charlie: it is never clear whether she is embracing a man, or the land. *Picture Bride* also layers these seductions atop each other: Does Riyo grow to love Matsuji, or does she fall in love with Hawai'i? These two narratives are inseparable insofar as Matsuji attempts to seduce Riyo with the landscape, but I would argue that Riyo's choice centers not on Matsuji or the landscape, but indeed represents her rejection of romantic, nostalgic beliefs in favor of contemporary political realities. This shift is expressed in the displacement of haiku by *hole hole bushi;* when Matsuji's haiku describing the beauty of nature is revealed to be hollow, Riyo replaces it with her own poem that describes the harshness of the land. The role the landscape plays in disabusing her of her fantasies of Japan is hinted at early on, when Matsuji points to the ocean view from the porch of his shack and tells Riyo that as the cane grows, it will block the view of the ocean entirely. The cycle of nature and the cane harvest on the island will hide the ocean: the immediacy of the present will dispel the fantasy of return to Japan.

Riyo's decision is forced upon her by her circumstances, but she also makes a conscious decision to invest her energy into the community of workers. She is on the one hand forced by economic necessity to become a Hawai'ian, but she also makes the deliberate choice to redefine her role as a worker in that economy. This paradox of agency—that Riyo has no choice but to become Hawai'ian, but she can decide what kind of a Hawai'ian she will become—expresses the contemporary Asian American storyteller's desire to show both that we have no choice but to be Americans, but that we choose to define ourselves as Asian Americans and not as Orientals; that is to say, we do not accept our position in U.S. politics but choose to redefine that role. An Oriental is often told "Go back where you came from," and the Asian American confronted with that sentiment surely envies the authority with which an African American can retort "You brought us here!" Thus, the Asian American storyteller describes the capitalist giant that recruited Asian labor to build this country. Pioneer narratives thus play on the contradictions of how people become Americans: they chose to become American, but they also had no choice but to be American.

In these immigrant narratives, the pioneer woman symbolizes the founding of communities: in the heterosexist imaginary, the arrival of women signals that the male workers are no longer sojourners, but first-generation Americans.[31] The men have given up their ties to Asia; it is only the women who continue to write letters and send money. The women are relied on to bear Asian traditions—to cook Asian foods, to observe Asian rituals, to honor Asian ancestors—while the men labor to create a new life in the United States. The sojourner, lured by the Gold Mountain to a land where wealth can be accumulated and returned to Asia, gives way to the first-generation American seduced by the American Dream; this man relies on the pioneer woman both to connect him to Asian tradition and to give birth to American children. The pioneer woman must therefore be persuaded that she has no choice but to become an American—and yet, she must demonstrate her agency, her right to define what it means to be an American. It is this paradox between agency and inevitability, between choice and lack of options, that accounts for the romance narrative, a narrative built around a structure of displaced agency, of inevitability, and of consent. The notion of consent yokes together the concepts of agency and inevitability: to romance a pioneer woman is to make her believe that she has chosen a life that she was forced to take—to gain her consent. The woman in a romance narrative does have a choice, but within a narrow range of options. She does not make her destiny, she accedes to it. She doesn't choose her lover, she accedes to the one that has been provided by the narrative.

In casting pioneer women as the first Asian Americans, the first to accede to an American identity, these stories depict Asian male national identity as always already secure. Matsuji, like Riyo, may define his identity as oppositional to white American identity; nonetheless, his decision to become an American precedes the diegesis of the film. In *Thousand Pieces of Gold,* Jim represents the Chinese sojourner who maintains his identity as a Chinese man; Hong King represents the Chinese American male entrepreneur, and he affirms his identity as an American whenever it is questioned. The relatively unproblematic assumption of American identities by these men is not surprising, for discourses of citizenship presume a normatively straight male subject.[32] In narrative terms, however, Asian men's choices are not dramatized; rather, they are hypostatized in a state of being rather than of becoming. There is no room in these narratives for fluid Asian American male subjectivity (to reiterate my own problematic position vis-à-vis these narratives). Which brings us to *Living on Tokyo Time,* a contemporary narrative of an Asian woman's migration and the effect she has on destabilizing an Asian American man's subjectivity.

Living on Tokyo Time

Steven Okazaki, a Sansei from Venice, California, graduated from San Francisco State University in 1976 and has remained in the Bay Area ever since.[33] He began his filmmaking career with short children's films, including *A-M-E-R-I-C-A-N-S* (1976), which was broadcast on CBS and PBS in 1977, and the dramatic short *A Little Joke* in 1978. In 1980 he made *Judy & Paul,* a documentary short about two survivors of the Hiroshima bombing, for KQED-TV's *Evening Edition,* and followed with *Survivors* (1982), a seventy-minute documentary focusing on more survivors of Hiroshima and Nagasaki; it was produced for WBGH and aired on PBS. Chinese American poet Genny Lim was the subject of *The Only Language She Knows* (completed in 1983 but not broadcast on PBS until 1987). Okazaki solidified his reputation as one of the premiere Asian American documentary filmmakers with *Unfinished Business,* a documentary on the *coram nobis* cases of internment resistors Fred Korematsu, Gordon Hirabayashi, and Minoru Yasui; the film aired on PBS and was nominated for an Academy Award in 1986.

Production on *Living on Tokyo Time* (1987), which would be Okazaki's first dramatic feature, began in 1984. Okazaki had encountered Ken Nakagawa at a local grocery store, where he worked as a boxboy; Okazaki got to know Nakagawa better when he began working at NAATA, and he became inspired to build a movie around Nakagawa's personality. Okazaki wrote a screenplay with his friend John McCormick, secured an AFI grant, and located some private investors. He auditioned many Asian American actors for the female lead opposite Nakagawa, finally finding Minako Ohashi, a theater student at San Francisco State who had sung in a Japanese rock band called Hanako. Production began in the winter of 1984 and continued through the summer of 1985, with most of the shoot taking place on successive weekends.[34] (Okazaki rented his cameras from companies who charged him for one weekday with the understanding that he would use the camera over the weekend, thus stretching Friday over three or four weekend days.) Judi Nihei, an actor and dramaturge with a long association with Okazaki's production company, served as assistant director, played the role of Sheri the waitress, and helped Okazaki cast many of the roles. Most of the actors came from the Asian American Theatre Company and Nihei's improv group, the National Theatre of the Deranged. Okazaki cast artist Kate Connell in the key role of Lana and also drew on figures from the Asian American community, including cameo roles for actor and performance artist Brenda Wong Aoki, lawyer Dennis Hayashi (who also produced), and Diane Wong; Hayashi and Dale Minami (Wong's then-husband) were both lawyers involved in the *coram nobis* cases (Nihei, letter to author, 3 May 1998). African American saxophonist Lewis Jordan also had a brief appearance; he would go on to be an important contributor to the Bay Area's Asian American jazz movement and can be heard on Mark Izu's album, *Circle of Fire.*[35]

Most of the editing took place at Film Arts Foundation; *Unfinished Business*'s Oscar nomination helped boost Okazaki's efforts to secure funding (the film's final budget was approximately $100,000). *Living on Tokyo Time* premiered at Sundance in 1987 and was well-received; Okazaki fielded distribution offers from several companies, including Miramax, Samuel Goldwyn, and New Line. After holding special screenings in New York and Los Angeles, he signed with Skouras Pictures, which had had success the year before with the Swedish film *My Life as a Dog.* The film opened in New York City in August 1987; it also showed on the Bravo cable channel.

Living on Tokyo Time was a modest financial success and a pioneering Asian American feature film.[36] It provided exposure for a number of actors who continue to be active in Asian American theater and films, including Mitzi Abe, Amy Hill, Ken Narasaki, Lane Nishikawa, and Sharon Omi. Minako Ohashi has gone on to work behind the scenes in media production; Ken Nakagawa is now a computer engineer. Since *Living on Tokyo Time,* Okazaki has produced one other dramatic feature, 1993's *The Lisa Theory,* a "theater piece" called *American Sons* (1995), and many documentaries, including the Oscar-winning *Days of Waiting* in 1990.[37]

Living on Tokyo Time begins with Kyoko, who addresses the camera in close-up, telling us that she moved to America after her fiancé had an affair with another woman. She finds a room at the YWCA and a job in the kitchen of a Japanese restaurant. When her visa is due to expire, one of the waitresses at the restaurant suggests she marry Ken, a Sansei with a going-nowhere job who plays guitar in a going-nowhere garage band: a slacker (before the term was coined). Ken knows virtually nothing about Japan, and he isn't much of a talker, but he seizes on Kyoko as his chance to connect with his roots; he likes being married and seems to think that he and Kyoko can make it work. After they sleep together, Kyoko realizes that Ken has "forgotten the plan." Following a disastrous INS interview, Kyoko suddenly returns to Japan. An epilogue and an on-screen epigram from Captain Beefheart—"You can't escape gravity"—imply that Ken has been brought out of himself somewhat by this experience.

Reviewer Joseph Gelmis favorably compared *Living on Tokyo Time* with *Chan Is Missing,* noting that both films possessed "idiosyncratic personalities . . . that overcome their technical limitations" (1987). Reviewers uniformly praised the film for getting the little things right—nuances of characterization among the supporting players, brief glimpses of life in J-town—but differed on the lead performances. On the one hand, *The Village Voice*'s Edelstein notes that "withdrawn, inexpressive people should not be played by withdrawn, inexpressive actors" (1987, 57); on the other hand, Gelmis describes Ken Nakagawa's performance as "passive, innocent, vulnerable—and, inexplicably, he's funny." These divergent evaluations of the quality of the lead performances emerge from different contextual expectations: framing the film as a "guerrilla production" (as Gelmis basically does) goes a long way toward inflecting the reception of an uneven film with occasionally amateurish acting. (Gelmis's comparison with *Chan Is Missing* is instructive; the roughness of that film invites an aesthetic response that accepts the unevenness of some of the performances. By contrast, *Living on Tokyo Time* has a more polished sheen—simply stated, it looks like a better-produced, better-scripted, better-funded production than *Chan Is Missing*—and thereby it puts itself in a different category. *Living on Tokyo Time* was probably a better-planned, certainly more tightly scripted film than the improvised *Chan Is Missing,* and its vitality is somewhat muted as a result.)

Revoking Choices

By bringing *Living on Tokyo Time* into the discussion, I should make clear that I do not see the film as responding to or commenting on a narrative pattern evident in the other films; after all, *Living on Tokyo Time* premiered three years before *Thousand Pictures of Gold* and eight years before *Picture Bride.* Whereas *Gold* and *Picture Bride* depict pioneering Asian American women, *Tokyo Time* is set in contemporary San Francisco. Indeed, it is precisely the differences in historical setting that I want to illuminate here, as well as the very different choices of narrative structure and what they tell us about the kinds of interventions that the filmmakers were attempting.

Given those caveats, it is amusing to note the uncanny ways in which *Tokyo Time* inverts the narrative patterns of the two later films. Reduced to the barest of plot points, the stories told by *Thousand Pieces of Gold* and *Picture Bride* are structurally quite similar: an older relative sends a young woman far away to marry. Upon arriving, she discovers that life in the new land is much harsher than she had been led to believe. She accepts her marriage in name only, not taking her "husband" to her heart, and devotes all of her energy to raising enough money to return to Asia, developing her entrepreneurial skills as a result. She makes friends with a kindred spirit who helps her to adapt to her new home while nurturing her dream of returning, but after she loses that friend she is advised to face the fact that there is no one waiting for her back home. Realizing that she is becoming an American, and that her mate has been patiently waiting for her to return his affections, she returns to him and yokes her future to his. Compare that story with *Living on Tokyo Time.* Betrayed by her lover, a young woman defies her family and travels to America. She marries in name only, so that she can become an American; however, she has no success earning money. She exchanges letters with her family and friends in Asia, who beg her to return. Realizing that her mate has been patiently waiting for her to return his affections, and confronted with the difficulty of adapting to another culture, she rejects her husband and returns to Asia.

What makes Kyoko's story different from Polly's and Riyo's? Narratively speaking, she doesn't have the friendships to nurture her sense of self and her incipient Americanness. When Lana suggests that Kyoko marry Ken, she doesn't have Kyoko's interests in mind; instead, she hopes that the marriage will force Ken to open up. By contrast, Kana tells Matsuji that he should romance Riyo, but only after she first tells him to stop gambling. Kana realizes that Matsuji has to change to be worthy of Riyo, and Lana hopes that Kyoko will bring about change in Ken. Even Polly has a larger network of friends than does Kyoko: the smithy who advises her that slavery is illegal, and Berthe, who advises her to go into business for herself. By contrast, Kyoko only encounters her coworkers at the restaurant and Ken at home; she is not part of a diasporic Japanese community (as Riyo is at Obon).

Of course, the biggest difference between Kyoko and her counterparts is that she has the resources to return to Japan when it doesn't work out for her in the United States. For all the emphasis on Polly's and Riyo's choices to commit to life in their new homes, neither has a life to return to in Asia. This is not to diminish the psychological importance of their decisions; after all, Riyo did not have to return to Matsuji and raise a family with him in order to remain in Hawai'i. It should also be acknowledged that economic factors encouraged the migration of Polly and especially Riyo, whose bodies were needed to contribute directly (with their own labor) or indirectly (with their service) to Asian migrant laboring communities. Despite anti-Asian legislation in the late nineteenth and early twentieth centuries, the U.S. economy depended on Asian labor.[38] By contrast, Kyoko offers nothing that the U.S. economy needs.

Whereas the pioneer women of *Thousand Pieces of Gold* and *Picture Bride* symbolize the founding of Asian American community, the Japanese American community in *Living on Tokyo Time* is already well established. It is, however, a community in which Sansei men and women rarely connect: counterman Lane is rebuffed by his female customers, a businessman harasses a waitress, and Ken's sister Mimi is married to her business partner, a white man. The great external threat facing J-town is not the "driving out" or the capitalist hierarchy of the sugar plantation; instead, J-town is threatened by outmarriage. It is important to note that *Living on Tokyo Time* does not portray Japanese American men as assimilationist: they do not pursue white women. Rather, the inability of Sansei men to connect with Sansei women is due to the inadequacy of Japanese American masculinity: Sansei men have no clue how to connect with Sansei women. Kyoko's role is thus updated from that of the pioneer women: she does not represent the foundation of first-generation Asian American communities, but the attempt to preserve and renew the Japanese American family, to re-create Japanese American marriage on the Nisei model. In *Living on Tokyo Time,* Nisei don't outmarry. Okazaki's film jokes that the only way to bridge the gap between twentysomething Japanese American men and women is to bring in new blood, to infuse J-town with a Japanese woman; it is too late, however, and Japanese American masculinity is not up to the challenge of romancing the immigrant woman, of getting her to consent to life in the United States.

Living on Tokyo Time may begin with Kyoko's narration, but it is ultimately Ken's story insofar as he is the one who undergoes transformation (albeit incremental). The film is ultimately less interested in Kyoko's efforts to plant her roots in American soil than in Ken's attempts to recover his Japanese heritage. Werner Sollors (1986) would identify this as a third-generation impulse, whereas Omi and Winant (1994) might see Ken's fascination with Japan as consistent with cultural nationalism. The cultural moment that *Living on Tokyo Time* depicts is the creation not of Asian American culture, but of a thoroughly Americanized Sansei's nostalgic desire to recover some cultural pride.[39] When the marriage of convenience proves to be untenable, it does result in transformation of the Sansei man; unfortunately, the Japanese woman returns to a Japan where she is still isolated, alone in a screened room, writing to her Japanese American ex-husband, inviting him to correspond with her. It is her isolation that removes *Tokyo Time* from the romance genre: the Japanese woman does not symbolize the founding of a new community, but a crisis of identity for Japanese American masculinity.

The narrative of immigration turns, then, on crises of agency: Did we choose to become Americans, or was that choice made for us by circumstances beyond our control? *Tokyo Time*'s Lambert, a blue-collar worker from Taiwan, critiques the narrative of immigration described by all three of these films. Lambert's cultural identity is illegible to Americans; everyone thinks he is from Hong Kong. When Ken asks him if he wants to go back, Lambert replies that it's too late; in Lambert's view, you become an American when you're not looking—it sneaks up on you until you've changed and you can't go back:

> LAMBERT: When I came to the United States, I never thought I would be working a job like this. $5 an hour! I thought I'd be rich by now.
> KEN: So? Can't you go back?
> LAMBERT: It's too late to go back. If you stay too long, you have to stay. Too hard to go back now.
> KEN: Well, maybe you'll strike it rich someday.
> LAMBERT: That is propaganda put out by rich people, to get poor people to work for no money by spreading those stories.
> KEN: You should become a musician. One hit record, and you got it made.
> LAMBERT: You are not as smart as you look. How many Asians you know with hit records?

Living on Tokyo Time. In a cameo appearance, Dennis Hayashi (left) looks on as Ken Narasaki tries to pick up Judi Nihei.

Ken implicitly equates economic security with feeling at home (if your job doesn't pay well, the answer is to go home; if you can't go home, the only hope is that "you'll strike it rich someday"). For his part, Lambert critiques the ideology of the American Dream from a class-conscious perspective, revealing that the transnational flow of capital strands workers who might imagine their identity differently if they were not rooted in bodies that cannot cross boundaries as easily as capital can. In Lambert's view, you can imagine that you could become the first Asian American rock star, but it's not likely to happen as long as Asian masculinity is represented by the likes of Ken.

If *Living on Tokyo Time* is pessimistic about the future of the J-town community, it nevertheless helps to construct a community in another sense: as a pioneering Asian American feature film, *Living on Tokyo Time* works to construct an Asian American film audience and to introduce Asian American characters into the U.S. pop cultural consciousness. In this regard, *Tokyo Time*'s cameo roles are revealing. Whereas *Picture Bride* features Toshiro Mifune, the charismatic star who symbolizes Japanese masculinity in the popular consciousness, *Tokyo Time* gives cameo roles to community leaders like lawyer Dennis Hayashi, who can be glimpsed watching the pathetic sexual innuendoes of a Sansei friend. Rather than building Asian American community on a heterosexist framework driven by transnational capital's dependence on immigrant labor, or imagining that community sustained by its cinematic heroes like Mifune, *Tokyo Time* seems to suggest that it is activists like Hayashi who are the true hope for Asian American community.

Living on Tokyo Time's pessimism is the inevitable result of its narrative structure, which refutes the simplistic resolutions of traditional romance narratives. But of course, the differences between the Japanese American communities depicted in *Picture Bride* and *Living on Tokyo Time* are also explained through historical changes between the two periods and the intervening event of World War II. The forced removal of Japanese Americans from the West Coast of the United States during World War II destroyed any lingering romantic notions of reciprocal love between Japanese Americans and their adopted country, and the long-term transformation of U.S.-Japanese relations after the war dramatically altered migration patterns between Japan and the United States.

The legacy of the WW II Internment is the subject of the movies in the next chapter. Rea Tajiri, Janice Tanaka, and Lise Yasui distrust the scientific gaze of ethnographic cinema and the seductive ideology of the romance genre. In both ethnographic cinema and romance narratives, cinematic convention articulates the terms by which Asian bodies will be accepted into the U.S. body politic. Cinema thus articulates an aesthetic of belonging, an aesthetic that contributed to a politics of exclusion that resulted in the imprisonment of 110,000 Japanese Americans following U.S. entry into World War II. The communities promoted by U.S. film genres are founded on the exclusion of Asian American subjectivities, as *Living on Tokyo Time* suggests with seriocomic melancholy; the Internment movies discussed in Chapter 3 attempt to transform that melancholia into full-fledged mourning.

CHAPTER 3

Articulating Silence

Sansei and Memories of the Camps

> Memories are not always an understood compilation of linear ideas. They seem instead to be fragments of stored, synthesized, edited sensory stimuli; bits of personalized perceptions. Film and television oftentimes play a major role in the process of subliminal inculturation by creating a criteria for self-evaluation. Consequently, our self-image, our role models, what we know and expect of our society and the world, are greatly influenced by the media. Somewhere caught between the crevices of concept and production lay the elements or perhaps the reflective shadows of who and what we are. This exquisitely complex structure of electrons prophetically examines nature.—Janice Tanaka, "Electrons and Reflective Shadows"

> This process—experimenting by turning persuasive discourse into speaking persons—becomes especially important in those cases where a struggle against such images has already begun, where someone is striving to liberate himself from the influence of such an image and its discourse by means of objectification, or is striving to expose the limitations of both image and discourse.
> —Mikhail Bakhtin, *The Dialogic Imagination*

The December 22, 1941, issue of *Life* magazine featured an article titled "How to Tell Japs from the Chinese."[1] At the bottom of the first page, below the close-ups of Chinese ("parchment yellow complexion") and Japanese ("earthy yellow complexion") faces, is a picture of a Chinese American journalist with a tag pinned to his lapel: "Chinese Reporter: *Not Japanese,* Please!" That spring, mass-produced buttons reading "I am Chinese" began appearing (not "I am Chinese American"), forming an ironic contrast to the famous photograph of a Nisei storefront displaying a banner (defiantly? defensively?) reading "I am an American."[2] In 1941–1942, the Asian American Movement was still a quarter-century away; examples of solidarity between Japanese Americans and other Asian ethnic groups in the United States were few and far between. Chinese Americans could still recall the "driving out" and knew that their own position was precarious at best.

The Internment of Japanese Americans was brought about by a crisis in vision, by the U.S. government's inability to see the difference between Japanese sympathizers and Japanese Americans. According to *Life,* the camera permitted the classification of visible differences between Japanese and Chinese, but the U.S. government's decision to imprison 110,000 Japanese Americans reveals that such systems of photographic classification were inadequate, as subjective in practice as ethnographic cinema. The preceding chapters have argued that cinema is a technology not of scientific objectivity but of subjective perception, not describing the world but justifying literal and metaphorical acts of colonization. If cinema does not record historical fact but instead enables the shaping of facts, then cinema becomes a technology of memory rather than history.

Lise Yasui and Ann Tegnell's *A Family Gathering* (1988–1989), Rea Tajiri's *History and Memory* (1991), and Janice Tanaka's *Who's Going to Pay for These Donuts, Anyway?* (1993) each depict a kind of archaeology of memory.[3] These two videos and one film confront the Internment's legacy for the survivors as well as their descendents, attempting to describe the violent effect Internment had on the continuity of memory for Japanese Americans, how repressed parental memories affected the lives of those born after the barbed wire was taken down. These movies thus attempt to represent that which should have been represented: they must somehow depict the absence of depictions of the Internment, and that paradox is evident in an ambivalent attitude toward the processes of cinematic representation. For example, Tajiri's *History and Memory* begins with an analysis of the absence of Japanese American faces in Hollywood movies and the effect that absence has on the self-image and desires of contemporary Japanese American women; but the video hesitates to address that absence by offering Japanese American faces, as if that act would confirm the logic of visibility (whereby that which is visible, i.e., represented cinematically, is legitimated).[4] Similarly, Tajiri's video invokes cinematic discourses (such as Hollywood movies and War Department propaganda films) to undermine them while it foregrounds its own processes of representation as if undermining itself.

Dominant cinematic representations clash with Asian American representations in Tajiri's *History and Memory,* so to interpret the video effectively we need a hermeneutic methodology that accounts for the interaction of discourses. This reading practice must be attentive to the power relations in texts and how those power relations shift as texts are brought to bear on each other, must be able to account for highly localized and indeed momentary reversals of power, for the ways the so-called margin can deploy its marginality to challenge the legitimacy of the center. For example, in *Racial Formation in the United States,* Omi and Winant advance a Foucauldian perspective when they argue against the "racism equals prejudice plus power" formula because " 'power' cannot be reified as a thing which some possess and others don't, but instead [power] constitutes a relational field. The minority student who boldly asserts in class that minorities cannot be racist is surely not entirely powerless. In all but the most absolutist of regimes, resistance to rule itself implies power" (1994, 188 n.65). In cinematic terms, surely the deployment of War Department footage in these Asian American texts indicates that their "power" has been mobilized in the service of an Asian American argument; however, I take it that the ambivalence that accompanies these textual operations is a sign of the power that adheres to the quoted footage. (This is evidenced in the fact that many students, after viewing *History and Memory,* respond, in effect, "But Japanese Americans *were* a security risk during the War." As I see it, they are responding to the pro-Internment perspectives expressed in Tajiri's video, even though Tajiri undermines those arguments.) To account for these shifting power relations, and the "double-voicedness" of quoted footage (which speaks with the "intent" of both the putative originating author and the appropriating maker), I propose an interpretive framework drawing on Mikhail Bakhtin's concept of dialogism.

Sansei and the Structuring Absence of the Camps

The three makers in this chapter are all Sansei women, but with widely varying experiences of the camps. Tanaka is (barely) old enough to remember the camps herself; Tajiri and Yasui were born after the war's end. Yasui was raised in a *hapa* (mixed-race) family on the East Coast; Tajiri and Tanaka grew up in Chicago and California.[5] The film/videos also vary widely; nonetheless, themes of parental reticence (metaphoric amnesia), imagined childhood memories, and pain recur throughout all three.[6] To account for the divergences and similarities in the three movies, we should briefly examine the contrasting contexts for each film/video's production.

Lise Yasui grew up in small-town Pennsylvania; the kids in her family were the only Japanese American children, indeed the only mixed-race children, in Williamsport. Her awareness of her Japanese American heritage came from her father's home movies (taken before she was born). During screenings of these films, her father told highly sanitized stories about the family; she later described these narrated screenings as "declarations of what he chose to remember." Looking back, Yasui decided that "the movies represented the boundary between the father she knew and the father whose real feelings might forever remain hidden from her" (Kessler, 1993, 309).

It was through another cinematic medium that Yasui first learned that her family had been interned: her father sent the children out of the room while he watched a televised documentary, *Nisei: The Pride and the Shame* (CBS, 1965). Years later, Yasui persuaded her father to tell her part of the story for essays on family history that she wrote in high school and college. She earned a bachelor's degree in psychology and entered that field after graduation; after four years she shifted gears and entered Temple University's film program and began work on a documentary about the camps and her family's experiences. By her own account, her production meandered until one night when her father finally revealed the family secret: her grandfather Masuo had committed suicide in 1957. Yasui had finally unearthed the "dramatic climax" around which she could organize her film, but it took her nearly a year to get permission from her family to proceed. (Yasui's Uncle Chop, the *chonan* or eldest son, was strongly opposed; Chop, actually the second-born son, had borne the mantle of chonan since his brother Kay had committed suicide at the age of seventeen. Years before, the Yasui family had rewritten their own history, no longer speaking of Kay, pretending that Chop had always been chonan.)[7]

A Family Gathering evolved into a thirty-minute documentary about Yasui's attempts to learn her family's past. Segments of the film approach conventional documentary style; for example, an early segment narrates the events of Masuo Yasui's emigration, marriage, and early years in Oregon. However, the voice-over narration for these relatively straightforward segments is continually peppered with such phrases as "I'm told" and

"I discover," foregrounding the process of discovery but also the mediated quality of the story. Masuo's story is not related by an objective narrator, nor in his own words, but is constantly relayed to us through Lise Yasui's occasionally doubtful narration. (Yasui herself never appears on-screen.)

A Family Gathering is structured around the medium that first introduced Yasui to her family's past: film. She explains her own childhood ignorance through recourse to home movies that show her "surrounded by blue-eyed relatives from my mom's side of the family"; the voice-over serves a dual function, both to call attention to young Lise's racial difference, but also to downplay its significance.[8] She next shows us footage of her grandparents and tells us memories she has of them, then reveals that her parents have told her that she never met her grandfather; Yasui notes that her father's home movies became the only images she had as a child, and they were shown with enough frequency that they became part of her memory. By film's end, when Yasui's voice-over tells us how she learned of her grandfather's death, she shows us the home movies again and informs us that she likes to remember her grandfather anyway, even though she now knows he died before she could meet him.

Yasui showed *A Family Gathering* around the country, garnering awards at the San Francisco International Film Festival and the Chicago Film Festival; it was also invited to festivals in Stockholm and Leningrad. In Chicago, the film caught the eye of the producers of PBS's *The American Experience* series. They asked her to expand the film to one hour, and she felt compelled once again to ask her family's permission.[9] During production of the expanded version, *A Family Gathering* received a 1988 Oscar nomination for documentary short subject; that recognition went a long way toward convincing her family that their story did not reflect badly on them.[10]

In contrast to Yasui's status as an emerging filmmaker, Janice Tanaka was already regarded as a pioneering video artist when she began work on *Memories from the Department of Amnesia* (1989) and *Who's Going to Pay for These Donuts, Anyway?* Her earlier works, including *Duality, Duplicity* (1979), *Manpower* (1980), *Beaver Valley* (1981), and *Mute* (1981), are structural examinations of American suburban life (not autobiographical, but often emphasizing a mother's point of view) and do not foreground Japanese American issues or otherwise direct attention to the videomaker's ethnicity. In the mid-1980s, Tanaka's work began to explore moral and ethical issues confronting American society, including *Superhuman Flights of Submoronic Fancies* (1982) and *Grass, or When the Rain Falls on the Water Does the*

Fish Get Any Wetter (1985). (Notice that Tanaka's titles began to get longer and more fanciful.)

Memories from the Department of Amnesia was completed after the death of Tanaka's mother, Lily Yamate. Depressed and unable to concentrate on her work, Tanaka finally decided to confront her emotions on video; she had intended to share the finished piece with only a few of her close friends, but their response to it encouraged her to distribute it. The thirteen-minute video has two parts: the first section, consisting primarily of abstract images set in a diner and a snowy landscape and accompanied by electronic music, conveys a sense of emotional dislocation; the second section, which features a conversation between Tanaka and her daughter on the soundtrack and processed images of family snapshots (with a series of character-generated dates and events from Yamate's life), offers several different perspectives on a Nisei's life. *Memories* is more explicitly personal than any of Tanaka's previous videos, and although the camps are an important aspect of Yamate's life, they are not emphasized.

Who's Going to Pay for These Donuts, Anyway? however, addresses questions of Japanese American identity (and memories of the camps) more directly. *Donuts* is a documentary, albeit a documentary that draws on the experimental video tradition; it aired on PBS's *P.O.V.* series in 1993.[11] Tanaka had last seen her father when she was three; he had been separated from the family when he was taken into custody by the FBI and subsequently placed in a mental institution. It was not until after her mother's death that Tanaka began actively searching for her father, eventually finding him in a halfway-house. *Donuts* chronicles the efforts by Tanaka and her two adult children to integrate Jack Tanaka into their lives; the video also explores the memories of Jack's brother Togo (whom the videomaker had seen intermittently during her childhood). Togo Tanaka, an English-language editor for the *Rafu Shimpo* (a Japanese American newspaper) had advocated cooperation with the U.S. government during the War, but Jack had protested incarceration; *Donuts* compares the stories of these two men and further compares Togo's cancer treatment with Jack's mental illness.

Experimental video techniques highlight segments that depict the disorientation of Jack's illness as well as the cultural dimensions of his behavior. For example, a sequence depicting a Japanese tea ceremony is intercut with footage of one of Jack's pastimes, fashioning fishing lures out of food packaging. Jack's meticulous clumsiness is contrasted with the precision of the ceremony, as a voice-over explains that the importance of the ceremony lies not in the tea itself, but in the serenity imparted by the ritual. This sequence is counterposed by an earlier segment depicting a doctor's examination of Jack, in which character-generated text points out that mental illness is diagnosed through behavioral tests, despite the fact that different cultures have different behavioral norms. *Donuts* also foregrounds its process by emphasizing the videomaker's own metaphoric schizophrenia at moments when she attempts (from behind the camera) both to interrogate her father and to connect with him; her occasionally patronizing questions (as when she asks him if he knows why he received a $20,000 check from the U.S. government) are simultaneously the words of a daughter assessing her father's mental acuity and of a filmmaker documenting the personal dimension of the movement for redress and reparations.

A comparison of *Donuts* with *A Family Gathering* is instructive. Yasui used the excuse of school assignments (essays and her film project) to get her father to talk about his past, whereas Jack's tenuous mental state made Tanaka's video both more pressing and more risky. Both films were impelled by the need to account for an ancestor's death and to explore the connection between that death and the camps, not to mention the void in the family's past; in Tanaka's case, that void was something more than metaphoric, as she did not know her father at all. Yasui's film chronicles her attempts to reconstruct what happened to her family and the circumstances leading up to her grandfather's death; Tanaka's video depicts her family's efforts to come to terms with the unexpected discovery that her father is still alive. Yasui's film is less impressionistic than Tanaka's video (drawing more on the documentary than the experimental tradition), and yet Yasui's film is still highly subjective and process-oriented. Whereas Yasui never appears on screen, Tanaka appears in her video in footage shot by other members of her family (including her father) and in footage where reflections in mirrors reveal Tanaka behind the lens of her own camera. Finally, each movie was presented under very different PBS banners, *The American Experience* (documentaries, usually on film) for Yasui, and *P.O.V.* (experimental video) for Tanaka.

Like Tanaka, Rea Tajiri is an established video artist. Much of her work is concerned with narrative structure in Hollywood films; for example, *Hitchcock Trilogy* (1987) juxtaposes a variety of experimental film techniques (scrolling text, appropriated footage, off-center framings of the human body) with Bernard Herrman's scores for three of Hitchcock's films. In *Off Limits* (1988), scrolling text presenting a first-person narrative adapted from the Hollywood movie *Off Limits* (1987) is contrasted with the soundtrack for the last five minutes of *Easy Rider* (1968); Tajiri's video tells us the former film was "made in America in 1987 about Saigon in 1968" and the latter was "made in America in 1968 about America in 1968." Tajiri also produced a short film titled *The Diary of Lennie Itoh One Year after the Death of Her Aunt Mako* (1986) that depicted "an adolescent Japanese American girl, her obsession with Hollywood images of romance, and her attempt to place her own images within that context" (Gee, 1990, 20), footage that Tajiri would incorporate into *History and Memory: For Akiko and Takashige*. (*History and Memory* was funded by grants from the NEA, the New York State Council for the Arts, and Art Matters.) In 1997, Tajiri completed her first feature film, *Strawberry Fields,* a road movie about a Sansei woman whose teenage sister commits suicide, setting her adrift in the American landscape until she ends up at the site where her parents had been interned; interestingly, Tajiri claims she resisted the idea of including the camps in her film until her collaborator/coscreenwriter Kerri Sakamoto insisted.[12]

History and Memory is perhaps the most complex of the movies discussed in this chapter. Unlike Tanaka, Tajiri's primary means of expression is not the manipulated image, but the organization and deployment (juxtaposition and editing) of image, sound, and text. Tajiri's video contrasts and conflates a wide variety of cinematic texts, ranging from Hollywood musicals to captured Japanese aerial footage. Material from members of her family is presented on the soundtrack as "captured sound," as studio-recorded rehearsed narrative performed by a nephew, and as a letter from an uncle read by Tajiri. Scrolling text presents factual information about the camps, family stories told from the perspective of an omniscient observer, and commentary on quoted film footage. Character-generated text may appear over the credit sequence of a Hollywood film, accompanied by the soundtrack to still another film as well as voice-over commentary. If the video has a central narrative, it is the story of how a Sansei analyzed her family's reticence to discuss the camps. Where Yasui's film focused on the difficulties she experienced gathering stories from her family, *History and Memory* emphasizes the variety of strategies Tajiri employed to prompt reminiscences. Where Tanaka's video is a gift from the videomaker to her children (to connect them to their unknown past), Tajiri's video is an offering to her parents (presenting them with images that represent the videomaker's coming to terms with pain and anger). To these and other cinematic efforts to explore the legacy of the camps, Tajiri adds two crucial components: an

History and Memory. Tajiri's video comments on Hollywood film: character-generated text overlays film credits.

analysis of the cinematic context for racial prejudice and an emphasis on exploring the connections of the internees to the land.

History and Memory returns continually to an image of a Japanese American woman filling a canteen in the desert, an image created by the videomaker to represent a picture in her head, an image of the one story she recalls her mother telling her about life in the camps. The conceit of her "grandfather's ghost," represented in the video by scrolling text across a black screen, is used to describe events that the family believes in but did not witness, as well as Tajiri's own imaginings of those events. An anecdote about Tajiri's sister, her collection of images of Hollywood stars, and her still camera, serves as a metaphor for Japanese American disaffection (dealing not with events directly, but with representations of events) and further introduces Tajiri's analysis of the Japanese faces depicted by non–Japanese Americans (in U.S. government newsreels and Hollywood feature films).

Who Is Speaking Here, Now? Bakhtin and Heteroglossia

It is the layering of cinematic texts, ranging from audio recordings and footage produced by the makers to "source footage" (in Tajiri's video, particularly), and the problem of interpreting such complex, polysemic movies that leads me to Mikhail Bakhtin's concept of dialogism, defined as the meaning created out of the interplay between contrasting socio-ideological languages, ways of speaking that convey the speaker's ideological investments. Bakhtinian concepts emphasize the interplay of perspectives as they are carried by contrasting discourses, even as Bakhtin is careful to note that these contrasting voices are deployed in the service of a unified authorial voice. Bakhtin notes that the "higher stylistic unity of the work as a whole" subordinates the different stylistic unities or language-types within it: thus dialogics are useful for Bakhtin only insofar as they figure in a text's unified meaning, which is revealed and structured by individual stylistic elements (1981, 262). Given the concern of Tajiri's, Tanaka's, and Yasui's movies with re-visioning the past, they evince discomfort with Bakhtin's "higher stylistic unity," a wariness of substituting one monolithic historical account for another. A totalizing hermeneutic impulse loses sight of the emphasis on *process* in these movies, emphasizing their resistance at the expense of their ambivalence toward cinematic representation. That said, it is clear that these movies *are* resistant (if not merely that)—they do propose a countercinema—and, as such, work to centripetally unify the polysemy of the various cinematic texts that constitute them.

Bakhtin's analysis of novelistic discourse (e.g., everyday speech and rhetoric) in his essay "Discourse in the Novel" suggests ways that we might construct a typology of different modes of cinematic specification (e.g., fictional narrative, compilation documentary, experimental video). He proposes a typology of novelistic discourse, specifically the categories of "direct authorial literary-artistic narration (in all its diverse variants)" and "various forms of literary but extra-artistic authorial speech (moral, philosophical or scientific statements, oratory, ethnographic descriptions, memoranda and so forth)" (1981, 262). (Bakhtin's typology also lists three kinds of speech that refer to the discourse of characters or other sources.) Authorial discourse is differentiated as artistic and extra-artistic narration, or what we might interpret as the difference between narration conceived with the specificity of the medium in mind, and narrative strategies not unique to film. We can zero in on medium-specific narration by asking what documentary film can do that other documentary forms (such as the journalistic article) cannot. The answer, it seems to me, is to be found in cinema's temporality. Cinema's soundtrack and image-track provide the possibility of simultaneous transmission of information, and the processes of postproduction provide the possibility of multiple discursive sources on a soundtrack and the layering of images. Thus, whereas prose forms can juxtapose quotations, either sequentially or not (e.g., a photo and caption and/or a sidebar alongside a body of text in a magazine), cinema can lay sounds and images on top of one another.[13] This kind of layering does indeed appear in all of the movies in this chapter; the dialogic potential of these texts is expressed in the very title of Tajiri's video, *History and Memory.* "History and memory" summarizes the two main discursive strands that operate in these movies, and their dialogic interaction is captured by that deceptively simple word "and." Rhetorically speaking, the "and" functions in at least two ways: to suggest contestation (history *versus* memory) or connection (history *with* memory). Rather than suggest that any given discourse (or, in Bakhtin's words, socio-ideological language) represents either history or memory, I think it is more useful to accept that the key discourses in these movies invoke both history and memory and propose distinct philosophies for relating the two. In other words, each discourse is itself "double-languaged," evincing the pull of history and memory, and the interaction of these already dialogized discourses results in second-order dialogism.

At this point I should explain how I am using the terms history and memory, or more precisely, discourses of history and memory. Historical discourse arranges facts about the past into a causal chain, laying claim to markers of objectivity to disguise its status as a reconstructed narrative.[14] Memorial discourse, which both remembers and commemorates, is characterized by linkages that are not necessarily causal; that is, two events are linked not because one can be said to have caused the other, but because one somehow explains or illuminates an aspect of the other. In Trinh T. Minh-ha's (1989) terms, historical discourse provides facts and memorial discourse provides truths; in other words, memorial truth lays claim to a universality that historical fact, in its insistence on specificity, does not. For example, Tajiri's video juxtaposes footage of a store in the Salinas Assembly Center with the mother's lack of memory; the footage dates from 1942, was shot by the U.S. Army Signal Corps, implies that it is part of a systematic documentation (that explains and justifies U.S. Army actions, proceeding through time in defense of its response to national "moments"), and asserts the physical existence of a canteen in Salinas. By contrast, the soundtrack dates from 1989, was recorded by Tajiri, reveals textual markers (e.g., poor recording quality) that imply that it is unsystematic (arbitrary, haphazard), and asserts that the canteen was not worth remembering.[15] Tajiri's mother does not remember a canteen, which is surely "wrong" but which carries the emotional "truth" of her experience of incarceration, thus suggesting that her recollection (or rather, absence of recollection) should be marked as "memory." Only a relational use of the terms history and memory is appropriate for a reading practice that seeks to account for power relations; otherwise, power would always inhere in history and not memory.

As stated before, I characterize Bakhtin conservatively; however, if these movies indeed evince second-order dialogism, they tilt the scales toward a more liberal interpretation, one that celebrates the instability and democratic potential of these multivocal texts. So it is worth remembering that Bakhtin notes that the "higher stylistic unity of the work as a whole" subordinates the different stylistic unities or language types within it; thus dialogics are useful for Bakhtin only insofar as they figure in a text's unified meaning, which is revealed and structured by individual stylistic elements (1981, 262). In this, Bakhtin reveals the debt his notion of the dialogic owes to dialectical thinking.

Like dialogics, dialectics can be taken as a theory of the interaction of multiple voices. A dialectical analysis conceives of competing voices as manifestations of a process by which contradictory ideas are reconciled and unified. It understands these conflicts among discourses as arising out of a fundamental power differential, in which one force is continually tested and refined by a second force. A dialectical hermeneutic—or rather, a dialogical hermeneutic that emphasizes the dialectical component of Bakhtin's concepts—would examine the ways memory tests history, and the ways history redefines and perfects itself to absorb what memory has to offer.

Although I am a pessimistic Bakhtinian, I have no desire to see the dialectic of history fulfill itself and absorb memory; instead, I am interested in preserving the special insight that memory can provide. Dialectics risks losing sight of localized resistance. For example, Fredric Jameson's *The Political Unconscious* (1981b) shows how dialectical thinking can be applied to the analysis of narratives; Jameson shifts focus from the dialectically opposed "parts" in favor of the unified "whole." For Jameson, it is a mistake to observe highly localized causality instead of the overall progression of the dialectic: in narrative terms, it is to focus on the forces that animate individual characters rather than the trajectory of the narrative that involves them. Although this might be true of a novel written by a single author, I think it is less true of films generally, and in particular is challenged by the multivocal movies examined here. Jameson's approach, if taken too far, robs the individual voices in a text of their agency, treating them as cogs in a dialectical machine.[16]

A Family Gathering

Lise Yasui and Ann Tegnell's *A Family Gathering* replicates many documentary conventions: intercutting talking heads with stock footage, providing foleyed sound effects to flesh out home movies and other silent footage. But in stark contrast to Felicia Lowe's *China: Land of My Father,* another PBS documentary, in *A Family Gathering* Yasui's voice-over works not to pin down the meaning of the image-track but to introduce ambiguity and call attention to the assumptions made about sound-image relations elsewhere in the film. Compared with Lowe's narration, Yasui's is slower, more hesitant; her voice is softer and less strident; and the syntax of her sentences is more essayistic (with passive voice constructions and elaborative clauses), less journalistic (relaying information in terse sentences). Yasui's voice-over opens up narrative possibities, whereas the voice-over in Lowe's film tells us what to think and feel.

This process of opening up the image to interpretation occurs whenever Yasui talks about her father's home movies. Robert Shu Yasui's movies are transformed over the course of *A Family Gathering,* at first representing the young Lise's unquestioned acceptance of her father's storytelling, then marking her growing awareness of the ways these movies mediate her access to the past, and finally coming to hold her conception of "the past" in a remarkable state of flux (a state in which the films become the marker of the sanitized past, the hidden past, the false past).

A Family Gathering begins with a zoom into a still photo of Masuo Yasui, the filmmaker's grandfather. Yasui's voice-over tells us that he was a pioneering Japanese American, a patron to the Japanese American community of Hood River, Oregon; the voice-over then tells us that one day her father told her that Masuo had been arrested by the FBI. "When I discovered this," the voice-over observes, "I wondered what else I didn't know." The photograph is followed by a slow-motion view of a rural countryside viewed (presumably) from the passenger side of a car; similar shots appear in many of the movies, where they seem to depict the process—the journey—of attempting to discover and document the past. The shot ends abruptly, followed by a few seconds of film leader (passing in slow motion) and grainy images (surely from a home movie) of an old Issei couple playing with some small children. Yasui's voice-over tells us, "I had a favorite memory when I was young: my grandparents came to visit." Significantly, Yasui does

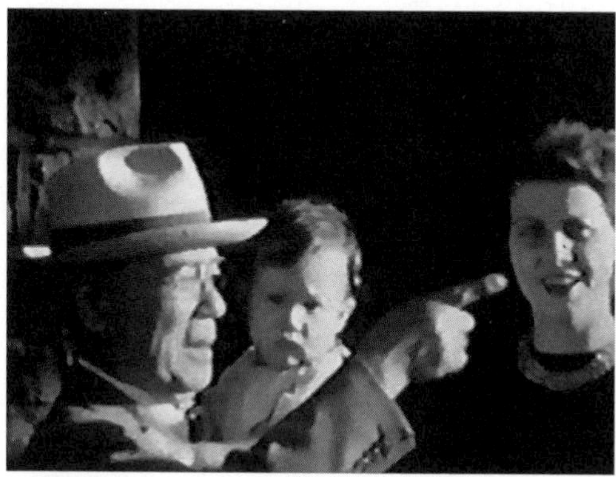

A Family Gathering. Home movies with Grandfather Masuo Yasui.

not employ the present tense (she states, "I *had* a memory," not "I *have* a memory"); the ambiguous phrasing could simply mean that she is specifying when the remembered events took place, or it could mean that she no longer has the same memory. And indeed, after telling us what she remembers of the day with her grandparents, Yasui's voice-over informs us that she has discovered that "the memory was one I'd made up—a creation drawn from all the stories I'd heard, and the images on my father's movie screen."

This sequence may not seem particularly innovative at first glance: the filmmaker uses home movies to represent her memories, memories that (it turns out) actually grew out of home movies (*these* movies, presumably). But the succeeding sequence tellingly recasts the previous one: we again see the leader, but this time accompanied by the sound of a projector on the soundtrack; that sound continues, along with foleyed sound effects, under grainy images, this time firmly attached to the filmmaker's youth ("This is me in 1959," the voice-over informs us). These two sequences, both built on home movie footage, depict radically different conceptions of representing the past. The nonfoleyed movie footage takes on a less determinate quality, while the foleyed footage (even though built on the illusion of sound-image conjunction) becomes grounded and (through inference) more objective.[17]

Yasui's voice-over next transforms the footage once again, by specifying the circumstances under which it was viewed: her father showed these films *often,* and when he did he offered narration. "Whenever they [Yasui's grandparents] appeared, my Dad would tell me about their early years—glimpses of a past I wanted to feel a part of." Once again, Yasui's use of the past tense opens up an ambiguity: Does she no longer want to connect with the past glimpsed through the movies? She thus establishes that this footage is not merely convenient material appropriated by the filmmaker to illustrate her story; rather, these home movies *are* the story: some of them become assimilated into memory, some of them remain "simply" home movies, and the context in which the movies were screened provides the impetus for Yasui's project.

Bakhtin reminds us to pay attention to the "double-voicedness" of quoted footage and the "double-languagedness" that the footage thereby carries. The graininess of the 8mm movie image is like an "accent" that indicates the original context for these films. The appropriation of this footage by Yasui redirects the footage, investing it with authorial intention, but the footage continues to signify its original context. Indeed, the footage lends much of its meaning to *A Family Gathering because* it is appropriated; furthermore, similar uses of 8mm footage in experimental-documentary films have established such appropriation as a cinematic convention (akin to the turns of phrase in Dickens's novels that Bakhtin highlights).[18] But it is crucial to note here that Yasui radically repositions the 8mm footage by means of contextual cues such as voice-over and sound effects, inflecting the quoted footage in myriad ways, so that while the home movies retain their own "voice" and "language," Yasui's authorial "voice" variously invokes the "language" of autobiographical interiority (memory) and the "language" of autobiographical exteriority (childhood events) in turn.

As *A Family Gathering* continues, Yasui's voice-over next takes on a more professional tone, narrating the story of Masuo and Shidzuyo Yasui's arrival in Hood River and the family they raised there. The flat quality of this sequence suggests that this story may have been reconstructed by Yasui from historical documents, but the voice-over soon shifts gears and reveals that this information is also mediated through her father's storytelling: "My dad was often told this history, memories he passed on to me." Once again, Yasui's voice-over opens up an ambiguity, this time in the shift from history to memories. Is Yasui conflating history and memory here, perhaps to indicate her suspicion of the historical accuracy of her father's stories? Perhaps the conflation echoes the process by which home movies became her memories? Or perhaps the locution underlines a typological distinction: stories told to her father are history, but when those stories are passed on to another generation they become memories.

The film continues the pattern thus far established, of moving from straightforward recitations of history to the ambiguities attending that history's transmission. The next sequence depicts Yasui's abortive first attempt to gather material for her film; her voice-over now informs us that she felt "frozen behind the camera" and was unable to interact with her family in front of the lens. This sequence gives way to a talking-heads sequence in which Masuo's children describe their father's arrest and the mounting resentment against Japanese Americans; the images of talking heads are interspersed with stock footage of the incarceration of Japanese Americans. This sequence closes with an actor's oral interpretation of one of Masuo's wartime letters on the soundtrack, while the image-track shows slowed (optically printed) footage of Masuo's postwar years, eventually dissolving to a close tracking shot over his handwritten text. What are we to make of the home movie footage this time? The images give us an old, visibly happy man, while the soundtrack gives us an actor's portrayal of a younger, sadder man. Perhaps this sequence depicts the disjunction between Yasui's false memories of her grandfather and the research she has since undertaken; perhaps her use of an actor's voice in place of her grandfather further highlights that disjunction. In any case, the sequence brings us back to the ambiguity of the home movies and sets us up for the next sequence, in which those images are transformed by Yasui's voice-over yet again.

Once again optically printed leader and the sound of a projector precede grainy images (with foleyed sound) of Robert Yasui playing with a small boy (Lise's older brother). Yasui's voice-over begins: "As a child I thought of my father's past as inseparable from mine. I never had the sense that he'd lived a life other than the one preserved in our movies. . . . I expected that one day, my dad would tell me about the traumas of his past, but he never did. Instead he showed home movies. I began to see them as a statement, a declaration of what he chose to remember. . . . For me they represented the boundary between the father I knew and the father whose real feelings about his past might always remain hidden from me." This statement sets Robert's home movies apart from the film that surrounds them, suggesting that the former represent the past he prefers to remember, while the latter (*A Family Gathering* as a whole) is an attempt to discover that hidden past. Yasui thus emphasizes her father's voice in the double-voicedness of this appropriated text, employing her own authorial position to call attention to the originary language from which the 8mm footage emerges. Paradoxically, this very moment when Yasui declares her estrangement from the home movies also marks the most radical appropriation of that footage, as she uses it to stand for both what she does know and what she does not know about her father. The home movies are now set up as a wall that the filmmaker will break through, just as the filmmaker seeks to break through her "screen memories."

The conclusion of *A Family Gathering* develops this trope, restating the idea that the past—more specifically, her father's *feelings* about the past—lies beyond the wall of those movies. We see the scenes of Yasui's grandparents one more time—as before, without the leader, without the sound of a projector—as she recontextualizes them one more time: "I'm aware of the history that lies behind these images—the moments of togetherness recorded here I no longer take for granted. It's a past my family made for themselves, and it's a past they gave to me." But even these statements maintain the ambiguity of the images. Does the "real" history (and the true feelings about the past) lie behind this footage—do Robert's home movies continue to mask the painful past? Or does Yasui mean that she is aware of the history that motivated the production and repeated projection of these images (in the sense that the painful past compelled the creation of a happier illusion)? Perhaps the history she is referring to is the various transformations she has wrought on the footage over the course of *A Family Gathering.* What about the "moments of togetherness recorded here": Does she refer to the reunion of her father with his parents, or does she still include herself in the gathering? Finally, what does Yasui mean when she says "It's a past my family made for themselves"? Does she mean the home movies are her father's representation of the past? Does she simply mean that our families "make" their past by living it, and bequeath it to us? Or is it the process of continually projecting these movies that creates her family's past? If so, then her father's process succeeded, for it created a (false) past in the memory of the young Lise.

Yasui asserts that she will continue to treasure the memory of the time spent with her grandfather, even though she knows now that they never met. Her final words are "This is what I'll remember." But what is "this"? The home movies? Her screen memories? Perhaps she refers to her own film, *A Family Gathering,* or perhaps she just refers to the voice-over itself? The process Yasui's film takes us through, a complex process of realigning and re-interpreting the ambiguities of these home movies, brings us full circle.[19] We undertake the journey to return to where we started; in Yasui's case, she still loves her memories. But of course, those memories are not exactly the same as the ones she "had" when she was young, so, in a sense, she has indeed abandoned those childhood memories; she now knows the story "behind" those memories, a story that explains how movies came to stand in for memory, and that has produced a movie about that story. Yasui's film is an elegy, not to the death of her grandfather, but to its own process of recovery.[20]

Who's Going to Pay for These Donuts, Anyway?

"When you have a past it is easier to believe that the present has a reason . . . perhaps with this insight, one may begin to look to the future with hope." So Janice Tanaka concludes near the close of *Who's Going to Pay for These Donuts, Anyway?* These comments are occasioned by her daughter's wedding and by her son's tentative overtures toward reconciliation with his father. The past restored to them is their discovery of Jack Koto Tanaka, Janice's long-absent father. *Donuts* documents the Tanaka family's wary reunion, a reunion like the dance at Becky's wedding, where the young couple circle in slow motion as Natalie Cole's "Unforgettable" plays. That song, Cole's electronically imagined duet with her father (from an album in which Cole finally comes to grips with her father's legacy),[21] seems an apt metaphor for *Donuts,* an experimental video that reconnects Jack to his past while it connects his family to him. This connection is important not only for Tanaka and her children (who discover the past) but for Jack (who discovers his progeny): Tanaka's father begins signing his name "Jack Koto Tanaka Sr. and Family" after meeting his grandchildren. His legacy allows him to reclaim and update his own name, to overlay his family onto his life.

This layering of intertexts, of the present on the past through the electronic manipulation of audio and video, is expressed in Tanaka's video not merely through her mastery of the processed image, but also through the confusion wrought by the camera. Throughout *Donuts,* we discover different ways that the camera, by preserving moments in time, threatens to obliterate crucial differences by preserving certain similarities. When Jack is shown a photo of himself, his wife, and baby daughter, he wonders who the man is and if the woman is Janice. For Jack, the man in the photo does not look enough like himself to be recognizable, but his wife looks too much like his daughter and he confuses them. The video goes on to explore other similarities, always reminding us not to forget crucial differences, when it compares Jack with his wife Lily, with his brother Togo, and with his daughter's ex-husband.

Thanks to this plethora of lives to juxtapose with Jack's, Tanaka is able

Who's Going to Pay for These Donuts, Anyway? Jack Tanaka turns the camera on his granddaughter Becky . . .

. . . as she shoots him.

to distance herself from Jack's past. But it might also be argued that she is indeed the center of this film, insofar as her children are part of the text as well. If the project of *A Family Gathering* was to connect Yasui to her grandfather, the project of *Donuts* is to connect Becky and David to their grandfather.[22] Whenever Tanaka is off-screen, she is nevertheless present as the link between Becky and Jack: she is both their biological link and the metteur-en-scène who brings them together before the camera. Becky also functions at times as an on-screen surrogate for Tanaka. This collapse of Becky and her mother is especially pronounced in a sequence in which Becky and her grandfather sit and talk on the couch while Tanaka interjects from behind her camera. Because Jack is often featured in close-up, Becky is sometimes excluded from the frame, and it becomes difficult to distinguish the mother's voice from the daughter's. In a later sequence, when Jack and Becky turn their video cameras on each other, Becky's face is obscured by the camera and she looks even more like her mother.

In bizarre counterpoint to the scene where Jack mistakes a photograph of his wife for Tanaka, Tanaka's children attribute their strong resemblance to their grandfather to the coincidental resemblance of their own father (a Mexican national) to Jack. Tanaka herself notes this coincidence when she lays a photo of her ex-husband over one of her father as a young man.[23] In voice-over, she notes, "Past and present collide with such unconscious force, I find myself standing in footprints that do not wholly belong to me." Gallardo's absence from the film (and his son's implied resentment of him) make the parallels to Jack's absence from Tanaka's childhood all the more striking.

Finally, Tanaka's distance from her father is preserved by the split personality she fosters as videomaker, akin to Yasui's experience of conflict between her roles as filmmaker and daughter. "When's the last time you saw your daughter?" the filmmaker asks, and Jack tells a story about seeing his daugher on the street a few years back. "Instinctively . . . [I knew] 'that's her!' " Then the filmmaker asks, "Who am I?" "Well, you're about the same thing!" replies Jack. Jack jokes with his daughter, perhaps aware that she is evaluating his memory, perhaps aware that she is hiding in her role as videomaker. Elsewhere, Tanaka's voice-over notes: "Observing the effects of the past could only be dealt with from behind the distancing lens of a camera."[24]

Donuts documents another confusion, however, a confusion that ends up structuring much of the video. Tanaka had earlier admitted that as a child she sometimes thought Uncle Togo was her father because she saw him more often; ironically, she had fallen out of touch with Togo as well and used *Donuts* to learn more about his life, too. Togo's wartime experiences and more recent battle with cancer are contrasted with Jack's incarceration and institutionalization, producing some eerie parallels. Jack's tongue rolls constantly due to the effects of overmedication; Togo's salivary glands were removed as part of his cancer treatment. Both men need lubrication (literally) to speak: late in the video, the two brothers sit in a cafeteria and discuss old friends; on the wall between them is a sign noting that the restaurant provides drinking water only on request.

Tanaka's deployment of postproduction techniques (of image processing and sound mixing) call up the layering that I suggested was unique to cinematic documentation, after Bakhtin's typology of artistic (medium-specific) and extra-artistic (quoted/incorporated) documentary prose. In demonstrating how photographs capture moments in time, Tanaka implies

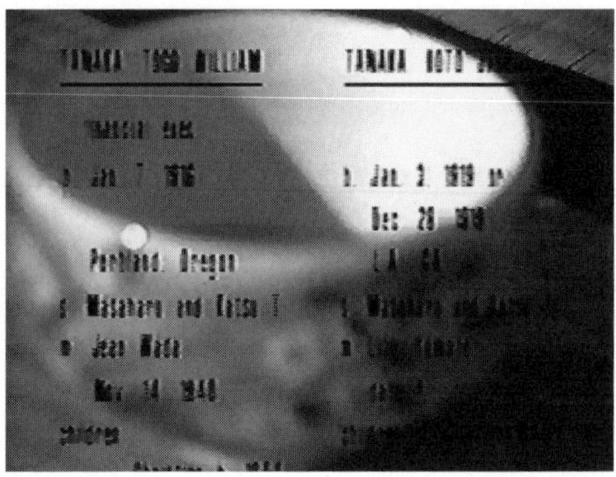

Who's Going to Pay for These Donuts, Anyway? Brothers Jack and William are compared.

that the very act of photographing creates a layering of past and present independent of their further cinematic layering. On top of these traces of the past, Tanaka often superimposes a "time line" of key dates and events in a person's life, each entry serving as a prose snapshot, and the succession of entries providing a narrative that moves forward in time, cutting through the photographic images they are layered on.

In *Memories from the Department of Amnesia,* Tanaka employed the device of a time line to emphasize the disparity between the observable facts of a person's life and the more subjective, day-to-day experience of living with someone. *Amnesia* sets out a series of dates and events in Lily Yamate's life, which appear on the screen at a measured pace. This time line is contrasted with the conversation of Janice and Rebecca about Lily, conversation that is buoyant, full of laughter, laughing at and with Lily, and speaking directly to the impact the woman had on their lives, enumerating the ways her sense of fashion, her attitudes toward events around her, and her philosophy of living contributed to the attitudes of her daughter and granddaughter. By contrast, the time line seems almost meaningless, but there is a sense in which the time line critiques itself. Even without the comparison with the soundtrack, the time line leaves tremendous gaps, leaping over years and years. We see a pattern, perhaps a sad downward spiral, but we do not know what is causing the pattern and the time line offers no explanations. It is as if the time line knows it is an inadequate represention.

A similar time line appears in *Donuts,* but it functions quite differently.[25] In *Donuts* two scrolling parallel time lines contrast the lives of Jack and Togo. Togo's time line, on the right, is full of facts verifiable in the public record, noting accomplishments, degrees received, and other successes. By contrast, Jack's time line on the left is replete with uncertainties, large gaps punctuated with question marks. The connection to the two brothers' differing political opinions is obvious; Tanaka's video mentions Jack's status as a de facto political prisoner only obliquely. At the conclusion of Jack's visit to the doctor, a character-generated banner notes, "20 volts administered to the genitals is considered torture, 170 volts administered to the head is called treatment." The story of Jack and Togo's father, a former Samurai who spent his days in camp forging a sword while Jack languished with the FBI and Togo was threatened by angry internees, also runs across the screen.

All in all, Tanaka's video does not spend nearly as much time as Yasui's film (or even Tajiri's video) laying out the context for the Internment itself, which is in keeping with the video's emphasis on the *aftermath* of the camps. However, Tanaka does include information on divisions within the Japanese American community, through a reenactment (on the soundtrack) of a debate between two men, one sympathetic to the Japanese American Citizens League's policy of cooperation, the other calling for resistance to the U.S. government.

Like Yasui's film, Tanaka's video attempts to work through parental "amnesia" to reconstruct a connection to the past. Of course, in Yasui's case, that amnesia is metaphoric, the product of wishful thinking, whereas in Tanaka's case, those gaps in memory can be attributed to mental illness, although Tanaka may never know for sure whether that illness can be attributed to FBI abuses.[26] But although both *A Family Gathering* and *Donuts* have mused on the role of the camera in constructing a past and present that isolates them from "true feelings" about the past, neither film explores the relationship between race prejudice and popular culture in depth; that project is taken up by Rea Tajiri.

History and Memory: For Akiko and Takashige

Like *A Family Gathering* and *Who's Going to Pay for These Donuts, Anyway?*, Tajiri's *History and Memory* attempts to account for the filmmaker's memories of events she never witnessed (she was born after the war's conclusion) and a parent's failure to remember events that she did witness. Also like the other movies, Tajiri's video meditates on the relationship of the cinematic image to memory; but unlike the other movies, Tajiri emphasizes

Hollywood movies and other images from popular culture to understand not only the context of racial prejudice that produced the camps, but also the response of Japanese Americans to their situation.[27] For example, the video pursues a lengthy digression to explore a story about Tajiri's sister, who as a teenager held the world at a distance through the lens of her camera, taking a picture of a boy she had a crush on and enshrining it in a box full of pictures of (white) Hollywood movie stars.[28] The absence of Japanese American faces from this box prompts Tajiri the narrator to wonder "what effect the movies had on our lives." In the next sequence, Tajiri reconstructs the events of Pearl Harbor, placing documentary footage next to staged reenactments by the likes of John Ford and clips from *From Here to Eternity.* Tajiri presents a four-tiered taxonomy of images, mental and cinematic:

> There are things which have happened in the world while there were cameras watching, things we have images for.
>
> There are other things which have happened while there were no cameras watching, which we restage in front of cameras to have images of.
>
> There are things which have happened for which the only images that exist are in the minds of the observers present at the time.
>
> While there are things that have happened for which there have been no observers except for the spirits of the dead.[29]

Tajiri can locate herself within this taxonomy only with difficulty. She notes that she "could remember a time of great sadness before [she] was born." After opening with scrolling, character-generated text, the first photographic image in the video is that of a Japanese woman filling a canteen with water in the middle of a desert. The voice-over identifies this image as a "fragment," an image that Tajiri has always held onto to represent one of the few stories her mother told her about the camp. Over the course of the video, her frustration with her mother's memory gaps becomes evident, but that frustration is balanced by respect for the value of those gaps. Tajiri's video seeks to fill in those gaps, but it does not seek to paper them over, for that would risk effacing the trauma that compelled her mother to forget. By video's end, Tajiri states that her pain came from not being able to connect this image of her mother's canteen with any narrative, but that in confronting that pain she was able to forgive her mother her loss of memory and make of the image (presumably, the video reconstruction that Tajiri created with herself as her mother) a gift to her mother.

Tajiri attempts to restore her mother's Americanness. To do this she must position herself in a tradition that opposes U.S. injustice, specifically a Japanese American tradition. It is by asserting her opposition to U.S. policies of injustice that Tajiri reclaims her mother's right to be a U.S. citizen. Literature about the Internment and especially about the *coram nobis* cases and the movement for redress and reparations makes this rhetorical point repeatedly: that Japanese Americans who resisted incarceration were themselves protectors of civil rights and thus more "American" than the military and governmental officials charged with defending the U.S. Constitution.[30] But Tajiri's project cannot simply build on this rather banal irony, for she locates herself within not only a Japanese American tradition but also a cinematic tradition, a tradition that may itself oppose so-called dominant cinema but one that is nevertheless implicated by the dominant. The movement for redress and reparations represents a triumph of the public sphere: protests of the expulsion of Japanese Americans are enacted in the U.S. legal system, thus confirming the logic that upholds the public sphere rather than working to undermine it. Tajiri's video challenges the dominant cinematic logic of representation (analogous to the dynamics of access to public sphere visibility), and it attempts to do so without reconfirming that logic.

To accomplish this, Tajiri's video attempts to evaluate the connections between narrative and the cinematic image. The video opposes itself to linear narratives of cause and effect, seeking instead an understanding of the need for narrative. At the end of the video, Tajiri's voice-over says, "For years I've been living with this picture [of my mother's hands filling a canteen] without the story, feeling a lot of pain, not knowing how they fit together, but now I found I could connect the picture to the story. I could forgive my mother her loss of memory and could make this image for her." If the video *History and Memory* depicts that process of connecting picture to story, it is not a linear narrative process. The ambivalence of Tajiri's cinematic project is evidenced in this attempt to attach narratives to images without relying on linear notions of narrative. The video seeks to preserve space for the emotional truth of gaps in memory, for the emotional truth of memories of events that never happened, emotional truths that can be contradicted by the historical record. While offering a critique of cinematic institutions (such as Hollywood) that promote a representational logic whereby the visible is legitimated, the video hesitates to offer up images of its own, for that would confirm that logic of visibility. Tajiri's video seeks to make a space for memory (and gaps in memory) within cinema, attempting to relocate that which is oral and private in a space that is literate and public, while retaining an aura of indeterminacy not usually found in public discourse.[31]

One of the methods Tajiri deploys to incorporate unsubstantiated narratives is the conceit of her grandfather's ghost, represented by white character-generated text scrolling up a black screen, usually accompanied by artifically abstract sound effects of nature (e.g., birds chirping, with a hint of digital echo). The spirit witnesses events from overhead and conveys actions in present tense; at the beginning of the video, the spirit describes a scene of a man and a woman arguing in what might be the front yard of a house in the suburbs. Then italicized text, also in the present tense, says, "The spirit of my grandfather witnesses my father and mother as they have an argument about the unexplained nightmares their daughter has been having on the 20th anniversary of the bombing of Pearl Harbor," and goes on to enumerate some of the losses suffered by Japanese Americans during their so-called relocation. The italicized text seems to motivate the argument scene, which is described dispassionately, with more interest in physical setting than in the topic of conversation. But lest the absence of passion be associated with objectivity or historical truth, locating the point of view with "the spirit of my grandfather" seems to place the text in an imaginative space of enunciation.

Before the italicized text is completed, a voice-over (spoken by Tajiri) intones conversationally (we hear an intake of breath), "I don't know where this came from but I just had this fragment, this picture that's always been in my mind." As the voice-over continues it describes Tajiri's mother filling a canteen in the desert, again in the present tense, and we are presented with a cinematic image that seems to fulfill that statement: a medium shot, from a high angle, perhaps echoing the overhead shot described by the text a moment before. The voice-over could just as easily be referring to the picture of the couple arguing, or the picture of the spirit watching from above. As the video progresses, we come to understand that the image of the woman with the canteen is an enactment of Tajiri's memory fragment (its careful composition as well as the color and quality of the image suggest that it is not stock footage, in any case). The savvy viewer might guess that the woman in the image is in fact Tajiri herself, standing in for her mother.

Within the first two minutes of the video, we've been given four overlapping elements: text, italicized text, voice-over, and an image (not to mention the sound effects). Each element seems to describe an event in the past but speaks of it in the present—in the case of the voice-over, "I just [always] had this fragment," suggesting that the videomaker cannot conceive of a time *before* this fragment existed. Each of these elements seems both to reinforce and undercut the truth-claims of the other elements: by specifying the enunciator as a "spirit"; by denying knowledge of the origin of the image ("I don't know where this came from"); by speaking in the first person; by invoking the flat, objective style of a screenplay—each of these rhetorical moves locates the truth of each element outside the text, evoking a higher authority, albeit an authority or authorities that cannot be specified or confirmed.

Thus far, the interplay among the various cinematic "fragments" has been restricted to elements that purport to come either from the videomaker's consciousness or subconscious, depicting events seen by Tajiri, her mother, and the spirit of her grandfather. The two styles of scrolling text take a "long view," referring not just to the specificity of the Tajiri family in 1961, but also to the effect on 110,000 Japanese Americans after Pearl Harbor. By contrast, the voice-over and the image to which it refers are particular to the Tajiri family, and the lack of temporal specificity (i.e., the suggestion that this image cannot be traced to an originating moment, that it is unmoored from narrative) locates references to the canteen outside of the enumerable experiences of the Internment shared by Japanese Americans. Tajiri could be said to be deploying many different authorial voices, each nearer or closer to the author. Bakhtin notes that "the intentions of the prose writer are refracted *at different angles,* depending on the degree to which the refracted, heteroglot languages he deals with are socio-ideologically alien, already embodied and already objectivized" (1981, 300; emphasis in original). The more "alien" discourses employed by Tajiri operate at a sufficient refraction to give voice to the shared language of Japanese Americans, while the "spirit of her grandfather" (an authorial conceit through which Tajiri distances herself from the narrated actions, but that paradoxically is too "close" to her to offer significant refraction) remains in a personal voice and speaks to familial experiences.

The image of the woman and the canteen returns intermittently throughout the video; I have already mentioned how it appears again at the conclusion. The image of the canteen not only frames the video as a whole, it reveals the workings of the video in miniature, while also standing in for Tajiri's impetus in making the video: to attach narrative to image.[32] This

History and Memory. Tajiri remembers her mother talking about a canteen in Poston . . .

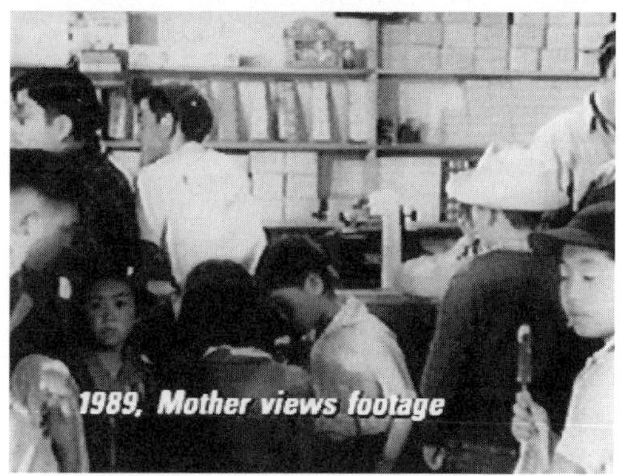
1989, Mother views footage

. . . but her mother does not remember a different kind of canteen at Salinas.

last function of the canteen image is evoked by voice-over at the beginning and end of the video, by means of an ambiguous pronoun, "this," which can be taken to refer either to the image of the canteen or the video as a whole (at the beginning, "I don't know where this came from," and at the end, "I could forgive my mother her loss of memory and could make this image for her").[33] The trope of the canteen thus marks a synechdochic confusion, a confusion exacerbated by the trope's refiguration into a different kind of canteen (the Salinas camp store, mentioned earlier in this chapter) and a different kind of memory.

In the Salinas canteen sequence, a subtitle states, "1989, mother views footage," and we hear Tajiri's mother and father speaking. This portion of the audio track is heavily marked by room tone. Tajiri's mother says, "What is this? Canteen. They didn't have a canteen in Salinas . . . Assembly Center. We had one in Poston. I don't remember this. My goodness, I don't remember this." The ambient sound suggests that the voices were recorded during the first screening of the footage (and not re-created in a recording studio). References to "this" suggest that the voices are speaking about a specific object in front of them, a pro-(audio)filmic event, also implying that the footage is before (in front of, as well as prior to) the moment of the soundtrack's inscription. The subtitle, "1989, Mother views footage," is a provocative attribution that on the one hand places the Tajiri family anterior to the footage (in 1989), and on the other hand locates that process of viewing in the present tense—putting the audience of *History and Memory* (the video) in the same audience as Tajiri's mother: regarding the screen, aware of other audience members, attending to some of their verbal comments, and seeing not them but what they are commenting on. This positioning of the audience means that we must first perceive the image and then understand the soundtrack's relation to it, thus prioritizing the image.

The temporal organization of this sequence—overlapping soundtracks and image-tracks to suggest the evaluation of historical documentation—is in stark contrast to the overlapping, loosely associated elements at the beginning of the video. The Salinas canteen sequence creates a sense of immediacy to emphasize the definitiveness of the physical evidence (in this case, the image-track) with the gaps in memory (relayed on the soundtrack). This hierarchy—images as documentation, audio as subjective recollection—supplemented by the "grandfather's spirit," is also evident in other sequences, even those that are more loosely organized. Following the Pearl Harbor sequence, with music continuing (Lester Bowie's Brass Fantasy performing "I Only Have Eyes for You")[34] and mixing with artificial wind sounds, the spirit's perspective is again conveyed in scrolling text, but this time the voice-over is different. It is first of all not Tajiri's voice, but that of her father; the ambience of the room and a barely detectable hum of a tape recorder imply that this voice is a textual element gathered and later edited for the video (as opposed to the videomaker's own voice-over, which betrays no room tone, presumably speaking from the postproduction space of a recording studio). This voice-over is again followed by an image, this time a family photograph of a house to which the voice-over refers; it also intersects with the story told by the scrolling text. In the same dispassionate tone as before, the scrolling text describes the removal of a house, and italicized script again marks the text as emanating from the point of view of "the spirit of my grandfather."

However, in this instance, the grandfather's spirit does not go on to enumerate facts about the Internment that would position this story as one of

History and Memory. Too many stories, too few facts: When was this picture taken?

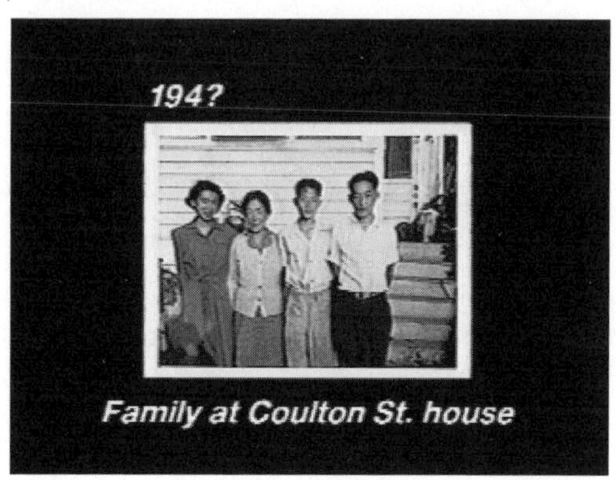

many similar Japanese American stories. Instead, it is the voice-over that refers to the larger pattern into which this story fits, noting, "At that time, a Japanese [alien] could not own any property . . . so [our mother] bought the house in my name." The voice-over also establishes credibility by making fewer claims about the disappearance of the house ("whether it was stolen or destroyed or whatever we'll never know"), whereas the grandfather's spirit states boldly that the house was stolen.

The image with which this sequence concludes, unlike the image of the woman with the canteen, is a snapshot, presumably from a family photo album. However, like the image of the canteen, the originating moment of this image cannot be specified; character-generated text dates it as "194?" Like the image of the canteen, this photograph precedes the videomaker as an image associated with an event she never experienced, but this time the problem is not a lack of narrative but an overabundance of narrative.

As if the conflicts among her family's own narratives were not enough, not to mention the conflicting narrative strategies brought together in the Pearl Harbor sequence (which combines restagings with documentary footage), Tajiri next turns her attention to a series of Hollywood texts. The first, *Yankee Doodle Dandy,* is paired with the War Relocation Authority film *Japanese Relocation.* Both films were produced in 1942, and both (Tajiri implies) evoked patriotism to justify the racist projects of the war. "We're one for all and all for one / behind the man behind the gun" sings the chorus in *Yankee Doodle Dandy,* and Tajiri repeats that soundtrack under Army Signal Corps outtakes of life in the camps: clearly, not all Americans were *behind* the man with the gun.

But the most complex series of interpolations of a Hollywood film can be found in the various uses to which Tajiri puts *Bad Day at Black Rock* (1955), a film that revolves around the mystery of a Japanese man who is never seen, a film in which Asian Americans like to imagine a Nisei in the Spencer Tracy role.[35] Tajiri employs the credit sequence of *Bad Day at Black Rock* to stand in for the trains that bore Japanese Americans into the American desert. The absence of Japanese faces echoes the ways "we were excluded from view" by the U.S. government. The wildflowers and the well that Tracy finds on Kimoko's land echo the planting and irrigation undertaken at the camps by the Japanese Americans.[36] And perhaps most provocatively, Tajiri compares herself with Tracy, stepping off a train in a small town, threatening to remind the locals of something they would rather forget.

Tajiri's identification with the Spencer Tracy role is not emphasized—just another intertextual reference in a video bursting at the seams with them—but I want to tease out the implications of this comparison. Tracy arrives in Black Rock to deliver a medal to a Japanese American man who cannot be found. He soon realizes that the entire town is covering up Kimoko's murder and teases out the truth by guessing at what is not being told to him. Without recourse to the established communication infrastructure (the telephone and telegraph), Tracy realizes he is going to have to rely on himself to survive. Whereas he had been overwhelmed by his pain when he arrived in Black Rock, his actions there show him that he has the resolve to go on living despite that pain.

Tajiri arrives in the small town of Parker, Arizona, not far from the Poston site. She perceives discomfort in the people she encounters, who would rather forget about the camps. To figure out what happened, she has to put together "fragments" of memories about the camps, and to get her message out she relies not on mainstream media but on the alternative distribution networks of video art and progressive film and video festivals. In making the video, Tajiri observes that she can give up the pain with which she had been living.

The parallels between Tracy and Tajiri as protagonists may seem a bit improbable. For the most part, when *History and Memory* cites Hollywood films, it is to provide a context for anti-Japanese sentiment in U.S. culture; Tajiri does not posit the protagonists of Hollywood fictions as points of identification; indeed, the review of *Come See the Paradise* (1990) quoted by Tajiri's video singles out and then rejects Dennis Quaid's character as "the Virtuous-White-Guy-Who-Audiences-Can-Relate-To-And-Who-Of-Course-Gets-The Girl."[37] *Bad Day at Black Rock*'s Tracy would seem an even less likely candidate for identification; but as a Hollywood production centering on Japanese American experiences from which Japanese American faces have been excluded, *Black Rock* is as "distant" from Tajiri's authorial voice as any of the footage her video appropriates. Tajiri's identification with Tracy is an attempt to bridge two "socio-ideologically alien" languages, and the resulting refraction emphasizes the difficulty of investing her intentions with the "social intentions" of the Hollywood film (Bakhtin, 1981, 300). Tajiri thus relies on the "alienness" of the quoted footage to destabilize the unity of her own film. Although she resists the exclusion of Japanese faces from *Black Rock,* she cannot revise that movie but must instead maintain it in a productive tension with her own video. The attention to "refraction" is what sets Tajiri's video apart from a film like *Come See the Paradise,* a film that attempts to incorporate so many discourses (the Issei father, the Nisei daughter, the pro-JACL Nisei son, the No-No Boy, not to mention the white husband of the Nisei daughter) that it collapses into "well-directed, professional mush" (in the words of Tajiri's nephew, quoted in the video).

Fragments and Sparks

Unlike documentaries about the movement for redress and reparations, which retell the events of the Internment in linear fashion, these three movies about the camps move forward and backward in time, using appropriated footage to layer past and present. Whereas the redress films propose a political identity for Japanese Americans specifically and Asian Americans generally, these three movies about memory seem specifically Japanese American in their subjectivity. But Tajiri's video, more than the others, seems to reach out to speak to Asian American cultural identity as well, via its critique of popular cinematic culture.

Although the adaptation of Bakhtin to film studies has generally tended to address how individual characters represent discourses, in the epigraph to this chapter Bakhtin (speaking of the creation of fictional characters) reverses that formulation. Although critical approaches to Sansei narratives about the camps have tended to focus on contrasting generational attitudes (thus interpreting individuals as part of larger collectives), the movies in this chapter focus on the individualized experience of parents and grandparents. Insofar as these movies are documentaries about an ancestor's experiences, their assessment as Asian American texts requires that the particularities are resolved with the greater sweep of Japanese American history. But insofar as these movies are not documentaries but meditations on the process of identity formation (in an experimental film tradition), they actively *create* characters (who just happen to have the same names and faces as real people) to stand in for discourses, in the manner Bakhtin describes. Each of these movies posits an *imaginary* relationship with a character from the past (a dead grandfather, or indeed the spirit of a grandfather; a mother with a canteen; a father before the onset of illness), a character created by the maker out of cinematic "fragments."

The fragments of parental narratives and memories out of which cinematic subjectivities are fashioned are not pieces of a jigsaw puzzle with one correct solution, but fragments that might plausibly be re-formed in a variety of ways. Indeed, the discontinuous past ensures that many of these fragments have been lost—left behind, destroyed, or sold to profiteers, like the property that Japanese Americans lost when they packed only what they could carry to the camps. It is of course the missing pieces that are treasured the most, and their absence can be marked only with reference to the fragments that have been saved; of the fragments that remain, it is their edges that fascinate, the points of fracture, the surfaces that suggest the shape of what is missing. The danger of handling fragments, of working with their edges, is that your fingers will wear them down, obliterating the sharp lines that provide a clear outline of the missing pieces.

In *History and Memory,* Tajiri describes a wooden bird that her mother kept in her jewelry box; whenever Taijiri wanted to play with the bird, her mother told her, "No, Grandma gave me that. Put that back." (Twenty-five years later, Tajiri found a picture in the National Archives of her grandmother and her classmates in Poston 2's bird-carving class.) The wooden bird is a fragment of the past, and Tajiri's mother guards it carefully, hoping to preserve its fragile edges from the clumsy handling of young Rea's fingers. As long as its edges remain sharp and distinct, they will show the outlines of that which is missing, the fragments of wood out of which the bird emerged—the traces of Grandmother's fingers. Grandmother's carving was the friction that shaped the bird, and preserving the object's distinctiveness preserves the subjectivity that formed it: bird-carving class becomes a moment that lasts.[38] Bird-carving class also lasts (is memorialized) in *History and Memory,* where the bird becomes the object that is engaged with Tajiri's subjectivity. Tajiri *becomes* the missing pieces that surround this fragment, *becomes* the gap in memory, the link that marks the discontinuous past.

Michael M. J. Fischer, discussing U.S. ethnic autobiographical writing, notes that what "seem initially to be individualistic autobiographical searchings turn out to be revelations of traditions, re-collections of disseminated identities and of the divine sparks from the breaking of the vessels" (1986, 198). Reading autobiographical writing, Fischer does not find fragments of broken vessels, but *sparks* from the breaking of those vessels. These sparks emerge from the moment of shattering, illuminating brilliantly (but briefly) the forces brought to bear and casting the sharp edges of fragmentation into silhouette. Fischer argues that these sparks are preserved in literature, but the preservation of sparks in film and video seems more plausible: these sparks are the flickering electrons that constitute the video image. In the epigraph that opens this chapter, Janice Tanaka describes "the crevices of concept and production" evident in video explorations of memory, crevices that mark "who and what we are." Aren't these crevices the edges between fragments, crevices created by friction so that the pieces can no longer fit together into a seamless whole, a continuous past? Tanaka's electrons are Fischer's sparks, emerging from the crevices to reveal lost traditions and (re)collect disseminated identities.[39]

How is one to see sparks when there is too much ambient light? Of what use is a flashbulb in the glare of a television camera? Whereas Japanese American makers worked in the shadows cast by the camps, Asian American travelogue movies work in the bright spotlight of pervasive representations of Asian landscapes. Whereas Tajiri becomes the missing pieces that make fragments of the past into a tenuous whole, the Chinese American makers and the Vietnamese American filmmaker discussed in Part 2 are confronted with too many puzzle pieces, enough fragments to reconstruct China and Vietnam many times over—and not enough space to insert themselves.

II *Travelogues*

CHAPTER 4

Decentering the Middle Kingdom

ABCs and the PRC

Chinese-Americans, when you try to understand what things in you are Chinese, how do you separate what is peculiar to childhood, to poverty, insanities, one family, your mother who marked your growing with stories, from what is Chinese? What is Chinese tradition and what is the movies?—Maxine Hong Kingston, *The Woman Warrior*[1]

Whatever the camera reproduces is beautiful. The disappointment of the prospect that one might be the typist who wins the world trip is matched by the disappointing appearance of the accurately photographed areas which the voyage might include. Not Italy is offered, but proof that it exists.—Max Horkheimer and Theodor W. Adorno, *The Dialectic of Enlightenment*

In the opening section of *The Woman Warrior* by Maxine Hong Kingston, the narrator reports that her mother told her stories about China that "tested our strength to establish realities" (1989, 5). It is the child's job to apply the lessons gleaned from the Chinese story to life in the United States: "to establish reality" might mean "to interpret the story in multiple contexts," except that presumes that the contexts of Chinese and American life are distinct and separable for the Chinese American child. For Kingston, the contexts for these stories were not only familial ("insanities, one family, your mother") but also shot through with the cultures of childhood and poverty—and the movies. Kingston posits that for Chinese Americans to understand themselves, they must determine what in them is Chinese, but it is impossible to know what is Chinese within you because China has been defined *without you,* by your family but also by U.S. culture.

This chapter examines three movies (two films and one video) that document the journeys of American-born Chinese (ABC) to the land of their parent's birth.[2] Felicia Lowe has stated that she consciously conceived of her film as a countertravelogue (telephone interview, 28 July 1994), and at the very least these movies add a subjective dimension to ethnographic depictions of China. However, that subjectivity can reveal itself in an awe-struck fascination with Chinese difference and a romantic desire to deny that difference; countertravelogues are not inherently self-critical. Each of these films evinces ethnographic tendencies, whether deliberately, in disguised fashion, or unknowingly. The very inspiration for these projects—the parent—is the key, for each movie is at its clearest when distinguishing between China and the Chinese parent, and at its muddiest when China and parent are collapsed. These movies face the very problem of cultural context to which Kingston alludes.

Kingston's dilemma—that of separating what is Chinese from what is peculiarly familial—arises from not knowing where a text (like a parent) ends and a context (like China) begins. The journey to China might be thought of as an attempt to construct a filter through which one can regard one's parents and childhood: the things that are filtered out are Chinese, the things that can still be seen must be familial.[3] But how are we to use China to evaluate our parents if our parents have already created our impressions of China? How can we see China without also seeing the stories that have been told about China? To journey to China in an attempt to contextualize and possibly discredit the stories one has heard is to put one's own identity at risk; it is hardly surprising, then, that we find it easier to see a China that has already been narrativized than a China that contradicts those narratives.

These travel movies made by immigrants' children do not simply document the child's journey *to* China, but evaluate the parent's migration *from* China. China is implicitly the culture that got left behind; therefore, these films posit that Chinese American identity is not hyphenate (made up of equal parts China and America), but hierarchical, with Chinese identity suppressed by an American subjectivity. The narrative of "return" to China is thus one of recovery, implying that a Chinese cultural identity has been buried or left behind. But to posit the Asian American experience as one in which "original" cultures are exchanged for "American" culture is to accept that ethnicity is innate and a priori rather than fluid and constructed out of the intersection of permeable (as opposed to discrete) cultures. To draw a strict boundary between cultures helps preserve a stable notion of Americanness, and ensures that immigrants will never be fully assimilated. Rather, the possibility of assimilation is the carrot dangled before their children, but the imaginary boundary further ensures that they will not be active shapers of an American identity but beneficiaries of a prefabricated identity.

The pervasiveness of these assumptions is revealed by the plethora of Asian American literary and cinematic narratives about generational conflict, a theme common enough that Lisa Lowe refers to it as a trope.[4] In "Heterogeneity, Hybridity, Multiplicity: Marking Asian American Differences," Lowe critiques the trope of generational conflict in Asian American literary texts, arguing that "interpreting Asian American culture exclusively in terms of the master narratives of generational conflict and filial relation essentializes Asian American culture, obscuring the particularities and incommensurabilities of class, gender, and national diversities among Asians" (1991b, 26). Lowe calls for sensitivity to diversity among Asian Americans, and notes that diversity is sufficient to preclude the possibility of a singular Asian culture inherited by Asian Americans, and therefore to preclude the possibility of an a priori Asian American culture. Instead, Lowe seeks "to define ethnicity in a manner that accounts not only for cultural inheritance, but for active cultural construction, as well" (27).

This does not mean that "active," resistant cultural strategies necessarily evade the master narratives of generational conflict to be found in narratives of assimilation. In Lowe's view, the Asian American cultural nationalist position conforms to the binary logic that insists that Asia and America are discrete entities: when "Asian American feminists who challenge Asian American sexism are cast as 'assimilationist,' as betraying Asian American 'nationalism,' " "assimilation" and "nationalism" are deployed as a "false opposition" (1991b, 31). Both positions rely on essentialism, on the reduction of generational conflict to cultural difference, on a binary logic that attributes old cultural values to the older generation and new values to the younger. Furthermore, that essentialist position begs the question Are cultures that distinct to begin with? Lowe cites the feature film *A Great Wall* (Peter Wang, 1985), avowedly a narrative about culture clash between Chinese and Chinese Americans, and argues that the film depicts a China that has already absorbed Coca-Cola and the Gettysburg Address. The Great

Wall itself becomes "a monument to the historical condition that not even ancient China was 'pure,'" representing China's perceived need—and its failure—to police its borders (37–38). By failing to allow for the permeability of cultural spaces, the trope of generational conflict fails to account for the complexities of cultural mixing and hybrid identities. Thus it begs the question If your parents were essentially Chinese, then why travel to China at all (as Chinese culture is available in your parents' home)?

The essentialist trope of generational conflict works only if migration flows in just one direction, from China to the United States, from Chinese culture to American culture. By journeying to China, makers collect on their parents' return tickets, giving the lie to one-way cultural flow. Thomas Wolfe's dictum "You can't go home again" is thus not a lament but our saving grace: it provides for a multiplicity of Chinas and a multiplicity of Chinese and Chinese American identities.[5] Although journeys to China may be inspired by romantic visions of reunification with one's inner self, that destination can never be reached, for that China no longer exists. That is why these makers do not simply tell their own stories (to China and back) but must incorporate their parent's narratives: the China of the past cannot be accessed through a geographical journey, but only through a temporal one. It is only by examining a parent's narrative of migration that one can account for temporal changes, so as to realign the China one sees with the China that one's parent saw.

The disparity between China as seen and China as previously narrativized is recoupable within the logic of narrative itself, as transformation. Narrativizing the journey to China incorporates a multiplicity of Chinas, rejecting (as Lisa Lowe does) the notion that China exists as a discrete space. Thus, the visit to China is not an attempt to see what is there now, but to find traces of what was there before. The visit attempts to substitute a spatial for a temporal migration. Therefore, these movies are forensic: they examine what has been left behind in an attempt to reconstruct what has happened; they search the tangible present to access the intangible past. In so doing, the makers reveal that they are not seeking China, but its transformation: thus, they are interested not only in what in them is Chinese, but in what in them is *not* Chinese; they are interested not just in their parent's identity with China, but in what compelled their parent to disidentify with China. In other words, by reconstructing the narrative of a parent's departure from China, the child hopes to understand how the parent's needs were not met by China. As the child does this, the journey comes into its own, completely eclipsing the destination.

Points of Departure

The two films and one video that I examine in this chapter each seek connection with the China of their ancestors and/or of their living relatives. The movies range from a 1979 PBS documentary to a 1987 video documentary that draws on experimental video traditions. Each of these movies is, explicitly or implicitly, a travelogue, and it is no accident that they each emerged in the late 1970s and early 1980s: before then, travel to and from China was restricted by international politics, most notably the Communist Revolution, which not only spurred migration from China but made reentry difficult. In the mid-1960s, when immigration reform opened the door for the migration of Chinese relatives of Chinese Americans, travel *to* China was still difficult. It was only with the end of the Cultural Revolution that China became accessible again (note that it is specifically *mainland China* that has inspired cinematic investigation, not Taiwan, Hong Kong, Singapore, etc.).[6] Movies about personal journeys to China were thus not possible before the late 1970s, and concern about the fate of relatives in China became an important motivation for such journeys.[7] Similarities of timing aside, the particular family histories that motivated each of these movies, as well as the details of production, vary widely.

Felicia Lowe's *China: Land of My Father* (1979) was produced on 16mm for KQED in San Francisco. Lowe had worked at KQED for several years, and when the opportunity arose for her to join a group of mostly print journalists traveling to China, she immediately asked the station for funds. (Around this time, Lowe won an Emmy for a series on financial planning for women and received a nomination for a series on breast cancer.) When they turned her down, she sought funding from all the stations in the San Francisco Bay area with no luck. By chance, Lowe discovered that a friend of hers knew PBS's Barry Chase ("probably the only time the old boys' network worked for me"), and Chase was familiar with her work for the series *Turnabout.* Meanwhile, Lowe made plans with a reporter for *Good Morning America;* the two of them would split the cost to hire a camera operator and would engineer sound for each other's projects. Three days before Lowe boarded the plane, CPB and KQED came through with funding and a December 25 airdate (leaving Lowe with eight weeks turnaround time). The next year, the program aired nationally on PBS (Lowe, telephone interview, 28 July 1994).

Lowe's film is a very conventionally shot and edited documentary that

China: Land of My Father. Sorting through photos: Felicia Lowe's trip to China is motivated by a desire to connect her son to his grandfather.

relies heavily on voice-over narration. No doubt this is due in part to Lowe's time and budgetary constraints (the project had an extremely low shooting ratio), but it can also be attributed to PBS's preference for traditional documentary structures. Despite Lowe's stated intention to counter traditional travelogue documentaries, *China: Land of My Father* replicates many of the traditional features of such documentaries, for example, reciting statistics about contemporary China and making obligatory visits to established sites such as the Great Wall. The film's subjective dimension emerges in Lowe's perspective as an immigrant's daughter and in the rendezvous with her father's family that closes the film.

China: Land of My Father begins with scenic views of the Chinese countryside at sunset and narrates the story of Lowe Wing-Sun, the filmmaker's father. The images of China give way to footage of Lowe's family going through picture albums, as Lowe's narration shifts into first person and expresses her desire for her own son to know more about his heritage. Lowe accompanies a group of journalists touring China and intersperses information about China with commentary on her emotional journey (her attempts to communicate using the rare dialect of her father, etc.). While visiting a Chinese news agency, she meets a woman whom she describes as her "soulmate," Sung Meiyu, a mother and a student at Beijing's Institute of Journalism, who asks Lowe "How do American women balance their careers and their families?" Lowe visits Sung's home, where the two women talk about mothers' roles in the workforce. As with the rest of the film up to this point, this visit is shot and edited as a traditional documentary (with establishing shots and talking heads); it is only Lowe's voice-over relaying her own impressions that hints at a subjective approach.

Eventually, Lowe departs from the tour group and journeys to meet her father's surviving family, consisting of her grandmother as well as several aunts and uncles. As with the earlier visit with Sung, this segment is visually conventional, but Lowe's narration adds a subjective dimension to the "objective" account of family life in this small village. At film's end, Lowe tearfully says goodbye to her grandmother, and the film closes as it began, with images of the same Chinese countryside.

In contrast, Richard Fung's *The Way to My Father's Village* (1988), produced on video, begins with a seemingly unmotivated image of a brick path, a stylized enactment of a bureaucratic interview, and an almost parodically authoritative, British-accented narrator who relates the story of the birth and North American migration of Fung's father. Fung, a Toronto-based videomaker and activist, is perhaps best known for his videos about Asian Canadian queer issues.[8] Funded in part by the Ontario Arts Council, *The Way to My Father's Village* documents a videomaker's visit to China, but unlike Lowe's film, Fung's video reaches beyond the temporal boundaries of the journey itself, documenting Fung's research into his father's story and the process by which he assembled the video. This process is captured not only in Fung's commentary on the video's production but in the clear disjuncture between images and narrated events. For example, the video's opening sequence depicts the story of Eugene Fung's arrival in Vancouver, journey across North America to Halifax, boat journey to Trinidad, and eventual retirement to Toronto. That narration on the soundtrack is accompanied by contemporary video footage of a ferry crossing a body of water, the view out the window of a jumbo jet, and so on. In fact, it is common documentary practice to use stock footage or contemporary footage with somewhat tangential connections to the voice-over narration. However, the striking disparity between the sound and image-track in *The Way to My Father's Vilage* hints that this video will not provide the coherent diegesis or story space of Lowe's *China: Land of My Father.*

Following the summary of the facts of Eugene Fung's life, the video shifts gears and presents a nonlinear, impressionistic portrait of Eugene's family life. Richard Fung's voice-over, its lilting Trinidadian tones in stark contrast to the British-accented narrator, describes his emotionally distant relationship with his father and notes his curiosity about the gaps in what he knows of him, those events in his past of which his father would not speak; the image-track presents home movies of Trinidad, interspersed with character-generated intertitles that echo phrases from the voice-over.

A taped conversation with Eugene's niece and nephew follows, and it, too, departs from linear documentary construction. Rather than presenting talking heads speaking to an off-camera interviewer, the interviewer/videomaker sits at a dining room table alongside his cousins while the video camera circles them. Although there are indications that the interview has been edited for the video, the long-takes and rambling narrative suggest that Fung has taken pains *not* to streamline the footage and impose a linear narrative. Unlike a talking-heads sequence, then, which either rehearses testimony or edits out tangential comments, this sequence takes on the intimate tone of a conversation over tea, without, however, constructing a coherent diegesis.

Like Felicia Lowe, Fung seems to have journeyed to China as part of a package tour and parted that tour's company to journey to his father's village (accompanied by his mother). Unlike in Lowe's film, however, Fung never appears before the camera in China, and his voice-overs discuss the omissions, mistakes, and frustrations of his project. The visit to Eugene's village is offset by images from the rest of the tour, each section framed further by a series of narratives about China from previous visitors (ranging from Marco Polo to Roland Barthes). Fung's video does not close with images of the Chinese countryside, but returns to Toronto; Fung makes it clear that he experienced no mystical reconciliation with the land of his father.

Lisa Hsia's *Made in China* (1986) differs from the other two movies in that it depicts a long-term visit: Hsia stayed with her cousin's family for five years while attending the University of Beijing. (The film was supported by grants from the Corporation for Public Broadcasting, New York State Council on the Arts, the Rockefeller Foundation, and two other foundations.) As such, Hsia's film is not primarily about retracing her parents' experiences in China; however, Hsia does avowedly frame the journey as one in which she tests American preconceptions about China and constantly compares the narrative of her childhood in Chicago with that of her relatives in China.

As a portrait of family life in contemporary China, Hsia's film follows a thematic structure rather than a chronological or linear one. Her position in the film is neither that of an outsider trapped behind the camera (as Fung portrays himself) nor that of a native tour guide. Footage of Hsia's Chinese family at times echoes the journalistic approach used to depict Lowe's visit with her Chinese "soulmate," but as we also see Hsia participating in that family life, the film sheds some of its "ethnographic tone." "The key to learning about China was not to go the 'protected foreigner' route, [however,] it wasn't wise tramping around pretending to be a local, either," states Hsia in voice-over, and the solution she hits on is to let her family be her guide. By insinuating herself into her Chinese family, Hsia can experience China as a "local," but only because her family buffers the "foreigner."

This complex inside/outside (local/foreigner) authorial position is evident in the interaction of various cinematic registers (types of footage) in the film's China sequences (leaving aside for the moment the combination of animation, silent home movies, and still photos to depict Hsia's U.S. childhood). The China experience proper is represented through three distinct cinematic registers: 8mm sync-sound home movies shot by Hsia, 16mm footage shot by two camera operators, and animation by Michael Sporn. Hsia's 8mm footage documents the family's domestic space, and her family responds as an American family would to home movies: they address the camera, that is, they address Hsia behind the camera (e.g., one of the boys performs his Charlie Chaplin impersonation). The animated footage depicts Hsia's solo encounters with "institutional China" (an altercation with a traffic cop, a visit to a clinic). And the 16mm footage operates in three distinct documentary modes: (1) verité footage of the family (diegetic footage in which Hsia and her family "ignore" the camera); (2) a hybrid talking-heads style, where Hsia's cousin Xue Su directly addresses either the camera or an interviewer (Hsia) off-screen; and (3) journalistic/ethnographic/tourist shots of Beijing street scenes (tai chi exercises, a dragon kite), in most of which Hsia does not appear.[9] These five distinct types of footage articulate different positions along the insider/outsider axis: the home movies at one extreme, the ethnographic shots at the other, with the verité, animation, and direct address falling in between.[10]

Hsia's voice-over perpetually draws comparison between the United States and China, whether noting contemporaneous events in the two countries, comparing the independence and privacy afforded her in the United States with her restricted role in her Chinese family, or speculating about growing up in China. Footage shot in the diegetic "present" in China is constantly juxtaposed with representations (snapshots and home movies) of the diegetic "past" in the United States. For example, the film begins with Hsia's departure from China, presents animation to depict her childhood ignorance of things Chinese, shows an old photo of an extended Chinese family in the 1930s, cuts to verité footage of Hsia presenting gifts to her Chinese hosts, gives us a glimpse of Hsia's 8mm footage, narrates childhood in Chicago with reference to family snapshots, returns to verité footage of Hsia's mother's visit to Beijing, cuts back to an American childhood by way of home movie footage, and so on—all in the first ten minutes. The rapid juxtaposition of divergent eras, cultures, and modes of cinematic representation serves to level out the various cinematic cues on first screening, but a close analysis reveals the complex process of signification alluded to in the preceding paragraph. On the surface, Hsia's film seems far less radical and self-reflexive than Fung's video, stylistically closer to *China: Land of My Father.* But careful attention to the film's enunciative process reveals a sophisticated, constantly shifting theory of Chinese American identity and history. The film's title, *Made in China,* is an ambiguous, punning reference that seems to imply an essentialist take on Asian American identity. But does the title refer to Hsia, her family, or the film itself (the last certainly being "made" in China, even if postproduction was in the United States)?

Losing Yourself in the Landscape

In these movies, the journey to China is always in pursuit of something other than China, something that is both of the self and beyond it. The object of these cinematic texts is potentially (and simultaneously) China, the parent, and the child. Inspired by an autobiographical impulse, these movies are not literally autobiographies, yet in journeying to China to find the self, they document subjectivities that threaten to disappear into the landscape.[11] Take, for example, a particularly fascinating passage in *China: Land of My Father,* wherein Lowe narrates her first impressions of the landscape: "These first images of the Chinese countryside are surprisingly familiar. The lush, green fields remind me of California's Sacramento Delta and the many summers I'd spent there as a child. I understand for the first time why so many Chinese settled in the Sacramento Valley: it was just like home."[12] Later, as she nears her family's village, she notes, "I'm sure my father crossed the same rivers and tributaries forty years earlier when he left the area." Lowe identifies with her father by imagining the moment when he *left* China instead of looking for traces of the China that he knew: she projects her own response onto her father, imagining that he journeyed to the United States and settled somewhere that reminded him of home, thus marking his journey from China while affirming his memory of it. Lowe, rather than reveling in her "homecoming," looks out her train window and sees California, and now sees California as not-China. Thus, China becomes the source, California the pale imitation—but of course for Lowe, Sacramento existed before Canton.

Lowe's vision of California as surrogate China is an intervention that asserts that China is not an inscrutably foreign place, but one with significant continuities with the United States. However, to accomplish this rhetorical move, *China: Land of My Father* must also acknowledge China's differences; it must participate in a tradition of representing China as foreign in order to question that tradition. The ways that each of the three movies takes up this problematic depends greatly on the child/narrator's identification with China. In other words, the degree to which a movie foregrounds its participation in the discursive construction of China is inversely related to the child's forging of emotional bonds with China.

China: Land of My Father

The child that seeks to understand the parent often wants to understand how parent and child are both alike and different. The parent must be established as both the same and different, as both native and foreign. In this context, Lowe's complicated assertion that China is like and is not like California begins to make sense. On venturing deeper into rural Canton, her narration observes: "I'm more taken by this scenery than any place I've seen so far. We'd stayed in many cities, but the majority of the population lives in the countryside, so it seems more like the *real* China to see people actually working in the fields. The faces look hauntingly familiar; they look like the Chinese people in America, but wearing different clothes. The reason is simple: I learn more than 90% of the early immigrants come from this southern province." Lowe thus makes two paradoxical assertions: first, that the real China is rural (and, by extension, timeless in an "Orientalized" sense), and second, that this "real" China is also the birthplace of Chinese America. Lowe seeks herself in the heart of China and thus must assert that the land she visits is both genuinely foreign and fundamentally related to her own heritage.

Lowe's discourse about the "real" China does not take place between her relatives and her or between other Chinese and her, but between Lowe and her tour companions—and between Lowe and her U.S. television audience (to whom she speaks in voice-over). In the film's only extended passage without voice-over, Lowe and two fellow tourists (both apparently white women) sit on the train and discuss what they've seen so far. Lowe's friends emphasize getting away from the tour, from the hotel rooms and other enclosed spaces, and visiting marketplaces and shops: they are most interested in spaces that reveal the way modern life is lived in China. For her part, Lowe shifts the conversation to a temple they visited, one she describes as the first "genuine" temple that they saw. At first, her words echo her companions', in that she emphasizes getting away from the tour and its sanitized sights; but whereas Lowe's companions find "genuine" China in the rhythms of modern life, Lowe finds "genuine" China in a preserved temple and in a three-thousand-year-old tree that she is able to touch. She tells her companions that the tree provided evidence of "continuous growth," and the image dissolves to Lowe on the Great Wall. The "genuine" China for Lowe is the past, not the present.

This difference between Lowe's tour companions and Lowe herself is crucial, for it reminds us that her desire for an exoticized, ancient China, as constructed by her voice-over, cannot be attributed simply to an Orientalizing vision of China desired by the PBS audience, for that vision is not shared with Lowe's companions, presumably print journalists and thus, in a sense, a surrogate PBS demographic. Lowe is not so much complicitous with her audience's demand for an Orientalized China as she is herself seeking an Orientalized China; the foreignness of the China that she sees is held in a productive tension with her own (perceived) ability to penetrate that foreignness. This tension is figured in Lowe's dialect, an offshoot of Cantonese. Lowe cannot speak Putong hua (official Mandarin), the people's language, and thus her contact with contemporary, modern China is mediated. When she encounters Cantonese speakers, she is better able to communicate (although still mediated by the dialects) until she finally encounters her family (who speak her dialect) and is able to assert unmediated conversation. Lowe's own knowledge of the Chinese language marks the tension between accessibility to and exclusion from China, and parallels her assertion of an "inborn and indestructible" connection to her family.

Lowe's simultaneous desires to affirm her connection to and separation from China surface whenever she is in contact with the Chinese people (not counting her relatives). In Canton, she sees the faces of Chinese Americans. When she converses (via an interpreter) with Chinese people on the street of an unnamed city, she explains their interest in her by surmising that

Made in China. The camera distances the photographer from the subject.

China: Land of My Father. The camera as ice-breaker.

they might have relatives in the United States. Lowe attempts to understand their interest in her as a manifestation of displaced desire to identify themselves with her; in actuality, it is Lowe who projects her own desires onto them.

The narrators of *The Way to My Father's Village* and *Made in China* are also guilty of projecting their own expectations onto China and the people they encounter, but Fung's video and Hsia's film differ from Lowe's film in their emphasis on the processes by which "China" is constructed; this self-reflexive strategy constantly refers to prevailing attitudes toward China (gathered from people "on the street" and from classic texts by Marco Polo, Roland Barthes, and others), and to the role the camera plays not only in framing what is before it, but in actually affecting the profilmic. For example, Fung describes the process of exclusion and inclusion that governed his image making, and Hsia relates an anecdote about how her use of a camera marked her as an outsider (both these stories are elaborated below).

In contrast, Lowe's film makes virtually no reference to a tradition of cinematic representations of China nor to the effect her own camera has on the profilmic (even though she is traveling with a tour of U.S. journalists).

Lowe's film is extremely unconventional in its own right: its emphasis on a subjective (as opposed to impersonal) perspective marks it as an important precursor to the stylized discursive approaches of contemporary documentaries. The eight years between *China: Land of My Father* (1979) and *The Way to My Father's Village* (1987) witnessed both the gradual acceptance of self-reflexiveness in theatrical documentaries (e.g., *Sherman's March,* McElwee, 1986) and the increasing codification of a distinct video aesthetic for documentary. This shift might be marked by the differences between 1970s documentaries on PBS, and PBS's *P.O.V.* series of independent makers in the 1990s.[13] Furthermore, the conventional tone of Lowe's documentary is also a function of the expectation that she prove she can make a conventional documentary. The work of a woman of color in television production in the 1970s would have been scrutinized for signs of "affirmative action bias." Indeed, although critics have argued that women and people of color have pioneered new modes of documentary production (modes that reject documentary conventions designed to promote the illusion of objective truth), it could also be argued that such "marginalized" filmmakers bent over backwards to make conventional film product.

Does this mean that self-reflexive movies are inherently less problematic, are better able to interrogate received views of China? If a movie calls attention to the processes by which China is constructed, does it necessarily follow that such a movie is able to see China in a fresh light? Richard Fung grapples with that very question in a video about the land of *his* father.

The Way to My Father's Village

If Richard Fung's video *The Way to My Father's Village* foregrounds the camera and its role in shaping the profilmic, that self-reflexivity is not merely a function of shifting conventions or of authorial style; rather, the formal differences between Lowe's and Fung's work underline a fundamental difference in the two makers' experiences of China. Whereas Lowe seeks connection, Fung finds estrangement. This end, however—connection or estrangement—is subordinated to the process (the means to the end); indeed, the title cards emphasize process by presenting the title of Fung's video in two successive screens (separated by an intervening image), "The Way" and "To My Father's Village," thereby suggesting that the journey is as important as the destination. Fung's piece does not describe China but the attempt to capture China on video.

When Fung arrives in his father's village, he is not reminded of a North American landscape; instead, his eyes and camera are immediately drawn to the tower of the house built by his family, instantly recognizable thanks to an oft-seen photograph of the same house. The landscape is different—other houses were built since the photograph was taken—but the house is unmistakable. The awareness that the landscape has changed but is the same, that the video camera is recording what a still camera did years before, indicates that Fung cannot see China without seeing how China has been previously represented. As he admits at the end of this sequence, he left the village without remembering to ask to see the house where his father was born. The house for which there was already a photograph was more important to Fung, or at least more immediate. Fung thus realizes he has been positioned as a tourist, taking photos of things that have already been photographed to prove that he had been there. More important, Fung realizes that as a videomaker and tourist, he did not seek out objects from his father's past, but objects that he and his father had seen representations of and heard stories about.

Whereas *China: Land of My Father* involves vaguely remembered stories from long ago, *The Way to My Father's Village* includes more recent reminiscences about China. *The Way* is constructed around a series of narratives about Eugene Fung, Richard Fung's father. The video begins with an apparently staged bureaucratic interview: an off-screen woman's voice asks "What is your name?" and a man's voice replies "Eugene Fung," giving way to a sync-sound image of a woman's hands typing. Disjunction between soundtrack and image, voice and printed page, and (by implication) between modes of narration are subtly suggested by the distortions that creep into the "record": Richard Fung's voice (his body is in frame, but his head remains off-screen) reports that his father's occupation was businessman, but the hands type "proprietor." After some more "facts" are recorded, the segment returns to the image of a foot path; a legend reading "1279 A.D." appears and a cultured, British-accented voice concisely sketches out a history of the Hakka people, and then begins to narrate specifically the story of Eugene Fung's birth and migration to Trinidad (via Hong Kong and Canada) as a young man. This narration is accompanied by images that

The Way to My Father's Village. Searching through Eugene's documents.

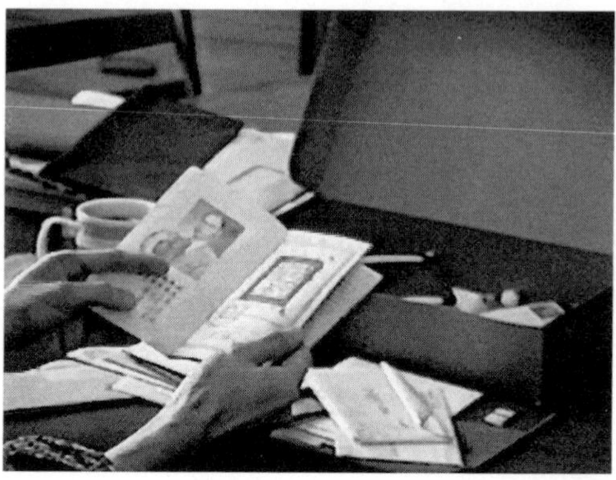

depart subtly from standard documentary practice. Hakka illustrations are given to us as freeze-frames shot off a television monitor; instead of a map of China we see a close-up on the cover of an atlas as a hand opens the book to the map of China; instead of images of Canada, we see abstracted, obviously contemporary landscapes that connect with the narration allusively, even tangentially (i.e., a shot over the railing of a ferry illustrates the narrated journey by train across Canada to Halifax; a view of a wing from the portal of a jumbo jet illustrates Eugene's migration to Toronto and his death following a stroke).

The segment concludes and is punctuated by an intertitle that reads "HISTORY and memory." If the section that just preceded the title consisted of facts that are a matter of public record ("HISTORY"), the section that follows consists of ephemera ("memory"): images from home movies are interspersed with textual reminiscences, as Fung's voice-over tells how little he knows about his father. This section, like the one that precedes it, begins with reference to public documentation as Fung goes through a box containing a marriage license, passports, and other documents, while the voice-over comments that these documents don't tell much. But Fung's voice-over is not positioned as the presenter of the "truth" of memory or Eugene's identity, because the voice-over doubts its own access to Eugene. As Eugene's youngest child, Fung tells us, "I was always aware that I'd come in near the end of a story. Everyone in my family talked about the past . . . [for example, how] my father would whip out his belt at any sign of disobedience. They all said that I was lucky, but I felt excluded."

The opening sequences of *The Way* set up the framework of interlocking narratives and positions toward "documentation" that structure the video.

The Way to My Father's Village. Fung's cousins show a picture of a house built in China after Eugene's departure.

At least two narratives are presented via voice-over: the objective facts and the subjective recollections, each with its own gaps. Each section begins with a "staged" moment of reflection (the recording of information on a bureaucratic form, and the attempt to read meaning from between the lines of those forms). Home movies and photos represent interventions into time, and official photographs document identity and attach facts, figures, and documentable events to the body. Finally, both introductory sections combine sound and image (voice-over and visual footage) in a way that emphasizes their temporal disjuncture. In the history section, contemporary footage of a journey across Canada "illustrates" (alludes to) the narrated journey; in the memory section, the voice-over refers directly to the documents, home movies, and snapshots, positioning the voice postimage, so that sound can interrogate the image. For example, the voice comments in reference to photos of the family at the beach, "Besides, I never remember my father being that relaxed," acknowledging that snapshots are simultaneously "candid" and "posed."[14]

As if to acknowledge the inadequacy of these accounts of his father's life, the history and memory segment is followed by "Tony and Dorothy," an interview with Eugene's nephew and niece. In this interview, Tony and Dorothy talk not about Eugene, nor about their father (Eugene's brother), but mostly about themselves, their village, and the house in the photograph. When Fung arrives at his father's village, his camera documents things from Dorothy's and Tony's stories: the bamboo poles on which laundry was hung (and from which the Nationalist armies hung the heads of alleged Communists), a pair of chairs that are no longer in the house with the tower but now reside elsewhere, the house itself that Eugene never saw except in a photograph. Fung's camera thus seeks to document the stories that he was told, to verify the existence of the family narratives' settings, emblematized in the shot of the two chairs (which once sat in a house that Eugene had never seen and that now sit elsewhere). The two chairs have no meaning without the narrative that gives them meaning—more precisely, the video image of the chairs has no meaning for Fung without Tony and Dorothy's narrative—and the narrative is the only thing that connects the chairs to Eugene.

Fung's video continually reminds us of the distance that separates videomaker and father, whether that distance is cultural or linguistic ("He never taught us his language—there's a real finality in that," notes Fung. When in China, Fung has to ask his mother questions in English; she translates them into Cantonese for a woman who can interpret Hakka). China is mediated by previous representations and narratives about China. When visiting Shanghai, Fung's camera is unable to capture what is in front of it, seeking out the famous park with the "No Dogs or Chinese" sign immortalized in Bruce Lee's *The Chinese Connection* (1972) and Han Suyin's *The Crippled Tree:* Fung's voice-over announces, "By the way, you can't see it, but to the left there is a park here in Shanghai. . . . There was a sign here. It read, 'No Dogs or Chinese Allowed.'" Just as he was compelled to photograph the tower of the house in his father's village, here the compulsion to record that which has already been documented is so strong that the soundtrack attempts to compensate for the camera's failure to capture an image.

Fung's video seems, almost of its own accord, to reiterate (rather than critique or amplify) representations of the past. In photographing Shanghai, Fung admits in voice-over that he intentionally excludes white tourists from the frame, for "they spoil the purity of the image I'm trying to capture." He admits that his camera attempts to find a China that has not been penetrated by the West, a spatially and/or temporally removed China. Fung's voice-over undercuts that attempted construction, allowing space for those tourists in his video—reinscribing them. The visual exclusion of tourists is marked as a deliberate act; the temporal disjunction between videography and voice-over, production and postproduction, Fung as editor and Fung as camera operator, reveals the videomaker in his Canadian studio as ashamed of his own actions in China. Thus Fung foregrounds the act of constructing his video—not just to call attention to its construction, but to emphasize the shifts accompanying production, the project's historical evolution, and the videomaker's awareness of his complicity in representing China as exotic.[15] In other words, although the video might be seen as an attempt to construct a Chinese filter through which to view Eugene Fung, the videomaker is aware that the task of constructing an accurate filter is beyond his capabilities, at least without resorting to simplifying China (i.e., excluding tourists from the image). That process of simplification insists on a static vision of China as temporally and historically removed. But by titling his video "The Way" and not "My Father's Village," Fung emphasizes the journey through space and time that his video attempts to document, thus preserving temporal and spatial fluidity. He thus admits that the China to which he has access is spatially and temporally removed from the China he seeks, and in admitting that, he allows for the ongoing historical transformation of his "Chinese filter." The problem with the documents—passports, but even snapshots—is that they lack narrative, they record a moment in time (as Fung notes, the photos "were taken before I was born; if I had been there they might trigger a memory"). More specifically, the snapshots do not evoke Fung's memories, but narratives about the past that were assigned to the snapshots by family members who *were* aware of the events the photos depict. Fung's video attaches his *own* memories and thus a new narrative—the story of his journey to China—to those still images.

But the video seems always aware that the narrative it constructs runs the risk of distorting the still image even more. For narrative cannot be restored to a still image once severed from it; instead, a new narrative must be constructed and attached to the image. For example, the bureaucratic interview that begins the film is an attempt to render Eugene's life into a comprehensible narrative, referring to documents that locate him in time and space (visas and such). A passport photo offers a narrative, but it imposes bureaucratic order on the photograph (itself different from the snapshot in that it is posed, organized for legibility); the official stamp on such a photograph is a marker of another subjectivity imposing its own sense of narrative. (Note the historical irony that many Chinese immigrants employed false papers to enter the United States, and the inadequacy of these official narratives is evident.) Fung thus attempts to attach a narrative that has meaning *for him,* emphasizing his subjectivity and thereby the image's objective primacy within the narrative.

Made in China

The passage of time and its effect on narrative is taken up in a different way in *Made in China,* which documents the experiences of Lisa Hsia, a second-generation Chinese American, who stays with her Chinese cousins when attending Beijing University. *Made in China* begins with a moving-picture family portrait, snapshot-style, marking the occasion of Hsia's departure by train. After this introductory sequence, we see an animated sequence of a cartoon Hsia sitting and knitting; the voice-over tells us she was a typical girl except for constantly being reminded of her "difference;" this difference is rendered in an audio collage of overlapping taunts and more or less good-natured inquiries about her ethnic heritage. This audio collage gives way to a montage of "on the street" interviews with white Americans who describe their impressions of the Chinese. At the beginning of the film, then, stereotypical misperceptions are located outside of Hsia, in the surrounding white populace. By film's end, Hsia's voice-over will refer to her *own* preconceptions about China, followed by a recapitulation of the audio collage, suggesting that her own attitude before her visit be aligned with those testimonies. Hsia's film thus echoes Fung's video, which seems at first to interrogate the exotic portrait of China painted by Marco Polo, Matteo Ricci, Roland Barthes, and others, but which later seems to admit that Fung too is complicitous in replicating these visions of China.

Although both Fung's video and Hsia's film are interested in finding out what role China had in making them, the two works interrogate the role of picture taking and filmmaking in constructing these personal narratives in slightly different ways. For Fung, the home movies and photographs predate his birth and thus indicate a father who preexisted his consciousness. The impetus behind Fung's video, then, is to attempt to determine which photographs reveal the truth of who his father was; Fung is concerned with the demand that photographs make on the viewer to provide narrative context. In *Made in China,* however, the home movies document Hsia's childhood, and as such they stand in for the narrative of her life in the United States.[16] Hsia's home movies, unlike Fung's, presumably stimulate her memory. The tension between competing narratives for Hsia, then, is akin to the classic diasporic question: Who would I have been if we had not left? *Made in China* presents its home movies and family snapshots as the baseline against which a childhood in China is imagined.

When we are first formally introduced to Hsia's Chinese family, she tells us that her aunt immediately welcomed her as if she had known her all her life; soon after, she notes that her aunt "treated me like the daughter she'd never had, which was wonderful, except that it meant she would consider me a child until I married. Whether I was three years old or twenty-two, it didn't matter: she considered me a kid, incapable of doing anything myself." Hsia thus positions herself within the alternative narrative of Chinese daughter while simultaneously marking her inability to fit that role due to her American identity. When she tells us how all-American her childhood was, we are shown a series of photographs in a family album that attest to her family's not particularly Chineseness (e.g., a young Hsia in a Girl Scouts uniform); the sequence is underscored by the Beatles' "When I'm Sixty-Four" (1967). The film later returns to this topic of her all-American childhood with a montage of home movies showing such activities as clearing the yard, skipping rope, and riding a bike; this sequence is underscored by the Beach Boys' "When I Grow Up (To Be a Man)" (1964). The use of these two songs is instructive: the lyrics look to the future, while the recordings themselves connote a specific period in America's past (the period of Hsia's youth, presumably).[17] In looking forward, both songs' lyrics articulate an interest in how one's life will turn out, in the narrative lines that one envisions for oneself; the recordings themselves locate the snapshots and home movies in the filmmaker's childhood (and vice versa).

The home movie sequence ends with a shot of a child (Hsia?) on her bike, followed by shots of the adult Hsia cycling with the Chinese masses. These shots lead directly into the animated sequence of Hsia's encounter with a Chinese policeman. In this sequence, Hsia's voice-over informs us that she sought to blend in with the Chinese, only to find that her ignorance of certain customs caused her to run afoul of a traffic cop; she escapes by pulling out her camera and taking a photograph, which makes the policeman realize that she is *not* Chinese but an "honored foreign guest." In attempting to immerse herself in an alternative personal narrative, one in which she is an anonymous Chinese, Hsia finds it necessary to extricate herself by reverting to her role as tourist/documentarian.[18]

The trope of parallel childhoods continues through another home movie montage sequence, this time of childhood vacations to Egypt, Greece, and Thailand. In the film's penultimate sequence, Auntie tells stories about her own youth and the Cultural Revolution. The sequence begins with Auntie sharing traditional Chinese embroidery that she had to put to prac-

keep photos of people who
had political problems

Made in China. China's Cultural Revolution left a legacy of mutilated photographs . . .

. . . and censored photo albums.

tical use during the Cultural Revolution, highlighting the disjuncture of traditions effected by China's political evolution. A brief insert of home movies illustrates Hsia's comment that she was eight when the Cultural Revolution began (the year she attended Disneyland) and eighteen when it ended. Auntie next pulls out her own photo albums, and the first image we are shown is of Auntie at twenty-two; Hsia's voice-over informs us that that was her age when she arrived in China, explicitly connecting the trope of cross-generational identification and parallel childhoods. The sequence ends with Auntie pointing to mutilated photographs where friends and relatives with "political problems" were excised, followed by pages of empty photo mounts where photos of Hsia's American family had been.

A photo album already marks the boundary between public and private memories: it is as private as the closet where it is kept and as public as the coffee table where it is displayed. How, then, to interpret this blank page in the Chinese photo album? It represents the excision of the American family from the public face of their Chinese cousins, yet that absence is

Made in China.
Making new snapshots.

still marked by the photo mounts. These mounts, then, preserve the space for reinsertion of those photographs, just as Fung preserves the space for reinsertion of white tourists into his video record of Shanghai. The blank pages near the end of the film recall the family photos at the beginning, and their absence here might be read as an indication of the ultimate impossibility of conceiving of parallel childhoods, the "What if we hadn't left?" But the photo pages, bookending the film as they do, remind us that the film itself arranges time into its own version of narrative: we have been led to believe in Hsia's gradual incorporation into her Chinese family over the course of the film. The film itself has straddled the Chinese and American narratives, doing the work of connecting and contrasting them. The film's narrative articulates the forces that impelled departure from China and compelled "return."

Photographs and Stories

These movies interrogate China as a point of departure for a series of potential narratives. The act of traveling to China in *China: Land of My Father* and *The Way to My Father's Village* involves an imaginative reversal of identifications with the forces that led fathers away from China. *Made in China* speculates on the potential lives that Hsia might have led had she been born elsewhere. I have argued that these films are most successful when they emphasize (and thematize) the *processes* by which the makers constitute China, and thereby illuminate the process of *becoming* (of identity formation).[19] It is when these films refer to China as if it were a tangible, fixed object that their hypotheses are at their most precarious: attempting to secure China definitively risks reversing the process of constructing the maker's subjectivity. It is only in the process of departing from China that subjectivity emerges. Richard Fung understands himself best when he understands his father least, and Felicia Lowe recognizes that forging a connection with her family in China will strengthen her as she leaves China behind.

The process of "returning" to China, identifying with an ancestor or the landscape, and attaching new narratives to old images, emphasizes the discontinuity of cinematic investigation into the past. If Fung traveled to China hoping to attach his father to a photograph of a house, he left China with that photograph irrevocably attached to himself, not to his father. The investigation of the past continually throws the maker on the shoals of the present.

Images of the past fascinate not because they connect the past to us, but because they reveal the *arbitrary* relation of the past to ourselves. In *Camera Lucida,* Barthes describes the process of seeking the one photograph that captures his mother's essence, settling on a photograph of her as a child, taken at the Winter Garden long before he was born. This is the photograph that captures his mother best, and it is not a photograph that depicts her maternal relation to Barthes, but the specter of her discontinuity:

> In 1865, young Lewis Payne tried to assassinate Secretary of State W. H. Steward. Alexander Gardner photographed him in his cell, where he was waiting to be hanged. The photograph is handsome, as is the boy: that is the *studium.* But the *punctum* is: *he is going to die.* I read at the same time: *This will be* and *this has been;* I observe with horror an anterior future of which death is the stake. By giving me the absolute past of the pose (aorist), the photograph tells me death in the future. What *pricks* me is the discovery of this equivalence. In front of the photograph of my mother as a child, I tell myself: she is going to die: I shudder, like Winnicott's psychotic patient, *over a catastrophe which has already occurred.* Whether or not the subject is already dead, every photograph is this catastrophe. (1981, 96; emphasis in original)

The Winter Garden photograph is catastrophic—Barthes's mother is already dead—and by dying in this photograph, she dies before Barthes is born. A photograph of the past erases the present: the photograph is like a time traveler who returns to the past and murders his or her own ancestor. The narratives we attach to images connect them to us, but the images themselves possess the specter of our own death. It is hardly surprising, then, that Fung's process of *becoming,* "the way" he finds his connection to the past, is to tell stories, for narratives contest the discontinuous past represented by cinema. The narrated story asserts the connection of the still image to the present through its existence in continuously unfolding time. Our connection to the past is an illusion, however, as illusory as the process of ventriloquism through which soundtrack and image-track assert their ontological connection[20]—but the shadows in Plato's Cave do not produce sounds, it is the mind of the viewer/auditor that associates sound and image. Cinema expresses both the desire to connect to the past and the fundamental disconnection with it, a desire for continuity built on an underlying discontinuity. The process of constructing Asian American subjectivity is thus akin to the process of film/videomaking foregrounded by Fung's video: by narrating the process of videomaking, Fung emphasizes the choices he could have made, the moments in the past where divergence might have taken place—the selection of images that, once taken, mark a catastrophic murder of the present.

These movies paper over the discontinuous past (proposing a means of connecting past to present) while marking that very discontinuity; pointing to the gap in the past and simultaneously attempting to fill it, they stumble when they trick themselves into believing that their efforts are more than makeshift. Lowe's search for the "real" China succeeds too well, for the only China she can see is the one she set out to find. Fung searches for a pure China as well, but by narrating his failure to find it, he permits both China and his father to exist apart from his own image of the past. Hsia's figure of the censored photo album reveals the discontinuity of the photographs themselves (the catastrophe they reveal) as well as the revisionist political history that impelled their removal: the absence of an image marks both its discontinuous existence and the historical rupture represented by its censorship. The truth of the past would not be the recovery of the missing photos, unless the photo album could somehow mark the history of their absence and return, for the restoration of the photo album would not accurately depict the photos' prodigal years, when retaining the past was relegated to memory. Similarly, Chinese American movies cannot simply narrativize images, masking their discontinuity, but must instead mark the historical rupture occasioned by the image's narrative detachment. When Fung's photograph attaches to him, and not to his father, then Fung becomes the link that marks the discontinuous past, the past that separated the photograph from his father. Linking the past to the present, these makers become the splice that holds together the discontinuity of a jump cut.

CHAPTER 5

Lost in the Media Jungle

Tiana Thi Thanh Nga's Hollywood Mimicry

War as a succession of special effects; the war became film well before it was shot. Cinema has remained a vast machine of special effects. If the war is the continuation of politics by other means, then media images are the continuation of war by other means. Immersed in the machinery, part of the special effect, no critical distance. Nothing separates the Vietnam war and the superfilms that were made and continue to be made about it. It is said that if the Americans lost the other, they have certainly won this one.
—Trinh T. Minh-ha, from soundtrack of
Surname Viet Given Name Nam

As an intentionally organized materiality, the body is always an embodying *of* possibilities both conditioned and circumscribed by historical convention. In other words, the body *is* a historical situation, as Beauvoir has claimed, and is a manner of doing, dramatizing, and *reproducing* a historical situation.
—Judith Butler, "Performative Acts and Gender Constitution"

The war in Vietnam and the antiwar movement in the United States were major inspirations for the Asian American Movement. According to William Wei, the movement

> began in the late 1960s and was primarily the result of the convergence of two historical developments: the emergence of college-age Asian Americans and the public protests surrounding the Vietnam War. . . .

> Moved by a mixture of moralism and idealism, Asian Americans participated in the civil rights, New Left, women's liberation, antiwar, and other movements organized to change the country. But it was mainly the antiwar movement that brought them together psychologically and politically, making them aware of their "Asianness," their membership in a pan-Asian community, and the need for an Asian American Movement. (1993, 1–2)

Yen Le Espiritu emphasizes the racial dimension of the antiwar movement, noting that Asian Americans did more than coalesce across Asian ethnic lines in the United States, that "pan-Asian political consciousness became transnationalized, encompassing the political struggles not only in America but also in Asia" (1992, 44–45).[1] Asian Americans defined themselves in the context of the antiwar movement, and indeed the very term Asian American was coined in this context (32).

The role of Asian Americans has not been thematized by the majority of popular media accounts of the antiwar movement, and Asian Americans who grew up in the 1970s were probably too young to be aware of the formative role the movement played in raising pan-ethnic, transnational consciousness for Asian Americans. However, the impact of mass media representations of the war on later generations of filmmakers and visual artists cannot be overestimated. Thi Thanh Nga (Tiana)'s *From Hollywood to Hanoi* responds to parental nostalgia for prewar Vietnam and the abundance of U.S. media representations of the war in Vietnam; it depicts a filmmaker who attempts to assemble a subjective and coherent sense of the past out of a wide variety of cinematic material, a filmmaker torn between the desire to reframe famous sights and the inability to escape famous sites.[2] This problematic position—simultaneously producing and being produced by cinema—is figured in the citation of stereotypic performances of "Orientalness" by Tiana, performances documented on film and cited by *From Hollywood to Hanoi.* These performances of mimicry emerge from Tiana's tenuous position as both subject and object of cinematic discourse, and therefore emerge from a space of "hybridity," Homi Bhabha's term for the space created by contradictory disavowals of racial difference in colonial discourse, disavowals that permit the colonial subject to escape from the colonizer's efforts to interpellate him or her as the object of colonial power.[3]

Tiana's use of generic conventions (to tell stories through shorthand) and of her own body echo the work of other Vietnamese American women artists of her generation, particularly Hanh Thi Pham and, to a lesser extent, Trinh T. Minh-ha. Each of these artists has attempted to convey the ways young Vietnamese women are interpellated by Vietnamese and U.S. ideologies about women's roles, viewing the struggle of the young woman from the vantage of an older woman. Tiana's perspectives are particularly interesting, because her younger incarnation seems to embrace "Oriental" roles (in a way that Pham does not), while her older incarnation implicitly critiques that role playing.[4]

From Hollywood to Hanoi

Thi Thanh Nga was born in Saigon in the early 1960s. Her father, the press secretary for South Vietnam, moved the family to the United States in 1966. Leaving her family as a teenager, Thi Thanh Nga renamed herself Tiana: as an actor she went under the name Tiana Alexandra, and she made music videos under the name Tiana Banana.[5] In 1988, she visited Vietnam with a group of U.S. veterans and was inspired to make a film, returning twelve times in the next three years. She and her cameramen trained a Vietnamese crew and shot seventy-five hours of 16mm footage, resulting in a five-hour rough cut. According to Tiana, feedback on her rough cuts was always the same: "Everyone said I was trying to do too much. They wanted to know my story. Why was I doing this or that? Where was I from? How had I grown up in America?" She added material on her childhood and cannibalized footage from her film career. During the 1992 film festival season, *From Hollywood to Hanoi* screened at London, Telluride, Chicago, and Hawai'i before beginning a run at the Film Forum in New York in the winter of 1993–1994.[6] A reedited version appeared on Cinemax in the summer of 1995 as part of their Vanguard series of independent films.[7]

Following an on-screen epigraph (from the poem "Who am I?" by Tru Vu),[8] *From Hollywood to Hanoi* opens with a clip from a B-movie, in which Tiana appears as a motorcycle-riding, high-kicking vice cop. "Hollywood was home," a voice-over informs us. The film next rapidly juxtaposes file footage of Vietnam on fire, newsreel footage of Ho Chi Minh, on-the-street interviews with so-called Amerasian teenagers raised in the United States, and home movies of Tiana's childhood, while the voice-over relays Vietnamese folklore and Tiana's father's stories about life in prewar Vietnam. As the sequence progresses it describes life in suburban America, now intercutting the war footage with clips from Tiana's various "Hollywood" incarnations: as Tiana Banana in music videos, in a workout video called "Karatecise with Tiana," and playing a Vietnamese woman opposite Rod Steiger. Via this fast-paced montage, the film presents a young woman whose Hollywood career has been built on cannily reproducing and occasionally rearticulating stereotypical Asian women's roles, but Tiana's voice-over indicates the limitations of such a career: "I thought I had it made, but really, my career was going nowhere."

This "prologue" out of the way, *From Hollywood to Hanoi* shifts gears slightly: the voice-overs shift to present tense and adopt the conceit of a letter to the United States. (Many of the voice-overs describing Vietnam begin "Dear Dad," and the film as a whole is dedicated "For Dad.") The body of the film is a portrait of contemporary Vietnam (the hotels, the nightlife, the availability of U.S. consumer goods),[9] but more than that, the film depicts Tiana's search for traces of the past. Her film is trapped in the web not just of familial representations, but of U.S. media representations. She tours the Chû Tîch tunnels, visits the street where Buddhist monks set themselves on fire, travels to My Lai, and meets Le Duc Tho. But in addition to these sights that Americans have all seen via the news media, she also digs deeper with her camera, visiting a hospital ward treating conjoined twins,[10] a scientist researching the effects of Agent Orange (and a lab filled with dead, deformed babies in jars), and speaking at length with children left behind by U.S. servicemen. *From Hollywood to Hanoi* contests previous cinematic representations directly, which means that it is beholden to those representations: even when documenting images downplayed or ignored in the U.S. media, those images are always in reference to (and elaborations of) U.S. actions. Other than a few references to Vietnamese culture (the traditional bamboo swing of a betrothal ceremony, the children's practice of riding the backs of water buffalo), all of Tiana's images of Vietnam are replications, elaborations, or rebuttals of U.S. images. As such, these images are addressed to the audience at large (not just "to Dad"). In a sense, *From Hollywood to Hanoi* searches not for Vietnam, but for the war in Vietnam.

Does *From Hollywood to Hanoi*'s reliance on familiar representations of Vietnam reveal an indebtedness to Hollywood that the film cannot escape? After all, Oliver Stone's name is above the title (as executive producer). Does the bountiful availability of Vietnam footage seduce this film into "a cultural logic of affluence,"[11] deterministically restricting the remobilization of these images? In other words, does cinematic shorthand lead to a short circuit of the film's critique of U.S. representations of Vietnam? Or does the film's shorthand point to the mechanism of "splitting," the redirection of the colonizer's discourse at its loci of ambivalence?

From Hollywood to Hanoi refers to popular U.S. visions of Vietnam as it constructs alternative visions. It is not just that there is more than one Vietnam in the film: Vietnam is presented as the object of multiple discursive formations. These multiple discursivities are balanced by multiple authorial presences in the film. By inscribing herself into the text repeatedly, and in multiple incarnations—especially clips from her "Vietnamese" roles in Hollywood fictions—Tiana uses her own body (or, more precisely, representations of her body) to call attention to the discursive construction of the various representations of Vietnam that the film cites. To explicate the functioning of Tiana's various incarnations in the film, and their relation to the notion of Tiana as author, I draw on insights gleaned from Bhabha's theories of colonial discourse, theories that identify the loci of ambivalence that permit the colonial to expose its mechanisms. In particular, Bhabha's analysis of mimicry as an articulation of colonial ambivalence toward the colonizer, and of stereotype as an anxious colonial discourse that produces the possibility of its own overthrow, provide useful frameworks for understanding the logic at work in Tiana's various incarnations; the recontextualization of Tiana's performative personae is an example of Bhabha's "hybridity."[12]

"Hollywood was home. . . . but really, my career was going nowhere." This pronouncement, over an action movie clip, signals *From Hollywood to Hanoi*'s narrative strategy: we are presented with condensed excerpts from Hollywood fictions (as if demonstrating how quickly we can process generic cues); whereupon a first-person voice-over resituates the clip, positioning it as a line on a performer's résumé. That résumé is further contextualized as a metaphoric search for home, a quest that had seemed successful but was ultimately revealed to be ongoing. Beginning in medias res, *From Hollywood to Hanoi* backs up to trace how the filmmaker has come to this point. Tiana narrates her childhood in the United States and the images of Vietnam that entered her consciousness from the surrounding culture, tracing her evolution from apparently all-American kid to her various Hollywood incarnations. These various identities are all defined in relation to high school culture and mass media images; for example, she asserts that she was high school Homecoming Queen, then admits that a tall blonde beat her out: "I got over it; I got a black belt instead. Jane

Fonda: try *my* workout tape!" After showing us clips from her "Karatecise with Tiana" video, her voice-over comments, "Dad wanted us to become model Asian Americans . . . No way!" The sequence of these clips implies a cause-and-effect relationship: Tiana was rebuffed when she attempted to assimilate into Middle America (the Homecoming pageant), so she responds by marketing stereotypic Orientalness (martial arts expertise) via a modern medium (the workout tape), thus estranging herself from her father. These quick clips trace the complex development of Tiana's Asian American female identity vis-à-vis U.S. culture.

The opening sequence of *From Hollywood to Hanoi* takes Tiana from the late 1960s to the late 1980s, from preadolescence to adulthood. Footage of the war in Vietnam provides a concise summary of the war's depiction in the U.S. news media. Intercutting the story of Tiana's own life suggests the interrelatedness of these two narratives, fostering an illusion of contemporaneity. However, midway through the sequence Tiana's voice-over announces, "I tried to tune out memories of the war but couldn't," and following this comment the images of Vietnam drop all pretense of chronology, becoming detached from specific historical events in the war; furthermore, the two narratives of warfare and suburban life, parallel and thus distinct to this point, suddenly merge. The "fall" of Saigon in 1975 is juxtaposed with one of Tiana's 1987 film roles. The family's relocation to California is implicitly associated with the late 1970s to early 1980s period of Vietnamese migration, but the contemporaneous events in Tiana's career are elided.

The merging, mixing, and elisions between the two narratives can be traced to Tiana's evolution through a variety of pop culture incarnations, from suburban Homecoming Queen, to pop star, to a succession of postmodern "Oriental" caricatures (reaching its apotheosis in a music video called "Lust in de Jungle," which depicts Tiana as a dragon lady in a bustier, and her role "as Rod Steiger's warbride" in *Catch the Heat* [1987]). In a sense, the montage suggests a progression from Daddy's girl (a supposedly nonracially marked youth) to rebellious young woman (mimicry of U.S. pop icons, stereotypic "Oriental" roles). This progression is mirrored by Tiana's father and mother, whose efforts to be all-American (through churchgoing and a job at Voice of America) give way to a Vietnam-identified phase in San Jose. Tiana's film portrays her father as giving up his political hopes for Vietnam (represented in this montage by his job with VOA)—that is, a view of Vietnam as a modern nation—replacing those aspirations with resignation to life in the United States and nostalgia for Vietnam's cultural achievements (represented in the montage by his interest in Vietnamese philosophy), a fantasy of the glorious premodern Vietnam. Tiana's mother, meanwhile, is portrayed in a state of arrested development and wishful thinking (the voice-over tells us dismissively, "She prayed—a lot"), attempting to assimilate into American middle-class respectability. (Significantly, Tiana's mother is not spoken of or seen later in the film.)

So, while Tiana's father progresses from a role in Vietnam's government, through a transitional phase as a patriot in exile, and finally becomes a model immigrant whose only contact with his homeland is through nostalgia, Tiana herself passes from suburban adolescent ashamed of her Asian heritage, to a rootless ("not destined for San Jose") adult who hopes to sort out Vietnamese and American cultural influences; this latter stage is charted by the remainder of the film. But to get from childhood to adulthood, from "hating gooks" to examining the U.S. construction of the Vietnamese, Tiana passes through a series of prefabricated personae, mimicking "whiteness" with a difference (martial arts workout tapes) before inhabiting Asian stereotypes (the warbride). It is as if, before "speaking" through film in her own "voice," Tiana passed through stages of mimicking other's speech. That linguistic paradigm brings me to Homi Bhabha, whose writing has theorized postcolonialism through reference to Lacanian and Derridean theories of language.

Hollywood Mimicry

In "Of Mimicry and Man: The Ambivalence of Colonial Discourse," Homi Bhabha describes the process of "almost the same but not quite" (1994, 89) in colonial discourse (later, he abbreviates this formulation as "not quite/not white" [92]). Mimicry is, by definition, not a perfect copy, but an *almost* perfect copy. Acts of mimicry reveal the ambivalence of colonial discourse, and that revelation "does not merely 'rupture' the discourse, but becomes transformed into an uncertainty that fixes the colonial subject as a 'partial' presence" (86); that is, the mimic becomes visible in the discourse by demonstrating the discourse's own uncertainty, its own ambivalence. This is a process that Bhabha elsewhere calls "hybridity" or "splitting," that moment/site where the colonial recognizes that the signifier has split from what it means to signify.[13] Mimicry disrupts the authority of colonial discourse by calling attention to the colonizer's presence (88).[14]

Bhabha makes a similar argument about the "stereotype" in "The Other Question"; it too evinces "splitting" and thus reveals the discursive contradiction of colonial authority. But the stereotype, as projection of the colonizer's fantasy onto the colonial, is a discursive construction of the creation and maintenance of racial and cultural hierarchies (whereas the mimic reveals the exercise of colonial power). The stereotype serves to populate a vision of the world that is fixed and unchanging, a world in which the distinct inferiority of nonwhite races is established and unquestioned. The visibility of otherness is crucial, for Bhabha does not claim that power always inheres in the colonizer; he criticizes Edward Said's formulation of "Orientalism" for not recognizing the fluidity of Foucault's conception of power, noting, "Subjects are always disproportionately placed in opposition or domination through the symbolic decentring of multiple power relations" (1994, 72); in other words, colonial discourse changes over time, it has a historical dimension, hence Bhabha's reference to the "play" of power. The stereotype, however, is itself fixed and arrested, and thus lays the workings of colonial power bare. When Bhabha notes that the stereotype is a simplification, it "is not a simplification because it is a false representation of a given reality. It is a simplification because it is an arrested, fixated form of representation that, in denying the play of difference . . . constitutes a problem for the *representation* of the subject in significations of psychic and social relations" (75). The very existence of the stereotype proves that its vision of colonial subjects is a fiction, or else the stereotypic vision would not need to be repeated.[15] The stereotype is advanced to conceal history: "the process by which the metaphoric 'masking' is inscribed on a lack which must then be concealed gives the stereotype both its fixity and its phantasmatic quality" (77).[16] Ultimately, Bhabha argues that mimicry and stereotype both fail in controlling the colonial; the process of splitting allows for the colonial's entry into discourse. Although mimicry may indeed reveal the mechanisms of colonial discourse, the mimic himself or herself is not necessarily liberated.

In citing Bhabha to explain Tiana's incarnations (as mimic and stereotype), I am not claiming that Tiana's mimicry is necessarily and exclusively resistant, that the process of mimicry automatically leads the mimic to an awareness of splitting. I am also making no claims about the agency of that mimicry, whether it was imposed on her by Hollywood mechanisms, or whether she deliberately inhabited stereotypical forms to subvert them. In sum, I am not applying Bhabha's theories to Tiana as represented on film

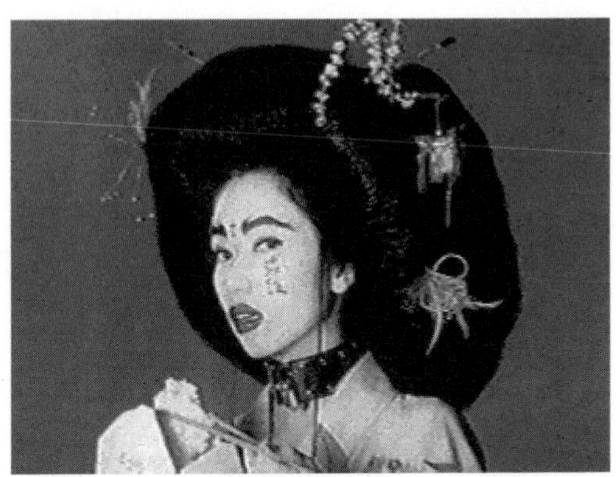

From Hollywood to Hanoi. Postmodern geisha?

(as actor Tiana Alexandra or singer Tiana Banana), but to *From Hollywood to Hanoi* as a text and to Tiana as authorial presence in the film. The film itself (not Tiana) enacts Bhabha's narrative of mimicry.[17]

This split, between film and Tiana, between author/narrator and actor/performer, is evident in the representation of Tiana's career, from which all references to agency have been excised. The specifics of the "creation" of her various personae (in collaboration with an agent, record company executives, etc.) is elided by the declarative statement "I tried to be everybody from Judy Garland to Jane Fonda to Tina Turner," a voice-over that "miscaptions" the image-track. In the absence of any narrative detailing the creation of these various media personae, what are we to make of the citation of these incarnations in the film? To make sense of the citations, we have to consider them in the context of the montage sequence that contains them and its own narrative logic; the point is not to speculate on whether Tiana's images were foisted upon her, or to argue that her co-optation by the system is expressed in her claim that she originated these parodic identities, but to consider the distance between these incarnations of Tiana (in the diegetic past) and the authoring presence of Tiana (in the enunciative present). This distance, what Bakhtin calls the "greater or lesser proximity" of the author toward language he or she incorporates,[18] indicates the author's ideological perspective toward her younger self.

Tiana's performative incarnations are placed in a narrative that traces her assimilation of American popular culture, her growing estrangement from the nostalgia of Vietnamese Americans of her parents' generation, and her ultimate decision to visit Vietnam in search of "home." Her career in Hollywood is located (in the montage) immediately following her rejection of her father's ideal of "model Asian Americans," suggesting that her Hollywood career be understood as enacting a narrative of teenage independence. In viewing these images, however, I am struck by their coy artificiality: these personae are not being inhabited but performed; that is, surface appearance is emphasized over interiority. Several of these personae are presented as still images, and the moving images of Tiana-as-Cyndi-Lauper pierce the fourth wall (she makes eye contact with the camera/audience), so that none of the images functions as part of a narrative, but rather as direct address; the brevity of each of these images further serves to isolate them, to resist the attachment of interiority (through narrative development) that might hint at the complex negotiation of personae undertaken by Tiana's star discourse. These images are frozen, arrested from developing, and in the absence of such complexity, the authorizing/narrating presence of Tiana emerges, self-aware and capable of narrating its own developing subjectivity: in the voice-over statements "I tried to be . . . Tina Turner" and "I was ashamed to be Vietnamese," the verb tense not only locates these actions and feelings in the past, but implies that they have since been repudiated (I *no longer* try to be Tina Turner, I am *no longer* ashamed to be Vietnamese). The point is not that Tiana's voice-over is "real" while the various images of performing personae are constructions and therefore "false," but that the voice-over inscribes itself in a process of ongoing development, while the images are arrested,[19] distancing Tiana-as-author/narrator from Tiana's past performative personae (even as all of these Tianas, especially author/narrator, are produced by the film).[20]

At this point, let me digress to point out that the arrested development of Tiana's images is by no means an inherent quality of still frames; I am not opposing them to an inherent narrativity of the motion picture. Hanh Thi Pham's photographs also exploit her own body, also adopt iconic poses, and also reference culturally significant images, and yet they also possess a narrative thrust (an argument, if you will) and a bracing clarity of emotional attitude. For example, in "Number 9, Expatriate Consciousness" (1991–1992),[21] Pham's naked torso, her right fist raised in the "fuck you" gesture, faces left in front of an upside-down, crossed-out image of Buffalo Bill Cody (the cross-out recalls the syntax of graffiti, in which a rival gang's or artist's symbols are inverted) and a romanized Vietnamese phrase that declares "Not as your servant." In this piece, Pham is drawing on established conventions of depicting the female body, just as Tiana had, but the image is staged so as to call attention to the interrelationship of its different

From Hollywood to Hanoi. Tiana mimics Cyndi Lauper.

components, thus evoking a sense of the artist's subjectivity. By contrast, the eye takes in Tiana's still images almost in one "gulp," and the viewer (this viewer, anyway) is left uncertain as to who the authoring presence of this image is: Is it the woman depicted, or a photographer behind the lens? Whereas Pham clearly deploys conventional iconography for her own ends, Tiana seems trapped in convention as much as she responds to it. Erica Lee refers to Pham's art as "continually break[ing] through each chrysalis that society presents to her" (1994, 134);[22] Tiana seems more complicitous in inhabiting society's chrysalises.

From Hollywood to Hanoi, in emphasizing the surface and not the interiority of Tiana's personae, foregrounds their performativity; as such, they suggest Bhabha's "mimicry"—Tiana is almost, but not quite Cyndi Lauper. Her performance clearly references Lauper but is just as clearly *not* Lauper but an imitation. (Lauper's persona is, of course, already a performance—as indeed most, if not all, public personae are—and should not be mistaken for the "real" Lauper.) In Bhabha's terms, Tiana-mimicking-Lauper is supposed to mediate discourse (specifically, star discourse): while supposedly serving to disavow difference (Tiana is Lauper) the mimicry instead reveals the disavowal (Tiana is *the Asian* Lauper). Mimicry thus lays bare the mechanisms by which "Hollywood's" (and here we should note that Tiana speaks of Hollywood as if it were a monolithic entity) star factory molds Tiana, and thus neatly aligns with the film's implicit argument that the U.S. media interpellated her as an American ("along with the rest of the nation, we were glued to the six o'clock news"). Her hatred of gooks and shame at being Vietnamese is attributed to the media's imposition of a racist, patriotic identity—Tiana as mimic American—and that iden-

From Hollywood to Hanoi. From the music video for "Lust in de Jungle."

tity is framed by her junior high role in *Rebel Without a Cause* and high school role as Homecoming Queen. The observation that "actually, that tall blonde took the crown . . . I got a black belt instead" hints that Tiana's mimicry of all-Americanness was problematic, that she was more intelligible—more visible or "knowable"—as an Asian rebel than as Daddy's girl/Homecoming Queen. What the six o'clock news started, Hollywood attempted to finish.

In this context, her progression from Cyndi Lauper wannabe to "Lust in de Jungle" is striking. The voice-over does not provide any commentary on "Lust in de Jungle," not even the barest contextualization provided by the earlier "I tried to be . . . Tina Turner." Instead, "Lust in de Jungle" immediately follows a montage of particularly bloody footage introduced by the voice-over "I tried to tune out memories of the war but couldn't." This comment retroactively inflects the Lauper persona as an attempt to escape from suburban memories of the six o'clock news into pop culture, to disavow history and its constitutive effect on Tiana's identity in favor of star mimicry. "Lust in de Jungle" emerges as the return of the repressed, the perverse attachment of history to Tiana Banana's body, not the previously narrated history as a suburban American, but as an exotic, sadomasochistic Asian dominatrix, a pop culture stereotype: timeless, fixed, and originary, "lust/lost" in the savage jungle. This image of Tiana as jungle whore is immediately followed by news reports of My Lai. Unlike Tiana Banana's previous incarnations, then, which were located in a narrative of emerging independence and rejection of a suburban valuation of "model Asian Americans," "Lust in de Jungle" emerges from (becomes aligned with) the parallel narrative of the war. Whereas the montage sequence as a whole alternated between its two narrative streams—American life and the war in Vietnam—implying their parallel simultaneity but insisting on their separation, the two previously distinct narratives merge at this point. "Lust in de Jungle" marks the moment when the war and the popular media completely overwhelm Tiana's identity. No longer able to disavow her Vietnameseness and mimic Americanness, she instead inhabits a stereotype.

The My Lai sequence next gives way to Tiana's role in *Catch the Heat:* "I had finally arrived—as Rod Steiger's warbride." The return of Tiana's voice-over serves not to restore the balance between the parallel narratives, but to further collapse them together. Where exactly has Tiana arrived: at the pinnacle of Hollywood or the depths of Vietnam? Indeed, the voice-over mischaracterizes her role opposite Steiger; she is not a warbride at all, but an undercover cop masquerading as a dancer to infiltrate Steiger's drug smuggling operation.[23] *From Hollywood to Hanoi*'s voice-over revises Tiana Alexandra's film career, claiming the racially and sexually stereotyped role of warbride (instead of the "merely" sexually stereotyped role of dancer/undercover cop). The ironic disjunction between Tiana's voice-over and the excerpt from her movie is emphasized by the character's silence: Tiana Alexandra (as Checkers Goldberg, the implausible character's implausible name) wears an impassive, inscrutable face; voice and body are alienated. The excerpt ends with Tiana/Checkers shooting Steiger.[24] Removed from the narrative context of *Catch the Heat,* where the scene might have had some emotional impact, the ludicrousness of the scene (which produced laughter from the film festival audience with whom I screened the film) suggests that Tiana-as-narrator posits Tiana-as-actor's "arrival" as signaling the loss of her own agency, co-opted by a Hollywood stereotype. Regardless of whether Tiana-as-stereotype became aware of Bhabha's process of splitting, the narrator of *From Hollywood to Hanoi* seizes on that splitting to rework the discourse.

From Hollywood to Hanoi depicts Tiana's dawning awareness *through discourse* of how her subjectivity has been constructed, a narrative structure that recalls Bhabha's arguments about the opening created by colonial discourse from which the colonial subject can speak. This emphasis on the give-and-take of discourses and subjectivities reveals the film's attitude toward storytelling. Not only is Tiana's story told through traditional (if not master) narratives of teenage rebellion and independence, it is told with reference to her position *within* stories ranging from *Rebel Without a Cause* to *Catch the Heat.* This thematization of metanarrativity offers a model by which we might evaluate the film's strategy of juxtaposing contrasting narratives of Vietnam. If Tiana's American years were marked by her enacting roles in stories, her Vietnam years were marked by the telling of stories, as her voice-over tells us that her father educated her in Vietnamese folklore and poetry: "His favorite [of the poems he read to me] was about a turtle who brought Vietnam a magic weapon that saved our land. In the Sixties, our magic weapons came by air. The skies filled with wonder." The accompanying image-track presents footage of a Vietnamese puppet show depicting the turtle with a magic sword, followed by stock footage of missiles fired from a plane and a helicopter descending from the sky. Her father's nostalgic tales are shown to be no match for the realities of modern warfare; but given the film's strategy of evaluating narrative discourses through juxtaposition, this moment should not be read as rejecting one story in favor of another. Instead, the film calls attention to the process by which these two stories are produced (and the process by which the film brings them together); as Bhabha notes in the introduction to *The Location of Culture,* "What is theoretically innovative, and politically crucial, is the need to think beyond narratives of originary and initial subjectivities and to focus on those moments or processes that are produced in the articulation of cultural differences" (1994, 1). When he speaks of "originary and initial subjectivities," Bhabha refers to essentialist notions of distinct racial and cultural difference, but I think his words are also applicable to *From Hollywood to Hanoi*'s practice of cinematic juxtaposition: the film itself does the work of articulating cultural differences by arranging cinematic images and sounds so that they speak to each other.

However, it is Tiana's mastery of her father's narrative modes that gains her access to government officials (and, by extension, enables her to locate her uncle, who had been presumed dead). A poem composed by Tiana, "Dear America, Dear Vietnam," secured her an interview with former premier Pham Van Dong and senior Politburo advisor Le Duc Tho. She attempts to play dutiful daughter to both men, donning traditional Vietnamese attire; both men speak to her in French and compel her to recite more poetry. Tiana's use of the poetic mode provides her entry, but restricts the kinds of questions she can ask, exemplifying the skepticism I expressed earlier toward the application of Bhabha's theories. In mimicking a dutiful overseas Vietnamese, she is unable to ask the questions that she would like, is unable to speak the language of filmmaker; her discourse may evince splitting, but Tiana herself is unable to break out of that discourse.

Elsewhere, Tiana attempts to adapt tropes for her own use but succeeds only in replicating their economies of difference. When she first arrives in Saigon, she is taken to the Saigon Floating Hotel ("owned by the Japanese and managed by the Australians"), a posh hotel that she ultimately rejects because it caters to foreigners and thus seems cut off from Vietnamese life. In the hotel's restaurant she encounters two white men, presumably Australian, one of whom tells her, "Vietnam is like a beautiful girl, and I'm afraid beautiful girls tend to get raped on college campuses—the foreign investors, the foreign colonialists have tended over a long period of time to get the best advantage out of Vietnam." Tiana's reaction to this offensive metaphor[25] is implied by the film's immediate cut to another hotel, and the voice-over's announcement, "I decided to stay at the Nine Dragons Hotel." However, the film itself repeats the metaphor of Vietnam as woman and foreigners as rapists, by presenting Vietnamese women as victims and white men as aggressors; significantly, no white women speak in the film. The Vietnamese men are for the most part government officials or professionals (such as doctors), whereas the "common folk" of Vietnam (both North and South) are virtually all women (examples include several street vendors, several older women who have relatives in the States, and a survivor of My Lai). This distinction holds for Tiana's family as well: her uncle talks about being a political prisoner, while her aunt testifies to her difficulties in caring for her family, and her female cousins play with her makeup kit, try on clothes, and talk about sex.[26]

The "Vietnam as beautiful girl" trope also lurks behind Tiana's interviews with so-called Amerasians living in Saigon. The split between female victims and male "activists" reasserts itself, in that only one of the two women speaks on camera, and she testifies to the discrimination that Amerasians face in Vietnam. In contrast, four men are permitted to speak, and two of them name their American fathers and express the intention of tracking them down.[27] Furthermore, as offspring of U.S. servicemen, the Amerasian children themselves symbolize the metaphoric "rape" of Vietnam by the United States, again repeating the trope. (One Vietnamese mother names her U.S. "husband" as well.)

An obvious source for the trope of "Vietnam as beautiful girl" is the *Kim Van Kieu,* the nineteenth-century epic poem about a Confucian heroine who becomes a prostitute to prevent the humiliation of the men in her family. Thanks to her virtue, she endures and is eventually reunited with her first lover. The life of Kieu "has repeatedly served as a metaphor for

Vietnam's destiny" and figures prominently in two films by Trinh T. Minh-ha, *Surname Viet Given Name Nam* (1989) and *Tale of Love* (1995).[28] *Surname Viet Given Name Nam* takes its name from what Trinh calls "recent socialist tradition," in which an unmarried woman will respond to a male suitor by announcing that her husband's surname is Viet and his given name is Nam. Trinh's film relies heavily on restaged interviews with contemporary Vietnamese women to discuss women's positions vis-à-vis socialist Vietnam, and in the process of doing so traces the rearticulation of Vietnamese history and folktales, as well as epic poems like the *Kim Van Kieu*. Trinh's first fiction film, *A Tale of Love,* centers on a Vietnamese American woman named Kieu who is researching an article on the *Kim Van Kieu* for a feminist journal. To support herself, she poses for a photographer who continually veils her body; this, and her explicit statement that writing is a form of loving, extend the idea that the tale of Kieu offers a metaphor of love to describe the Vietnamese citizen's duty, here transposed to the American context.

From Hollywood to Hanoi makes no mention of the *Kim Van Kieu,* and this is significant for two reasons. First, given Tiana's emphasis on the poems that her father told her as a child, the absence suggests that the tale of Kieu is not consonant with his vision of Vietnam. Second, *From Hollywood to Hanoi*'s emphasis on the legacy of the U.S. war serves to privilege that war, rather than frame it as another in a long series of wars fought on Vietnamese soil. It is not Vietnam that is compared with a woman, but the Vietnam known to the United States.

Furthermore, the trope of Vietnam as woman functions in *From Hollywood to Hanoi* as part of a larger strategy of personifying the events of the war. The impact of Agent Orange is personified by Viet and Duc, conjoined twins (their names represent North and South) who reside in a Saigon hospital. Tiana explicitly compares herself to them, seeing in them a metaphor for her own bicultural identity ("two beings trapped in one body") produced by war. The important difference is that Tiana's film depicts her own bifurcated identity as a formation of media *discourses*—it is a psychic bifurcation, after all—not the war itself (or, more precisely, as a production of U.S. military action). To counter this distinction, *From Hollywood to Hanoi* foregrounds Tiana's body's performative history, grounding the film's narrative in her ongoing transformation.[29] (The centrality of Tiana's body to this film suggests that the autobiographical mode is incompatible with explicit reference to the *Kim Van Kieu;* by contrast, Trinh's films juxtapose a variety of speaking voices, and this dialogic approach facilitates introduction of the tale of Kieu.)

Bodies and Distances

Tiana's film offers an important corrective to U.S. media representations of the war in Vietnam: she insists that My Lai was not (just) an American tragedy by permitting a survivor to speak; she reminds us that Agent Orange wreaked havoc on Vietnamese parents and children as well as on U.S. soldiers. However, her strategy of putting a Vietnamese face to the war serves to further reproduce the trope of Vietnam as woman. Bhabha's theories of hybridity suggest that, by inhabiting a stereotype and by investigating the trope of Vietnam as woman, Tiana finds a space from which to speak; however, that space restricts her to rebuttal.

From Hollywood to Hanoi surpasses mere rebuttal when it advances an image of Vietnam that is more than merely oppositional to U.S. accounts. "For most Americans, our New Year celebration was a military offensive"; this statement points out that Vietnam is not a country but a war for most Americans, and glimpses of Tet celebrations and Vietnamese traditions hint at the culture obscured by the war. Vietnamese culture is glimpsed through the teachings and stories of Tiana's father, but Tiana comes to see his stories as entrapment by (rather than connection to) the past. The more nostalgic her father becomes, the less she is able to reconcile her Vietnamese heritage with her American life and the more she is thrown back on U.S. perspectives of Vietnam and, consequently, on the reduction of Vietnam to a "mere" war: "In the Sixties, our magic weapons arrived by air."

Tiana's estrangement from the San Jose Vietnamese American community affirms her Americanness. *From Hollywood to Hanoi*'s lengthy prologue, the montage sequence, depicted the complex weave of her American life with her perceptions of the war (gleaned from U.S. media), and in a sense, the film attempts to illustrate how all Americans have similarly woven representations of the war into our lives. The film's dedication, "For Dad," suggests that Tiana is particularly invested in inscribing her father into this narrative, in making him see the war through her eyes. She brings her father a souvenir NVA helmet from Vietnam, "since they're now being made in Danang, his home town." She attempts to align her father's vision of Vietnam with her own through the medium of the souvenir helmet, a gift that not only positions the giver and receiver as tourists, but also demands an ironic relationship to the war and its commodification. Tiana's father rejects the gift, however: "This is taboo. I didn't see that except on TV, but we don't like it here." It is the TV image of Vietnam that concerns Tiana: the television's intimacy may have made Vietnam into "the living-room war," but television also fostered an ironic distance, a distance that Tiana's helmet comments on; she hopes that her father will view the helmet in its ludicrousness, as a camp statement about the touristic commodification of the war. But although her father is able to acknowledge that the helmet has no real connection to his Vietnam ("I didn't see that except on TV"), he cannot take the next step that would align him with her subjectivity: he cannot "split" the signifiers and see the helmet as a symbol that has divorced itself from its material context (the war) and functions (for Tiana) as a signifier of the war's *mediation.* For Tiana's father, the helmet is still a helmet and cannot be seen as a media effect; even though he "didn't see that except on TV," the helmet's materiality refers him not to representations of the war, but to the war itself. For all the splitting that Tiana's own subjectivity (as constructed by the film) undergoes, that splitting is a function of growing up in the shadow of Hollywood, where image *is* reality, where mediation aspires to materiality.

Tiana's estrangement from the Vietnamese American community (as figured in the film) is analogous to Tiana-as-author/narrator's estrangement from her (earlier) performative incarnations, but the narrator's studied perspective does not serve to reverse the narrative of teenage rebellion and restore Tiana to her father's good graces—and not surprisingly, for the repudiation of those personae is undertaken by the film's rhetoric, not by Tiana herself. The discursive separation of author/narrator from her acts of mimicry further splits the discourse at Bhabha's site of hybridity. For while I am skeptical of the subversive potential released by mimicry and the stereotype[30] (I argued earlier that for the colonial subject to free himself or herself from colonial discourse is not the same as being free of colonial oppression), I am more sanguine about the possibility of locating subversive potential in the author's distance from acts of mimicry and stereotyping. In other words, to the extent that *From Hollywood to Hanoi* constructs an authorial/narrating presence that is distinct from Tiana's performative personae, the film capitalizes on the production of splitting and critiques the production of Hollywood discourses of the "Orient." By mixing her own performances of "Orientalness" into her retelling of the war in Vietnam, the film splits open the production of racial difference via cinematic discourses.

The splitting of "Orientalist" cinematic discourse is accomplished through a narrative disjunction between the figure of the author and her performative past; furthermore, the author/narrator positions her earlier incarnations at the intersection of two narratives, marking points where Tiana's American life intersects with representations of Vietnam. *From Hollywood to Hanoi*'s narrative rearranges the past, emphasizing discontinuity of past and present (the author's Bakhtinian distance from her past life) and renarrativizing those moments of discontinuity. *From Hollywood to Hanoi* thus produces the subjectivity of Tiana (as figurative author/narrator) through a cinematic narrativization of a discontinuous past. The film's strategy of not just reconnecting present to past, but of understanding the historical motivations for discontinuity—for a form of historical amnesia—aligns it with other constructions of subjectivity via Asian American cinema. The qualified success of Bhabha's splitting—finding a place within cinematic discourses from which to speak—highlights the ambivalence toward cinematic processes of signification that I have argued typify Asian American cinematic investigations into memory. *From Hollywood to Hanoi* suggests that the ambivalent critique of cinema undertaken by Asian American makers is a function of awareness of their own constitution by cinematic discourses. The articulation of subjectivity through cinema is thus an attempt to depict the process of mass media interpellation *in reverse,* producing Asian American subjectivities from that space where endlessly repeating mass media discourses position us obsessively. But the ambivalence expressed by Asian American cinema echoes Fanon's (imagined) rejoinder to Bhabha: the production of resistance from the incoherencies of colonial discourse is a textual operation that does not automatically lead to material changes in the circumstances of media production.

Elaine Kim, speaking of the rapid proliferation of Asian American literature and the discursive redefinitions that literature proposes, offers these words of caution: "In the midst of rejoicing about these works and about the possibilities created by new social realities, we should remind ourselves that boundary crossing must not be merely an aesthetic and intellectual exercise: we must beware lest our texts cross boundaries that a majority of our people still cannot" (1992, xiv). The dialogic distance between the author/narrator of *From Hollywood to Hanoi* and her textual instantiations, her various personae, is in part an attempt to illuminate this disjunction between border-crossing texts and border-enclosed people, between a discontinuous conception of the past that allows for the construction of resistant subjectivities and the all too continuous past that traps the body in place. The tension between personifying Vietnam (as a woman, as conjoined twins) and demonstrating the material effects of the war on Vietnamese bodies (abandoned Amerasian children, survivors of My Lai) is a productive tension, one that interrogates the paradox of the cinematic investigation of memory. That interrogation continues in the next section: Chapters 7 and 8 continue the examination of how cinematic border crossings affect the body and the body politic, and Chapter 6 searches for an absent, overnarrativized body.

III *Performing Transformation*

CHAPTER 6

Becoming Asian American

Chan is Missing

It was almost ten years ago. A small group of us perched on the rickety chairs at the old Collective for Living Cinema loft in Manhattan got a first glimpse at a low-budget, black-and-white feature by then experimental filmmaker, Wayne Wang. The appeal of *Chan Is Missing* (1981) went beyond its social relevance or the familiarity of the characters and themes. There was something original about the film, and something very Asian American.
—Renee Tajima, "Moving the Image"

Where's our jazz? Where's our blues? Where's our ain't-taking-no-shit-from-nobody street-strutting language?—Wittman Ah Sing, in Maxine Hong Kingston, *Tripmaster Monkey*

Sometime in the early 1980s, sometime between the inauguration of Ronald Reagan and the murder of Vincent Chin, a new voice began to intrude on the cultural consciousness of the United States. That voice belonged, depending on who named it, to Wayne Wang, a Hong Kong–born Chinese American filmmaker; to Asian American filmmakers as a group; or to Asian Americans as a filmgoing community. The film *Chan Is Missing* (1981) announced that Asian Americans could be artists, could be commercial filmmakers, and could support Asian American filmmaking, as well as successfully market Asian American films to wider audiences.

Part 1 of this book interrogated attempts to delimit Asian American history through a variety of cinematic modes: ethnography, romance narratives, and home movies. The contrasting formal approaches that characterize each of these modes determine the ways the Americanness of Asian Americans is evaluated. In Part 2, travelogue films provide the occasion for reassessment of Western discourses about Asia, exploring the impossibility of seeing Asia through a lens that can be separated from the Western cinematic apparatus. Can cinema express Asian American identities that escape containment by Western regimes of vision and discourses of citizenship? Part 3 of this book examines films that attempt to trace identities in motion, subjectivities in the process of redefining Asian Americanness and the Asian diaspora, films that attempt to convey the heterogeneity of Asian American experiences without delimiting them. Given this diversity of experience, how can there be a voice that is distinctively Asian American?

Chan Is Missing works to destabilize notions of Chinese American identity, even while the film is marketed as an Asian American text; ultimately, I argue, the destabilization of Chinese American identity not only allows for, but actually contributes to the construction of Asian American subjectivity. This can be accomplished only by focusing on process rather than end result, on the act of "becoming" rather than the state of "being," otherwise we risk arguing "merely" that *Chan Is Missing* elaborates the fragmentation of Chinese American identity without suggesting what it offers in its place.[1]

Chan Is Missing is a useful text for examining the contingency of identity, for the film lends itself to multiple reading formations, generic and otherwise. Surely the appeal of *Chan Is Missing* to those of us who teach film is due in no small part to the different cinematic traditions the film evokes. Its narrative structure allows us to discuss it as an arthouse film; the film plays with the conventions of detective fiction, and thus contributes to a discussion of investigative narrative structures and epistemology; its claustrophobic visual style, combined with grainy black-and-white cinematography, suggests film noir; the film's low-budget aesthetic intersects with an auteur-based approach (insofar as it can be compared with other first features like Spike Lee's *She's Gotta Have It* [1986]); scenes that draw on direct cinema conventions locate the film in a tradition of international "new wave" films (such as John Cassavetes's *Faces* [1968]); and so on. Just as the identities of its characters are destablized by the film, so the identity of *Chan Is Missing* is destablized by a multiplicity of interpretations drawing on different aspects of cinematic history. But how many subject positions can one film occupy?

The Interval: Being and Becoming

In the introduction to his study of literatures of subjective fragmentation and alienation, Phillip Brian Harper argues that postmodernism erases certain markers of difference (race, class, gender, and sometimes sexual orientation) in its effort to decenter white male subjectivity.[2] Critiquing Habermas, Lyotard, and Jameson, Harper notes that "however differently they might interpret the political meaning of subjective fragmentation . . . [these three] theorists conceive of that meaning in terms of macro-level social and economic structures, leaving aside considerations of more contingent political phenomena, in particular those having to do with the social identities of the various subjects who manifest fragmentation in the postmodern context" (1994, 9). In Harper's analysis, social identities are contingent political phenomena, which is to say that social identities function instrumentally and are therefore already fragmented insofar as they are not essential.

Chan Is Missing foregrounds the heterogeneity of Chinese American subjectivities, thereby arguing for the fluidity of Chinese American identity. If the film did no more than that, it would simply exemplify postmodern fragmentation, and its discourse would be recuperable by postmodern discourses that efface markers of social marginality. But *Chan Is Missing* also suggests the *contingency* of Chinese American subjectivities, and in so doing paves the way for Asian American subjectivities that might learn from Chinese American heterogeneity. To describe subjectivity as contingent suggests that subjectivity is not a thing to be located, but a process from which the world is perceived. Instead of positing subjectivity as that which seeks closure, the contingent subjectivity foregrounds its own impermanence, its inadequacy as a coherent identity formation. In a different context, Trinh T. Minh-ha notes: "Meaning can neither be imposed nor denied. Although every film is in itself a form of ordering and closing, each closure can defy its own closure, opening onto other closures, thereby emphasizing the interval between apertures and creating a space in which meaning remains fascinated by what escapes and exceeds it" (1991, 49). Like the progressive documentary film practice that Trinh describes, contingent identities maintain an instrumental gap between subject and object, creating and maintaining the space where meaning is exceeded. That space is akin to the space between "Asian" and "American," a space I have refused to bridge with a hyphen.

The presence/absence of the hyphen underscores the need to stabilize momentarily a position from which to speak, and to destabilize that position immediately. Taking a text such as *Chan Is Missing* and discussing the ways it mobilizes notions of hyphenate identity is "[to venture] into that distance that has not been abolished but expanded to infinity by postmodern criticism: the gap between the politics of production, and of regimes of consumption" (Morris, 1988, 268). To seize on a text is yet another attempt to hold together and keep apart the terms on either side of a hyphen; that is the distance or gap to which Morris alludes. We who would discuss hyphenate identity seize on Wang's film to do so, but our interpretations of the text must not lock down the range of meanings found in the gap between text and reader, but take advantage of the gap between the production of the term and the uses to which we put it. The question then becomes how exactly to mobilize such a label.

In *Chan Is Missing,* many courses of action are identified as being Chinese and others as being American, but a Chinese American course of action is difficult to identify. The realm of Chinese American—the gap between production and consumption—cannot be named, because it is constantly being negotiated by the characters in the film. Being Chinese American is not a matter of resolving a duality, for proposing to draw from two cultures inevitably results in not belonging to either. George, director of the Newcomers' Language Center, points to an apple pie baked by the Sun Wah Kuu bakery as an example of Chinese American negotiation: "It is a definite American form, you know, pie, okay. And it looks just like any other apple pie, but it doesn't *taste* like any other apple pie, you eat it. And that's because many Chinese baking technique has gone into it, and when we deal with our everyday lives, that's what we have to do."[3] But ultimately, such a negotiation proves untenable because it does not create anything new; it merely borrows forms.[4] Jo rejects the apple pie analogy, referring to it as George's "spiel," in his quest for a notion of identity that does see the duality, but creates a space in the gap between the two terms. As Trinh notes in *When the Moon Waxes Red,* "There is indeed little hope of speaking this simultaneously outside-inside actuality into existence in simple, polarizing black-and-white terms. The challenge of the hyphenated reality lies in the hyphen itself: the *becoming* Asian-American" (1991, 157). The apple pie cannot be Asian American because it does not manifest the process of "becoming": it is an expression of the uneasy encounter of two cultures, not revealing the process of accommodation so much as revising Asian techniques to produce American goods. To be Chinese American is to be constantly in the process of becoming, to negotiate the relationship between cultures; to be a Chinese American artist (whether baker or filmmaker) one must do more than introduce Asian themes into American forms: the artist must reveal the process that produces new cultural expressions and thereby preserve a sense of contingency. When an artist asserts that there is one way successfully to balance Chinese and American influences, that artist implicitly asserts that Chinese Americans exist in a fixed space, fulfill a fixed role. Rote actions are successful only when events operate predictably, and with rote responses one will not discover anything new, will not evolve, will not accept the challenge of becoming Asian American.

How, then, is the challenge of becoming Asian American explored by a film that draws on film noir conventions? Is a detective film with Chinese American characters simply an apple pie made in a Chinese bakery? Don't genre films, with their predictable events, call for the very rote actions (on the part of characters, and indeed, on the part of filmmakers as well) that fix their characters in a state of being rather than a process of becoming? When Jo and Steve argue about their course of action, Steve asserts: "Hey, I understand the situation man. . . . Here's how I see it. If you're sick, you go see a doctor, right? If you're going nuts, you go see a shrink. If you need some money, man, you go to a bank or a loan company. You know, somebody rips off your money, if you don't have no friends who can take care of it, you go to the cops and let *them* take care of it" (W. Wang, 1984, 64). Steve thus advocates a rote response: if someone does this, then you do that. He is frustrated by the lack of results, and so advocates conventional methods of resolving his problem. Jo, on the other hand, does not believe that conventional methods will work; "It's none of their [the police's] damn business" (64), he says, for he knows that Chan's disappearance is not conventional and therefore the police (who are bound by rote responses) will not be successful. When Jo says, "I'm no Charlie Chan," he is also saying This only appears to be a Charlie Chan case, a genre film; but we don't know what will happen next, we're just making this up as we go along. In other words, Jo is willing to wait and see what happens next, what kind of a film this is "becoming."

One way of reading *Chan Is Missing*'s critique refuses to fixate on the questions it poses about the nature of hyphenate identity, and instead emphasizes the process of becoming. The film affirms through its textuality the impossibility of being, the insistence on becoming—in its refusal of closure, and by questioning identity, appropriation, narrative, and temporality. (These terms overlap; for example, appropriation is narrativized, temporality is expressed narratively, identities are appropriated as means to narrative and other ends.) But although *Chan Is Missing* may critique fixed notions of identity, it must be emphasized that many of the discourses that surrounded the film, discourses that contextualized its position in the marketplace, located it in relation to putatively fixed identity constructions. These discourses of the popular media place Wayne Wang's films between the constructed poles of Asian American and mainstream American film markets.

Wayne Wang[5] was born in Hong Kong in 1949 ("Really I was born when Hong Kong was born" [Thomson, 1985, 24]); his father named him after John Wayne (W. Wang, 1984, 101–2). He came to the United States to attend college in the late 1960s, earning a bachelor's degree in painting at the California College of Arts and Crafts, where he also studied film history and production. Returning to Hong Kong in the early 1970s, Wang quickly found work as a director for a Hong Kong television comedy, but he was not satisfied working in the Hong Kong industry. He returned to the San Francisco Bay Area and became an administrator and English teacher for a Chinatown community organization (experiences he would draw on for *Chan Is Missing*); during this period he also learned "how to write grants and turn them in on time." Wang also developed a program for KRON-TV and occasionally worked on Loni Ding's *Bean Sprouts,* a series of half-hour programs for Chinese American children (Thomson, 1985).

Wang's first film after returning from Hong Kong was supposed to be a thirty-minute video documentary on cab drivers. After securing $10,000 from the American Film Institute, he decided to make a feature instead. He and his crew shot the film over ten successive weekends and then settled down for the arduous process of editing and postproduction, going steadily deeper into debt; during this period, Wang supported himself by writing bilingual science curricula for San Francisco State University (Chiu, 1982, 17). Eventually securing a grant from the NEA, Wang completed the film on a budget of $22,500. After good response at a few festivals (key among them the New Directors/New Films festival in New York), the movie was picked up by New Yorker Films (Patterson, 1983). The result was an extremely rough, immensely likable film that earned critical raves and more than recovered its investment.

According to Sterritt, "Though its initial audience has not been an ethnic one, Chinese viewers are being wooed through newspaper ads, and Wang would like to see a trial run in a Chinatown theater" (1982, 18). This statement, though anecdotal, indicates the underdevelopment (or outright absence) of venues for Asian American feature films in 1982. *Chan Is Missing* succeeded because it appealed to arthouse audiences and also brought Asian Americans into the theaters. In Asian American newspapers, articles about *Chan Is Missing* and its director often cited its mainstream success and quoted reviewers in mainstream publications (e.g., Lam, 1981), as if to announce to the Asian American audience that, first, the film is not an amateurish production, and second, this is the film that is teaching whites about Chinese Americans. Reviews in the Asian American press often simply advertise the screenings (Lam, 1981); but the lengthier reviews usually refer to how white reviewers see Chinese Americans and how Asian American texts are received by non-Asian audiences (Lau, 1982).[6] Wing Tek Lum points out that many texts produced by Asian Americans are not produced *for* Asian Americans: "*Chan Is Missing* . . . does not have the same tone of voice as some of the other artistic works which have come out of [the Chinese American] community—the grossest examples being the tour guides and cookbooks—where one again has the feeling that the readership which the author has chosen to write to is really the larger society, there being so much explaining, so many footnotes, sometimes so much apology for not being white" (1982, 9). Lum takes care to point out that the tourist mentality can be found in texts, not just in their reception; he thus positions *Chan Is Missing* as *from* and *for* the Chinese American community.

By contrast, the majority of mainstream reviewers take one of two critical approaches, and often include both approaches despite their seeming incompatibility. The first approach is to locate the film within a tradition of filmmaking represented by "canonical" U.S. films and foreign films that had arthouse success in the United States: several reviewers compare the film to *Citizen Kane* (Ansen, 1982; Seitz, 1982) and mention *The Third Man* (Denby, 1982; Ebert, 1982a); the *Variety* review cites *L'Avventura* ("Caught," 1982), and Hatch (1982) reviews *Bob le Flambeur* in the same column, emphasizing *Chan*'s appropriation of gangster iconography. The film is often positioned vis-à-vis arthouse cinema through references to its low budget, often favorably (Ansen; Canby; Denby; Ebert, 1982a; Hatch; Kauffmann, 1982; Sterritt, 1982; *Variety*) but not necessarily so (O'Toole, 1982; Seitz), and/or through reference to the film's release strategy; one reviewer

(Siskel, 1982) even alludes to the manner in which other reviewers have hyped the film's budget. The second approach is to describe the authenticity of Wang's film and praise it for presenting a "true portrait" of Chinatown (Ebert, Hatch, Siskel), often citing a specific stereotype that the film challenges; in other words, by addressing certain stereotypes head on, the film is perceived by mainstream reviewers as representing an authentic Chinese American perspective.[7] The first approach locates *Chan Is Missing* in a tradition of arthouse cinema; the second asserts the essential uniqueness of the film. Although seemingly contradictory, these two approaches are of course entirely compatible, and indeed correspond to complementary marketing strategies.

Charlie Chan Is Dead—Long Live Charlie Chan!

When *Chan Is Missing* begins, two San Francisco cab drivers, Jo and Steve, are searching for their friend, Chan Hung, who has apparently absconded with $4,000. When the film ends, the money has been recovered but Chan has not been found, and Jo no longer knows who Chan Hung is. Each clue they find only raises more questions—indeed, the clues aren't even real clues: they include a gun that may or may not have been fired, a newspaper with the important article torn out, a spot on the wall where a picture used to hang, a series of former addresses no longer occupied by Chan, and a Polaroid photo in which Chan's face is obscured by shadows. Given the inconclusiveness of these clues, Jo is forced to rely on the testimonies he gathers from various people who knew Chan, but the incompatibility of these stories evacuates them of any explanatory force.

Chan Is Missing can be interpreted as a revisionist Charlie Chan film; indeed, the marketing of the videocassette release of the film refers to Jo and Steve as "two 'subgumshoes' " who are "walking self-mockingly in the footsteps of Charlie Chan and his Number One Son." At one point, Steve introduces himself by pointing to Jo and saying, "That's Charlie Chan, and I'm his Number One Son—The Fly!" (W. Wang, 1984, 52) The videocassette's "self-mocking" label seems appropriate; the characters themselves seem aware that they are trapped in a pop culture stereotype—trapped, not in the sense that they have been placed there by the dominant, but in Linda Hutcheon's sense of a strange kind of critique, purveying and challenging their position. Later, while puttering around in his kitchen, Jo invokes

Chan Is Missing.
Absent clue no. 1.

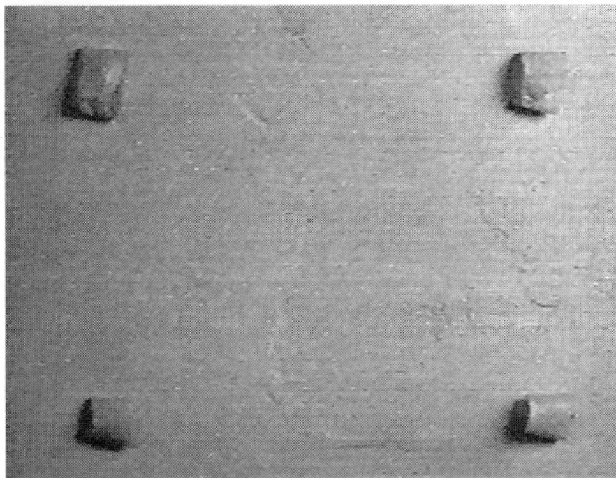

Chan Is Missing.
Absent clue no. 2.

Chan Is Missing.
Jo's photo of
Chan Hung.

Charlie Chan in voice-over: "I guess I'm no gourmet Chinese cook, and I'm no Charlie Chan either, although I did start watching some of his reruns for cheap laughs. Charlie says, 'When superior man have no clue, be patient. Maybe he become lucky!' The next night, I was cleaning out the cab Chan Hung was driving the day he disappeared. I found a letter in Chinese and a gun under the front seat" (57–58). In this scene, it is not only Jo who mocks his adopted role of Charlie Chan, but the narrative itself that is bound up in the complicitous critique. Jo asks for a clue, and he gets one; the film's soundtrack underscores this moment of deus ex machina by hammering out melodramatic music when the gun is discovered. The overdetermined emphasis on this narrative moment mocks the unfolding of the narrative, and thus mocks the generic expectations of a Charlie Chan film.[8]

In 1935's *Charlie Chan in Paris,* Charlie whimsically notes, "Perfect crime like perfect doughnut—always has hole!" Charlie's doughnut reference alludes to the inevitable slip that will allow the detectives to capture the criminal, but I prefer to think of the doughnut in other way: as a metaphor for a mystery with a missing center. Whereas the typical Classical Hollywood detective drama[9] is characterized by a relentless narrative acquisition of clues that eventually climaxes in the solution of the mystery, in *Chan Is Missing* each clue seems to take the narrative farther from a possible solution. Rather than closing down the narrative possibilities, each clue opens up the range of possible answers to the question Where is Chan Hung? Jenny, Chan's daughter, further deflates the narrative tension by returning the money to Jo and Steve, thereby removing the impetus to find Chan. If Jo's investigation continues, it is because the real problem posed by the narrative is not Where is Chan Hung? but Who is Chan Hung? As Jo states at the end of the film, "I've already given up on finding out what happened to Chan Hung, but what bothers me is that I no longer know who Chan Hung is" (W. Wang, 1984, 73–74). If no one knows who Chan Hung is, then who can know if he has been found?

> Mr. Lee says Chan Hung and immigrants like him need to be taught everything as if they were children. Mr. Fong thinks anyone who can invent a word processing system in Chinese must be a genius. Steve thinks that Chan Hung is slow-witted, but sly when it comes to money. Jenny thinks that her father is honest and trustworthy. Mrs. Chan thinks her husband is a failure because he isn't rich. Amy thinks he's a hot-headed political activist. The old man thinks Chan Hung's just a paranoid person.

> Henry thinks Chan Hung is patriotic, and has gone back to the mainland to serve the people. Frankie thinks Chan Hung worries a lot about money and his inheritance. He thinks Chan Hung's back in Taiwan fighting with his brother over the partition of some property. George thinks Chan Hung's too Chinese, and unwilling to change. Presco thinks he's an eccentric who likes mariachi music. (74)

Jo's investigation, rather than closing in on Chan, serves only to widen the hole in the doughnut.

Chan Is Missing's lack of closure is a manifestation of the process of becoming which the narrative describes. Any definitive answer to the questions Who or where is Chan Hung? would serve to close off the process of becoming and solidify the film into a "became." That the narrative of the film is closely tied to the notion of hyphenate identity is underlined by the two questions which are actually the same question: Who is Chan? and Where is Chan? Textually, the tie between narrative and identity is manifested in the destabilization of the identities of the various characters who seek to hypostatize Chan. As the narrative "progresses," for example, Steve's identity begins to evaporate, as if the increasing indeterminacy of Chan's identity undermines everyone else's identity. The reasons for this are underlined in the suggestion Presco offers to Jo and Steve in their search for Chan: "Look in the puddle" (W. Wang, 1984, 34)—look to your reflection to answer your question.

Early in their investigation, Steve asks Jo if his feelings about Chan Hung are being influenced by his feelings for his ex-wife; both were FOB (fresh off the boat). By doing so, Steve reveals an assumption that all FOBs are alike, or more specifically, that Jo would react to all FOBs in the same way. Steve tells a story about Chan that reveals how the older man's inability to acculturate himself embarrasses the supposedly well-adapted Steve: after seeing Chan take off his jacket and give it to a friend who had admired it, Steve told Chan that he liked his pants—was he going to take them off, too? Jo tells us in voice-over, "Steve doesn't realize that the joke about the pants is really on him. Chan Hung told me he sometimes play up being an FOB just to make Steve mad" (W. Wang, 1984, 28).

The encounter between Steve and Chan is a drama that resonates throughout the Chinese American community and has been dramatized before in playwright David Henry Hwang's *FOB*. In the prologue to *FOB*, an assimilated Chinese American "lectures like a university professor" at a blackboard:

> F-O-B. Fresh Off the Boat. FOB. What words can you think of that characterize the FOB? Clumsy, ugly, greasy FOB. Loud, stupid, four-eyed FOB. Big feet. Horny. Like Lenny in *Of Mice and Men.* Very good. A literary reference. High-water pants. Floods, to be exact. Someone you wouldn't want your sister to marry. If you are a sister, someone you wouldn't want to marry. That assumes we're talking about boy FOBs, of course. But girl FOBs aren't really as . . . FOBish. Boy FOBs are the worst, the . . . pits. They are the sworn enemies of all ABC—oh, that's "American Born Chinese"—of all ABC girls. Before an ABC girl will be seen on Friday night with a boy FOB in Westwood, she would rather burn off her face.
>
> . . . How can you spot a FOB? Look out! If you can't answer that, you might be one. (1990, 6–7)

In the course of Hwang's play, the ABC is forced to revise his estimation of FOB's; meanwhile, the audience comes to understand that the image of the FOB is entirely a creation of the ABC, and a creation that the ABC depends on to stabilize his or her own sense of identity. Similarly, Steve's identity is threatened by the destabilization of Chan Hung: Chan's process of becoming forces Steve to confront the fact that his identity is not fixed, that he too is in the process of becoming rather than being. As the investigation continues, and Jo begins to speculate about Chan's identity crisis, Steve becomes more and more adamant: "That's a bunch of bullshit, man. That identity shit, man—that's old news, man, that happened ten years ago" (W. Wang, 1984, 62). Jo asserts that the identity crisis is never over (that hyphenate peoples like Steve as well as Chan are always becoming), to which Steve replies that everybody has a role in "the game." Steve tells a story about an old friend of his, and then invokes his experience in Vietnam, "getting shot at by my own peo—; 'ey! The Chinese are all over this city. Why are you tripping so heavy on this one dude, man?" (63) Steve almost refers to the Vietnamese as his own people,[10] but he stops himself; is it because he realizes that he is Chinese, not Vietnamese? Or is it because Marc Hayashi, the actor who plays Steve, realizes that he is Japanese?[11]

The instability of Steve's identity—and that of the ABC in Hwang's play—is clearly tied to his insecure masculinity. Steve's references to combat in Vietnam, not to mention his repeated use of the interjection "man," hint at the threat to his masculine identity posed by Chan Hung. Chan's inability to assimilate threatens Steve's perception of himself as American and as a man. Similarly, the ABC in Hwang's play reveals his biases when he allows that "girl FOBs aren't really as . . . FOBish." Juxtaposed with his claim that

Chan Is Missing.
Steve plays cop.

"Boy FOBs . . . are the sworn enemies . . . of all ABC girls," the boy ABC reveals that he thinks it is okay for ABCs to date FOB girls, but that FOB boys should stay away from ABC girls. The FOB stereotype, as articulated by Hwang's character, is rooted in the exchange of women in a sexual economy: women assimilate more easily than men, because women are sexual possessions and can be more easily absorbed into U.S. society.[12] *Chan Is Missing* reveals a similar logic; for example, Chan Hung's wife rejects her husband because he was unable to assimilate ("He doesn't even want to apply for American citizen. He's too Chinese" [W. Wang, 1984, 46]), and Chan's daughter Jenny mocks Steve when he uses American idioms awkwardly (see below). As is often the case, the more Steve's masculinity is threatened, the more recourse he has to masculine posturing, as evidenced by his assertion that he understands "the game" better than Jo or Chan.

Steve's metaphor of "the game" suggests that everyone's actions are prescribed by certain rules, that interpersonal dynamics are reducible to a repertoire of gambits. "The game" is Steve's description of his own reliance on situationally determined rote responses: "If you're sick, you go see a doctor." For Steve, succeeding in the game is a matter not of always reacting the same way, but of recognizing and adjusting to the situation at hand; indeed, whenever Steve encounters someone new, he immediately riffs off the situation. When Jo and Steve visit Chan's hotel room, they are given some information by one of Chan's neighbors, who calls out to them from behind a closed door. The unseen speaker queries, "You Chinese, Jo?" Steve turns the question around: "Are you Chinese?" Then the voice asks, "Hey Jo, you police?" When the voice refuses to answer their questions, Steve squats down, makes a gun with his hand, and says "Let's go in the other way—got your magnum?" (W. Wang, 1984, 41–43). Steve adopts the posture of a cop, assuming the identity that the voice suggested for him.

The fluidity with which Steve shifts should not be mistaken for the process of negotiation that I have described as the process of becoming; instead, Steve reserves the right to shift from one fixed subject position to another. The fixity of the subject positions that he serially inhabits is emphasized by their mediated quality: each subjectivity is made available to him from pop culture. When I say that Steve adopts the posture of a cop, the word "posture" should remind us that such role playing involves the performance of visible actions metonymically associated with the roles in question. What, then, does it mean to say that Steve is a self-mocking Charlie Chan?

To celebrate Steve as a deconstructed Charlie Chan is to privilege the notion of postmodern critique. Such a reading assumes that Steve's situationally driven role playing displays his virtuosity. But Steve does not maintain any of his roles long enough to explore its uniqueness; instead, he isolates each subjectivity from its unique sociocultural context, so that it is evacuated of any political force. Instead of restoring markers of difference and hence historical specificity to the center, he confirms the emptiness of the postmodern subjectivity: the hole in the doughnut. This is evident in the reactions he elicits. The key scene in which Steve identifies himself as Chan's "Number One Son—The Fly!" begins with his misidentifying himself: "I'm Steve Chan—Choy—Chan—Choy" (W. Wang, 1984, 52). Even the spectator who does not already know that *Chan Is Missing* evolved from an improvised script is likely to read this line as a "blooper," a moment of rupture. In the spirit of improvisation, the other actors modify the trajectory of the scene to account for the dialogue: the scene continues with Jenny's friend mocking, "This dude doesn't even know his name!" While shaking her hand, Steve adopts the posture of a streetwise ghetto kid, clasping her wrist and rapping, "What's happening!" He then goes on a riff about Mrs. Chong's mahjong club, to which the girls reply, "Who do you think you are, anyway, you think you're Richard Pryor, something like that?" Steve reverts to his "normal" voice until they say goodbye, when he suddenly shifts into Chinese Uncle mode: "I got some spare change, go get yourself an ice cream cone, man." The offer is rejected: "Who do you think we are, kids?" (51–54). The girls refuse to play along with him, to accept the roles that he is suggesting for them, leaving him trying on various identities, hoping he will find one that works. Steve's self-conscious awareness of his position as a mock Charlie Chan does not occasion a critique of that role, but instead reveals that he accepts the terms that the text lays out for him. Steve is trapped in a generically defined role.

"I'm Steve Chan—Choy—Chan—Choy. . . ." Steve's Chinese American identity is not in a process of becoming (of evolving from position to position), but of shifting from subjectivity to subjectivity, just as he oscillates between Choy and Chan. His character emblematizes the process by which Chinese American identity is interrogated by the film. His various subject positions are deployed in response to interpellation ("Are you police?") and situation ("What's happening!" to begin a conversation; "Get yourself some ice cream" to end one) and, most important, in contradistinction to Chan Hung, Steve's FOB other. This last dynamic is reversed by Presco's suggestion to "Look in the puddle": he advises that Chan Hung is best found by examining oneself. And indeed, everyone who offers an opinion of Chan first looks in the puddle—defines his or her own identity—and then depicts Chan as he best complements that identity. Steve sees Chan as an FOB; Chan's wife sees him as an unsuccessful, unassimilated Taiwanese; Mr. Lee sees him as a small child who needs to be led by the hand. Each person sees Chan as the thing that he or she is not, or does not want to be. As such, each person sees Chan as something to get beyond, or rather, as something to avoid. "To get beyond" suggests that subjectivities exist on a continuum of becoming, emphasizing process and movement. However, each of the characters in *Chan Is Missing,* with the possible exception of Jo, attempts to fix Chan's identity, and in so doing fixes his or her own identity. It is crucial that the differing opinions about Chan are all expressed in his absence: Chan becomes the "other" who can be made to stand in for all insecurities, and through him the Chinese Americans can momentarily become one with the dominant.

It is telling that the suggestion to "look in the puddle" does not come from within the Chinese American community, but from Presco, who runs the Manilatown Senior Center.[13] At the Center, where Chan Hung went to enjoy mariachi music, the Filipinos know Chan as "Hi Ho" for the crackers he carries in his pockets. Thus, it would be wrong to suggest that the Filipino American community is more aware of the processes of becoming, for they too have assigned Chan a stable identity (as Hi Ho). By suggesting that Jo and Steve "look in the puddle," Presco does not abandon his own understanding of Chan, nor does he ask Jo and Steve to accept his own interpretation. However, by taking the advice from Manilatown to

Chinatown, Jo is provided with an opportunity to seek Chan in the interval between Chan's Filipino and Chinese identities. And it is in this interval where Chan has been lost, and where Asian American subjectivity may be found.

Voicing the Interval

If the figure of Steve emblematizes the paradoxes that attend to the performance of multiple identities, Steve also emphasizes the link between identity and the acquisition of a voice.[14] Given the multiplicity of voices in the film, what is the distinctively Asian American voice that Renee Tajima heard when she first saw *Chan Is Missing* in 1981? If there is such a thing as an Asian American voice, what does it have to say?

The characters in *Chan Is Missing* repeat themselves over and over again; it seems that everybody whom Jo encounters has a favorite rap. George uses the anecdote of the apple pie and has a rehearsed spiel about Chinatown politics. Henry talks about solidarity with the people in China (except when cooking, when he sings "Fry me to the moon" over and over). Mr. Lee gives advice over the phone on how to make business arrangements with Chinese people. Frankie says, "You don't know the Oriental people—when they say they haven't got it, they got something" (W. Wang, 1984, 31–32). The faceless voice of Chan's neighbor recycles clichés from television shows like *Dragnet* and *The Rockford Files.* Everyone who is asked to speak to the specificity of Chan Hung's position instead takes refuge in prefabricated speeches.

The need to find a voice is expressed in the tension between the two epigraphs that began this essay. Wittman Ah Sing, the protagonist of Maxine Hong Kingston's *Tripmaster Monkey,* refers to African American culture and bemoans the lack of similar hyphenate cultural expression for Chinese Americans. Wittman can conceive of an Asian American voice only in terms of already existing voices of subcultural expression, which would seem to ally him with Steve and his various appropriated identities. But both *Chan Is Missing* and *Tripmaster Monkey* demonstrate the ultimate untenability of appropriating voices; it is as if the characters seize on the first thing at hand in an effort to plug the doughnut hole, without really understanding what that doughnut is. By romanticizing African American cultural forms as resistant ("ain't-taking-no-shit-from-nobody street-strutting language"), Wittman and Steve fail to interrogate the extent to which American culture has absorbed African American cultural forms, as well as the specific processes of negotiation and contestation that produced African American culture(s).

The conflict between different modes of expression—between different voices—is described in *Chan Is Missing* by a lawyer (Judi Nihei) researching a paper on "the legal implications of cross-cultural misunderstandings" (W. Wang, 1984, 17). When a police officer asked Chan, "You didn't stop at the stop sign, did you?" Chan answered, "No." In Chinese grammar, the answer must agree with the logic of the question ("No, I did not *not stop*"), whereas most native speakers of American English understand answers to agree with the logic of the statement ("No, I *did not* stop"). The lawyer, interested in the misunderstandings that result from this encounter, explicates the cross-cultural confusion in an attempt (presumably) to foster cross-cultural understanding. On the one hand, her voice is put in service of the two voices that preceded hers; on the other, her voice intervenes in their conversation, taking advantage of the confusion occasioned by the meeting of two voices to convey her own message.[15]

Following from this example of the interaction of hierarchized voices, it is important to maintain a distinction between the voice of *Chan Is Missing* and the voices of its characters, for the one contains and mediates the others. This is the only way I can make sense of Tajima's claim that there is something very Asian American about *Chan Is Missing*. If we understand hyphenate identity in the terms Trinh T. Minh-ha proposes, as a process of becoming, there can be no hypostatized Asian American voice, just encounters between difficult-to-place voices that can be interpreted by third parties as Asian American. I can understand my own voice to be Asian American only by standing apart from it, for if I try to arrest the process of becoming that my voice is undergoing, I remove myself from the realm of hyphenate identity and assert that I have a position somewhere. Perhaps, then, the importance of *Chan Is Missing* for the Asian American community is that it forces Asian Americans to reevaluate our own positions vis-à-vis our own identities.

I have argued that Asian American subjectivity cannot be founded on any notion of stability; this is especially true given the diversity of Asian Americans, who represent a wide range of Asian ethnicities and cultures, different histories in the United States, and different generational removes from Asia. In this, I am echoing Lisa Lowe, who suggests that "it is possible to utilize specific signifiers of ethnic identity, such as Asian American, for the purpose of contesting and disrupting the discourses that exclude Asian Americans, while simultaneously revealing the internal contradictions and slippages of [the term] Asian American. . . . I am not suggesting that we can or should do away with the notion of Asian American identity . . . [but that we] explore the hybridities concealed beneath the desire of identity" (1991b, 39).[16] Wayne Wang's films explore the contradictions of Chinese American identity, and in so doing propose a space for Asian American subjectivity. *Chan Is Missing* takes the interrogation of identity as its central project, presenting a variety of perspectives on Chan Hung from a variety of puddles. Detective films are frequently described as if they were jigsaw puzzles; I have proposed the metaphor of the doughnut. Each character in *Chan Is Missing* holds a doughnut that contains the possibilities for Chinese American identity in its center; each character glances in the puddle and takes one bite from the doughnut in an attempt to find his or her access to the center. The big doughnut made up of all the little doughnuts—a doughnut akin to the construction of Chinese American identity that the spectator viewing *Chan Is Missing* is left with—is almost meaningless, almost wholly "hole." Whereas each character fixes Chan in an attempt to fix his or her own identity, the spectator is not allowed to occupy any one of these fixed perspectives but instead must negotiate all of them. Thus, each character's bite out of the doughnut, each character's attempt to limit the range of identities for Chan Hung opens up the interval in the spectator's doughnut, widening the space for spectatorial subjectivity and, by extension, Asian American subjectivity. By showing us why it is impossible to know precisely who we are as Chinese Americans, *Chan Is Missing* shows us how we might discover how we can become Asian Americans.

But while *Chan Is Missing* may emphasize the process of becoming, setting identities in motion, evolving subjectivities encounter resistance from those who are invested in affirming the legitimacy and solidity of established identity formations. At the end of *From Hollywood to Hanoi,* when Tiana returns to the United States with a helmet that is meant to signal her ironic relationship to the line drawn between North and South Vietnam, her father refuses to adjust his own identity as a South Vietnamese government official in exile. *Chan Is Missing* may show us how Asian American cinematic identity can be spoken from the interval, from liminal space, but we must not forget that even liminality is faced with recuperation by identity formations that are founded on the myth of origins and essences.

In this chapter I have attempted a reading that continually opens up the figure of Chan Hung, but it is more often the case that movies are interpreted in the light of fixed categories of identity; after all, Steve does not welcome the destabilizing of his identity, for it threatens the stability of his worldview. The next two chapters examine movies that purport to advance transitional identity formations and the threat that these liminal identities pose to essentialist discourses of the family and of national identity.

CHAPTER 7

We're Queer! We're Where?

Locating Transgressive Films

> I made my choice; I shouldered my way into the country in which I felt minority discourse empowered me rather than enfeebled me. This time I was crossing a border because I wanted to cross it. This time I was repossessing a "homeland" I had willed into existence, not inherited. —Bharati Mukherjee, *Days and Nights in Calcutta*

> In Europe and in every country characterized as civilized or civilizing, the family is a miniature of the nation. —Frantz Fanon, *Black Skin, White Masks*

The varied and contradictory perspectives that the characters in *Chan Is Missing* have of Chan Hung reveal that self-identity is dependent on the construction of a coherent reading of an/other identity. *Chan Is Missing* thus leads to a twofold insight. First, each character defines Chan differently, suggesting that he is the locus of multiple identity formations and to focus on one formation is to miss others. Second, none of these identities is stable, but each is in a process of becoming something else (the immigrant becomes the American, the husband becomes the father, etc.). The process of becoming reveals that there is no pure state of being because there are no fixed subject positions. No identity is any more or less stable than any other; nevertheless, certain subject formations are culturally constructed as if they were pure, self-evident categories. The lesson of *Chan Is Missing:* the desire for stable self-identity leads us to view an/other identity as fixed. Identities are in motion, but we deal not with identities themselves but with representations that seem to arrest their movement, as if we were seduced by the stillness of a snapshot into believing that the subject was itself motionless.

In this chapter I bring sexual identity to the forefront. Specifically, I look at two feature films, Deepa Mehta's *Fire* (1996) and Ang Lee's *The Wedding Banquet* (1993). Both films depict the conflicts between traditional family structures and the expression of homosexual desire, conflicts that illuminate the heteronormativity of national identities. Both movies beg the question of national identity because they were produced transnationally, which is to say that each film was funded by private investors and/or government agencies in at least two different countries.[1] In these films, transnational investment depends on the fiction of distinct national identities even as it apparently transcends those borders.

When nations are implicitly defined by ethnic homogeneity, as they are in cultural nationalism, then homosexuality threatens ethnic minorities and hegemonic national unity alike. The reception of *Fire* recalls responses to the character of Chan Hung: disparate audiences in India and North America apparently agree that *Fire* depicts the conflict between cultural and sexual identities, even as these audiences disagree about the meaning of these identities. *The Wedding Banquet* dramatizes a similar conflict, but in contrast to *Fire,* Lee's film somehow appealed both to audiences invested in gay identity and to audiences invested in Taiwanese national identity. On the one hand, the representation of homosexuality in these movies demystifies the heteronormativity of racial identity formations (because race is predicated on biological reproduction), and therefore these films serve to destabilize identity. On the other hand, these movies were unable to effectively interrogate the myth of racial purity that undergirds virtually all conceptions of national identity, thereby failing to challenge national identity. My interest in these films thus emerges from the ways they are implicated in the twinned desires to open a space for fluid conceptions of identity and to cling to a secure subject position. Are transnational films inherently conducive to maintaining multiple, contradictory readings in a productive state of tension, thereby challenging essentialist notions of identity that would fix these narratives? Or do these films exploit their audiences' desire for a fixed identity by enabling them to reject the contradictions of diasporic subjectivity by articulating multiple subject positions that ultimately become reified and static?

The contradictions in these films can be attributed in part to the contradictions of transnationalism as a concept.[2] Transnational films, as commodified narratives, reveal the uneven alignment of transnational business practices and transnational cultural formations. Mohammed A. Bamyeh argues that transnational phenomena are translated into the spheres of culture, the economy, and government according to each sphere's own logic:

> While the interaction of such logics *may* create a "total" or "integrated" phenomenon, its absence will lead only to a fragmented existence of the transnational phenomenon within separate spheres and the imprisonment of its various aspects within the contours of distinct trajectories. This fragmented existence continues to typify transnationalism today. The contemporary transnational economy has not led to the formation of transnational culture, even as it enhanced transnational systems of communication. Neither does the globalization of the state system correspond to the globalization of culture or the economy; very often, the state machinery has been used . . . to undermine the potentials for cultural globalization by consciously inventing or accentuating national distinctions and traditions. (1993, 67)

It is film's status as an industrially produced cultural artifact that makes the application of the transnational label difficult. Although we can define transnational films as those funded and produced in two or more countries and released internationally, this definition does not account for reading formations in different locations.[3] Of course, diverse audiences interpret films from other cultures according to their own "ways of seeing" (61), but I would like to extend this question: How do diverse audiences accommodate understandings of the transnational production of film into their interpretations?[4] How does promotion of a film or filmmaker as transnational affect interpretations of where a film is coming from (its *enonciation*)?

The international arthouse cinema is a gatekeeper that selectively promotes films to international audiences. Writing in a festival catalogue for a Korean film festival hosted by University of California, Irvine in 1998, Chris Berry offers speculative remarks on the marketing of national cinemas on the international arthouse circuit.[5] Berry argues that the international film festival circuit introduces new work and suggests trends which are then exploited by the "globalized art-house cinema" (1998, 40). Unlike Hollywood, which promotes its films primarily through genre labels and movie stars, the international arthouse circuit markets its films through national categories and auteur filmmakers: "This occurs regardless of the fact that [some of the most successful] film movements [French New Wave, Italian Neo-realism, New German Cinema, China's Fifth Generation] . . . are atypical of production in their countries of origin and most auteurs are also exceptions to the rule rather than representative of the cinema of their country" (44). I would add that the four movements Berry specifies all claimed to be revolutionary departures from their national traditions. On the international circuit, then, national films are promoted as authentic visions of the cultures they depict, often with intimations of repression and censorship in their countries of origin. In the West, sexually themed arthouse films are particularly appealing, in part because they energize discourses about Western sexual liberation and freedom of personal expression, in contradistinction to putatively backward countries.[6]

Transnational films with sexual content reveal fissures in the international distribution network. For example, in the U.S. context, arthouse films might be rated X or NC-17 or be unrated, suggesting that explicitly sexual films must be carefully marketed to emphasize their cultural significance. Just as the very notion of arthouse cinema plays on film's liminal status between popular culture and high art, so is sexuality an expression both of the marketplace's lowest common denominator and high culture's fascination with transcendence. Add transnational film production and a diasporic film audience into the mix, and the result often is a film that attempts to transcend nationally based identity politics, which is nevertheless marketed to an audience as the ultimate expression of cultural exoticism.[7]

These contradictions are apparent when one considers that diasporic audiences often romanticize their countries of origin, preferring films that express dominant ideologies. Rather than appreciating films that dramatize the fluidity of transnational identity, diasporic audiences often interpret such films in nationalist and essentialist terms, most dramatically evident in the attacks on *Fire* as anti-Hindu.[8] The everywhere apparent attack on fluid transnational identity from supposedly stable subject positions can result in what Sheng-mei Ma (1998) has called "immigrant nostalgia," what I would call a nostalgia for essentialism. Fluid subject formations are continually recuperated by essentialism, just as Chan Hung's indeterminacy in *Chan Is Missing* leads the other characters to cling tenaciously to their assumed identities.

In this chapter, I examine the tension between contradictory readings of *Fire* and *The Wedding Banquet* emerging from diverse audiences positioned differently vis-à-vis the transnational cinema marketplace. Drawing on reviews from a variety of journalistic sources and secondary accounts of reception whenever possible, I argue that *Fire* and *The Wedding Banquet* were both read as allegories of nationalism. In the case of *The*

Wedding Banquet, the homophobic logic of cultural nationalism (articulated comedically) accounts for the movie's uneasy marriage of progressive politics and Taiwanese-style "family values"; although fundamentally incompatible, the impulses of "queer nation" and "Taiwanese nationalism" are both metaphoric counternationalisms (resisting heteronormativity and mainland Chinese nationalism, respectively). In the case of *Fire,* by contrast, both the avowedly progressive West and the neoconservative (specifically, Hindu nationalist) East interpreted queer desire as a Western construct (even as they assigned contrary values to putative Western influence).

Fire

Filmmaker Deepa Mehta was born in Amritsar in the early 1950s, the daughter of a film distributor.[9] She studied philosophy at Lady Shri Ram College in Delhi and after graduating took a clerical job with the Cinema Workshop, a small company based in New Delhi. "It took me all day clumsily typing with two fingers to complete the simplest task. They shook their heads and apprenticed me for editing instead. I learned how to edit, do camera work and sound, and helped with television programs." She married filmmaker Paul Saltzman, moving to Canada with him in 1973. The couple made documentaries for Sunrise Films, including *The Bakery* (1974) and *At 99: A Portrait of Louise Tandy Murch* (1975), with Mehta editing and sometimes writing the scripts. In the 1980s, Mehta divorced her husband, directed the award-winning documentaries *Traveling Light: The Photojournalism of Dilip Mehta* (1988) and *Martha, Ruth and Edie* (1988), and took a few roles so that she could learn the process from the actor's perspective (earning a Gemini nomination for her role as a Sri Lankan refuge in CBC-TV's *In Limbo*).

Her first feature film was *Sam and Me* (1990), with a screenplay written by Ranjit Chowdhry, who also starred and would play featured roles in Mehta's next two films. *Sam and Me* won honorable mention at Cannes in the competition for the Camera d'Or. Steven Spielberg hired her to direct a few episodes of *Young Indiana Jones Chronicles,* where she met cinematographer Giles Nuttgens and production designer Aradhana Seth. Miramax tapped her to direct *Camilla,* starring Jessica Tandy and Bridget Fonda, but Mehta did not have final cut; after the movie flopped, she decided to return to independent filmmaking.

Mehta began work on the screenplay for *Fire* in April 1995, finishing in September. The role of Radha was written with Shabana Azmi in mind, and after some initial reluctance Azmi accepted the role. Unknown actor Nandita Das was cast as Sita. Mehta had briefly considered seeking funding from Telefilm Canada (Kirkland, 1997), but that would have required 40 percent of the film to be shot in Canada (although it need not be *set* in Canada: Canada could stand in for India) and the hiring of Canadian actors (Melwani, 1996). In the end, Mehta raised money privately, with approximately 90 percent of her budget coming from Canadian sources and the rest from Indian sources (Kirkland, 1997).

The crew were prepared for controversy when they arrived in New Delhi to begin production (Mehta had selected producer Bobby Bedi, in part for his experience guiding another controversial production, *Bandit Queen*), but media attention was focused on Mira Nair's production of *Kama Sutra,* already underway. *Fire* was shot in thirty days.

Fire tells the story of a joint family household in New Delhi. Ashok is the patriarch of a middle-class Hindu family that runs a small shop selling food and renting videos. Ashok's wife, Radha, is barren; Ashok has sought solace by following the spiritual teachings of a guru who preaches abstinence. Ashok's younger brother, Jatin, returns home with his new wife by an arranged marriage, Sita. In this joint family household, the women are primary caregivers to Ashok's mother, Biji, rendered mute by a stroke. When Sita discovers that Jatin is engaged in an affair with Julie (a Chinese woman who speaks English with a North American accent), she turns to Radha for comfort: these two women, both abandoned by their husbands, become lovers. When Ashok discovers them in the act, Radha and Sita decide to leave the family. After a confrontation between Radha and Ashok in which Radha's clothing is set on fire, Radha meets Sita, but as the film ends, the extent of Radha's injury is unclear.

Fire entered the international film festival circuit in 1996, appearing at the New York Film Festival, the Chicago Film Festival (winning Best Film and Best Actress for Azmi), the Vancouver International Film Festival (Best Canadian Film from the audience, and Honourable Mention for Best Canadian Film from the jury), the Mannheim-Heidelberg International Film Festival (Special Jury Award), Rencontres Internationales de Cinema à Paris (Best Foreign Film), the 1997 Barcelona International Film Festival (Best Foreign Film), and the 1997 Outfest in Los Angeles (Best Film and Best Actress for Azmi). *Fire* was rolled out in the fall of 1997, opening in August in New York[10] and Los Angeles, September in San Francisco, and October in Boston, Chicago, and across the Southwest.

In interviews promoting *Fire,* Mehta announced that the film was part of a projected trilogy. *Earth* was based on Bapsi Siddhwa's novel *Ice Candy Man* (released in the United States as *Cracking India*) and began production in February 1997, premiering at the Toronto Film Festival in 1998. Mehta began work on the screenplay for *Water* in the fall of 1998 and also plans to adapt Vikram Seth's novel *Suitable Boy.*

Tongues of *Fire*

Fire's distributor, Zeitgeist films, set up an official Web site for the movie, a press kit without the middleman. The site includes links to Web sites devoted to Indian cinema, links to South Asian diasporic groups (organizations for gay South Asians, women's support groups, etc.), and has several sections written by Mehta, including her account of the movie's reception at Indian film festivals (notably the Trivandrum festival in January 1996), and a brief essay called, "Why *Fire* Is in English":

> I thought about translating *Fire* into Hindi [the script was written in English or Hinglish], but more for the Western audience rather than the Indian one. Western audiences find a "foreign" film easier to imbibe, easier to accept in its cultural context, if it is in its indigenous language. "A foreign film can only be a foreign film if it is in a foreign language." And if it isn't, then somehow it is judged (albeit subconsciously) as a Western film disguised as a foreign one. All very complex but true to a large extent. Well, how to explain to people in the West that most middle-class Indians speak Hinglish? Eventually, I decided to go for the authenticity of spirit of *Fire* rather than people's expectations of what a foreign film constitutes.

Mehta reveals herself to be a master rhetorician in the closing lines of this passage. "How to explain?" she asks quite rhetorically, for the question answers itself while including the reader as confidant. Her appeal to "authenticity of spirit" implies a distinction from mundane realism, begging the question of whether Hinglish is indeed accurate and appropriate or only authentic in spirit. Finally, note the slippage from "people in the West" to "people" in the final sentence, and the inverted commas that set off "foreign" in the first but not in the final sentence; at the very least, these slippages confirm that the reception of the film by Western audiences was foremost in Mehta's consciousness, that Western audiences were, if not catered to, then at least accommodated, even as the first part of the passage blasts Western audiences who are charmed by subtitles.

Mehta's justification for using English was received and duly reported by many U.S. reviews and journalistic accounts of the film, an indication of the promoters' success in shaping the film's reception by non-Indian (diasporic) audiences. On this issue, at least, Mehta's authority to speak for a culture was not questioned. Why, then, was *Fire* dubbed into Hindi for its 1998 release in India? Did Mehta suspect that Indian audiences would find English-speaking characters "easier to imbibe" (i.e., easier to dismiss)? Or did the producers decide that an Indian audience would never believe that middle-class characters would address their servant in English (even if they spoke English with each other)? "Why *Fire* Is in English" is not explained to Indian and diasporic audiences, only to Western ones.

If *Fire* was aimed at the Western market, surely that is not surprising given that the lion's share of the film's budget was raised from Canadian sources. Mehta's dubious justification for using English anticipated the confusion about this film's "national" identity. The film's setting, the filmmaker's biography, the sources of funding—these different geographic components suggest contradictory national labels, and while these different categories may carry different weights, they also highlight the film's status as both a cultural artifact and a commercial product. It is not surprising, then, that these contradictions were foregrounded when *Fire* competed for awards, for awards are also attempts to recognize both the cultural and commercial achievement of a film.[11]

Independently produced feature films depend on the international film festival circuit to attract the interest of distributors, and festivals segregate films by national origin for award consideration. At the 1996 Toronto International Film Festival, *Fire* screened under the "Perspective Canada" banner: "It means that the mandate decided by the government about what is a Canadian film does not apply in this case. By choosing it to open Perspective Canada, they just said, 'It is Canadian'" (Mehta, quoted in Gerstel, 1997, B6). By doing so, they may also have been repeating the myth of Canada as polyglot nation:

> Working with what Mehta calls "a motley international crew"—a British cinematographer, Canadian producers, Indian cast and art department—

> Mehta borrowed and reshaped things from Western and Eastern traditions in the service of her vision. While Mehta cites Indian filmmakers, like Guru Dutt, as filmic influences, she admits, "My approach to photography is Western." Indeed, while working in India—the world's largest film producer—she depended on Western conventions of camera set-up and location sound to get the film done. In one way, it is this patchwork of international styles that makes her film particularly Canadian. For Mehta, "Canada is not a melting pot, but a mosaic of different people. Here I am Indian living in Canada, and my sense of living in both places gives me the freedom and space to create myself." (Bowen, 1996)[12]

Fire's Canadian identity was thus argued in terms of Western cinematic conventions of film production and the film's multinational crew (in a system where a multicultural mosaic supposedly signifies Canada's multicultural society), and *not* the story content. However, Western critical reception of the film suggests that it was repeatedly read as if its story *itself* was multicultural, a motley mix of India and the West.

Migratory Spectatorship

Reviews of *Fire* in the mainstream North American press interpret the film as telling a story of sexual awakening wherein two women separate themselves from a patriarchal family structure to pursue their sexual identities. This reading pits Western feminism against Indian culture and further equates the relationship between the two sisters-in-law as "closeted" before they leave the household. By contrast, Gayatri Gopinath argues that *Fire* signifies on Anglo-American narratives of homosexuality. That is, scenes of "secrecy and disclosure, as well as gender inversion and cross-dressing" should be read in relation to South Asian cultures as well as with reference to "coming-out narratives," which Gopinath, following Martin Manalansan, identifies as an Anglo-American genre (1997, 472–73). Manalansan critiques contemporary gay transnational politics for privileging a Western understanding of gayness and constructing a teleology that casts non-Western practices as " 'premodern' or unliberated" (1997, 486). For Manalansan, the coming-out narrative is itself meaningful only "within the context of the emergence of bourgeois civil society and the formation of the individual subject that really only occurs with capitalist and Western expansion" (488). According to Manalansan, the International Lesbian and Gay Association's *Pink Book* reproduces this logic when it imposes concepts like "coming out" on non-Western nations (488–89), assuming "that practices that are not organized around visibility are 'closeted' " (490) and thereby failing to account for the particularities of different cultures.[13]

This is not to say that *Fire* does not address the specificity of Hindu tradition: the film's critique of the Hindu ideals of femininity and wifely devotion is foregrounded by the names Radha and Sita.[14] However, in the context of a coming-out narrative, this critique implies Western conceptions of sexual identity.[15] *Fire*'s narrative is thus understood as not just a movement from heterosexual wife to lesbian lover, but from East to West. So, despite Mehta's deliberate setting of the story in New Delhi—"Deepa could have easily set it in Toronto. . . . She did not want to set it in the West because she did not want people to think what happens could be blamed on the West" (Shabana Azmi, quoted in Roy, 1997)—many reviewers attribute the film's progressive politics to the West. For example, New York *Newsday* encapsulates the film's plot as a "Florid, erotic cross-cultural romance" (John Anderson, 1997, B8). What exactly makes this story cross-cultural, given that it is set in India and all the characters are Hindu? The review clarifies the cultural hybridity when it refers to the film as a "ménage à trois of Indian esthetics, American mores and feminist aggravation." This reviewer assumes that the movie's depiction of burgeoning lesbian sexuality must be indicative of a (North) American (not to say Canadian) sense of morality, that feminism is un-Indian (and un-American), and that Indian artistic sensibilities are at odds with women's sexuality.

The *Newsday* review is by no means atypical of mainstream North American reviews, and is perhaps driven by the use of English (not subtitled Hindi) and the assumption that therefore this story is not truly set in India. The attribution of cultural hybridity to the film may also indicate that it is the filmmaker herself who is being read, not her film. When migration is understood as a linear process, a process of giving up Asia for North America, the act of returning to Asia is incomprehensible except as a critique of Asia, an affirmation of the superiority of North American subjectivity. In other words, when transnational identities are collapsed into migrant identities—when India is the only site not considered to be part of the Indian diaspora—then the gesture of return cannot be understood except as regression. But if transnational identities are understood as distinct from migrant identities—not Asian (adjective) American (noun) and therefore relatively stable in national terms, but both Asian and American (or indeed, neither Asian nor American) and relatively unstable in national terms—then we are not talking about a linear teleology, but a circular narrative. In other words, North American conceptions of ethnicity understand Mehta as having chosen North America over India (instead of maintaining multiple allegiances); they therefore read the film as articulating a similar evolution, as leaving behind Indian patriarchy for Western sexual liberation.

Fire's structural similarity to familiar Western narratives of lesbian awakening (in which lesbianism is posited as the result of spousal neglect) suggests why many Western critics found the film to be tamer than the title led them to expect. However, Gopinath notes that such a reading fails to account for the specific location of middle-class joint family life in New Delhi. The domestic space of the family is built on gendered expectations (e.g., the women are the primary caregivers for their mother-in-law) and an understanding that heterosexual marriage depends on restricting the desires and mobility of the wife (manifested in observance of Karva Chauth, when Hindu wives fast to ensure the well-being of their husbands). Gopinath observes: "The attraction between Radha and Sita is enabled by those spaces of female homosociality that are sanctioned by normative sexual and gender arrangements. Whether rubbing oil into each other's hair or massaging each other's feet during a family picnic, the women exploit the permeable relation and the slippages between female homosociality and female homoeroticism" (1998, 634). Because domestic space permits and even encourages female homoeroticism, home cannot be equated with the closet and leaving home is not equivalent to coming out.[16] Rather, leaving home has specific resonances in *Fire:* throughout the film, when Radha and Sita venture outside the home they are always seen in Islamic or otherwise non-Hindu spaces, and at the film's conclusion, the two women meet in a Sufi temple.[17] Specifically, the women are not rejecting the closet, the home, or India, but Hinduism's role in constructing the middle-class family; fundamentalist Hindu protests during *Fire*'s Indian release corroborate this interpretation.[18]

In December 1998, the Hindu fundamentalist group Shiv Sena (which has ties to the Bharatiya Janata Party) closed down theaters in Mumbai, Surat, New Delhi, and other locations. *Fire*'s distributor, Shringar Films, suspended all screenings, and the Ministry of Information and Broadcasting sent the film back to the Censorship Board (which had previously passed the film) for review. On December 7, Mehta petitioned the Supreme Court to direct that the security of theaters be protected so that audiences could view the film without fear, and to investigate the violence. Shabana Azmi publicly alleged that the timing behind the attacks on the film (which had already shown for almost three weeks without incident) was motivated by the BJP's poor showing in elections the week before (Mackinnon, 1998). On December 14, Bal Thackeray announced that the Shiv Sena would withdraw its opposition to *Fire* if the characters named Sita and Radha were renamed Sabhana and Saira.[19] Shiv Sena thereby narrowed their objections to the film, no longer claiming that lesbianism was anti-Indian, but that it was anti-Hindu.

Western reviews that attribute lesbianism and progressive feminism to Western influence evince the same logic as Shiv Sena. Mainstream North American reviews suggest that *Fire*'s combination of feminist sensibility and Indian setting is novel, as John Anderson does in the *Newsday* review cited above. But such reviews can also be read as imposing the narrative teleology of migration to the West on Mehta and (by extension) her film:

> Deepa Mehta's *Fire* is a feminist-based critique of modern Indian society, particularly of marriage, from a Westernized point of view. (Stone, 1997, D3)
>
> Perhaps bold and novel in India, its feminist messages seem dated by American standards. (Van Gelder, 1996, C16)
>
> Clearly, feminism has been slow to emerge in India. (Carr, 1997, D6)

These reviews rate India's feminism as less developed than the West's, implying that Indian culture, given time, will evolve into something approximating that of North America.[20] Indian culture is cast as inhospitable to notions that the progressive West takes for granted. For example, noting Sita's comment to Radha, "In our language, no word exists for what we are to each other," critic Roger Ebert avers, "It is of course the Indian context that gives this innocent story its resonance. Lesbianism is so outside the experience of these Hindus, we learn, that their language even lacks a word for it" (1997, 38).[21] Ebert thus assumes first that the English spoken in the film stands in for the characters' true language, and second, that the word Radha refers to must be "lesbian." Both assumptions reveal that the Western critics apply their own understandings of what it means to be lesbian or feminist.

In the case of *Fire*, Indian and North American audiences both interpreted the characters' cultural and sexual identities as conflictual. Furthermore, both audiences found the film's discourse on identities troubling:

it deconstructed Hindu national identity and did not go far enough (by Western standards) in affirming queer identity. Responses to *The Wedding Banquet,* by contrast, suggest that the film manages to appeal to audiences invested in a queer identity as well as audiences invested in Taiwanese national identity, despite the fact that the film is unable to articulate a coherent space for gay Taiwanese American subjectivity. Whereas *Fire* was read as promoting Western feminism, *The Wedding Banquet* attempts to reconcile ethnic/national and gay male identities through a misogynistic narrative. Both *Fire* and *The Wedding Banquet* were produced outside the mainstream film industry, but Lee's film won him the opportunity to direct the pseudo-independent features *Sense and Sensibility* and *The Ice Storm.* Somehow, *The Wedding Banquet* negotiates its liminal status as a transnational film, appealing as both/and rather than either/or.

The Wedding Banquet

Filmmaker Ang Lee was born in Taiwan in 1954 and grew up in the town of Tainan, the eldest son of a high school principal.[22] By Lee's account, his entire family was shocked when he failed his college entrance exams; he later entered the Academy of Arts. In 1978 he transferred to the University of Illinois to study theater, then entered NYU's film production program to get his MFA. While attending NYU, Lee married Jane Lin, also from Taiwan, whom he had met at Illinois; Lin, a microbiologist, supported the family. After Lee's thesis film, *A Fine Line,* won him Best Director and Best Picture in NYU's 1984 competition, he signed with an agent but was unable to sell a script in Hollywood. He won a Taiwanese government contest with two Chinese-language scripts, *The Wedding Banquet* and *Pushing Hands,* which led to an offer from Central Motion Pictures. *Pushing Hands* (1992) was shot in New York on a budget of $480,000; the film broke even in Taiwan and won three Golden Horse Awards (out of nine nominations). He was then given the go-ahead to shoot *Wedding Banquet* (1993), which was coproduced by New York–based Good Machine Productions, for a total budget of $750,000; production was completed in four weeks. Lee rewrote the screenplay with his scriptwriting partner, James Schamus. Lee had written the first draft in 1988 with Neil Peng, inspired by a mutual friend of theirs from Taiwan who was living with his white boyfriend (Pacheco, 1993); according to Hornaday (1993), the script was also inspired by Lee's impromptu proposal to Lin on the occasion of a visit from his parents in 1983, and by the wedding-night conception of their first child. The first draft was written in Chinese, translated into English for the second draft, and then translated back to Chinese (Schamus, 1994, xi).

The premise of *The Wedding Banquet* is simple: Wai-Tung, a businessman in his thirties who emigrated from Taiwan ten years earlier, marries Wei-Wei so that she can get a green card: in exchange, Wai-Tung will be able to end his parents' matchmaking efforts without revealing his five-year relationship with Simon, his white lover. Complications begin when Wai-Tung's parents, Mr. and Mrs. Gao, fly to New York to stage an elaborate wedding banquet: Wei-Wei seduces Wai-Tung on their wedding night and realizes some three weeks later that she is pregnant. After Mr. Gao (a retired general) suffers a mild stroke, Wai-Tung finally "comes out"[23] to his mother and tells her that Simon is his lover: they agree not to tell his father. After leaving the hospital, Wai-Tung's father reveals to Simon that he understands and accepts his relationship with Wai-Tung, but he makes Simon promise that it will be their secret; he has pretended ignorance so that he can have a grandchild.[24] On the way to the clinic to procure an abortion, Wei-Wei has a change of heart and asks Wai-Tung and Simon if they will help her raise the child. The film concludes with an air of bittersweet melancholy as Mr. and Mrs. Gao board a plane to return to Taiwan.

Lee cast Sihung Lung as the family patriarch; May Chin was a Taiwanese pop star and TV actor; Mitchell Lichtenstein was best known for his role in Robert Altman's *Streamers* (1983), for which he won Best Actor at the Venice Film Festival. Winston Chao had never acted before: Lee coached him for over a month. Chin and Chao spoke their English lines phonetically; likewise, Lichtenstein's Mandarin.

The Wedding Banquet grossed over $4 million in Taiwan, making it the most successful film ever shown there; at its U.S. premiere at the Seattle International Film Festival, it won the Audience Award. The film would go on to earn over $30 million worldwide, leading *Variety* to label *The Wedding Banquet* "the most profitable film in the world in 1993" (Huang, 1994).

Lee went on to direct *Eat Drink Man Woman* (1994), shot in Taiwan in fifty-six days on a budget of $1.5 million. He then produced Sylvia Chang's next film, *Siao Yu,* a green card melodrama that began shooting in New York in fall 1994 (Chang, 1994). Next, Emma Thompson tapped Lee to direct her screenplay of Jane Austen's *Sense and Sensibility* (1995); the success of that film seems to have convinced the American film industry that Lee can make films on non-Chinese subjects. The impact of *The Wedding Banquet* and the films that followed was such that *A. Magazine* listed Ang Lee on its 1995, 1996, and 1997 lists of influential Asian Americans; in January 1997, New York Mayor Rudolph Giuliani appointed Ang Lee to a pro-immigration commission (David Henry Hwang, Zubin Mehta, and I. M. Pei were the other prominent Asian Americans; Harlan, 1997).

Preserving the Family: Conservativism and Conservation

The Wedding Banquet was a breakout hit, sharing the Palme d'Or at Cannes (with *Orlando*) and cowinning a Golden Bear for Best Picture at the Berlin International Film Festival. This success was due in no small part to the movie's blending of the sexually risqué and progressive in its queer themes, and with the reaffirmation of a traditional moral order. Of course, this is the very definition of comedy: a story that allows the audience to indulge in transgression, yet whose narrative resolution preserves social mores. But in another sense, this film has it both ways: it is both naughty and nice, and ultimately extremely flattering to a U.S. audience. Generically speaking, the film is neither a comedy, with a plot that culminates in marriage, nor a tragedy, with a marriage setting the plot in motion; the wedding falls squarely in the middle of *The Wedding Banquet*.[25] Structurally then, *The Wedding Banquet* could be placed in the small genre of the green card comedy, films in which characters marry for expediency midway through the film and then deal with the consequences in the second half; the expected resolution is that the characters will fall in love.[26] In the process, green card comedies demystify marriage,[27] calling attention to the state's interest in restricting access to the economy through the institution of marriage.[28] In critiquing the state's linkage of marriage and citizenship, *The Wedding Banquet* calls attention to the ways national identity is predicated on heteronormativity, and as such, it begs the same question as *Fire* (in relation to Hindu nationalism).

The Wedding Banquet presents a fairly sanitized, nonthreatening depiction of gay men, as if to demonstrate that gay men can be bourgeois, too. There are brief glimpses of queer subculture—for example, Wai-Tung is flanked by drag queens in a briefly glimpsed photograph, and Simon is seen staffing an Act Up table—but it is very polite: no dog collars, no leather, no depictions of anal sex or sexual promiscuity—indeed, the only depiction of nonmonogamous intercourse is Wai-Tung's night with his wife; presumably, conservative distaste for promiscuity is mollified by the assertion of heterosexuality.[29] Whereas same-sex desire in *Fire* threatens constructions of unified Hindu national identity even as that desire paradoxically arises from the space of the family, in *The Wedding Banquet* homosexuality is no threat to the family structure at all. Indeed, Wei-Wei becomes pregnant because she and Wai-Tung engage in unsafe sex (as Simon angrily points out); Wai-Tung's identity as a polite, bourgeois gay man is thus called into question on two levels: not only can he be sexually aroused by a woman, but he does not follow safe sex orthodoxy.[30] Wai-Tung is all but straight.

Ultimately, *The Wedding Banquet* is an exceedingly conservative film despite its veneer of progressive politics: it may depict the viability of nontraditional (i.e., heterosexual nuclear) families, but it does so on the backs of women. For although some critics understand the film to conclude with the construction of a new family unit (S. Ma refers to Simon, Wai-Tung, and Wei-Wei as a ménage à trois [1998, 150]), that unit is not an alliance of equals, but is structured by tremendous economic disparities. In this family, Wai-Tung is the breadwinner, Simon the wife, and Wei-Wei the nanny, a role consistent with her status before the wedding (illegal immigrant from an "underdeveloped" country, mainland China; whereas both Simon and Wai-Tung come from developed economies).[31] My pessimistic reading is sanctioned, I think, by reference to Lee's other films, in particular *Eat Drink Man Woman,* where the modern, sexually liberated businesswoman undergoes a series of humiliations (she loses her savings in a bad investment, is crudely propositioned by her best friend) and gives up a promotion so that she can stay home and care for her father (metaphorically, by cooking for him, if not literally).[32] In *The Wedding Banquet,* it is Wei-Wei who is reined in, giving up her bohemian life to play the role of a dutiful Chinese daughter-in-law. Yet despite the sexist narrative, *The Wedding Banquet* was promoted (and by all accounts received) in the United States as a contemporary comedy about transgressive modern sexuality. How is it that these various conservative threads can be woven together so as to appear progressive?

As a transnational film, *The Wedding Banquet*'s economic success can be attributed to its masterful deployment of its contradictory political impulses. By articulating homosexuality as a Western phenomenon, the progressivism of Western audiences is flattered and they are encouraged to attribute the film's sexism to Taiwanese culture. In the film, the Taiwanese patriarch acknowledges Simon's relationship with Wai-Tung through the same gesture that he had earlier made to Wei-Wei: a monetary gift and thanks for "taking care" of Wai-Tung. Simon is therefore acknowledged as Wai-Tung's true wife, consistent with his attention to domestic detail (cooking, cleaning, anticipating Wai-Tung's needs). S. Ma points out that the father's acceptance of Simon comes only after the pregnancy; he is thus assured that his gay son has reproduced (1998, 155). If Wei-Wei can perform the one wifely duty that Simon cannot, the reverse is also true: Simon shows up Wei-Wei's inadequacies as a wife. As is consistent with Hollywood melodramas, the independent woman is punished for her failure to cultivate domestic skills. Thus, rather than celebrate Simon and Wei-Wei as unstereotypical constructions of masculinity and femininity, they are ultimately revealing of a heteronormative cultural nationalism.[33] Simon's domesticity "reinscribes the notion that homosexuality, understood erroneously as the feminization of the male, is a particularly 'Western' construct" (Dariotis and Fung, 1997, 206). The incompatibility of gay and Taiwanese immigrant identities is visually conveyed in the scene where Wai-Tung, Simon, and Wei-Wei clean house in preparation for the Gaos' arrival. Jeanette Roan notes, "[This] process involves not only the removal of photographs, videos, posters, and other paraphernalia, but more importantly their replacement, most conspicuously by scrolls of Wai-Tung's father's Chinese calligraphy. The 'degaying' of the apartment then, must also be understood as a simultaneous 'ethnicization' " (1994, 9), casting Wai-Tung as filial Taiwanese subject (particularly in his portrait in military uniform).[34] The association of Chinese calligraphy—the aesthetic deployment of China's written language—with heteronormativity is further reinforced by the spoken language, in that Simon and Wai-Tung are able to argue about their relationship in front of the Gaos as long as they speak English: English becomes the language of gay desire.[35]

The dual wedding ceremonies also reinforce the association of Chinese tradition with heterosexuality. Wai-Tung and Wei-Wei's civil ceremony is a legal transaction, permitting Wei-Wei to acquire a green card; the inadequacy of this deception is comically foreshadowed when Wei-Wei vows to marry Wai-Tung "in sickness and death." By contrast, as Roan points out, the Chinese wedding does not seal a legal contract, but rather insists on marriage as "fulfilment of the patrilineal imperative to reproduce" (1994, 7). The traditional invasion of the bridal chamber (*Nao-tung-fang*) concludes with the married couple compelled to shed all their clothes and get into bed, crudely promoting heteronormativity. Insofar as the American civil

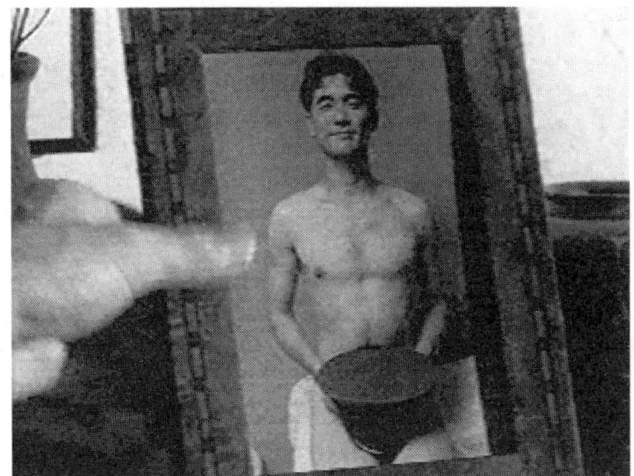

The Wedding Banquet. The queer portrait is removed . . .

. . . and replaced with the Taiwanese national subject.

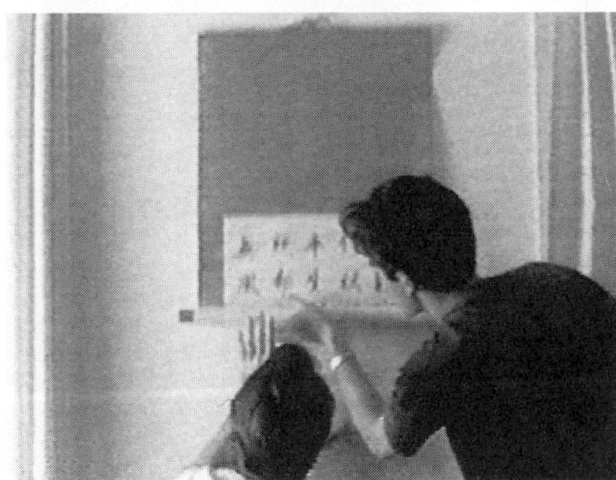

The Wedding Banquet. General Gao's calligraphy is hung.

ceremony is a fiction that evacuates heterosexual union of its procreative function, the film accomplishes the neat trick of associating the American wedding with homosexuality itself. David Ansen aptly summed up this overlay of binary oppositions in the pithy aside, "Old Taiwan meets gay New York" (1993, 61).

It is the transnational character of *The Wedding Banquet* that permits it to weave its conservative threads into a seemingly progressive pattern. By integrating a veneer of cultural critique into a narrative that affirms bourgeois values, the film is perfectly suited for the arthouse cinema's framing of cultural exoticism. In this case, cross-cultural relativism permits the film to cross over. Stanley Kauffmann was on to something when he speculated: "*The Wedding Banquet* won the Golden Bear award, the top prize, at this year's Berlin Film Festival. Why? Was it for reasons of cultural diversity? The director and most of the actors are Chinese. Was it for social liberalism? The center of the story is a homosexual pair. Perhaps the combination of the two factors was irresistible" (1993, 25). The words Kauffmann stops just short of saying are "politically correct." *The Wedding Banquet* is an international film about an interracial gay couple, which wins it plenty of P.C. points. The transnational character of the film opens up a slipperiness of authorial attribution that is then reflected in readings of the film, which forgive political shortcomings by attributing them to the film's transnational character.

As is often the case with fiction authored by ethnic minorities, *The Wedding Banquet* was promoted as simultaneously particular (ethnically Taiwanese and therefore different) and universal. This trope was invoked specifically through reference to Lee's scriptwriting partner, James Schamus, with many reports citing a variation of the story that Schamus tells in his introduction to the published screenplay for *The Wedding Banquet:* "There was many a time when I, working with my American assumptions, would be re-working a scene and finding myself frustrated by Ang's insistence that the psychology of the characters I was sketching was not naturally Chinese. My initial inclination was to study even harder the Chinese poems, stories, and histories I had been accumulating as research, usually to no avail. Finally, in frustration, I'd simply give up and write the scenes as 'Jewish' as I could make them. 'Ah-ha,' Ang would respond on reading the new draft. 'Very Chinese!' (1994, xi). Elsewhere, Schamus claimed that, if anything, "Ang is secretly Italian" (quoted in Lasky, 1994, 9). The universality of the film's themes—the tension between individuality and family responsibility—was frequently cited as the basis for Lee's selection to direct *Sense and Sensibility* (e.g., Warren, 1995).

Schamus's rhetoric of universality posits the interchangeability of ethnicities, eliding cultural differences. His universality is consistent with multicultural discourses that seek to encourage assimilation while preserving difference at the level of cultural expression (so that it can be safely consumed). *The Wedding Banquet* renders homosexuality safe for multicultural consumption, permitting homophobic audiences to overcome their ethnic/cultural differences and unite on the importance of the nuclear family. On the other hand, queer audiences can attribute the film's conservative politics to its Taiwanese identity (ethnic or cultural national).[36] The various appeals to Wai-Tung's affection—from his parents, from Wei-Wei, from Simon—are attempts to interpellate Wai-Tung, to fix him as the subject of a specific, established identity formation. Because Wai-Tung is located at the center of competing interpellations, his experiences structure the film's narrative resolution. To obtain narrative pleasure from the film's conclusion, the spectator cannot ponder the consequences for other characters: the Gao family does not bother to interpellate Wei-Wei, they simply assume that she will naturally fulfill the role of heterosexual daughter-in-law.[37]

By contrast, *Fire*'s open-ended narrative does not resolve the contestation of Hindu nationalism. It is intriguing that Hindu nationalists in India did not blame Ashok for failing to preserve the Hindu family; even more interesting, the film's conclusion was apparently not interpreted as punishing Radha for violating the ideals of wifely devotion. This suggests that Radha's true crime against the family, from a Hindu nationalist perspective, was being unable to bear a child. Wai-Tung may be gay, but his sperm is still a valuable form of transnational capital; by contrast, Radha has no eggs with which to barter. If Radha had borne a child, then perhaps all would be forgiven, as it was for Wai-Tung. Her true crime against the Hindu family was not her exploration of her sexuality (which did not, after all, interfere with her service to the family), but her failure to bear children, but she is presumably punished for the former and not the latter. *Fire* thus reveals the contradictions that structure the joint family household, and so even if Radha is punished, Hindu nationalists are unable to recuperate the film's conclusion.

Transnationalism, in confounding the assumed identity among culture, politics, and economics, commonly reconfigures the ways we conceive of the world. For example, Katharyne Mitchell's analysis of transnational capital and Canadian multiculturalism focuses on Vancouver, where supporters of development have accused their slow-growth opponents of racism for objecting to luxury condominiums marketed exclusively in Hong Kong: "[The] attempt to shape multiculturalism can be seen as an attempt to gain hegemonic control over concepts of race and nation in order to further expedite Vancouver's integration into the international networks of global capitalism" (1996, 223). Yet, as *Fire* and *The Wedding Banquet* demonstrate, discourses of multiculturalism that attempt to mediate conflicts between race and nation can do so only if the role of women is not questioned. The subject of women's duties to the family and the state are taken up in the next chapter.

CHAPTER 8

Paying Lip Service

Narrators in *Surname Viet Given Name Nam* and *The Joy Luck Club*

> I began to write stories using all the Englishes I grew up with: the English I spoke to my mother, which for lack of a better term might be described as "simple"; the English she used with me, which for lack of a better term might be described as "broken"; my translation of her Chinese, which could certainly be described as "watered down"; and what I imagined to be her translation of her Chinese if she could speak in perfect English, her internal language, and for that I sought to preserve the essence, but neither an English nor a Chinese structure. I wanted to capture what language ability tests can never reveal: her intent, her passion, her imagery, the rhythms of her speech and the nature of her thoughts.
> —Amy Tan, "Mother Tongue"

> Languages are not strangers to one another, but are, a priori and apart from all historical relationships, interrelated in what they want to express.—Walter Benjamin, "The Task of the Translator"

It has been the goal of this book to examine the ways that Asian American cinema signifies on cinematic discourses, the conventions and traditions that govern the legibility of movies and supposedly ensure their objectivity. The movies that I've examined are very much aware of their implication in cinematic discourses, which is to say, these makers are aware of how their subjectivities have been constituted (to a greater or lesser extent) by cinema. Another way to put this is to note that each of these movies uncomfortably bears the burden of representation. Asian American movies are still few and far between, so that each movie labors under the expectation that it will represent the totality of "the Asian American experience." No movie can do so much. Nor do any of these movies do so little: each speaks to much more than (an) Asian American experience.

These issues are, of course, connected by *darstellen* and *vertreten,* aesthetic representation and political representation. Every aesthetic decision is also political: every choice about how to say something affects those who are spoken for. Trinh T. Minh-ha's decision to employ actors to reenact interviews conducted several years earlier and many thousands of miles away calls attention to the presumed immediacy of the interview, highlighting its mediation. Speaking of *Surname Viet Given Name Nam,* Linda Peckham notes, "The artificial subject points to the absence of the 'real' speaker, an absence that suggests internment, censorship and death, as well as the survival of a witness, a record—a history" (1989, 33). To make a film, whether a documentary or fiction, is to translate human experience into a text; in Peckham's words, it is to make a speaker into "a record—a history." No text can hope to depict (darstellen) human experience in its wholeness, but can only speak for it (vertreten).

The paradoxes of representation are multiplied when a movie takes on the task of translating speech or adapting a text.[1] A feature film adapted from a novel is, in a sense, a representation of that novel, but the immediacy of the cinematic signifier suggests a closer relationship to the depicted events and characters than the novel could hope to evoke (in George Bluestone's [1957] words, whereas linguistic signifiers bear a conceptual relationship to their signifieds, photographic signifiers share perceptual similarities with their signifieds). So, although we might conceive of a cinematic adaptation as twice removed from the events that it depicts (the diegesis it constructs), cinema's representational immediacy serves to obscure that mediation. A similar dynamic is evident when a literary or cinematic text attempts to marshal a multiplicity of voices to convey diverse perspectives: the more diverse the voices, the more the text that contains them is authenticated as a representation of those voices. Such a movie or book may intend to articulate the limits of its ability to represent, but the filmgoer or reader will receive such a text as a unified whole unless the text's discursive strategies are continually foregrounded and problematized. Amy Lawrence notes, "The ideal of a coherent, unified text mirrors the fantasy of a coherent unified spectator" (1992, 179). The spectator's desire for unity, what Christian Metz (1982) calls the passion for perceiving, is served by cinematic conventions that, for example, translate foreign speech via subtitles; spectatorial frustration with a text that neglects or withholds translation arises from the inability to become one with the text.

In this chapter, I seek to compare the different strategies that the makers of *Surname Viet Given Name Nam* (1989) and *The Joy Luck Club* (1993) employed in adapting books for the screen. In the first film, an interrogation of cinematic convention serves to affirm the inadequacy of cinematic representation; the second film exploits cinematic conventions to resolve a complicated set of narrative arcs into a single narrative through-line. *Surname*'s narrative fragmentation refuses to articulate a unified notion of Vietnam or Vietnamese womanhood; such a strategy is especially disturbing to an exile community that turns to film to construct an image of its homeland. By contrast, *The Joy Luck Club* was promoted as a film in which Chinese American women could see themselves reflected.[2] That marginalized Asian American communities should desire to see themselves represented as coherent, centered subjectivities is not surprising (as we saw in Chapter 7). Metadiscursive movies that depict the difficulty of constructing coherent narratives from fragmented histories are, in a sense, telling their audiences what they already know and in that sense are distinctly unpleasurable.

The Wedding Banquet proposed that Taiwanese nationalist identity is maintained through the appreciation of traditional practices (the banquet) and arts (such as calligraphy); *From Hollywood to Hanoi* suggests that the filmmaker's father turns to Vietnamese poetry and folklore to preserve Vietnamese culture in exile. *Surname Viet Given Name Nam* likewise describes the preservation of traditional values, emphasizing the ways such diasporic practices have become commodified, as in a Vietnamese American beauty pageant. Commodification tends to arrest identities in motion, in large part by making ethnicity available for consumption both by diasporic Asians and by U.S. culture at large. Multicultural consumption involves translation, the adaptation of Asian traditions for diasporic contexts, and it is the paradox of translation that it arrests tradition as it distorts it. A number of cinematic conventions attempt to ameliorate the distortions inherent in linguistic translation, literary adaptation, cultural transmission, and multicultural consumption; Trinh T. Minh-ha's *Surname Viet Given Name Nam* evinces a distrust of cinematic conventions akin to that expressed by *Bontoc Eulogy* and *On Cannibalism* (discussed in Chapter 1).

Surname Viet Given Name Nam

Trinh Thi Minh-ha was born in Hanoi in 1952 and grew up in Saigon.[3] She left Vietnam in 1970 at the age of seventeen, arriving at Wilmington College in Ohio before training as a composer and ethnomusicologist at the University of Illinois, where she earned both an MFA and a PhD. From 1977 to 1980 she taught music at the Institut National des Arts in Dakar; she returned to Senegal in 1981 to shoot her first 16mm film, *Reassemblage* (1982), a film not "about" but "near by" Senegal. She completed the manuscript for *Woman Native Other* (1989) in 1983; over the course of the next six years it was rejected by thirty-three presses and eventually published in 1989, virtually concurrent with the first screenings of *Surname Viet Given Name Nam. Woman Native Other* includes pointed critiques of conventional ethnographic practice, critiques that Trinh had put into practice with *Reassemblage* and continued with *Naked Spaces: Living Is Round* (1985). Trinh followed *Surname Viet Given Name Nam* with *Shoot for the Contents* (1991) on China. The latter film evolved out of a project that examined India and China; in *Cinema Interval,* Trinh describes Vietnam as "the site where Indian and Chinese cultures meet" (1999, 201). According to Kaliss, *Surname* and *Shoot for the Contents* initated a series of films about " 'civilization and culture' that will move on to India and Europe and 'explore the relation between video and film' " (1989, 30). In 1995, Trinh released her first 35mm film, *A Tale of Love,* a narrative feature centering on a Vietnamese American woman named Kieu. In addition to teaching women's studies and film at Berkeley and San Francisco State, Trinh has written and edited many books and journals in French and English. Many of her books and virtually all of her films were produced in collaboration with her husband, Jean-Paul Bourdier.

Surname Viet Given Name Nam was germinated when Trinh came across Mai Thu Van's book, *Viêtnam: Un peuple, des voix* (1983) in a bookstore in France. Mai was born in New Caledonia; her mother was part of a Vietnamese village that had rebelled against French rule and had consequently been sent to the nickel mines (15). Mai arrived in Paris at age twenty-three in the mid-1960s to work and study (18). In the fall of 1978 she traveled to Vietnam to research Vietnamese women (20); it took her several years to earn the trust of the women she worked with (most of the interviews included in the book date from 1981–1982). She translated the interviews into French and published the book in Paris in 1983.

In deciding to "adapt" the interviews in Mai's book, Trinh undertook the somewhat unintuitive task of restaging interviews, interviews that had been conducted in Vietnamese and published in French. Trinh now proposed to reenact the interviews, translating them yet again and casting first-generation Vietnamese American women, most of whom spoke English as a second or third language. In a 1989 interview, she stated: "In the casting process, it was important for me to hear about their own life stories before I decided on the voices that they would be incorporating. Within the range of their personal experiences, which were sometimes worse than those they were reenacting, they could drift in and out of their roles without too much pain. But in selecting them for who they are rather than simply for who they can play, I was not so much looking for authenticity as I was interested in seeing how they would draw the line between the differing fictions of living and acting" (1992, 194). Woven through the interviews is super-8 footage shot by Trinh, documentary stock footage, Vietnamese folks songs and sayings, and translated Vietnamese poetry; the sum is a poetic essay on women in North and South Vietnam and the United States.

Viêtnam: Un peuple, des voix includes Mai's essays on socialism and the everyday life of Vietnamese women, but the lion's share of its pages are devoted to interviews. Mai includes conversations with eight women labeled "Les voix du Nord," voices of the North, conducted in and around Hanoi. Another section includes interviews with seven women conducted in Ho Chi Minh City, labeled "Paroles du Sud," words of the South. An interview with Phan Thi An, president of the Vietnamese Women's Union (l'Union des femmes du Viêtnam), divides the two sections; unlike the other interviews, this one is in essay form. The book is illustrated with photos, some of which might depict the interviewees, for example, a photo of women in a hair salon precedes the interview with "Nhung, 23 ans, coiffeuse." However, these photos may simply be loosely associated with the text (and thus comparable to Trinh's use of stock footage and poetry in *Surname*).

For her film, Trinh selected two women each from the North and South. In the end, she decided to use two doctors, a medical cadre, and a foreign embassy restaurant worker. In an interview with Isaac Julien and Laura Mulvey, she admits that her final choices were not as diverse as she had initially planned: "These women are helping other women—devoting their skill to relieving not only the physical but the psychological pains of other women—[making] them stand out as those whose interactions with women's bodies and mental health allow them to evaluate women's condition with both depth and scope" (1992, 203). In selecting a representative sample of the interviews collected in Mai's book (already a representative sample of the "many voices" of Vietnam), Trinh contends with documentary's foundation on synecdoche, the use of a part to represent the whole.

In staging these interviews for the film, the questions and interjections of the interviewer were edited out. In some cases, the questions were incorporated into the answers, as when Cat Tien says, "You asking me if there are social services to help them? You must be dreaming!" In Mai's book, Cat Tien responds, "Vous rêvez chère Madame . . ." when Mai asks, "Y a-t-il des services sociaux pour les aider?" (1983, 176). By referring to an absent interlocutor, such dialogue calls attention to the textual mediation of the interviews, referring not just to Mai's book but to the original interviews on which the book was based—the ur-text of the ur-text that germinated Trinh's film.[4]

Surname's overall form is quite simple. The first half of the film is devoted to staged interviews; after a brief voice-over interlude in which Trinh discusses her rationale for selecting and framing the interviews this way, the second half of the film is devoted to "real" interviews with the women who performed the reenactments. Stock documentary footage of women in Vietnam is intercut throughout the film, mostly in the first half, and footage of Vietnamese American women is intercut mostly in the second half. Poems and folk songs are featured throughout the film; the poems are generally presented as intertitles in English translation, and Vietnamese songs are generally translated in English subtitles. Although this overall structure is simple, the absence of explicit signposts, the delayed revelation that the early interviews are staged, and the fluidity with which the film intercuts between texts and various sources of footage all tend to confuse filmgoers on their first encounter with the film. But on close examination, the various logics that govern the juxtapositions emerge.

Each staged interview is introduced in the same manner. A sequence of folk song or poetry illustrated by stock footage (allusively associated with the words on the soundtrack) precedes each interview; over the course of the poem or song, the footage is increasingly step-printed, which is to say that the footage is increasingly mediated as the poem or song progresses.[5] The footage next yields to a series of stock photographs over which the camera pans; however, unlike traditional documentaries in which the camera moves fluidly to isolate narratively significant detail, here the camera moves in abrupt, jerky movements. This brief interlude is then followed

their children exposed to war, deprivations epidemics and diseases? The woman is alone, she lives alone, she raises her children alone. She gives birth alone. It's a sea of solitude! The revolution has allowed the woman access to the working world. She works to deprive herself better, to eat less. She has to get used to poverty.

Surname Viet Given Name Nam. Redundant and obtrusive text calls attention to subtleties of transcription and problematics of translation.

Surname Viet Given Name Nam. Unconventional mise-en-scène for a "talking head" sequence.

by an English intertitle that functions as an epigraph, excerpting a brief passage from one of Mai's interviews, and which identifies the interview that follows by name, age, and profession of the interviewee, and the date of the interview conducted by Mai.

The mise-en-scène of the interviews offers the first clue that they are staged; for example, Ly is shown preparing food in an abstract space featuring stylized lighting, while the camera scans away from Thu Van's face to focus on her hands. The differing degrees of facility with English and the differing abilities as "actors" also hint that these interviews are not genuine. As the film progresses, the stagings become increasingly mediated: Thu Van paces from left to right, occasionally leaving the frame, and her words are superimposed on the image; Ly faces away from the camera.

The second half of the film consists of relatively conventional interviews with the actors: they speak to an off-screen interviewer in fluent English and Vietnamese (we occasionally hear Trinh or Bourdier interject a question), and these interviews are intercut with footage of the women at work or play. During the "documentary" footage the women avoid looking into the camera as they go about their business, consistent with standard documentary practice. In addition to the four women who reenact the interviews on screen, we also meet the young woman who provides the American-accented English voice-overs; instead of speaking to the off-screen filmmaker, Lan engages a friend in conversation. Thus, whereas in the first half of the film Lan is featured off-screen, as a voice-over narrator, in the second half she is the one character who does not interact with an off-screen voice.[6]

In a sense, the second half of *Surname* can be understood as a separate film that refers to the first.[7] Kim and Yen both talk about their motivations for agreeing to appear in the film, and Yen also mentions the difficulty she experienced in setting aside time to make the film while simultaneously working, caring for her family, and organizing her younger brother's wedding (which we see briefly on screen). Kim and Yen both situate acting in the larger context of film production and reception, as when Kim reports that a friend commented "Maybe you'll act so well that the Americans will notice you and you'll be a Hollywood star in the future." Thus the interviews in the second half call attention to the material conditions surrounding the film's production, conditions that are hinted at in the mise-en-scène of the film's first half. Of course, there are other elements that can be traced across the film, for example, letters from one of Trinh's sisters, read by Trinh on the soundtrack in both halves of the film. These letters, and footage of the wedding of one of Trinh's younger sisters, serve to inscribe Trinh's own "extracurricular" life in a manner similar, if not precisely akin to the lives of the actors.

The stylized mise-en-scène and framing of the film's first half convey the ways that meaning exceeds translation and representation in documentary film generally; paradoxically, these techniques of estrangement call attention to Trinh's intervention, metonymically representing her control in selecting and framing interviews. Trinh has somewhat less control over her actors in the second half. In an interview with Laleen Jayamane and Anne Rutherford, Trinh reveals, "I asked the women to choose how they wanted to be presented as we moved to their own stories. The choices they came up with were often disturbing to me. I was expecting something that relates intimately to their daily existence and instead. . . . For example, one woman wanted to be seen at a fish pond" (1992, 167). Trinh's discom-

Surname Viet Given Name Nam. Khien at the fish pond.

fort with the fish pond relates to her initial desire to show the women in their everyday activities; speaking about the film after its completion, she used this anecdote to illustrate the ways certain conventions of documentary representation structure her own experience, namely, her initial belief that the truth of Khien's life would be better represented by showing her working-class home and not her desire for a space of serenity: "I realized afterwards . . . how important this fish pond is, both for her personally and for the film. She is a working-class woman living at the time in a very small apartment with a large family, and having always been such a richly significative symbol in Asian cultures, the fish pond seems to point here to a dream space, a space of meditation where you can rest and retreat from the pressure of daily work . . . when you want something true to someone's life, what you get usually goes much further than the mere details of that person's daily existence" (168). In this interview, Trinh seems to forget for a moment that the artificiality of cinema precludes the possibility of capturing "daily existence." Indeed, the institution of cinema has often been described by Western commentators in terms similar to those that Trinh uses to describe the fish pond: a dream space, an escape from the mundane. As an independent filmmaker, Trinh thus reveals her desire to make cinema speak the truth of Vietnamese American women's lives, even as she is aware that cinematic convention traffics not in truth but in truth effects.

In the interview, Trinh suggests that she was forced to adapt to the women's self-presentation. She connects the selections of setting to the women's dress in the second half of the film.[8] She notes that progressive middle-class Americans (i.e., the audience for political documentary) have internalized a convention of dressing down to signify solidarity with the working class (a practice that working-class audiences might read ironically):

> There is no legacy of pride in dressing down among poor people or among people coming from Third World nations. On the contrary, the latter dress up when they are in a public situation—like being on film and being watched by thousands of spectators. So the women in my film also chose to dress up. I was time and again disconcerted by the combination of showy colors, but finally I stood by their choices because that's how they wished to be presented. As a result, the question of dressing became one of the threads of the film, as it wove in quite pertinently with the question of (de)territorializing the woman's body and Vietnam as a nation. So all in all, the person who was very narrow-minded in this instance was myself, not the women. (1992, 168)

In these interviews, Trinh emphasizes the evolution of the film project. In a sense, she suggests that the project has a life of its own (her initial resistance to the women's attire was ultimately untrue to the film), but in another sense, she is simply using the occasion of the interviews to ascribe a split between Trinh as on-set director and Trinh as editor.[9] The metaphor of weaving implies that she did not have complete control over the colors provided by her collaborators, but just as the weaver ultimately determines the pattern based on the available materials, so Trinh determines the shape of the film by selecting and juxtaposing elements from the interviews.

Although *Surname Viet Given Name Nam* may call attention to processes of textual mediation, the film does not foreground its own construction to the same extent that it problematizes translation. The actors may have selected their clothes and suggested some settings, but surely Trinh influenced the selection of some of the locations. For example, whose idea was it for Lan and her friend Sue, both students at Berkeley, to climb trees? These images are accompanied by Ho Xuan Huong's poem "The Jackfruit" (in Nguyen Ngoc Bich's translation) on the soundtrack, narrated by Lan. Was the poem recorded before this scene was shot, or did the images provide the inspiration to incorporate the poem?

Interspersed throughout the film are scenes of Khien and Hien in the audience of an outdoor festival; it may be the San Jose Miss Vietnam 1988 Pageant that is likewise interspersed throughout. It seems unlikely that Trinh came upon this pageant fortuitously. When one contestant answers a question about what Vietnamese values should be preserved in the United

Surname Viet Given Name Nam. Lan mimics a jackfruit hanging from a branch.

States, Trinh juxtaposes step-printed footage of the pageant with a folk saying about the "three deferments and four virtues" that should be observed by proper Vietnamese women. Did Trinh suggest that Khien and Hien attend this pageant, did they attend coincidentally, or did Trinh tag along after they had already decided to attend? Trinh may have been thinking of this pageant as well as some of the women's choices for self-representation when she said, "I have problems with forms of presentation that tend to commodify ethnicity" (1992, 194). How can a filmmaker critique ideologies without condemning the people who reproduce those ideologies? One might read Trinh as exposing the lack of sophistication of the women she recruited for her film; I for one take her admission that "[these choices of self-representation] embarrass me . . . at least initially, but afterwards I understood, because they are so much a part of myself as well" (194) as her acknowledgment that she is interpellated and implicated by the commodification of ethnicity as well.

Faithfulness to the Text

Trinh's film argues that a critique of ethnic commodification requires a simultaneous critique of cinematic conventions; however, *Surname Viet Given Name Nam* also reproduces ethnic commodification, as Trinh's ambivalence about the ways her interviewees chose to represent themselves reveals. Can conventional narrative films (i.e., movies that do not critique cinematic convention) also incorporate an ambivalent critique of ethnic commodification? I want to move now to a discussion of *The Joy Luck Club,* a feature-length narrative film that on the surface has little in common with *Surname.* However, in deploying multiple narratives about Chinese and Chinese American women, *The Joy Luck Club* invokes many of the same discourses about representation, representativeness, and women's negotiation of migration between Asian and U.S. patriarchies. *The Joy Luck Club* features multiple narrators who invoke folk sayings to make sense of their experiences, and if we factor in discourses about casting (ranging from the filmmakers' criteria for verisimilitude to affinities the actors express between their lives and those of the characters they play) we have an extratextual equivalent to the metatextual second half of *Surname.* If *The Joy Luck Club* is less critical of ethnic commodification than is *Surname,* this is ultimately due to its uninterrogated discursive structure: whereas *Surname* reveled in the multivocality of the book that inspired it, the film of *The Joy Luck Club* attempts to construct a linear narration from the multiplicity of speaking voices that make up the novel.

Trinh took the discrete interviews from Mai's book and intercut among them throughout the first half of *Surname;* screenwriter Ronald Bass suggested doing the opposite with *The Joy Luck Club,* taking the novel's various short stories and reorganizing them. Amy Tan's best-selling novel[10] consists of four groupings of four short stories, with each section introduced by an italicized story written in pseudo-mythic style (characters are not named but called "the mother" and "the daughter"). The enunciative present of the novel takes place after the death of Suyuan Woo, the founder of the club; her stories are narrated by her daughter June.[11] Otherwise, the first group of stories is narrated by four Chinese immigrant women and emphasizes their childhood; the second group is narrated by their Chinese American daughters, who tell generally comic stories of their own childhood; the third features the daughters narrating tales of their adulthood, mostly comic stories about their romantic relationships; and the final section returns us to the mothers, who tell mostly tragic tales from their adult years. In their screenplay, Bass and Tan reshuffle the stories, taking the four stories narrated by Lindo and Waverly and grouping them together. They also integrated two of the italicized stories (attributing them to different characters) and invented a party where the seven surviving women mingle as a framing narrative.

The press kit for *The Joy Luck Club* emphasizes—and most articles about the film faithfully report—that Bass agreed to work on the screenplay on the condition that all sixteen stories in Tan's novel were retained in the film, and indeed early drafts of the screenplay do feature elements from all sixteen stories. This plan was abandoned soon after producer Patrick Markey (representing Disney's Hollywood Pictures division) came aboard and cut two of the stories—"The Moon Lady" and "Half and Half"—because, taking place on a lake and at the beach, they would have been extremely expensive and time-consuming to shoot (Hajari, 1993). Furthermore, for unstated reasons, only a fragment of the story "The Voice from the Wall" was retained, with the result that the Ying Ying–Lena storyline was severely compromised.[12] The artistic success of the film's narrative structure can be debated, yet the film generally handles the complexity of its shifting point-of-view structure with aplomb. The screenplay makes canny use of flashbacks, falsely cueing the audience that we are returning to the enunciative present of the party in order to facilitate the narrative shifts from the mothers to the daughters. For example, Lindo's tale of her childhood betrothal is motivated by an interior monologue. When the story ends, we return not to the party but to the recent past; this return is facilitated by a close-up of Lindo staring abstractly ahead, echoing the beginning of the flashback. After shifting to Waverly's story—within which Lindo narrates a story (this time motivated by Waverly's presence as interlocutor)—we return to Lindo at the party after much time has elapsed, again lost in a reverie. Lindo smiles as if she had been replaying a cherished moment with her daughter in her mind. If the entire preceding sequence represents Lindo's memory, how are we to account for Waverly's narration in the midst of Lindo's story? *The Joy Luck Club* presents many narrative conundrums like this one, but these moments pass by barely noticed due to the forward progress of the narrative. Whereas *Surname* foregrounds its enunciation by calling attention to the artificiality of shifts from interview to interview, *The Joy Luck Club* attempts to disguise these shifts, for, generally speaking, commercial cinema prefers not to draw attention to its enunciative techniques.

Identifying with *The Joy Luck Club*

An article that appeared in the *New York Times* the Sunday before its New York opening called attention to another narrative challenge for *The Joy Luck Club:* its large cast. "It is in fact difficult to assemble a large cast in which one character is not mistaken for another. The conventional solution is to pepper a cast with blonds, redheads and brunettes and different ethnic types. But the 'Joy Luck Club' does not have that liberty."[13] Faced with casting over fifty female roles (in two languages, English and Mandarin)—a task made more difficult by the fact that in some cases three actors of different ages would portray the same character at different stages in her life, not to mention the aspiration that mothers and daughters would bear some resemblance—Wayne Wang devised two rules when casting the film:

> First, no Caucasians would play roles written for Asians. "During the 'Miss Saigon' controversy," he said, "there were a lot of people who said, 'Talent is talent, and anybody can play any character with makeup.' But it never happens that an Asian actress can go out for a major Caucasian role and get it. Until that day comes, there is no equity, so it was important to me that these roles all go to Asians."
>
> Rule two was that actresses of various Asian backgrounds would be considered for specifically Chinese roles. "Because there are so few good roles for Asians, I didn't want to eliminate Japanese or Vietnamese or Koreans," Mr. Wang explained. "The important thing was that they felt right for the role and would fit into the ensemble." (Avins, 1993, 2:14)

Wang's argument, as presented by the *Times,* is based purely on equity. He never says that a non-Asian actor cannot play an Asian role, only that such casting denies opportunities to Asian actors. However, by formulating the argument this way, Wang sidesteps the implications of casting non-Chinese in *The Joy Luck Club;* for example, when non-Asian filmmakers cast Rosalind Chao as a Korean on *M*A*S*H* or as a Japanese on *Star Trek: The Next Generation,* many Asian Americans are displeased. Wang goes on to argue that there are other aspects of performance that might affect ethnic realism—for example, he admits that an actress was not cast because her speech rhythms were more Japanese than Chinese—conceding that realism is the ultimate deciding factor but leaving open the question of who defines realism.[14] After all, did Wang foresee the complaints of some Mandarin speakers that all the Chinese characters in *The Joy Luck Club* spoke with Beijing accents?[15]

These and other discourses speak to the appropriateness and ability of the various actors cast in *The Joy Luck Club.* Promotional materials for narrative films often stress affinities between actor and character, laying claim to performative authenticity. For example, *Parade Magazine* reported that Ming-Na Wen brought her mother with her when she shot scenes in Shanghai ("A

Mother and Daughter," 1993), and in the *New York Times* Wen described her first encounter with the novel: "For the first time, I felt I was reading something that was completely talking to me" (Avins, 1993, 2:14).[16] It is commonly reported that the narratives of ethnic "cross-over" films resonate with ethnic actors in a way that mainstream projects do not. By mentioning the amateur actors who attended open casting calls for the film, publicity for *The Joy Luck Club* lays claim both to the authenticity of these narrative representations and to their scarcity in the cinematic marketplace, simultaneously affirming that the narrative is original (insofar as Chinese American women's experiences have been marginalized by mainstream film) and commonplace (in telling a story that all Chinese American women know).[17] In the film's press kit, casting director Heidi Levitt states, "Every woman who came in had a story, whether it was about a sister, aunt or grandmother, that reflected these characters," and San Francisco casting director Robin Gurland commented, "When I initially read the book and then the screenplay, I thought that the characters' tragic lives were unique. . . . If anything the stories in the novel were minimized compared to the ones I heard from the women who auditioned."[18] Indeed, even the story's central narrative is attested to: in an interview, Wang referred to an extra who, overhearing the dialogue in the film's final scene, reported that she had left her baby during the war (Tibbetts, 1994, 5).[19] Furthermore, actor Kieu Chinh reported that abandoning the babies reminded her of leaving her father behind when she left North Vietnam. (According to Baker [1993], Wang encouraged Chinh to perform this scene in Vietnamese if it allowed her to draw on her experiences.)

The notion of auditors identifying with the stories they are told is alluded to in the film, when Rose tells her husband, "I died sixty years ago . . . for my daughter's sake." Rose's identification with her grandmother seems less bizarre in an early draft of the screenplay, where the writers suggest that the same actor should be cast as the adult Rose and as her own grandmother in the stories related by Rose's mother, An-mei.[20] This story is based on the life of Tan's own grandmother, named Jing-mei (Tan, 1991a), a name that Tan gave to *Joy Luck Club*'s central character, Jing-mei Woo (also known as June). Like June/Jing-mei, Tan has both an English and a Chinese name: Amy and An-mei. Many critics have assumed that June is patterned after Tan (e.g., Tseo, 1996), in part because June's stories draw from Tan's experiences with the piano and working as a business writer.[21] Thus, readers familiar with the biography of Amy Tan can interpret her as June, Rose's mother An-mei (who shares Tan's Chinese name), and Rose (whose grandmother is based on Tan's grandmother).[22] Perhaps this is what Tan meant when she said, "All Chinese people are family to one another in some unexplainable way" (1989b, 302).

If I find assertions about the authenticity of the film (its connection to "real women's experiences") problematic, it is because they echo an assertion in the narrative itself: that daughters *can* go home again, returning to the motherland and indeed to unity with their mothers.[23] Following a dinner party where the Woo family hosts the Jongs, June comes to realize that her anger with her mother results from misunderstanding her mother's words. Suyuan had stated that Waverly and June had differing styles, which June interpreted to mean that Waverly was more stylish; in the kitchen, Suyuan makes clear that she means that June is morally superior to Waverly. Suyuan caps off this scene by telling her daughter "I *see you,*" meaning she sees who June really is. When mother and daughter embrace, it is as if June is able to return from the realm of the Lacanian symbolic to that of the imaginary, where visual apprehension (being seen) supplies a truth that cannot be achieved by language (due to verbal misunderstanding).[24] *The Joy Luck Club* enacts a fantasy of reconciliation and reunification, and this fantasy is echoed whenever the film's promotion asserts an identity between actor and character.

There remains, however, one identification that does not deny historical rupture. Tamlyn Tomita reveals her keen awareness of her position in Hollywood when she is quoted in the film's press kit: "Ming-Na, Lauren, Rosalind and I often vie for the same projects because we're all Asian women of the same age range. . . . And Lisa, Kieu, Tsai and France are the women we grew up watching, they were our role models in the industry. To bring us all together and to hear each other's stories about surviving in the industry—those are secrets being passed between us." By mentoring the actors who play their daughters, *The Joy Luck Club*'s veteran actors become metaphoric mothers. It is, of course, a sign of commercial cinema's recuperative power that an anecdote about the limited roles Hollywood offers Asian American women is deployed to promote a movie coproduced by Walt Disney and Oliver Stone.

Although many of the promotional discourses for *The Joy Luck Club* called attention to the film's production, these narratives did not emphasize the film as a mediation but its continuity with Tan's novel and with the experiences of Asian American women (the sole exception being Tomita's commentary, which pointed not just to the material circumstances governing the production of *The Joy Luck Club* but indeed to the structure of the mainstream film industry generally). These discourses of continuity were in keeping with *The Joy Luck Club*'s fantasy of cross-generational reconciliation, of unity across historical discontinuity; in short, the affirmation of the movie as an effective and accurate translation of the book is part and parcel of the story's governing logic of reunion. By contrast, *Surname Viet Given Name Nam* self-reflexively highlights the mediation of translation and adaptation, thereby emphasizing the discontinuity of the film from the experiences to which it refers. The film's wariness of translation preserves the fundamental discontinuity of the women's experiences that it represents. Thus, movies that signify on cinematic conventions (designed to assure legibility, veracity, and authority) work against ethnic commodification, and movies that aspire to transparency of technique promote the consumption of ethnic difference. The words Ming-Yuen S. Ma's video *Slanted Visions* uses to describe Oriental cooking techniques in a parody of televised cooking shows—"conceived through ancient wisdom, perfected by generations of practice"—could just as easily describe cinematic conventions. The cooking show, like promotional discourses surrounding mainstream movies, purports to reveal the secrets behind the construction of complex cultural products, but in actuality affirms the mastery of the chef. Rather than highlighting the artificiality of a movie's effects, promotional discourses flatter the spectator by sharing the filmmaker's expertise, aligning the spectator with the author figure. By contrast, Trinh T. Minh-ha's film attempts to construct the filmmaker as *reader,* remobilizing these texts for her own purposes, setting identities in motion.

Afterword

The Asian American Muse

> We have been trying to theorise identity as constituted, not outside but within representation; and hence of cinema, not as a second-order mirror held up to reflect what already exists, but as that form of representation which is able to constitute us as new kinds of subjects, and thereby enable us to discover places from which to speak. —Stuart Hall, "Cultural Identity and Diaspora"

> But then the cinema has never stopped being a palace of dreams. Even in the serious cinema there is some emphasis on the ideal. Imagine casting a film with only ugly or even, just ordinary-looking actors. The cinema cannot replace the novel or autobiography as the precise and serious medium of the age while it is still too intent on charming its audience! —Hanif Kureishi, *Sammy and Rosie Get Laid: The Script and the Diary*

The previous three chapters discuss a number of movies that attempt to articulate liminal Asian American identities, arguing that these redefinitions of subjectivity were typically interpreted from putatively secure and stable positions that ignored the play of these representations. As cinematic identity grows less and less secure, audiences frequently respond in incomplete fashion, attempting to locate cinematic identity firmly within the bounds of comprehensible, stable, and unchanging identity formations. Although cinema can promote hybridity by bringing formerly distant cultures into contact, historically cinema has been more concerned with promoting national identities. In this reception context, movies that articulate ambiguous Asian American identity formations threaten the discursive stability of the nation-state; articulations of the complexity of Asian American identity are branded as disloyal or anti-American.

Assimilationist narratives tend to pose the dilemmas of identity in terms of a choice between the United States and the country of origin, conventionally and conveniently dramatized as a choice between individuality and the family. Such narratives imply that identity is a matter of cultural choice on the part of the child (even as race is constructed as immutable) and assume that the parents' identities are fixed. But what of the parents' choice to start a family in the first place? Consider the act of adoption as an alternative family narrative, one that involves the parents' choice to incorporate an individual into the family, potentially contending with cultural and/or racial diversity. The phenomenon of international adoption calls into question the correspondence of nation and family that Frantz Fanon identified as characteristic of civilization.

Chinese babies (mostly girls) began to be adopted in large numbers by Americans in the last decade of the twentieth century, concurrent with the coming-of-age of Korean Americans and Vietnamese Americans adopted in the wake of U.S. military involvement in Asia. Asian adoptee makers thus arrived in a cultural context already receptive to the narratives they had to offer, but, as with the Chinese American makers who attempted to find their way across oft-traversed discursive terrain, Asian adoptee makers have often risked reproducing hegemonic discourses of essentialism and assimilation. By way of conclusion, I want to consider how the borders among Asian American, African American, and white subjectivities are taken up by two distinct sets of adoption narratives: documentaries and memoirs about Korean adoptees raised by white American families, and feature films about Asian children adopted by African American families. These diverse films and videos succeed in putting identities in motion to the extent that they problematize racial discourses, but when these movies slip into essentialism, they arrest the motion of Asian American cinematic identity.

Most of the movies made by Korean American adoptees have focused on the search for Korean parents. Kimberly SaRee Tomes's *Looking for Wendy* (1998) focuses on the adoptee's U.S. identity: Tomes muses on the nature of hybridity using the metaphor of her adoptive father's research in genetics. Her video is atypical, however; the majority of Korean American adoptee movies have dealt with journeys to Korea. Both the experimental film *Great Girl* (Kim Su Theiler, 1994) and the dramatic short *Subrosa* (2000, made by Korean Canadian Helen Lee, not herself an adoptee) depict adoptees searching for their mothers, and *Searching for Go-Hyang* (Tammy Tolle, 1998) documents two sisters who successfully locate their mother and siblings. Two more documentaries, Nathan Adolfson's *Passing Through* (1998) and Deann Borshay Liem's *First Person Plural* (2000), also document journeys to Korea, and, in addition, emphasize the largely supportive reactions of the videomakers' U.S. families.

Although exceptionally intimate and frequently introspective, none of these movies is sentimental: none of the adoptees achieves unmediated reconciliation and reunion with their Korean families. But if Korean American adoptive identity is represented in its complexity, the desire for wholeness that seems to motivate the search for biological parents suggests a longing for an essential subjectivity. In Borshay's *First Person Plural,* the videomaker's investigation of her Korean roots is prompted by a series of dreams, suggesting that her true identity is innate and cannot be repressed. Borshay discovers that her birth name is not Cha Jung Hee but Kang Ok Jin and that one of the Korean officials overseeing her adoption sent her to the United States in place of the girl that the Borshay family had sponsored. If the video at first hints that Borshay's U.S. identity is a construction and her "true" identity is Korean, her Korean identity is shown to be equally a construction, an uneasy hybrid of Cha and Kang. Her trip to Korea results in a renewed intimacy with her adoptive mother; rather than narrating a return to an essential Korean identity, the video instead charts the dynamic equilibrium of the videomaker's investments in the Kang and Borshay families (haunted by the specter of her identity as Cha).

Even as *First Person Plural* charts a journey of self-discovery, its emphasis on a dynamic equilibrium keeps identities in motion. All of these movies, whether the makers successfully locate their birth parents or not, are characterized by a certain lack of closure that preserves not just the contingency of the adoptee's subjectivity, but also the indeterminacy of the various points of identification (Asian American, Korean, etc.). Like most quest narratives, these protagonists journey outward in search of answers but ultimately achieve a measure of solace by turning inward.

The introspective nature of *First Person Plural* and the other autobiographical movies about adoption offers a striking contrast to the extroversion of a number of feature films about the adoption of Asian children by African American families. Thematizing the potential for Asian American identification with African Americans, these films depict an ongoing process of transformation for Asian Americans, but at the cost of essentializing African American subjectivities. *Fakin' da Funk* (Timothy A. Chey, 1997) centers on a Chinese boy adopted by an African American family in the South; when the family relocates to Los Angeles, the young man's mannerisms consternate everyone he meets. (A subplot follows a female Chinese exchange student hosted by another African American family.) *Catfish in Black Bean Sauce* (Chi Moui Lo, 2000) begins with a similar premise: two Vietnamese siblings are adopted by an African American family. The film explores the conflicts and jealousies that arise when the biological mother is located and brought to live with her now-grown children.

In depicting the development of Asian American subjectivity vis-à-vis African American cultural expression, these movies threaten to reify blackness: the stability of African American subjectivity is taken for granted. African American cultural expression is consumed (or colonized) by these Asian American characters, even as they decry the commodification of Asianness by U.S. culture at large. For example, the narrative climax of *Fakin' da Funk* is a high-stakes playground basketball game between the good guys and a drug dealer who wants to recruit Julian (the adoptee) as a bag boy. This exceedingly conventional narrative is indicative of the mainstream aspirations of this feature film, suitable for promotion by the machinery of mainstream film and video distribution (indeed, *Fakin' da Funk* aired on the USA cable television network and is distributed on the rental video market by Blockbuster). African American cultural production is not realized in its own complexity but is reduced to a stable point of identification for the Asian American protagonist.

A meaningful exploration of African American culture requires consideration of the historical processes that produced it. In the desire to identify with African American subjectivities, these films pay insufficient attention to the gaps between the experience of Asian Americans and that of African Americans. This is not to say that Asian American and African American histories are incommensurable; theorizing the gaps between those histories can be a productive process, but one that is necessarily dependent on first theorizing the gaps within the respective histories of Asian Americans and African Americans.

In the introduction to this volume I suggest that gaps in the cinematic representation of Asian Americans characterize Asian American film and video. Although Asian American cinema is necessarily concerned with historicity—situating itself in relation to historical discourses, specifying the contingency of the place from which it speaks—it does not follow that Asian American movies are all concerned with history, with the past.[1] Asian American identity cannot be constructed out of the mere recovery of discontinuous history, as Fanon suggests when he argues, "We must not therefore be content with delving into the past of a people in order to find coherent elements which will counteract colonialism's attempts to falsify and harm" (1973, 233). This is in part because, as I have argued, no such construction will ever be fully coherent, a point acknowledged by movies like *First Person Plural* and those of Yasui, Tanaka, and Tajiri, which inscribe the process of forgetting as well as the process of remembering.[2] More important, Fanon cautions us that coherent identities are not "out there" waiting to be discovered, but are actively constructed. This is particularly true for Asian Americans, who have been deliberately divided along ethnic and cultural lines in some cases (as on the Hawaiian plantations) and lumped together as "Orientals" or "Asiatics" in others (as when the Asiatic Exclusion League asserted that Indians were not Caucasian but Asiatic). The narration of these histories can be deployed to unite or divide Asian Americans; in other words, the act of narration constitutes Asian Americans.

Stuart Hall concludes his influential study of cinema's role in producing identity by noting that "black cinemas . . . construct those points of identification, those positionalities we call *in retrospect* our 'cultural identities'" (1994, 402; emphasis added). Hall argues that cinema is not a mirror that reflects cultural identities back to us; rather, cinema constructs those identities. This retrospective action suggests that cinematic texts always lag behind us, yet we have no words to describe where we are now, looking back on cinema; we are somewhere ahead of cinema, already in motion.

If the stereotypic discourse of mainstream cinema does not correspond with Asian American identity (even as it shapes Asian American self-perception), neither does Asian American cinematic discourse (which signifies on cinematic convention) correspond with Asian American identity. Because no movie lives up to the ideal cinematic text envisioned by its maker, we can hardly expect movies to live up to their audience. And yet, in attempting to articulate an artist's perspective of the world, movies strive for an ideal representation of the world and of their audience (who make up that world). The paradox, then, is that cinematic identity is always more fully realized than the identity of its audience and yet always inadequate to its audience. Asian American identity is like the muse who inspires the artist: the artwork is never equal to the beauty of the muse herself, and yet its beauty always exceeds that of the muse because she provides only the initial inspiration.

To study Asian American film and video in an attempt to locate Asian American identity would seem a misguided task: such a study attempts to reconstruct the artist's muse rather than interpret the text at hand. This volume avowedly attempts to understand the material constraints on the production and reception of Asian American film and video, constraints that prevent makers from fully realizing their goals. In a world where Asian American cinematic identity could be fully realized, the muse of Asian American cinema would vanish; but then, in a world in which our identities could be fully realized, there would be no need for art at all.

But in an important sense, this volume is indeed an attempt to reconstruct the Asian American muse. In the introduction I noted that identities are not located in movies themselves, but are mobilized within the spectator. This is because spectators do not absorb movies wholly unaltered, but create imaginary constructs for each movie, constructs that correspond to the text that we suppose each movie aspires to be; if my interpretation differs from yours, it is because we each interpret different aspirations for the movie at hand. This volume, then, is inspired not by Asian American film and video, but by this author's sense of what Asian American cinema aspires to be. In that sense, my quest has been to imagine the muse of Asian American makers, that force that inspires their work. If this book in turn inspires Asian American makers to refine their work (in an attempt to refine my characterization of the muse that inspires them), I would be well pleased. If this book inspires a more critical audience for Asian American film and video, it will have achieved its own ideal.

NOTES

Introduction: Locating Asian American Cinema in Discontinuity

1 Sigmund Freud coined the term "screen memories" to describe substitute memories that we deploy to cover up those "real" memories that are too unsettling. I am indebted to Doug Johnson for the notion of cinema as screen memory; the metaphor is also explored by Marita Sturken (1996).

2 Throughout this book, I use the terms "filmmaker" and "videomaker" when appropriate; in place of the clumsy "film- and videomaker" or when comparing a filmmaker and a videomaker, I use the term "maker."

3 "Self-identity needs to be continually reproduced and reassured precisely because it fails to secure belief. It fails because it cannot rely on a verifiably continuous history. One's own origin is both real and imagined" (Phelan, 1993, 4).

4 On the ways that gender is constituted through performative repetition, see Judith Butler's work, particularly *Gender Trouble* (1990a), whose conclusion broaches the subject of parodic repetition.

5 In "Of Mimicry and Man," Bhabha argues that the colonial subject's imperfect mimicry disrupts the colonizer's discourse and allows the colonial to speak. "The Other Question" describes the anxious repetition of the stereotype that reveals it to be a fantasy of the colonizer rather than an accurate depiction of the colonial; this stereotype can be exploited for it gives the colonial access to the illusions of racial difference that legitimate colonial rule. In "Signs Taken for Wonders," Bhabha asserts that the translation of the Bible into the colonial's language concedes the very difference that it wishes to disavow; according to Bhabha, it is that concession of difference that opens the text up to subversive reinterpretation. (All essays are included in Bhabha, 1994).

Judith Butler's argument that heteronormativity and gender hierarchies can be destabilized by parodying the repetition through which they operate parallels Bhabha's analysis of the subversion of colonial discourse (see 1990a).

6 Muñoz (1999, 11–12) draws on Michel Pêcheux's *Language, Semantics, and Ideology* (1982), which discusses the three modalities of the "*reduplication* constitutive of the subject of discourse" (i.e., Althusser's interpellation); (Pêcheux, 1982, 155–59).

7 See Elaine Kim's introduction to *Asian American Literature* (1982), and Yen

Le Espiritu's *Asian American Panethnicity* (1992) for discussions of the strategic use of pan-ethnic Asian American identity.

8 Katya Gibel Azoulay argues that much celebration of "multiplicity" is a postmodernist fantasy that ignores the lived experiences of African Americans; instead, Azoulay defines "black identities" with reference to the Jews: "Jewish identity in the Diaspora is not merely—or even primarily—a religious affiliation but, historically and philosophically, engages questions about cultural identity and political identity referring to centuries of anti-Semitism culminating in the Holocaust. . . . It is an existential tension between bridging universalism and particularism" (1996, 135). Azoulay's comparison is based in part on the parallels between slavery and the Holocaust, parallels that limit comparison to Asian American identity. However, her argument about a tension between cultural and political definitions of U.S. racial terminology is very similar to my discussion of Asian ethnicities as cultural terms and "Asian American" as a political term.

9 My formulation of Asian American identity is strongly indebted to Lisa Lowe's "Heterogeneity, Hybridity, Multiplicity: Marking Asian American Differences" (1991b), although we differ in nuance. For a further discussion of Lowe's essay, refer to Chapter 4.

Kent Ono's "Re/signing Asian American" (1995) explores the limitations of the term Asian American with particular attention to experiences that the term either ignores or suppresses. I agree with Ono's contention that the term Asian American often masks important differences in the name of solidarity; however, I contend that the term is always already problematic, and that the foregrounding of its inadequacies sufficiently destabilizes the term to permit the interplay of heterogeneous conceptions of identity. Nevertheless, I share Ono's concern that a term like Asian American—or, by extension, the singular term "identity"—can be deployed (intentionally or inadvertently) to quash dissent.

Resistence to coercive Asian American identity can be seen whenever the articulation of discontinuous history fails to convince a subgroup that they share political and historical commonality. At worst, pan-ethnic Asian American identity marks an additive pluralism, in which Chinese American and Japanese American history becomes a norm against which, for example, Southeast Asian and South Asian history is measured. For a critique of Asian American pluralism, see Koshy (1996); see also V. Nguyen (2002).

10 In this context, "to signify on cinematic convention" means "to call attention to how cinema functions." The term is related to "signifyin(g)," the African American cultural practice of manipulating language. See Gates's *The Signifying Monkey* (1988) for an application of the concept to African American literary criticism.

11 In film studies, production histories are often tainted by their association with author-centered criticism, itself devalued since Roland Barthes proclaimed the death of the author in 1968. Insofar as Barthes engaged in a critique of interpretations that used biography to authenticate certain readings, his proclamation is welcome. And yet the coincidence of the widespread championing of the death of the author at precisely the moment when many marginalized peoples were asserting that they could be authors as well has been often remarked on, as when Henry Louis Gates Jr. notes "While we readily accept, acknowledge, and partake of the critique of [the Western male] subject . . . to deny us the process of exploring and reclaiming our [black] subjectivity before we critique it is the critical version of the grandfather clause, the double privileging of categories that happen to be *preconstituted*" (1992, 35–36).

12 In 1996, a similar project resulted in *Tenderloin Stories.* In 1998, *Kelly Loves Tony,* another video diary overseen by Nakasako, was completed. In 1999, *a.k.a. Don Bonus* and *Kelly Loves Tony* were released theatrically as *American Dreams* by Quentin Lee's Margin Films.

13 An ironic epilogue: Don auditioned for MTV's *The Real World* when they came to San Francisco in 1994; presumably, MTV adjudged him not real enough.

14 In their study of Korean American entrepreneurs, Light and Bonacich note, "The United States plays an important role in driving immigrants to its own doors . . . immigration policy . . . is intimately tied to foreign policy, including economic aid, trade, cultural influence, military assistance, and political interference" (1988, 125). JeeYeun Lee contrasts this model with "the push-and-pull view of immigration," in which people depart for the inherently superior "New World" (1998, 186–87).

15 Shortly after this scene, Ny turns in an essay titled "Surviving in the Jungle," which humorously reveals how the specificity of his experience lies in stark contrast with his teacher's expectations about what a "jungle" is like. Ms. Schaeffer asks him if he had a machete; Ny affirms that he did. Moments later he tells us that he has no idea what she was talking about.

16 The latter mode is certainly in keeping with many traditional modes of irony. For example, the ironic naïf often appears as "an *ingénu* who may ask questions or make comments the full import of which he does not realize" (Muecke, 1982, 64). Muecke observes, "In eighteenth-century literature [the ingénu] is very frequently a non-European, a visitor from China or Persia or a Red Indian, Tahitian or Brobdingnagian, who does not, like us, see the world through the obscured or distorting spectacles of creeds, customs and conventions but freshly with the eyes of common sense or rationality" (65). Muecke unfortunately does not explore the complicated politics of the ingénu (his "like us" presumes that the reader is European):

the ironic naïf is superior to the surrounding society because he or she voices the "truth," but is inferior insofar as that truth is unwitting; that is, the naïf is not smart enough to realize he or she is being ironic.

17 In ironic terms, because the subject is aware of self-observation, the subject combines the role of *eiron* and *alazon.*

18 Susan Koshy notes that collaborative autobiographies are typically guided by an impulse to introduce diverse voices, suggesting an "emphasis on concrete experience and sovereign subjectivity" in which the collaborating subject stands "in quasi-ethnographical relation" to the purported speaking subject (1996, 328).

19 Jameson, 1981a, 112. Jameson is speaking of Jean-Luc Godard's postmodern reflexivity in the context of a discussion of Hans-Jürger Syberberg's modernist realism.

20 Linda Hutcheon notes that the postmodern aesthetic critique is always "bound up . . . with its own *complicity* with power and domination . . . [acknowledging] that it cannot escape implication in that which it nevertheless still wants to analyze and maybe even undermine" (1989, 4).

21 Bakhtin would agree with Bhabha that the colonials can express their distance from the Bible's discourse through strategies of "refraction," highlighting their own skepticism toward the discourse that they incorporate. However, Bakhtin is more wary of the power that inheres in quoted discourses, discourses that represent socio-ideologically alien languages; for Bakhtin, the redeployment of alien languages is achieved through nuances of contextualization.

22 These are just a few of the categories that distinguish marginal cinema practice from the mainstream. For other categories, see, for example, Phillip Lopate's article on "the essay-film" (1996), Sharon R. Sherman's book on film and folklore, *Documenting Ourselves* (1998), and Patricia Peyton's guide to "social issue films" (1979). I would argue that Asian American feature filmmakers like M. Night Shyamalan are recognized as filmmakers only to the extent that the film industry does not perceive them as Asian American, whereas Hong Kong expatriates like John Woo succeed as Asian (not Asian American) filmmakers. Ang Lee may be an exception; however, the continually reiterated justification for his affinity to non-Asian-themed films like *Sense and Sensibility* and *The Ice Storm* indicates that this exception proves the rule.

23 Karl Marx, from whom Spivak borrowed the terms *darstellen* and *vertreten* (to represent), once drew precisely this distinction, when he warned that we should not get so caught up in interpreting the world that we do not attempt to change it. However, Marx himself advanced an interpretation that was so compelling that it changed the world. (I am grateful to John Durham Peters for this insight into Marx's distinction.) Craig Owens

offers a parallel to "Can the Subaltern Speak?" in " 'The Indignity of Speaking for Others': An Imaginary Interview." Amusingly, Owens's critique of those who would speak for others is cast in the form of an interview: he imagines an interlocutor who speaks to him (and thus, for him): "Marxism lacks an adequate theory of representation. (Louis Althusser's belated attempt to provide it with one tends to collapse representation into ideology.) . . . in the *Eighteenth Brumaire* . . . Marx uncritically assumes the traditional role of politically motivated intellectual—or artist—in bourgeois society: he appropriates for himself the right to speak on behalf of others, setting himself up as their conscience—indeed, as consciousness itself. But in order to occupy this position, he must first deny them (self-)consciousness, their ability to represent themselves. In other words, Marx overlooks the constitutive role of his own discourse, which is held to be merely representing—and representative" (1992, 261).

24 Butler, 1993, 219. Muñoz discusses the relevance of this passage to his theory of disidentification in the introduction to *Disidentifications* (1999).

25 Rizal's original Spanish is "el demonio de las comparaciones." The most recent English-language translation renders this phrase as "the devil of comparisons."

26 Of late, just as interest in split subjectivities has arisen in the mainstream of literary theory, straight white male documentary filmmakers have foregrounded their own postmodern subjectivities (as noted by Jim Lane, 1993). This assumption of marginal subjectivity is often accomplished through emphasis on class markers (I'm thinking here of *Lightning over Braddock, Sherman's March,* and *Roger & Me*), although I'd argue that the sexism these documentaries evince suggests that the filmmakers are not as marginal as they would like us to believe. See my discussion of Philip Brian Harper's critique of postmodernism in Chapter 6.

In another context, Fredric Jameson notes that art is particularly reflexive in a society where artists are marginalized: "As the position of the artist becomes jeopardized, reflexivity increases, becomes an indispensible precondition for artistic production, particularly in vanguard or high-cultural works" (1981a, 88). Reflexivity is not precisely the same as "double consciousness," however; all contemporary artists do not necessarily evince this modality of perception.

27 My focus on Asian American cinematic subjectivity as always already doubled is of course complicated by the politics of collaboration; *a.k.a. Don Bonus,* as a collaboration between an established maker and his student, poses an interpretive conundrum to which I have alluded in the preceding discussion of how irony depends on an attribution of authorship. The politics of Nakasako and Ny's collaboration deserves fuller examination than I can devote to it here, given that my project is concerned

primarily with how Asian American cinema situates itself in relation to dominant cinematic practices. Much of the most important work in Asian American cultural theory is devoted to the ways Asian American studies reproduces structures of domination and marginalization (on diverse Asian American populations) even as it contests U.S. hegemony, and in the light of that work my own project seems to belong to an earlier moment of Asian American cultural criticism. To the extent that Asian American studies, which on inception sought to transform the academy, has become institutionalized, it is invested in maintaining its own authority and legitimacy. (Of course, Asian American studies' position in the U.S. academy is far from secure.) However, because Asian American Studies describes an interdisciplinary field, its development across different disciplines is uneven and requires tactical, not to say strategic, interventions. Situated at the border between cinema studies and Asian American studies, this project has been shaped by the requirements of both fields.

28 "Consciousness awakens to independent life precisely in a world of alien discourses surrounding it. . . . When thought begins to work in an independent, experimenting and discriminating way, what first occurs is a separation between internally persuasive discourse and authoritarian enforced discourse, along with a rejection of those congeries of discourses that do not matter to us, that do not touch us" (Bakhtin, 1981, 345).

Discussing the video *Sa-I-Gu* in an essay entitled "Tradition and the Movies" (1999), David James argues that identity is created in a struggle with textual representations of mainstream and alternative media.

29 "As a living, socio-ideological concrete thing, as heteroglot opinion, language, for the individual consciousness, lies on the borderline between oneself and the other. The word in language is half someone else's. It becomes 'one's own' only when the speaker populates it with his own intention, his own accent, when he appropriates the word, adapting it to his own semantic and expressive intention" (Bakhtin, 1981, 293).

Anthony P. Cohen, in his discussion of metaphoric definitions of community, fixes on the symbolic constitution of boundaries: "The boundary encapsulates the identity of the community and, like the identity of an individual, is called into being by the exigencies of social interaction. Boundaries are marked because communities interact in some way or other with entities from which they are, or wish to be, distinguished" (1989, 12). Boundaries mark the very limit of our communities; metaphoric boundaries are the test cases by which we define who we are.

30 Yen Le Espiritu identifies two approaches to "ethnicity" in sociological literature: primordialism (seen in the work of W. Connor, Harold Isaacs, Pierre L. van den Berghe, and others), which describes ethnicity as a "community of culture"; and instrumentalism (seen in the work of Orlando

Patterson, Nathan Glazer and Daniel Patrick Moynihan, Edna Bonacich and John Modell, and others), which emphasizes the common interests that hold communities together. See Espiritu, 1992, 3–5.

31 For these reasons, the author also rejects the use of the hyphen when the term Asian American is being used attributively. For Asian Americans, precedent was set as early as 1930 with the foundation of the Japanese American Citizens League, which debated the hyphen question at its founding convention.

1 The Camera as Microscope: Cinema and Ethnographic Discourse

1 Igorrote (sometimes spelled Igorot) is a Tagalog word which, literally translated, means "mountain dweller" and refers to the people who live in the Cordillera mountains. As such, the term connotes the mainstream Filipino perspective of the tribal Filipinos.

2 The narrator of *Bontoc Eulogy* notes, "For the first time ever, native tribes who did not even know of each other's existence now lived side-by-side in the reservation." A fascinating photograph depicting representatives of various tribes gathered before the camera appears on the cover of *Amerasia Journal* 24 no. 2 (1998), a special issue devoted to "Essays into American Empire in the Philippines."

3 This narrative of evolution into civilized Brown Brother is told in a series of photographs called "Evolution of a Bontoc Igorot Man," presenting three profiles supposedly depicting the same man: in the first he is bare-chested and his hair extends down his back, and in the third he is clean-shaven, close-cropped, and wearing the uniform of the Philippine Constabulary (Breitbart, 1997, 25–26). See also "Two photographs of a Bontoc Igorot Boy, With the Second Taken Nine Years After the First" (de la Cruz and Baluyut, 1998, 24).

For my understanding of the ways the Exposition linked anthropology and U.S. imperialism, I am greatly indebted to Rydell's *All the World's a Fair,* which provides a fascinating account of the St. Louis Fair and a dozen others. Rydell notes that the 1903 Manila exposition, a dry run for the Philippine Reservation in St. Louis, served to "emphasize to Filipinos the long road they would have to travel before achieving the capacity for self-rule" (1984, 170); as such, the Manila exposition provided a corollary to the St. Louis Fair's thesis about the evolutionary potential of Filipinos.

4 Chapter 1 of Del Mundo's *Native Resistance* (1998) examines U.S. representations of the Philippines prior to 1904, focusing on cinema but also encompassing coon songs and other popular cultural forms. Of the surviving

films held by the Library of Congress, Del Mundo lists seven Edison films, all shot in the United States, and twelve Biograph Films, mostly actualities shot in the Philippines.

5 *Raising Old Glory over Morro Castle,* American Vitagraph (1899).

6 The image also recalls Theresa Hak Kyung Cha's video *mouth to mouth* (1975), which features close-ups of a woman's mouth forming different shapes; according to Helen Lee, the piece references *hangul,* the Korean script in which "consonants are said to be based on the shape of the human tongue, mouth, and throat when forming these letters" (1998, 322 n.9).

7 See Wise (1983) for a review of an exhibition of prints from the *Circle of Fear* series.

8 Reproductions of some of the photographs in the series can be seen in Kudaka's *On a Bed of Rice* (1995, 228) and in Machida (1994).

9 Unlike most fairs in the decade following the Louisiana Purchase Exposition, the San Diego Fair featured an extensive anthropological exhibit; see Rydell (1984, 219–27).

10 Throughout this discussion, I refer to the on-screen figure as Marlon, to the voice-over narration as "the narrator," and to the implied author of *Bontoc Eulogy* as Fuentes. I agree with Blumentritt's (1998) assessment that the narrator is a *character,* but to be absolutely precise I am drawing a distinction between the on-screen figure and the "disembodied" voice-over.

11 The footage of Hagenbeck's circus elephants shooting the chutes, and of a female dancer with the strength to hold a chair in her jaw, also comes from Coney Island; Fomoaley does not describe these scenes in his published account, however.

12 Blumentritt, 1998, 79. A possible but unlikely interpretation: when the storyteller dreams up a story, he or she attributes it to Markod to assert that it is not a lie. Unfortunately, *The First Grammar* does not make clear whether the Bontoc word *iitao* means "to dream" in this sense. According to the Oxford English Dictionary, the phrase "to dream up" does not appear until 1930, although the sense of "to imagine to be possible" is long established.

13 Following the advice of his consultant, Henry Pit-og, Fuentes opted to employ the alternate spelling "Markod," which is closer to the correct pronunciation. To this I would add that the "Markod" spelling is close to "Marlon," thus emphasizing the fiction of lineage. Seidenadel speculates that "Malkod" may be related to the word "malkut" in another dialect, meaning "the specters of dead people" (1909, 561).

14 De la Cruz and Balayut note that ethnographic photos like these "suggest how the entire population of the archipleago was cast as the 'criminal type' of civilization to be incarcerated and reformed" (1998, 28).

15 Describing these and other reenactments produced by James White for

Edison's Kinetograph Department, Charles Musser notes, "[Reenactments] avoided the expense of sending a cameraman to the Far East and allowed White to show the heroic actions of American soldiers—something unlikely to be filmed in the midst of a guerilla war" (1991, 146).

16 The film was most likely shot in New Jersey; National Guard units portrayed the U.S. soldiers (Musser, 1991, 146).

17 Rony draws a distinction between ethnographic film generally and the scientific research film specifically (1996, 14). The footage of the dancing child, strictly speaking, does not fall into the latter category; scientific research films often can be distinguished by the use of a grid or regular backdrop.

It seems to me that these movies also served to halt the flow of evolution by preserving that which might become extinct (i.e., people and/or their practices). In a sense, this is what Rony means when she states that all ethnographic film tells a narrative of evolution, meaning that it casts the ethnographic "other" as less evolved: the film attempts to preserve the "other" in a state of arrested development. See also Rydell's (1984) account of a controversy that arose when the U.S. government attempted to clothe the Filipinos on display: ultimately, the Philippine Exposition Board came up with another solution to prove that the Filipinos could evolve into modern, civilized people. Negritos were defined as imminently extinct, whereas other tribes were elevated as progressive (i.e., receptive to civilizing influences; 174–77).

18 I am alluding here to *Before Hollywood,* the title of a 1987 touring exhibition of early films curated by Jay Leyda and Charles Musser.

19 Later in the video we see a famous photograph taken at the St. Louis Exposition of Ota Benga, a Chirichiri man who was also exhibited at the American Museum of Natural History (the same museum that *On Cannibalism* visits) and later the Bronx Zoo (Rony, 1996, 187). Ota Benga's mouth is open, displaying his filed teeth, supposedly indicating that he was a cannibal (Breitbart, 1997, 67–68).

20 The recording is taken from a CD entitled *Batak of North Sumatra* (New Albion 046), featuring an ensemble directed by Rizaldi Siagian under the auspices of Festival of Indonesia, a nationwide arts festival sponsored by the Smithsonian Institution in 1991. *On Cannibalism* features "Batara Guru," from the Toba tradition, featuring an ensemble of *sarune bolon* (a double-reed instrument), gongs, and tuned drums.

21 It is possible that the term "hot dog" (strictly speaking, a frankfurter of pork and beef served in a bun) was popularized at the fair, but the *Random House Dictionary of American Slang* notes that the name was used as early as 1895, well before the Philippine-American War, so it is unlikely that the term arose from an association with eating dogs. However, the name

"hot dog" was banned from signs at Coney Island for a time because of the widespread rumor that the sausages contained dog meat; recall that Chief Fomauley gave his "life story" at Coney Island in 1905. It therefore seems likely that the name *stuck* because of the Filipino association. (The term's first recorded usage dates from 1894: it referred to a dapper gentleman.)

22 In *The Third Eye* (1996, 28) Rony quotes Letourneau's *Sociologie d'après l'ethnographie* (Paris: Reinwald, 1880), 4, quoted in Joy Dorothy Harvey, "Races Specified, Evolution Transformed" (Ph.D. diss., Harvard University, 1983), 139.

23 Because the resulting still images captured by the chronophotographe were not intended to be animated but rather viewed one at a time, Marey's invention is not cinema as we understand it; by using one camera instead of the multiple cameras employed by Muybridge, however, Marey's invention is a sort of evolutionary link between Marey's serial photography and the motion picture. This history of cinema's evolution from motion studies is commonly told in textbooks surveying film history, for example, Cook's *A History of Narrative Film* (1996), Sklar's *Film: An International History of the Medium* (1993), and Thompson and Bordwell's *Film History: An Introduction* (1994).

24 I am, of course, alluding to Laura Mulvey's "Visual Pleasure and Narrative Cinema" (1975), which actually uses the term "look" and not "gaze." Mulvey argues that the spectator is compelled to identify with the look of the camera—with the male gaze—to receive pleasure. In my essay "Recuperating Suzie Wong" (2000) I argue that spectators of color oscillate between this "sadistic" position of mastery and a resistant renarrativizing of films that shifts the balance of power to characters of color.

25 *Children of the Camps* is the title of a 1999 documentary (produced by Satsuki Ina, directed by Stephen Holsapple) about the psychological impact of incarceration on the Nikkei who were children at the time of World War II. I also take the title to refer to contemporary Asian Americans, who are, in the lyrics of a song written by Chris Iijima and Nobuko Miyamoto, "the offspring of the concentration camp" ("We Are the Children," *A Grain of Sand,* Bindu 9701–2); this song makes a brief appearance in a party scene in Rea Tajiri's *Strawberry Fields.*

2 Pioneering Romance: Immigration, Americanization, and Asian Women

1 The historical context Pateman refers to here is the shift away from domestic production and the concomitant shift away from women's control of certain trades. As a political theorist examining contract theory, par-

ticularly Locke and Rousseau, Pateman's analysis centers on the West of the eighteenth and nineteenth centuries.

2 According to Thomas Schatz, generic heroes' "identities and narrative roles (or 'functions') are determined by their relationship with the community and its value structure. . . . The static vision of the generic hero—indeed of the entire constellation of familiar character types—helps to define the community and to animate its cultural conflicts" (1981, 25–26). Schatz's *Hollywood Genres* and Steve Neale's *Genre* (1980) summed up much of the work on film genres from the 1970s, setting the terms for the debates in the 1980s. Alan Williams's review of Schatz's book, "Is a Radical Genre Criticism Possible" (1984), and Neale's response to Williams, "Questions of Genre" (1990), sum up the issues concisely. Grant's *Film Genre Reader II* (1995) collects many of the most important articles from the 1970s and 1980s (including Neale's "Questions of Genre").

3 "The classical film has at least two lines of action, both causally linking the same group of characters. Almost invariably, one of these lines of action involves heterosexual romantic love. . . . ninety-five [percent of the films in the sample] involved romance in at least one line of action, while eighty-five [percent] made that the principal line of action" (Bordwell, Staiger, and Thompson, 1985, 16).

The romance genre itself often focuses on lovers who attempt to escape from the forces turning their world upside down. I am grateful to David Shumway for discussing the historical backdrop of romance movies with me on the occasion of a visit to the University of Delaware on 11 November 1998, where he presented a chapter from his forthcoming book, *Modern Love: Discourses of Romance and Intimacy in 20th Century Filmmaking.*

4 My understanding of the Western has been strongly influenced by Robert Warshow's seminal essay, "Movie Chronicle: The Westerner" (1970).

5 In his review of *Thousand Pieces of Gold,* Dave Kehr discusses the characters in terms of contemporary identity politics, noting, "The only character in the film who seems truly of his time, Jim is, of course, made a heavy for it" (1991b, 7D).

6 It is a historical fact, of course, that Polly married Charlie Bemis, and I claim no insight into the real woman's motives; rather, I am analyzing the character of Polly as dramatized in the film. For further discussion of the distinction between being and becoming, see the discussion of *Chan Is Missing,* chap. 6.

7 See Deborah Gee's documentary video *Slaying the Dragon* for analysis of the representation of Asian American women in television news as well as popular film and television. Jessica Hagedorn's "Asian Women in Film" (1994) and Renee Tajima's "Lotus Blossoms Don't Bleed" (1989a) survey the limited range of roles for Asian women in popular film. Asian Ameri-

can actors' perspectives are included in Eugene Franklin Wong's *On Visual Media Racism* (1978) and Joann Faung Jean Lee's *Asian American Actors* (2000).

8 I am, of course, alluding to Laura Mulvey's "Visual Pleasure and Narrative Cinema" (1975). Note that I refer not to actual straight male spectators, but to a spectatorial position coded as straight and male. In her original formulation, Mulvey argued that all spectators, to derive pleasure from dominant cinematic texts, were positioned as heterosexual men. She revised her argument in "Afterthoughts" (1981), and much feminist film criticism since has been concerned with positioning female spectators, queer spectators, and others, vis-à-vis dominant cinema.

Mulvey's article saw publication after Julia Lesage's "The Human Subject" (1974), which argued that much feminist criticism drew too selectively from the psychoanalytic literature. In "The Difficulty of Difference," D. N. Rodowick (1982) extended Mulvey's argument by noting that her emphasis on sadism suppressed consideration of masochism. Gaylyn Studlar launches a more direct critique of Mulvey in "Masochism and the Perverse Pleasures of the Cinema" (1985). In "Film and the Masquerade," Mary Ann Doane (1982) proposed a model of spectatorial transvestism to account for female spectators in male spectatorial positions. Judith Mayne's *Cinema and Spectatorship* (1993) remains the best single source for an extended discussion of the above literature.

The bibliography lists the initial appearance of the articles cited above, all of which have been reprinted often. Both articles by Mulvey appear in Constance Penley's *Feminism and Film Theory* (1988), in Thornham's *Feminist Film Theory* (1999; along with Doane's essay), as well as Mulvey's own *Visual and Other Pleasures* (1989). Mulvey, Doane, and Studlar are collected in Mast, Cohen, and Braudy's *Film Theory and Criticism* (1992). Bill Nichols's *Movies and Methods, Vol. 2* (1985) includes Mulvey and Studlar.

9 The name Nathoy suggests Mongolian ancestry; McCunn's novel has been translated into Mongolian as well as Chinese; see Hesford, 1996, 59 n. 1. Priscilla Wegars is presently researching Polly Bemis's original name; she is not yet fully convinced that "Lalu" is correct. Given this uncertainty, and because the film version of *Thousand Pieces of Gold* focuses on her life in the United States, I refer to her as Polly. This is not to say, however, that the two names are not important in the film; Jim consistently refers to her as Lalu, and Hong King's use of both names on different occasions is an important signifier of his attitude toward her.

10 Hesford, 1996, 54. In the film, Jim is also given the Chinese name Li Po. Xing mistakenly states that Jim was added for the movie, and that he is a cowboy (1998, 128).

For simplicity's sake, I refer to the Idaho town where Polly Bemis lived from 1872 to 1894 as Warren. The town began as a camp named Washington, founded by Union sympathizers in the Warren Mining District (Confederate sympathizers founded a camp named Richmond). The Richmond camp died, and Washington became known as Washington in Warren's camp, later Warrens, and finally Warren (Wegars, letter to author, 22 Apr. 1998). The town (and its post office) officially became Warren in 1885, although it was still frequently referred to in print as Warrens and is still called Warrens by some (Wegars, letter to author, 26 Apr. 1998). See also Elsensohn's *Idaho Chinese Lore* (1970, 76).

11 Wegars is a curator at the University of Idaho's Alfred W. Bowers Laboratory of Anthropology and is presently writing what will certainly be the definitive historical account of Polly Bemis. Through the UI Enrichment Program, she offers a course comparing the historical record with McCunn's novel and Kelly's film; the program also offers a trip to visit Polly Bemis's cabin on the River of No Return. Until Wegars's book is published, the reader is referred to a Web site that she maintains detailing ongoing research under the auspices of the Asian American Comparative Collection: *http://www.uidaho.edu/LS/AACC/research.htm.*

12 According to Janet Chu, McCunn unsuccessfully sued to recover the film rights to her novel and is consequently prohibited from making any public statements about the film (1996, 94 n.3).

13 All information on the film's production and the filmmakers' biographies comes from the press kit for *Thousand Pieces of Gold* and from correspondence and phone conversations with Nancy Kelly and Kenji Yamamoto.

14 According to Wegars's research, drawing on documents unavailable to McCunn or Kelly at the time, the real Polly Bemis arrived in Idaho in 1872 and is listed in the 1880 census as living with Charlie Bemis; Charlie was shot in 1890, and the couple were married in 1894; again, I refer the reader to her forthcoming work,

15 Hesford, 1996, 56. Both Hesford and Wegars report that residents of Warren complained about this historical inaccuracy on the film's release. For a historical account of Chinese immigration and the driving out, I have relied on Wynne's *Reaction to the Chinese in the Pacific Northwest and British Columbia, 1850 to 1910* (1978), although other sources deal more specifically with Idaho. The chief virtue of Wynne's text is its comparison of the U.S. and Canadian responses to Chinese migration.

16 This specific aspect of his critique is most clearly stated in F. Chin, "The Most Popular Book in China" (1984). Chin's own versions of Chinese mythology are articulated in "Come All Ye Asian American Writers of the Real and the Fake" (1991a), and he puts his interpretation into fictional practice in his novel *Donald Duk* (1991b). The text that inspires Chin's ire is Maxine Hong Kingston's *The Woman Warrior* (1989), particularly her revision of Fa Mulan in the second section, "White Tigers." Elaine

Kim discusses the implications of this debate in " 'Such Opposite Creatures' " (1990).

17 Quoted in the press kit, Yamamoto explicitly connects the movie's narrative to contemporary concerns in multicultural America. Biederman (1995) attributes a similar motivation to Kelly: speaking on the occasion of a screening at the Autry Museum of Western Heritage, Kelly compares the social upheaval in late nineteenth-century China to "Los Angeles in recent years." Kelly is paraphrased in this article, so I am not completely convinced that she was comparing China with the L.A. of Rodney King; it seems more likely that she was invoking the racism of Warren in her comparison. Nevertheless, like Yamamoto's statement in the press kit, Kelly explicitly connects *Thousand Pieces of Gold* to contemporary cultural politics.

18 Wilmington's comments about the film's absence of conflict derive from his claim that the movie belongs to the Western genre: "In a way, this is classic Western filmmaking: the lucid lyricism of a John Ford, a Budd Boetticher, a George Stevens. But, since Kelly is dealing with different kinds of conflicts, the film, however simple, always seems to be opening up a new world" (1991, F8). Certainly *Thousand Pieces of Gold* develops several central Western themes (notably masculinity and cross-cultural negotiation), but Wilmington backs off from the genre label almost as soon as he invokes it.

Tom Schatz's distinction between genres of determinate and indeterminate space also suggests that *Thousand Pieces of Gold* is more usefully classified as a romance than as a Western. In genres of determinate space, an ideologically contested setting "is entered by an individual or collective hero, at the outset, who acts upon it, and finally leaves." Genres of indeterminate space, which take place in an ideologically stable setting, "generally involve a doubled (and thus dynamic) hero in the guise of a romantic couple. . . . The kiss or embrace signals the integration of the couple into the larger cultural community" (1981, 27–29). Obviously, I am not contending that *Gold*'s setting is ideologically stable, nor are Charlie and Polly integrated into the community at the film's end; but if we understand the key distinction as between a lone hero who cannot join the community that he (and it is invariably a male hero) protects on the one hand, and a doubled hero whose romance signals the birth of a new community on the other, then *Gold* clearly belongs to the latter category.

19 In the cast credits in the press kit, Toby is listed as "Ohio."

20 In 1882, 39,379 Chinese emigrated to the United States, but between 1884 and 1888 fewer than 50 Chinese entered each year. "That decline was not due to the overt hostility of the people but was the direct result of measures taken by the federal government" (Wynne, 1978, 284–85).

21 In the shooting script on deposit at the Autry Museum, dated 6 April 1989,

Hong King's citizenship papers are an important plot point (e.g., Hong King's second attempt to auction Polly's sexual favors follows Charlie's warning to Jim that "he's got his papers now, he'll think he can get away with anything" [55]). It is hinted that Hong King must bribe the judge to secure his papers; in this context, it can be inferred that the judge is stringing Hong King along or that he intends to grant him papers under the table; the shooting script can be read as consistent with historical fact. Unfortunately, the release version of the film does not explore this question.

22 Janet H. Chu notes, "Lalu/Polly becomes further interpellated as a subject in espousing the ideology of democracy and capitalism. In this way, Lalu/Polly, who was at one time the most disenfranchised member in the town, achieves economic independence, the promised reward of democracy" (1996, 77).

23 Hong King is the only Chinese male without a queue, the ponytail without which no Chinese man could return to China. Hong King thereby bodily performs his Chinese American identity. In this sense, I disagree with Janet Chu's statement that Hong King represents Chinese identity for Polly and Jim represents the model minority (1996, 84), for Jim keeps his queue and states his plan to return to China. I do, however, agree with Chu's argument that Hong King serves to indict Chinese patriarchy (vis-à-vis American freedom).

24 Hatta's maternal grandparents arrived on Maui in the 1920s; her father emigrated in the 1940s (Rich, 1995).

Except as noted below, all information about the film's production comes from the *Picture Bride* press kit. The reader will notice that details about the production's many setbacks and triumphs over those setbacks were not detailed in the press kit.

25 Hatta received her NEA grant while still enrolled in UCLA's MFA program and had to drop out to claim it; when UCLA changed its requirements, allowing an MFA to be granted on a body of work in the absence of a thesis project, Hatta was awarded her degree in 1991. According to the movie's press kit, "both of Ms. Onodera's great-grandmothers were picture brides." Presumably, this refers to two of Onodera's four great-grandmothers.

26 Cliff Eidelman's unused score was issued as *Music Inspired by the Film Picture Bride* (Varese Sarabande VSD-5651).

27 Inexplicably, the press kit states that the story begins in Tokyo in 1918.

28 Fires cleared the razor-sharp leaves (as well as the underbrush) from the cane when it was ready for harvest. For information on plantation life, see Ron Takaki's *Pau Hana* (1983); Gary Okihiro's *Cane Fires* (1991) focuses on Japanese workers; Edward Beechert's *Working in Hawaii* (1985) examines "the social relations of production" from before 1819 to statehood.

29 According to the press kit, she steals the strike fund. But this isn't clear,

as the container that holds the strike fund is not clearly shown, only her own canister.

30 This reading is consistent with another goal of the 1920 strikers: to secure paid maternity leave for female plantation workers (Takaki, 1983, 167).

31 Pre-1965 U.S. immigration policies served, discursively speaking, to construct Asian female immigrants as wives—as the wives of Asian male laborers and professionals, or as "war brides" of U.S. servicemen. The discursive construction of Asian female immigrant as "wife" continues into the post-1965 period in the "mail order bride" phenomenon. Prostitutes are the major exception to the discursive construction of female immigrants as wives. However, Gary Okihiro notes that Chinese prostitutes supported patriarchal families in China and the United States with their earnings (1994, 77–78); this historical reality is obscured, however, by the discursive connection of prostitutes with so-called bachelor communities. Because many "bachelors" were themselves married, the labels "bachelor" and "prostitute" suggest that the economy of sojourner laborers, defined in opposition to marriage, is part of a larger discourse linking marriage and migration. For more on Asian American women, migration, and work, see Asian Women United of California, *Making Waves* (1989) and *Making Waves II* (1996).

32 See Chapter 7 for a discussion of the relationship of male heterosexuality to nationalist discourses in the context of a discussion of homosexuality and transnational cinema.

33 Unless otherwise indicated, all information on the production of *Living on Tokyo Time* comes from my interviews with Okazaki or from publicity material provided by Farallon Films.

34 Viviano (1987) reports that *Living on Tokyo Time* was funded by sources in Tokyo and shot some scenes there as well; according to Okazaki, this is incorrect.

35 Asian Improv Records 0009.

36 The film turned a profit, but keep in mind the modesty of its budget.

37 For an extended discussion of *American Sons,* see Feng, "Redefining Asian American Masculinity" (1996b).

38 For an analysis of the role of Asian laborers in Hawai'i and of Hawai'i's dependence on them, see especially Okihiro's *Cane Fires* (1991). For a discussion of contemporary capitalism's dependence on Asian female labor, see Lisa Lowe's "Work, Immigration, Gender" (1997).

39 It might be interesting to compare *Tokyo Time* with another film about the recovery of cultural heritage, *A Great Wall,* which is also a comedy, but in which the Asian Americans are somewhat more successful in accessing Chinese culture. Not coincidentally, Lisa Lowe cites *A Great Wall* as an example of a film showing that China's and the United States's cul-

tural borders are already permeable (where Coca-Cola can be guzzled in the shadow of the Great Wall); see "Heterogeneity, Hybridity, Multiplicity" (1991b).

3 Articulating Silence: Sansei and Memories of the Camps

The title of this chapter alludes to King-Kok Cheung's study of Asian American women authors, *Articulate Silences* (1993).

1 This *Life* article is often confused with a similar piece, called "How to Tell Your Friends from the Japs," which ran in *Time* magazine the same week. The anecdotal confusion of these articles is evidence of their notoriety in Asian American circles. Milt Caniff's "Steve Canyon" taught soliders how to distinguish between "Asiatics" in the U.S. Army's *Pocket Guide to China;* Renov reprints three frames (1994, 107, Fig. 6).

2 Chinese American actor Beulah Quo, who grew up in the San Francisco Bay Area during the war, remembers wearing buttons that read "No, I am not." This button, which does not announce what one is but only what one is not, strikes me (a Chinese American who perhaps romanticizes the past) as speaking a certain defiance in its refusal of external labels; the refusal of a specific identity preserves the contingency and multiplicity of subjectivity. The button that announces "I am Chinese" fixes the identity of the wearer in a way that the "No, I am not" button does not.

3 This chapter also considers Tanaka's *Memories from the Department of Amnesia,* which also concerns the relationship of memory to history when evaluating the life of a parent, but in which the camps play a less central (if still important) part.

In this chapter I restrict my focus to movies about the U.S. Internment. For a comparison of Canadian Midi Onodera's *The Displaced View* with the videos of Tajiri and Tanaka, see Sumiko Higashi's "Melodrama, Realism, and Race" (1998). For a discussion of Japanese (North) American spectatorship and its relation to camp films and videos, see Kent Ono's "Re/membering Spectators" (2000).

4 I discuss Craig Owens's "phallacy of the positive image" (1992, 262) in the Introduction; see also Peggy Phelan's effort to establish "a theory of value for that which is not 'really' there, that which cannot be surveyed within the boundaries of the putative real" (1993, 1). Arguing against redressing marginalization through a politics of the visible, Phelan makes the case for a representation economy that maintains the indeterminacy of the "unmarked."

5 Tajiri was born in Chicago and studied in California (receiving her MFA from the California Institute of the Arts); Tanaka was born in California,

grew up in Chicago, and received her MFA from the School of the Art Institute of Chicago (Armstrong et al., 1991). Many Japanese Americans relocated to Chicago after leaving the camps; they were encouraged to leave the West Coast, and many Chicago factories offered work to Japanese Americans. To leave the camps, internees had to prove that they had been accepted into a university or had a job waiting for them.

6 All three movies also draw from documentary and experimental traditions; that hybridity is evident in the various generic categories applied to *History and Memory,* which appeared in the 1991 Whitney Biennial and won Best Experimental Video at the 1992 Atlanta Film and Video Festival and a Distinguished Achievement Award at the 1992 International Documentary Association Festival.

7 The events leading up to Kay's death are chronicled in Chapter 7 of Kessler's *Stubborn Twig* (1993); its aftermath is dicussed in Chapter 8. By the way, Chop's real name is Tsuyoshi; the nickname of "Chop Yasui" (Chop Suey) was given to him by white classmates (82–83).

8 Please refer to the introduction for a discussion of this passage and its implications for constructions of Asian American identity.

9 It bears noting that Yasui's deference to her family is by no means the rule for other filmmakers. Many documentarians have produced films with absolutely no regard for their subjects, and filmmakers who document their own families are no exception; indeed, many filmmaker-daughters have been exceptionally antagonistic toward their families. Lauren Kessler (1993), who chronicles the Yasui family through three generations, implies that values the Nisei inherited from their grandfather account for their reluctance to air the film, but Kessler does not explore Lise Yasui's respect for those values (i.e., whether she had internalized them; whether she disagreed with them herself but respected them; or whether she as a Sansei might even have deferred to her uncles and aunts so as not to put her own father in an awkward position). I am not willing to explain away Yasui's deference as a Japanese trait; after all, as Nisei, her uncles and aunts had evolved their own value systems and sense of familial responsibility in the United States, and if their values are not unproblematically attributable to Japanese cultural beliefs, then neither are Sansei Lise Yasui's.

10 Kessler, 1993, 313–14. Both versions of *A Family Gathering* are in circulation, and I have screened both. However, I have studied only the expanded version in depth, and consequently I restrict myself to general, comparative comments on the shorter version. The thirty-minute version is usually given as 1988, and the long version is usually given as 1989, although I believe it aired on PBS in 1990.

11 Tanaka had to edit four minutes from her fifty-eight-minute video for PBS broadcast; PBS had requested more extensive cuts so that they could

also show a brief statement from the videomaker, but Tanaka insisted on devoting as much time as possible to the video itself. Two scenes were shortened, and the rest of the time was made up by accelerating the credit sequence and removing a few frames from the black screens that punctuate the video (conversation with the author, 27 May 1994).

12 See the afterword for a brief discussion of *Strawberry Fields.*

13 However, I subsequently argue that contextual cues lead the audience to hierarchize the various elements presented in a cinematic text. For example, we often draw conclusions about the sources and circumstances of production of quoted footage, and thus infer a hierarchy in the relationship of the layered sounds and images. See the discussion of Tajiri's *History and Memory* in particular.

14 Refer to the discussion of Trinh Minh-ha's "Grandma's Story" in the introduction, wherein Trinh asserts that historical discourse denies it is a form of storytelling by distinguishing itself from "imaginative" storytelling.

15 Ben Xu defines "memory" as "beyond the actuality of events to the determination of their coherency as an existential situation" (1994, 5); "Our sense of what has happened to us is entailed not in actual happenings but in *meaningful* happenings" (4). Ono's "Re/membering" (2000) points out that this sequence implies that the U.S. Army intended to establish the normality and plenitude available to Japanese American consumers in the camps; the disavowal of the footage is also a disavowal of the footage's truth claim.

16 Note that the term history as I am using it (relationally) must be distinguished from the way the term is used in the Hegelian dialectic, in which the very force that drives the dialectical process is called history. Conflation of these differing concepts of history would absorb the Bakhtinian hermeneutic into the Hegelian dialectic, emphasizing the power inhering in history and the antithetical force of memory. Such a conflation would lose sight of the localized resistance of memory (just as Jameson's approach overemphasizes the totalizing efforts of the text as a whole).

17 It is these two different ways of deploying home movie footage that Robert M. Payne misses when he asserts that Yasui's film "never questions the cinematic relation between word and image" (1997, 70). Payne is comparing *A Family Gathering* to *Who's Going to Pay for These Donuts, Anyway?,* and I agree that *Donuts* foregrounds its interrogation of the ontology of documentary truth more so than *A Family Gathering,* but Yasui and Tegnell's film is engaged in a similar critique.

18 Michelle Citron's *Daughter Rite* (1979) employs step-printed home movies to allude to dreams and memories of childhood, and Marilee Bennett's *A Song of Air* (1989), a contemporary of Yasui's film, interrogates her father's role as metteur-en-scène of his movies.

19 A similar process animates Richard Fung's *The Way to My Father's Village,* discussed in Chapter 4. In Fung's case, that circle might begin and end in China, or it might begin and end in Canada.

20 Mention of *A Family Gathering*'s elegiac quality requires at least passing mention of Sumi Tonooka's score. Like Yasui, Tonooka is a hapa Sansei (in her case, African American and Japanese American) who grew up in Pennsylvania. Tonooka learned jazz in Philadelphia clubs and has recorded several albums. She has also composed a three-movement suite called *Out of the Silence,* scored for jazz combo, Japanese instruments, and voice; each movement provides a setting for a Japanese American poem, with the three movements depicting the Issei, Nisei, and Sansei. *Out of the Silence* is itself the subject of a documentary called *Susumu: A Tone Poem in Three Movements* (Gei Zantsinger, 1989). For more information on Tonooka and her compositions, see Davis (1986) and Asai (1995).

21 Elektra 61049.

22 Becky Gallardo is a much more visible part of this film than her brother, and indeed, was much more involved in connecting with Jack, flying in from Chicago to take part in the process and the video (personal interview, 26 May 1994).

23 I would be remiss if I did not mention the Oedipal implications of these sequences. However, I will waste no more paper elaborating on those implications.

24 For an elaboration on this statement, see Hong's (1993a, 1993b) interview with Tanaka.

25 Much of the time line sequence fell under the axe in the PBS version.

26 Tanaka's video also has much in common with the Chinese American movies discussed in Chapter 4: the use of bureaucratic documents to establish the facts on record; impetus from the death of a parent; and an expressed desire to explore the past for the benefit of one's children.

27 See Mimura's (2000) and Sturken's (1997) essays on *History and Memory.*

28 According to Darrell Hamamoto (1996), the character of the "sister" is actually a fictionalized version of Tajiri herself; as noted earlier, this footage was drawn from Tajiri's *The Diary of Lennie Itoh.* The photos all depict white men and women seated in open-air convertibles; this image of the freedom of the open road stands in contrast with the blacked-out windows of the trains that transported the internees into the desert.

29 Situating the Internment in relation to other traumatic events of the twentieth century, Sturken notes that some events are "relentlessly and copiously documented in camera images," whereas other events produce "few photographic images to capture the global public's attention" (1997, 692). As an example of the latter, Sturken cites the Khmer Rouge's acts of genocide. Tran T. Kim-Trang's *Ekleipsis* (1998), a video that explores hysterical

blindness among Cambodian women living in the United States, might be compared fruitfully with the movies discussed in this chapter.

30 See, for example, Sucheng Chan's *Asian Americans* (1991, 129), Don Nakanishi's "Surviving Democracy's 'Mistake'" (1993), and Ronald Takaki's *Strangers from a Different Shore* (1990, 392–93).

31 Because I read the image of the canteen as a representation of the process of creating *History and Memory,* I cannot agree with Robert M. Payne's argument that the video's conclusion affirms "the power of the image to validate history and memory" (1997, 74). Payne's reading confuses what the image represents with what it depicts.

32 The canteen thus marks the videomaker's investment in creating her own understanding of these events to sit alongside her mother's. Toni Morrison, describing the process of crafting fiction from autobiography, discusses her own negotiation with her mother: "I'm not going to ask my mother. . . . Because my experience when I do this with my mother is so crushing: she will give you *the* most pedestrian information you ever heard, and I would like to keep all of my remains and my images intact in their mystery when I begin. Later I will get to the facts. That way I can explore two worlds—the actual and the possible" (1990, 304).

33 Recall that *A Family Gathering* ended on a similar ambiguity: "This is what I'll remember."

34 *I Only Have Eyes for You* (ECM 1296).

35 Philip Kan Gotanda makes this point in his play about struggling Asian American actors, *Yankee Dawg You Die* (1995, 103–4).

36 See Ono's *Representations of Resistance and Subjectivity in Japanese American Discourse* (1993) for an argument about the political dimensions of the internees' agricultural renovations.

37 The review was written by Tajiri's nephew, Vincent Schleitwiler, who contributed to the *Chicago Tribune*'s "High School Movie Panel." As it happens, *Tribune* critic Dave Kehr (1991a) reviewed *Come See the Paradise* in the same edition.

38 I am alluding here to Theodor Adorno's essay, "Subject and Object":

> Primacy of the object can be discussed legitimately only when that primacy—over the subject in the broadest sense of the term—is somehow definable, when it is more than the Kantian thing-in-itself as the unknown cause of the phenomenon. . . . The test of the object's primacy is its qualitative alteration of opinions held by the reified consciousness, opinions that go *frictionlessly* [emphasis added] with subjectivism. Subjectivism does not touch the substance of naive realism; it only seeks to state formal criteria of its validity. . . . But what defines the prior object as distinct from its subjective trappings is comprehen-

> sible in the conditionality of what conditions it, in that which in turn defines the categorial apparatus it is to be defined by, according to the subjectivist pattern. The categorial attributes without which there is no objectivity as yet, according to Kant, are posited also, and thus, if you will, they are really "merely subjective." The *reductio ad hominem* thus becomes the downfall of anthropocentrism. That even man as a *constituens* is man-made—this disenchants the creativity of the mind. But since primacy of the object requires reflection on the subject and subjective reflection, subjectivity—as distinct from primitive materialism, which really does not permit dialectics—becomes a moment that lasts. (1982, 504)

Adorno describes the constitution of subjectivity vis-à-vis an objectivity that resists it. The object comes first, Adorno says, and the proof is that it tests the subject's hypothesis (it qualitatively alters opinions): without the object, the subject would be free to hypothesize freely, offering opinions without regard to their relevance ("frictionlessly"). Subjectivity is ephemeral, as it exists only as a momentary hypothesis—unless those hypotheses are continually tested against the object, which permits subjectivity to sustain itself, to become "a moment that lasts" (i.e., to transcend its ephemerality).

39 Tanaka is a video artist. But Lisa Hsia is a filmmaker. Perhaps instead of electrons, filmmakers find Fischer's sparks in the flashes of light that emerge from the film projector, interrupted by the blades of the shutter, flashing rapidly enough to produce "flicker fusion" and make discontinuous still images appear to move.

4 Decentering the Middle Kingdom: ABCs and the PRC

1 *The Woman Warrior* was published in 1975. Kingston's *Tripmaster Monkey* was published fourteen years later, in 1989. In the later book, Kingston's protagonist takes great pains to oppose the hyphenated "Chinese-American":

> When I hear you call yourselves "Chinese," I take you to mean American- understood, but too lazy to say it. You do mean "Chinese" as short for "Chinese-American," don't you? We mustn't call ourselves "Chinese" among those who are ready to send us back to where they think we came from. But "Chinese-American" takes too long. Nobody says or hears past the first part. And "Chinese-American" is inaccurate—as if we could have two countries. We need to take the hyphen out—"Chinese American." "American," the noun, and "Chinese," the adjective. From now on: "Chinese Americans." However. Not okay

yet. "Chinese hyphen American" sounds exactly the same as "Chinese no hyphen American." No revolution takes place in the mouth or in the ear. (1990, 327)

2 The land of a parent's birth—not of both parents' birth. In Richard Fung's case, his mother was three generations out of China, while his father was born there. Felicia Lowe visits her father's family, and Lisa Hsia visits her mother's cousins.

3 In other words, the metaphoric filter that I am describing is not a membrane or a mesh but a photographer's filter, more akin to a polarized cap on the camera's lens. The goal of this filter is not to *remove* an element from solution, but to mask aspects of the object being photographed for analysis; this filter does not directly affect the constitution of the object, merely its *appearance*.

4 Literary examples of generational conflict among Chinese Americans include C. Y. Lee's *The Flower Drum Song* (1957), Louis Chu's *Eat a Bowl of Tea* (1961), and Amy Tan's *The Joy Luck Club* (1989a). Cinematic examples include Ang Lee's *The Wedding Banquet* (1993) and Chinese Canadian Mina Shum's *Double Happiness* (1995), not to mention the film adaptations of the three novels cited above.

5 There have always been competing conceptions of Chinese American identity: Ling-chi Wang discusses the inadequacy of the two dominant paradigms, "assimilation (to the U.S.)" and "loyalty (to China)," in "The Structure of Dual Domination" (1995). While the "loyalty" paradigm represents China's definition of diasporic Chinese as "overseas Chinese" (see Aihwa Ong's "Chinese Modernities," 1997, for a discussion of the discursive role "overseas Chinese" play in the economic development of the People's Republic of China), diasporic Chinese have often emphasized the fluidity of their national identities (see Ong's "On the Edge of Empires," 1993). For a study of how Chinese Americans have defined their identity in transnational terms, see Arif Dirlik's "Asians on the Rim" (1996) and Joe Chung Fong's "Transnationalized Newspapers" (1996).

Discourses concerning "overseas Chinese" are most often deployed in the context of transnational capital: "overseas Chinese" are economic resources, either as markets for Chinese goods or investors in China's economy. As such, the notion of "overseas Chinese" is applicable to certain diasporic narratives and not others; for example, concern with China's human rights record motivates the flexible citizenships that Ong (1993) describes: these "astronauts'" concern for political and economic freedom sets them apart from Chinese nationals who return to China with expertise gleaned from study at foreign universities. Transnational identities are therefore a subset of the subjectivities produced by the diasporic migration of Chinese. This essay contributes only indirectly to an understanding of transnational subjectivites; rather, I emphasize how discourses about China have shaped Chinese American subjectivities.

6 Renee Tajima, in noting the historical significance of *China: Land of My Father,* calls Lowe's film "an anecdote to the Sinophile frenzy that followed normalization" (1991, 23); perhaps Tajima meant "antidote" as well.

7 An additional consequence of the Communist Revolution is to underline that Chinese Americans who trace their ancestry back to pre-1949 China *cannot* go home again, for the People's Republic of China is a different nation (Thomas Wolfe's famous observation at a further remove).

8 Fung's queer videos include *Orientations* (1985), a documentary about Asian Canadian gays and lesbians; *Fighting Chance* (1990), about the impact of AIDS on that community; *Chinese Characters* (1986), about Asian Canadians who watch gay male pornography; and *Dirty Laundry* (1996), an exploration of friendships and sexual attachments in the Chinese Canadian "bachelor community" that built the transcontinental railroad. Thomas Waugh situates Fung's videos within a Toronto art community and analyzes their construction of homoscape(s), "the transnational scene of sexual spaces, commodities, communications, and identity performance" (1998, 168). Waugh's major contribution is the equal weight he gives to Fung's community-based activist videos and his autobiographical videos.

Muñoz focuses on *Chinese Characters* and *My Mother's Place* (1990) in Chapter 3 of *Disidentifications* (1999); as the title indicates, the latter video can be read as a follow-up to *The Way to My Father's Village. My Mother's Place* explores Fung's Trinidadian roots, which *The Way* hardly touch on; if this chapter, for reasons of thematic coherence, privileges China as a constitutive component of Fung's cinematic identity, it is not because Fung's Chinese roots are self-evident, as the remainder of this chapter should make clear.

9 I speculate that there are purely practical reasons for these different cinematic registers and modes. Judging from the growth of the boys and Hsia's facility with the Chinese language, it seems fairly clear that the 8mm footage dates from early in Hsia's stay. The 16mm footage includes a visit from Hsia's parents and the distribution of gifts from the States, and so I think it is likely that a film crew on one or more occasions accompanied Hsia and/or her mother from the States to China, late in Hsia's visit. The 16mm footage also documents Hsia's departure from China, which might suggest that the gift giving was part of a follow-up visit after her studies in Beijing had already ended. Finally, the animated footage surely depicts events at which cameras were not present, events of a different profilmic order than footage of Hsia with her family, which (despite the verité presentation) was "staged" or at least "planned."

10 Of course, animated footage is radically different from the indexicality of verité and even direct address. The deliberate artifice of animation highlights the paradox of the insider/outsider axis: the animated footage shows us private spaces where cameras do not have access, and yet stylize those spaces in such a way that they cannot make claims to represent truth objectively.

11 These movies invite us to understand them as direct authorial expressions —voice-overs abet this process—but I have endeavored to keep maker and movie distinct. Thus, when I refer to the maker (as in, "Fung tells us . . .") I am describing a voice-over or other inscription of the maker's subjectivity; but when I refer to the movie itself (as in, "*Made in China* narrates . . .") I am describing a textual operation in the movie, without attributing any authorial intentionality to the movie's rhetoric. For more on the autobiographical mode and nonfiction cinema, see Jim Lane's "Notes on Theory and the Autobiographical Documentary Film in America" (1993). Albert Stone's *Autobiographical Occasions and Original Acts* (1982) remains the touchstone for any investigation into American autobiography, and Laura Marcus's *Auto/biographical Discourses* (1994) usefully discusses the use of autobiographical modes in discourses that are not, strictly speaking, autobiographical.

12 The sentimentality of this account de-emphasizes the role played by material factors such as economic discrimination and restricted opportunities for employment in determining settlement patterns. For an account of how Punjabi immigrants described the Sacramento Valley in terms of the Punjab, including an accounting of some of the material factors influencing settlement in California, see Leonard (1997).

13 The mid-1990s witnessed the emergence of a pop culture narrative of the evolution of documentary convention in the plethora of articles in the mainstream press about the Academy Award's nomination process for documentaries. I'm thinking of numerous articles and editorials by popular film critics about the shut-out of critically acclaimed documentaries like *The Thin Blue Line* (1988), *Roger & Me* (1989), and preeminently *Hoop Dreams* (1994).

14 Roland Barthes claims that all photographs are "posed" in that the act of capturing a moment in time makes a "pose" of motion, whereas cinema does not record poses but time's *passing*. See *Camera Lucida* (1981, section 33, 78–80).

15 In the terms suggested by Lisa Lowe's analysis of space in "Heterogeneity, Hybridity, Multiplicity" (1991b), the image-track attempts to construct China as a discrete space, but the voice-over reinscribes white tourists and thus reminds us of the permeability of the Chinese border.

16 This argument holds true for home *movies,* which function differently

from family portraits; for example, an old family portrait of Hsia's father's family functions in much the same way as the photo albums in Lowe's *China: Land of my Father.* The differing traditions of still photography (portraiture) and home movies account (in part) for this distinction in function.

17 Indeed, "When I'm Sixty-Four" harkens back to an early period of English music hall; it is doubly nostalgic.

18 Students of documentary filmmaking immediately recognize that the footage of the adult Hsia on her bicycle is staged for the camera and later matched to the animation, further highlighting the temporal disjunction of the narrative.

19 See Chapter 6 for an extended discussion on the relationship of process to hyphenate identities, specifically the ways that *Chan Is Missing* destabilizes states of "being" to promote the process of "becoming."

20 See Altman, "Moving Lips" (1980).

5 Lost in the Media Jungle: Tiana Thi Thanh Nga's Hollywood Mimicry

1 More recently, Asian Americanists have turned their attention to connections between Asia and the United States, following two decades in which Asian American studies, in an effort to distinguish itself from Asian studies, focused almost exclusively on North American issues. For a discussion of the reasons for this shift, see Sau-Ling Wong, 1995a.

2 For discussions of what media depictions of Vietnam in U.S. media tell us about U.S. culture, see Anderegg (1991), Dittmar and Machaud (1990), Jeffords (1989), and Lanning (1994). See also Gruner's (1993) analysis of representations of POWs. Cynthia Fuchs's (1993) review focuses on *From Hollywood to Hanoi*'s intervention into a cinematic history of the war.

3 Bhabha's theories are most commonly developed with regard to British colonialism in India, the situation from which he draws most of his examples. However, his emphasis on colonial textuality allows for the application of his ideas to the U.S.-Vietnam context, especially because *From Hollywood to Hanoi* depicts the United States (in the postwar period) as a *cultural* colonizer of Vietnam via pointed references to bootleg U.S. videotapes and readily available U.S. consumer goods. In this context, *From Hollywood to Hanoi*'s cinematic response (to cinematic colonialism) seems only appropriate.

4 Trinh T. Minh-ha's films counterpoise different generational perspectives, albeit not in the schematic fashion of older, wiser women and their younger, unaware counterparts. Indeed, the protagonist in *A Tale of Love*

(1995) is arguably more radical than her older friends and relatives, and the older women are not apolitical but rather too experienced to see the world as black and white: they know that women do things that they find politically distasteful when practical circumstances warrant.

5 The film credits her as simply Tiana, while a recent article in *Cineaste* is attributed to "Tiana (Thi Thanh Nga)" ("The Long March: From Wong to Woo," 1995). References in the text to Tiana are not intended to connote the familiarity of a given name. In the credits for her debut, Sam Peckinpah's *The Killer Elite* (1975), she appears simply as Tiana. In the credits for *Catch the Heat* (1987), she is listed as Tiana Alexandra. As her then-husband, Stirling Silliphant, was the screenwriter, it's possible that this role was written for her, and Silliphant may have had a hand in selecting her stage name. *From Hollywood to Hanoi* does not explicitly mention any of Tiana's stage names (except in the end credits, where the song performances are credited to Tiana Banana), but the film's publicity consistently lists her earlier screen incarnations.

6 Information on the film's production was culled from Anton (1994), Elley (1992), and Reddy (1994a, 1994b), and from the film itself.

7 The Cinemax version bears a copyright date of 1994, suggesting that it was not substantially reedited from the version I screened at the Seattle Asian American Film Festival in 1994. I have been unable to determine precisely where the film was reedited, or whether the edits were required by Cinemax; however, relying on copious notes taken on viewing the pre-Cinemax release print, as well as Goldstein's "Herself as History" (1994), I have identified one specific change (mentioned below). My main text, though, is the Cinemax version.

8 Nguyen Ngoc Bich, *A Thousand Years of Vietnamese Poetry* (1975, 210).

9 Hanh Thi Pham has also thematized the commodification of U.S. pop culture in Vietnam. A photograph entitled "Evening Stroll/Night Patrol" from her 1985 series *Along the Street of Knives* depicts an American couple peeking through the window of a Vietnamese home: they see a young girl playing with a Mickey Mouse doll. "Evening Stroll/Night Patrol" is reproduced in Machida, 1994, 106.

10 Greta Ai-Yu Niu (1998) argues that the phrase "Siamese twins" reveals a discursive construction of Asian bodies as monstrous: she titles her study "People of the Pagus" (after a phrase of Homi Bhabha) to describe bodies that mark and are marked by the borders and boundaries they cross. (Niu discusses the Pagus and conjoined twins Chang and Eng in the introduction and conclusion of her dissertation.)

11 Meaghan Morris, with reference to Geeta Kapur, points out that the post-modern jargon of "appropriation" implies an economy of abundance; appropriation is not necessarily empowering, then, but often serves merely

to confirm the marginal (impoverished) status of one who would appropriate (1988, 267–68).

12 The performative aspect of Tiana's various personae already implies an attitude of critique; the context of "performance art" provides all the irony that the performance itself does not (and indeed, the more disingenuous the performance, the more ironically it is received). However, *From Hollywood to Hanoi* is a performance piece only ambiguously; for example, it is unclear whether Tiana's music videos are commercial products or deconstructions of the music video form. I turn to Bhabha for assistance in assessing the ambiguity of *From Hollywood to Hanoi*'s discursive context.

13 "Splitting" is elaborated in the essays "Signs Taken for Wonders" and "Interrogating Identity," both collected in *The Location of Culture* (1994).

14 Mimicry is like a fetish (in the Freudian, not the Marxian sense): it "mimes the forms of authority at the point at which it deauthorizes them." The fetish pretends to cover that which is desired but is not actually there; the presence of the fetish is necessitated by an absence (the fetish would not be necessary if the object of desire itself were present). Thus, the fetish is an example of Bhabha's splitting: "Two attitudes toward external reality persist; one takes reality into consideration while the other disavows it and replaces it by a product of desire that repeats, rearticulates 'reality' as mimicry." Mimicry reveals the attempt to "normalize" colonial authority; it exists precisely to cover the contradiction between the exercise of colonial power and its foundation on an enlightened civil society (Bhabha, 1994, 91).

15 Bhabha's emphasis on repetition parallels Judith Butler's argument that the performance of gender reinforces heterosexual normativity, and that the necessity of such performances reveals that heterosexuality is not at all natural but rather a "regulatory fiction" (1990b, 279). Butler has developed this argument since the 1990 publication of *Gender Trouble;* elaborations can be found in, for example, "Imitation and Gender Insubordination" (1991), *Bodies That Matter* (1993), and "Performative Acts and Gender Constitution" (1990b).

16 Bhabha equates this process of perpetual disavowal, of forgetting and "attempts to forget the forgetting" (1994, 79), to "suture," Lacan's term for the ego's constant striving to stitch the imaginary and the symbolic. Individuals enter into a complex social system by learning societal codes (language in particular), but to function we must act as if those codes are completely transparent. In other words, we would like to believe that we exist whole unto ourselves, but at some level we know that our psyches have been constituted by our interaction with others. "Suture" describes the ego's efforts to maintain that contradiction. For Bhabha, the constant repetition of the stereotype is akin to the colonizer's efforts to suture together the

belief that the colonial is different with the repressed knowledge that the colonial is the same.

17 Bhabha's "mimicry" and "identification" are very similar concepts. "Of Mimicry and Man" draws examples from the Indian context, while "Interrogating Identity," as a tribute to Fanon, draws on Martinique and other examples of European colonies in the African diaspora. Those by no means insignificant differences aside, the main distinction seems to be that mimicry is imposed by the colonizer and is primarily administrative, and identification is enacted by the colonial and is primarily social. Given the coercive overdetermination of colonial situations, however, this distinction seems tenuous when applied to textual mechanisms. My decision to analyze *From Hollywood to Hanoi* in terms of mimicry and not identification, then, does not imply that Tiana's performative incarnations were externally imposed rather than inhabited (desired); I selected "Of Mimicry and Man" and not "Interrogating Identity" primarily because the former essay is more concise, and the latter engages in a lengthy dialogue with other texts (primarily Fanon's).

18 In "Discourse in the Novel," Bakhtin argues that we define ourselves ideologically when we first distinguish our position vis-à-vis inherited discourses (1981, 345). He frequently employs spatial metaphors to describe the act of quoting someone else's language and the greater or lesser degree with which we indicate our agreement with that language, that is, whether we "distance" ourselves from the words we speak. For a discussion of language as the border between the self and the other, see 293.

19 This disjunction between soundtrack and image-track points to the relative power of voice-over and image in documentary film. Synchronous sound and long-takes allow film footage to "speak for itself," but still images are reduced to "illustrating" the soundtrack.

20 In other words, I want to read Tiana's voice-over as participating in the construction of an authorial/narratorial presence, but I want to resist the notion that the film gives us access to the "real" Tiana as auteur.

21 Reproduced in color in *Asia/America,* 49, and in black and white in *Amerasia Journal* 20, no. 1 (1994): 161.

22 The images to which Lee refers are scattered throughout *Amerasia Journal* 20, no. 1 (1994): ix, 83, 161. See also Machida (1994, 49, 106), where Pham's photographs are reproduced.

23 Excerpts from *Catch the Heat* appear elsewhere in *From Hollywood to Hanoi:* the action sequences that illustrate Tiana's Hollywood career and the video that Tiana's Vietnamese cousins watch on TV. In none of these three scenes is the film identified by name, and the voice-over encourages the spectator to infer that these are three different movies, in effect padding Tiana's c.v.

24 *From Hollywood to Hanoi* omits a few shots that suggest that Steiger is shot by another character, not by Tiana.

25 The offensiveness of the metaphor is self-evident, but allow me to note that the mention of "college campuses" suggests that women in higher education are particularly susceptible to the "tendency" of rape. The "beauty" of a woman is presumably comparable to the exploitable resources of a (post)colonial country.

26 The gender split in Tiana's depiction of her family is also expressed in the contrasting attitudes of her male and female relatives to Tiana's gifts; her grandmother likes the hat Tiana brings her, but her father refuses the helmet. For more on the gender dynamic in Tiana's family, see, Lynda Goldstein, "Herself as History" (1994).

27 In the pre-Cinemax versions of the film, the names of the U.S. servicemen are captioned on screen; in the Cinemax print, their names are mentioned in the subtitles but are not emphasized.

28 From the transcript of the soundtrack of *Surname Viet Given Name Nam,* in *Framer Framed* (1992, 59). Huynh Sanh Thong has translated *The Tale of Kieu* into English. Like Tiana, Trinh T. Minh-ha left Vietnam before the fall of Saigon and hails from an educated middle class; however, Trinh is a good ten years older than Thi Thanh Nga. That age difference no doubt accounts for Trinh's emphasis on Vietnamese tradition and family relationships and Tiana's perspective on U.S. media accounts and American suburban life. For an extended discussion of *Surname Viet Given Name Nam,* see Chapter 8.

29 This rhetoric of transformation is captured in the title of Lynda Goldstein's essay on *From Hollywood to Hanoi,* "Herself as History" (1994). For a discussion of Tiana's bodily performance in the context of contemporary images of Asian women in cinema, see Hagedorn's "Asian Women in Film" (1994).

30 Judith Butler argues that the parodic performances of gender expose gender norms as phantasmatic effects of discourse; in her view, parody is a variation on the repetition of gender norms, and because repetition makes gender norms (and the constitution of subjectivity) intelligible, parodic variation contributes to destabilizing gender normativity. Butler's argument is very similar to Bhabha's notion of mimicry (repetition with difference), and I therefore level a similar skepticism about the subversive potential of parody. (Butler's reference to "subversive laughter" keys my skepticism: whereas Walter Benjamin saw laughter as subversive and liberatory, I tend to side with Adorno's contention that laughter instead serves to defuse critical engagement and position the laughing subject as an object of interpellation.) See Butler's *Gender Trouble* (1990a), particularly her conclusion.

6 Becoming Asian American: *Chan Is Missing*

1 In this chapter, my use of the concept of "becoming" is drawn primarily from Trinh Minh-ha's formulation. The concepts of being and becoming are famously explored by Stuart Hall in an essay that appeared in *Framework* in 1989 under the title "Cultural Identity and Cinematic Representation." It has been reprinted often under the title "Cultural Identity and Diaspora" (1994). Hall argues that cinema does not merely record identities but constitutes them. *Chan Is Missing* both documents Asian American identity's process of becoming and embodies that process; further, to the extent that *Chan Is Missing* helped usher Asian American cinema into public consciousness, the film marks the becoming of Asian American cinema itself. Bakhtin also uses the word "becoming" to refer to an individual's process of coming to consciousness vis-à-vis ideological discourses (1981, 342).

2 Craig Owens notes, "Postmodernism is usually treated, by its protagonists and antagonists alike, as a crisis of cultural authority, specifically of the authority vested in Western culture and its institutions" (1992, 166).

3 W. Wang, 1984, 50. Page references for quotations from the film's dialogue refer to Wang's published continuity script; however, when the script as published conflicts with what I hear on the soundtrack of the video release, I have opted to notate what I hear. My notations differ primarily in the way I have punctuated: I have attempted to indicate the rhythms of speech rather than grammatical logic. Although the continuity script has been an invaluable reference, it is no more than that—as is the script of any highly improvised movie. The principle actors (Wood Moy and Marc Hayashi) as well as some of the supporting players (in particular, Peter Wang and Judi Nihei) deserve credit for "rewriting" the initial script written by Wayne Wang, Isaac Cronin, and Terrel Seltzer.

4 The apple pie example does not combine American form with Chinese content—that might arguably result in something Chinese American—but rather combines American form with Chinese technique. Technique is not content, but another manifestation of form. Trinh tells us, "To excel only in the mechanics of a language, be it verbal, visual, or musical is to excel only in imitation—the part that can be formulated, hence enclosed in formulas. Form as formulas can only express form; it cannot free itself from the form-content divide" (1991, 162). (Chinese content would perhaps be Chinese ingredients, but not baking techniques.)

5 Wang's name rhymes with "hang." Whereas some Chinese Americans with Wang's surname pronounce their name "wong," which is closer to the correct Cantonese pronunciation, other Chinese Americans accept the

Americanized pronunciation; in this, Wang is not unlike the descendents of European immigrants who have Anglicized or shortened their surname.

6 Wang's published script for *Chan Is Missing* includes a detailed bibliography of reviews, of which I was able to track down only a small fraction, as Asian American newspapers have limited regional circulation. My thanks to the staff of Seattle's *International Examiner* for locating back issues for me, and to the University of Iowa's Interlibrary Loan staff.

7 In analyzing the mainstream appeal of Amy Tan's novels, Sau-ling Cynthia Wong argues that counter-Orientalist rhetoric (e.g., when characters directly refute stereotypes) exists alongside hints of Chinatown exoticism, and together the two discourses constitute a "complex, unstable interplay of possibilities [that] makes for a larger readership" (1995b, 191). I would go further: the voicing of a counter-Orientalist position legitimates the novels' "authenticity" and reframes their own tendencies to exoticize Chinese culture. Such a rhetorical approach appeals strongly to progressive whites because it condemns overt racism while celebrating (unassimilable) ethnic difference.

8 It is ironic to cite the music as underlining and mocking a moment of intertextual reference in the film, for the score itself has been lifted from Michel Legrand's score for *The Go-Between* (1971). The musical quotation would suggest that the film's narrative approach belongs more in the realm of pastiche than of parody, to use Fredric Jameson's terminology. (The excerpt is not noted in the credits.)

9 I do not mean to imply that there is any such thing as a typical detective movie; rather, I have chosen this locution in the absence of satisfactory generic terminology. I am uncertain whether the detective film is best described as a genre, a mode, or a tendency, and the conflation of the terms film noir and hardboiled detective drama only adds to the confusion. Insofar as this chapter is concerned with destabilizing terminology and the process of becoming, it rejects the notion that a rigorous definition of the detective film would assist us. Thus, I have used the word typical to call attention to the fluidity of the detective film.

10 Another interpretation: when Steve says he was shot at by his own people, he is referring to U.S. soldiers.

11 For more on cross-ethnic casting in Wayne Wang's films, refer to the discussion of *The Joy Luck Club* in Chapter 8.

12 The implication that women assimilate more easily than men is, of course, tied up with the U.S. attitude that it is more acceptable for white males to associate with women of color than it is for white women to associate with men of color. For a discussion of how these attitudes play out in U.S. films about romances between Asians and whites, see Gina Marchetti's *Romance and the "Yellow Peril"* (1994). Marchetti discusses the roots of this attitude

in, for example, rape narratives and captivity stories, two genres that revolved around attitudes toward non-Asian people of color, and how those genres were inflected when Asians were inserted.

13 Presco is played by Bay Area writer Presco Tabios. For an audience familiar with Tabios's poetry, the figure of Presco marks a space where actor and character are not distinct and separable. More than an in-joke, the casting of Tabios as Presco underlines the self-reflexive advice that Presco dispenses.

14 Galperin refers to Steve as "the most attractive and accessible of the film's characters . . . [because] Steve attracts our fallen nature, makes us realize who we are and more important what we must resign to become like Jo or to imitate the still greater example of Chan Hung" (1987, 1167). I agree with Galperin that Steve's character exhibits the contradictions of hyphenate identity most visibly, but I resist the implication that Jo represents a more successful negotiation of Chinese and American cultures. To speak of how Steve has "fallen" and what Jo has "resigned" suggests not only a cultural hierarchy, but also that the process of becoming forecloses even a partial "return."

Norman Denzin, on the other hand, is interested less in the voice than the gaze. Denzin's reading focuses on Jo and pays Steve only lip-service, which is perhaps inevitable given Denzin's argument: he discusses *Chan Is Missing* as an interrogation of the Charlie Chan movies, in which he (reasonably) privileges Chan over his various sons. He argues that Charlie is "rational, virtuous, mature, normal" when contrasted with "irrational, depraved, childish, violent, immature Westerners" (1994, 67), and he further notes, "Of course in the Chan series Number One Son played the part of the immature, irrational, childish Asian; yet even this conduct was neutralized, by having Charlie act as the traditional-white-paternal father figure" (86 n. 17). I would take Denzin's argument one step further: not only is Charlie the "Asian male [who] knew who he was, knew his place in society" (74), but by disciplining his awkwardly acculturated sons he does not merely "act as" a white *patriarch* but serves to enforce white *patriarchy*. Unlike the Number One Son, however, Steve is not contained by Jo, as revealed by Jo's attempts to explain Steve to Steve ("Two-faced, schizophrenic Chinaman" [W. Wang, 1984, 48]). Just as we should resist the temptation to read Chan Hung as a symbol of the diversity of Asian America, so should we as critics avoid reducing Jo and/or Steve to points of identification for the audience. Furthermore, we should not assume that our critical activity positions us as representatives of a unitary audience (a move Galperin risks) nor as completely divorced from it (which Denzin risks when he argues that in *Chan Is Missing* "this self has become so thoroughly Westernized, no otherness is any longer possible" [1994, 79]).

15 Of course, the alternately bored, confused, and bemused expressions on Jo's and Steve's faces suggest that the graduate student is not communicating as effectively as she might hope, either.

16 In personal conversation, Lowe revealed her desire to rewrite her essay, which relies heavily on Chinese American and Japanese American texts to interrogate Asian American subjectivity. However, I have argued that the deconstruction of the cultural term Chinese American opens up the interval in which we might locate the political term Asian American. I therefore contend that neither Lowe's nor my project reduces Asian America to its Chinese American components, but rather attempts to destabilize Chinese American texts in favor of Asian American subjectivity. (By contrast, Denzin's analysis conflates Asian American and Chinese American terms, e.g., "the Asian-American must take a stand on the American experience that is either Pro-Taiwan and assimilationist, or anti-American and pro-People's Republic of China" [1994, 76]. The flip side is that Denzin conflates *Blowup, The Conversation, Sex, Lies, and Videotape,* and *JFK* as "Hollywood" films [83].)

7 We're Queer! We're Where? Locating Transgressive Films

1 The claims I'm making here about the transnational production and reception of queer cinema could also be applied to Mira Nair's films. *Mississippi Masala*'s interracial relationship can be compared with *The Wedding Banquet; Kama Sutra* was produced and released simultaneously with *Fire* and drew much attention for its sexually explicit themes and allusions to a classic Indian text; and *The Perez Family* occasioned much discourse about whether a filmmaker from one nonwhite ethnicity could accurately depict another, thus suggesting fruitful comparison with similar discourses surrounding Ang Lee's *Sense and Sensibility* and *The Ice Storm.*

The films of Peter Wang, an American filmmaker who has made films in the United States, mainland China, Hong Kong, and Taiwan, are also compelling investigations of national identity (see L. Lowe, 1991b). However, *First Date* (1992, set in 1950s Taiwan) and Wang's other films present sexuality in a much less convoluted fashion than *Fire* and *The Wedding Banquet.* Because I am specifically interested in the connections between sexuality and transnational film production, I have set Wang's films aside.

2 The distinctions between transnationalism and globalization are frequently difficult to discern. Jameson notes that "as a concept, 'globalization' knows its own internal slippages," including an interchangeability with the term transnationalism. Broadly speaking, globalization evokes

the symbolic relationships between nations, regions, or groups, marking a postmodern conception of relations between nation-states as spatial thematizations of class struggles (Jameson and Miyoshi, 1998, xi–xiii). For Jameson, then, transnationalism might be said to describe a particular instance of globalization.

3 Sheldon Lu's *Transnational Chinese Cinemas* (1997) employs a different usage: in this case, transnational film refers to films originating in different sites, distinct nations that nonetheless are perceived as connected, for example, the Chinese diaspora of mainland China, Taiwan, and Hong Kong, not to mention Singapore and the United States. Under this framework, Taiwanese, Hong Kong, and Chinese American films all stand under one transnational umbrella; in this sense, all films produced by diasporic people are transnational. Diverse reading formations across the diaspora are accounted for insofar as each of these cinemas proposes a different perspective on Chineseness.

4 Readings themselves will not be informed by transnationalism unless and until cultures meaningfully interact; Bamyeh points out that contemporary borders are permeable to capital and cultural products, exerting the most control over the flow of *people:* "Historically, this is a novel occurrence. While populations have over time followed the pathways established by the movement of trade and capital, today such pathways are being made inhospitable to one of the most important ingredients of a meaningfully transnational world, namely large-scale human interaction and truly multicultural ways of life" (1993, 78).

5 Berry takes pains to specify that this piece is not a "scholary essay," but a "catalog essay" (1998, 39–40).

6 Mark Chiang hypothesizes that "the success of independent (that is, non-Hollywood) films in the international art house and film festival circuit is most often tied to that text's proximity to the culture and values of the transnational capitalist class" (1998, 376). His account of the international film festival circuit is similar to but distinct from my own. Because I am particuarly interested in the film's reception by critics who are mired in local identities, I argue that the "culture and values" that appeal to transnational audiences due to their fluidity also permit misapprehensions, allowing critics to read such "cultures and values" not as fluid but indeed as fixed. Cynthia Liu makes a similar observation when she notes, "The juncture this film [*The Wedding Banquet*] occupies . . . contributes to decontextualized readings founded in market-specific assumptions regarding gender and genre" (1995, 3).

7 The marketing of exotic sexuality is wholly consistent with Orientalism. Said's *Orientalism* briefly notes the centrality of sexuality to Orientalism but does not engage the topic. Hastings notes that Said thereby reduces

sexuality to a heterosexual and phallocentric axis (1992, 130), and Porter (1994) focuses on passages of sensual description as instances of literary discourse that reveal the Orient as a representation.

8 In the discussion of *Fire* and *The Wedding Banquet* that follow, I have been greatly influenced by the interpretations of Gayatri Gopinath and Mark Chiang, respectively; however, I am interested in somewhat different audience formations, and therefore my interpretations diverge from theirs. Gopinath and Chiang are both primarily (but not exclusively) interested in Asian diasporic audiences, whereas I am interested in contrasting Western, Asian, and Asian diasporic readings. In "Nostalgia, Desire, Diaspora," Gopinath proposes a queer diasporic reading practice that will "render queer subjects intelligible" and mark the ways that queer sexuality "works within and against hegemonic nationalist and diasporic logic": "A queer diasporic reading and viewing practice conceptualizes a viewing public as located within multiple diasporic sites and the text itself as accruing multiple, sometimes contradictory meanings within these various locations. In other words, I place these texts within a framework of a queer South Asian diaspora, one that allows us to conceive of both the text and the viewer in motion" (1997, 473). Gopinath argues that texts that reinforce heteronormativity, nationalism, and conventional understandings of gender in some sites can be remobilized and queered in the diaspora. Her approach enables us to hold various readings in tension, thereby embracing provisionality and rejecting linear, teleological interpretations. Gopinath considers the West insofar as it structures the readings of diasporic people; I want to place more emphasis on how North American readings of *Fire* reveal Western attitudes toward diasporic filmmakers.

In "Coming Out into the Global System," Mark Chiang hypothesizes that "the success of independent (that is, non-Hollywood) films in the international art house and film festival circuit is most often tied to that text's proximity to the culture and values of the transnational capitalist class" (1998, 376). For Chiang, subjects who identify with the system of transnational capital over their national identities constitute transnational culture. He illuminates the ways *The Wedding Banquet* signifies on Taiwan's problematic identity as a nation founded by exiled Chinese nationalists so that he can examine the articulation of transnational identity by the film. Chiang is not primarily concerned with how the film is interpreted by people who do not belong to the transnational capitalist class, whereas I am intrigued by *The Wedding Banquet*'s popularity with diverse audiences.

9 For background on Mehta's career, I have drawn primarily from Zeitgeist's official Web site for *Fire,* Mehta's "Outlook," and Melwani (1996).

10 Sakhi for South Asian women held a benefit screening in New York with the stars in attendance.

11 One need only think of the U.S. Academy Awards and the slippage between the concepts of foreign film and foreign-language film to see the contradictions in the ways that language, culture, commerce, and national identity are mutually implicated.

12 Katharyne Mitchell notes that Canadian rhetoric of multiculturalism has avoided metaphors associated with the United States, such as the melting pot (1996, 228). This is in part due to the fact that Canadian unity is partly a response to U.S. cultural and economic hegemony.

13 Of course, some diasporic Asians may employ the genre of the coming-out narrative themselves. Nayan Shah considers narratives authored by South Asians in North America and Europe and agrees that Western conceptions of queer politics can be problematic, as when he comments that the notion of a gay movement "is itself a Western construct" (1993, 121).

14 Sudhir Kakar argues that Indian culture expresses its cultural values through storytelling: "For most orthodox Hindus, tales are a perfectly adequate guide to the causal structure of reality" (1989, 2). I think Kakar is attempting to account for the centrality of folktales and mythology as well as the popularity of Bollywood films in constructing images of romance for Indians. He limits his study to heterosexual relationships; arguably, this is because the forms he examines are heteronormative, but unfortunately he does not even allude to homosexuality in his introduction. Kakar's slippage between Indian and Hindu (evident in the passage quoted above) is also troubling.

15 Of course, even within the United States, the relationship between coming out and sexual identity is complicated: as Eve Kosofsky Sedgwick notes in *The Epistemology of the Closet* (1990), coming out must be continually repeated, for heteronormativity requires alternative sexual orientations to be continually resignified. (My thanks to Jeanette Roan for this comment.)

16 In "Out Here and Over There," David Eng's (1997) point of departure is a discussion of the yearning for "home" in both queer and Asian American discourses.

17 I am indebted to Poonam Arora for this insight; more recently, Jigna Desai made a similar point in her paper, "All the Rage: The Globalizing of Queerness and the Mobilizing of Sexuality through *Fire*" (2000).

18 Jigna Desai (2000) offers a congruent analysis of the film in relationship to fundamentalist Hindu reception of the film. Gopinath discusses non-Hindu spaces in "On *Fire*" (1998, 635) and heteronormative nationalist ideologies (in "Nostalgia, Desire, Diaspora," 1997, 468–70).

19 "Thackeray's Terms," 1998, n.p. The name Sita had already been changed to Nita when the film was dubbed into Hindi, at the instigation of the Censorship Board (Kapur 1998). Saira is the name of actor Dilip Kumar's wife;

Kumar was one of Mehta's copetitioners to the Supreme Court. Sabhana invokes Shabana Azmi.

20 See Johannes Fabian's *Time and the Other* (1983) for a critique of the West's tendency to locate other cultures in the past. Note also that it does not occur to these writers that different cultural contexts may require different kinds of feminism. See Aguilar's "Lost in Translation" (1997) for a discussion of Asian women's responses to Western feminism.

21 The context for this statement is a conversation in which Radha agrees that it is easier for Ashok to see the two women engaged in lovemaking than it would be for her to attempt to verbalize their relationship. Sita's words thus make sense only in the context of the film's thematization of the visualizable, introduced via scenes of Radha's parents suggesting that the child Radha attempt to close her eyes and see the ocean while sitting in a field of flowers.

22 Biographical information is drawn from Ito (1997), Lin (1993), Melwani (1993), and T. Nguyen (1993).

23 I enclose this term in inverted commas to indicate that this film bears much the same problematic relationship to Western understandings of visibility and sexual identity as the discourses that Manalansan critiques.

24 Of course, he has no way of knowing whether his grandchild will be male. He has previously confessed to Wai-Tung that he married only after he was prevailed on to continue the family name as the only surviving son, and presumably this is why he has pressured Wai-Tung, an only child, to marry. My reading is based on the U.S. video release, which uses the word grandchild in the subtitles. According to Sheng-mei Ma (1998), the subtitle is a mistranslation: Wai-Tung's father does indeed refer to a grandson in Mandarin. However, Cynthia Liu (1995) argues that the Mandarin dialogue preserves ambiguity: it can be interpreted as referring to a grandson or a grandchild.

25 My argument echoes that of Mark Chiang, who also identifies the banquet as the hinge between the generic modes of comedy and melodrama; citing Jameson's *Political Unconscious* on "generic discontinuity," Chiang argues that it is this generic recombination that "signals the film's status as a transnational allegory masquerading as a national one" (1998, 381). By contrast, Sheng-mei Ma proposes that the film be understood in terms of Chinese/Taiwanese generic categories. Ma refers to the film as a "domestic tragicomedy." He thus distinguishes the films from "domestic melodrama" (following E. Ann Kaplan, 1991), which in U.S. film theory and criticism tends to emphasize female-centered storytelling (1998, 147–48). "Domestic tragicomedy" also echoes the Chinese term "*Chia-t'ing Pei-hsi-chu* (family tragicomedy)" (149); Ma's larger project is to situate Lee's films as "the most recent phase in the evolution of *Liu-shue-shen wen-shueh* (overseas student

literature)" (144). Along similar lines, Cynthia Liu draws a distinction between what she calls the "domestic drama" and the women's film (or chick flick) as that term is understood in the U.S. film marketplace (1995, 6).

26 See the discussion of *Living on Tokyo Time* in Chapter 2.

27 I am alluding to David R. Shumway's "Screwball Comedies: Constructing Romance, Mystifying Marriage," wherein he argues that "the major cultural work of [screwball comedies] is not the stimulation of thought about marriage, but the affirmation of marriage in the face of the threat of a growing divorce rate and liberalized divorce laws" (1995, 381).

28 My thanks to Martin Brückner for this observation.

29 A personal anecdote: after viewing *The Wedding Banquet* with my family, my grandmother asked her son (my father) about homosexuality, because she could not reconcile the film's depiction with her own understanding of gay couples. She had thought that gay couples were composed of impotent men who relied on each other for emotional support in a heterosexual world.

30 Jeanette Roan, drawing from D. A. Miller (1990), notes that Wai-Tung is "a character who, on the level of denotation, we have been told is gay, but without any corresponding connotative signs" (1994, 9). Ling-Yen Chua argues that Wai-Tung's homosexuality can be authenticated only through an interracial same-sex relationship (1999, 109); intraracial Asian homosexuality cannot be visualized.

31 Chiang notes that Wei-Wei's decision not to abort the pregnancy "is understood by Wai-Tung (and the film) only as ventriloquizing the father's imperative [to reproduce]" (1998, 383), noting further that "Wai Tung's reconciliation with Simon depends on Wei Wei's decision to have the baby" (384). For Chiang, Wei-Wei's pregnancy figures her dependence on the system of global capital, a system that Chris Berry reminds us motivates the story insofar as Wai-Tung "has come to New York with the prior aim of managing his wealthy family's real estate investments" (1996, 163). By contrast, Lawrence Chua reads this scene in terms of metaphoric Western colonialism: "The black man's colonial relationship with his white boyfriend . . . relegates the black woman to the role of incubator" (1995, 260).

32 Dariotis and Fung offer a more nuanced and positive reading of *Eat Drink Man Woman* than I do here, in large part because they consider Jia-Chien's relationship with her father in all its complexity; for example, the reason Jia-Chien is not literally caring for her father is because he has remarried, thereby breaking tradition and giving Jia-Chien the ability "to make a choice that is not based on binary oppositional structures [between Chinese tradition and Western modernity]" (1997, 210). Cynthia Liu, in considering *The Wedding Banquet* as well as *Pushing Hands* and *Eat Drink Man Woman,* states that "the narratives of Lee's trilogy exhibit a punitive ten-

dency in his constructions of the feminine" (1995, 9). Liu shares my interest in investigating the film's reconciliation of antihomophobic and misogynist politics (10), noting the paradox that the film strives to expand our notion of what constitutes family while shoring up a patriarchal figure at the center of those families (14).

33 Ling-Yen Chua points out that Simon's American family is described as completely dysfunctional, reading the white American family in contrast to the Chinese family (1999, 106).

34 An updated version of Roan's paper on *The Wedding Banquet* (1994) is included in her dissertation (2001).

35 Of course, we discover that Mr. Gao understands English after all, but this is consistent with his role as puppetmaster.

36 In this chapter, I have not attempted to account for a queer Asian reading position, working instead with the constructions of identity articulated in Lee's film. To reiterate, it is my contention that the film's representation of gay Taiwanese American identity is completely incoherent. Cynthia Liu attempts to account for a gay Asian male subject position and a lesbian (Asian?) female in the concluding section of "To Love, Honor, and Dismay" (1995). Liu also briefly discusses a billingual (Mandarin and English) spectatorial position and the ambiguities in the English subtitles. Not surprisingly, many critics reviewing Lee's film were also unable to conceive of ethnicity and homosexuality as congruous. For example, *The Advocate* reveals an Orientalist perspective in describing Wai-Tung and Wei-Wei as a "Taiwanese couple" and in calling the banquet "sort of a cross between the recent nuptials of Japan's crown prince and *Bachelor Party,*" betraying the belief that Asians do not party (Kort 1993).

37 See Chiang (1998) for a discussion of what Wei-Wei's mainland Chinese identity represents vis-à-vis the film's articulation of Taiwanese nationalism.

8 Paying Lip Service: Narrators in *Surname Viet Given Name Nam* and *The Joy Luck Club*

1 Much of the literature on adaptations, cinematic versions of literary texts, proposes replacing the notion of "adapting" literature with the metaphor of "translation." In this chapter I am not concerned with the problematics of cinematic adaptation of literary texts per se, and when I refer to translation I am referring to literal translation—as from Vietnamese to French and French to English—more often than not. Useful condensations of the theoretic and aesthetic questions raised by adaptations are presented in Andrew's chapter on "Adaptation" in *Concepts in Film Theory* (1984), and in

a review article by Michaels (1998). Corrigan's *Film and Literature* (1999), which reprints many key articles on the topic, is an extremely useful and accessible volume.

2 As a commercial film based on a best-selling novel by an Asian American author, *The Joy Luck Club* was frequently described as a test of the commercial viability of Asian American films, with the presumption that "Asian-themed" films would follow if *The Joy Luck Club* were successful. The film thus came to speak for the potential for diverse Asian American voices to be heard in the cinematic marketplace. I argue that the film's marketing campaign, which positioned the film as speaking to (for) all Chinese American women, might be seen to undercut this strategy (If *Joy Luck Club* succeeds in representing Chinese American women, then why is a follow-up film necessary?), but history has shown that Hollywood favors product that is aimed at a loyal and identifiable market.

3 Biographical information on Trinh is drawn from a number of sources, primarily from interviews given by Trinh and collected in *Framer Framed* (1992, 96) and *Cinema Interval* (1999, 211).

4 *Framer Framed* (Trinh, 1992) includes another ur-text and another mediated text that incompletely masquerades as an ur-text, namely, the "script" for the film, more accurately a transcript. The tran/script is illustrated with excerpts from Trinh and Bourdier's storyboard-like lighting schemes, text on the right, drawings and notations on the left, in some cases these illustrations are further juxtaposed with frame enlargements or stills from the film itself. Of course, if the reader does not interpret the storyboards as illustrations, as visual embodiment of the text of the tran/script, but interprets the tran/script and illustrations as one text, then the whole becomes yet another version of *Surname Viet Given Name Nam,* a version that, like the film, repeats certain passages in different modes. Goellnicht argues that the stills in *Woman/Native/Other* do not "concretize" (illustrate) the written text: because the photos are presented in collages, they call attention to their status as constructions (1997, 348–49).

5 A step printer is a machine that copies frames from one strip of film to another, allowing the filmmaker to arrange frames in any desired sequence (holding on a single frame, producing reverse motion, etc.). Step-printing can refer to any of these processes, but generally describes the repetition of frames at a fixed ratio, resulting in an extreme slow motion, methodical enough that it isolates gestures and de-emphasizes the continuity of movement.

6 The film's credits identify the actors by their full names. In this chapter, I use the given names of the actors, for several reasons. First, the given names are meant to connote not familiarity but anonymity, following Mai Thu Van's practice of identifying her interviewees only by given name.

Second, I am following the practice observed in *Framer Framed* (Trinh, 1992, 50n). Third, because some of the women give their surnames first and others adopt the Western convention of placing surname last, my use of first names here will assist the reader in distinguishing surname and given name.

7 Rhona Berenstein makes a similar point (1990, 161–62).

8 In an interview with Isaac Julien and Laura Mulvey, Trinh makes the same connection between the women's choices of location and the codes of dress (1992, 194–95). The juxtaposition of these separate interviews in the same volume is itself a commentary on the way that a seemingly spontaneous interview can be rehearsed.

9 In Chapter 4's discussion of *The Way to My Father's Village,* I argue that this split can be inscribed into the text itself.

10 By September 1993, when the film opened, Tan's debut novel had sold over two million copies and been translated into twenty-three languages; it stayed on the *New York Times*'s best-seller list for a year and a half (Hajari, 1993). For an account of the roles that Tan's agent, editors, and publishers played in developing and promoting the book, see Feldman (1989).

11 Suyuan's second husband, Canning, accompanies June to China and narrates part of Suyuan's story. In the film, June travels to China alone (which seems to contradict an earlier statement that she is not fluent in Mandarin), but Suyuan's story is still narrated briefly by Canning. To my knowledge, no critic of either the film or the novel has analyzed the effect of this lone male narrator who provides crucial information about the central story in *The Joy Luck Club.*

12 Coincidentally, Tan had already adapted "The Moon Lady" into a children's book illustrated by Gretchen Schields. She also performs the abridged audio version of her book, which excises the Ying Ying–Lena storyline entirely. (Apparently, a few scenes from this storyline were shot but did not make the final cut; see http://goldsea.com/Personalities/Nuyenfrance/nuyenfrance.html.)

13 Avins, 1993, 2:14. According to the article, both Tan and producer Janet Yang were approached by members of a preview audience and praised for their performances in the film. This was not an isolated case; filmmaker Jessica Yu (1993b) reports that she was repeatedly mistaken for Ming-Na Wen at the 1993 Telluride Film Festival.

14 In addition to an actor's performance, mise-en-scène can also construct ethnicity. For example, Tamlyn Tomita's costume in the hairdresser's scene (a white cashmere jacket over a red silk blouse and black slacks) went a long way toward helping this particular viewer see beyond her non-Chinese features, as those colors are favored by many Chinese American women and not by Asian American women of other ethnicities (in my experience).

Of course, some aspects of the mise-en-scène may receive less attention than a lead actor's wardrobe. Charlie Chin, who portrayed "band member #5," reports that he nearly lost his mustache when "the make-up person patiently told me that Chinese men didn't wear mustaches in the 1930's" (1993, 5).

15 This discussion took place on the Internet newsgroup alt.asian-movies during the fall of 1993. I am grateful to Michael Raine for this information. Although Wang apparently insisted on casting only Mandarin speakers in the roles of Chinese women, Russell Wong (in the role of a Chinese man) is clearly dubbed. For a discussion of Chinese mistranslations in Tan's novels, see Sau-Ling Wong's " 'Sugar Sisterhood' " (1995b). George Tseo (1996) also examines Tan's translations and comments on differences between the film's English subtitles and the spoken Mandarin.

16 See Ron Miller's emphasis on parallels between Polly Bemis and Rosalind Chao in Chapter 2's discussion of *Thousand Pieces of Gold.* I might also cite Chao's statement that she felt "a personal tie" to Tan's novel ("L.A. Woman" 1990), but this article can hardly be considered promotion for the film, as it was published in 1990.

17 For an account of the open casting call held in Flushing, Queens, in the fall of 1992, see C. Smith (1992).

18 Levitt and Wang are quoted saying essentially the same thing in Avins (1993); Levitt's name is misspelled Levin in that article.

19 In the finished film, the characters on the pier do not repeat this story; it is possible that Wang is misremembering an incident associated with filming the scene on the roadside. (Wang's imperfect memory is evident elsewhere in the interview, when he confuses the characters played by Christopher Rich and Andrew McCarthy.)

20 Rose's grandmother, played by Vivian Wu, is not named in the film, at least not in the English subtitles.

21 Asked point-blank "Which daughter is most like you?" Tan declines to single out any of the characters (Chatfield-Taylor 1989, 179).

22 I am indebted to Karen Gaffney, who first suggested this autobiographical interpretation as one of many possible readings of *The Joy Luck Club* in a seminar at the University of Delaware.

23 Hajari (1993) quotes France Nuyen (Ying Ying): "Joy Luck represents the fantasy of every misunderstood child. . . . You want to realize that your mother never really was mean to you. In real life that kind of communication rarely happens."

24 Taking a different psychoanalytic tack, Rey Chow argues that as the mothers *are seen,* reconciliation is forestalled. Chow's account highlights the paradox of the narratives of China: the mothers supposedly narrate what they saw, but the force of cinematic convention overtakes their

ability to describe their vision, rendering the mothers as spectacles to be seen. Chow argues that the mothers in *The Joy Luck Club* are "encrypted texts, gestural archives, and memory palaces" whose visual apprehensibility reveals "what Walter Benjamin calls the 'optical unconscious'. . . . The resulting aesthetic effect is not one of identity with but one of a distant fascination for this awesome 'animal' and 'being' which strikes us as spectacle and drama, and in front of which we lose control of our bodies—we cry" (1998, 107–8). Chow is speaking almost exclusively about scenes of the mothers in China, not of their encounters with their daughters in the United States, where they assert what it is that they see.

Afterword: The Asian American Muse

1 I am not using the term historicity to mean "historical authenticity." Rather, my usage derives from Tejaswini Niranjana's discussion of historicity as "that part of the past that is still operative in the present," itself derived from Foucault's declaration, "Effective history affirms knowledge as perspective" (from "Nietzsche, Genealogy, History," quoted in Niranjana, 1992, 37).

2 Thematizing amnesia is not the exclusive province of documentary and experimental movies. To take two recent examples, Rea Tajiri's *What Happened to Her . . . and the Strawbery Fields* (1997) describes the transfer of a mother's repressed memories to her daughter, and Quentin Lee and Justin Lin's *Shopping for Fangs* (1997) turns on a former refugee's traumatic amnesia. In both cases, the false memory generates new identity formations.

BIBLIOGRAPHY

Abrams, Joan. 1997. "Myths of Polly: Author, Historical Archeologist Digs Deep to Set Right the Life of One of Idaho's Legends." *Lewiston Morning Tribune,* 10 Jan., 1D+.

Abrash, Barbara, and Catherine Egan, eds. 1992. *Mediating History: The MAP Guide to Independent Video by and about African American, Asian American, Latino, and Native American People.* New York: New York University Press.

"Acclaimed Film to Be Shown at Art Academy." 1982. Review of *Chan Is Missing. Honolulu Star-Bulletin,* 17 June, D1.

"Adaptation Brings Joy to Tan." 1993. (Toronto) *Globe and Mail,* 18 Sept., C24.

Adler, Jerry. 1995. "The Rise of the Overclass." *Newsweek,* 31 July: 32–46.

Adorno, Theodor W. 1982. "Subject and Object." In *The Essential Frankfurt School Reader,* ed. Andrew Arato and Eike Gebhardt. New York: Continuum.

Aguilar, Delia D. 1997. "Lost in Translation: Western Feminism and Asian Women." In *Dragon Ladies: Asian American Feminists Breathe Fire,* ed. Sonia Shah. Boston: South End Press, 153–65.

Aguilar-San Juan, Karin, ed. 1994. *The State of Asian America: Activism and Resistance in the 1990s.* Boston: South End Press.

Albos, Marilyn. 1996a. "Filipino Docudramas in Asian Film Festival." *Filipino Reporter,* 25, no. 30 (25 July): 28.

———. 1996b. "Minority Voices Hit the Big Screen." *Filipino Reporter* 25, no. 41 (10 Oct.): 28.

Altman, Rick. 1980. "Moving Lips: Cinema as Ventriloquism." *Yale French Studies* 60, no. 1: 67–79.

———. 1989. *The American Film Musical.* 1987. Bloomington: Indiana University Press.

———. 1992a. "Introduction: Four and a Half Film Fallacies." In *Sound Theory/Sound Practice,* ed. Rick Altman. New York: Routledge, 35–45.

———, ed. 1992b. *Sound Theory/Sound Practice.* New York: Routledge.

Anderegg, Michael. 1991. *Inventing Vietnam: The War in Film and Television.* Philadelphia: Temple University Press.

Anderson, Benedict. 1998. *The Spectre of Comparisons: Nationalism, Southeast Asia, and the World.* London: Verso.

Anderson, John. 1997. "Slow-burning Issues Fuel *Fire.*" *Newsday,* 22 Aug., II B 8.

Anderson, Joseph D. 1996. *The Reality of Illusion: An Ecological Approach to Cognitive Film Theory.* Carbondale: Southern Illinois University Press.

Andrew, Dudley. 1984. *Concepts in Film Theory.* New York: Oxford University Press.

Ansen, David. 1982. "Chinese Puzzle." Review of *Chan Is Missing. Newsweek,* 21 June, 65–66.

———. 1993. "Straightening Up the House: Old Taiwan Meets Gay New York." *Newsweek,* 16 Aug., 61.

Anton, Saul. 1994. "A Search for Roots and Identity: An Interview with Tiana Thi Thanh Nga." *Cineaste* 20, no. 3: 46–47.

Armstrong, Richard et al. 1991. *1991 Biennial Exhibition.* New York: Whitney Museum of American Art.

Asai, Susan Miyo. 1995. "Transformations of Tradition: Three Generations of Japanese American Music Making." *Musical Quarterly* 79, no. 3 (fall): 429–53.

Asian Women United of California. 1989. *Making Waves.* Boston: Beacon.

———. *Making Waves II.* 1996. Boston: Beacon.

Auer, James. 1989. "Vietnamese Women Topic of Film Study." Review of *Surname Viet Given Name Nam. Milwaukee Journal,* 22 Oct., 8E.

Auster, Paul. 1990. *The New York Trilogy.* New York: Penguin.

———. 1991. *The Music of Chance.* 1990. New York: Penguin.

———. 1995. *Smoke & Blue in the Face: Two Films.* New York: Hyperion.

Avins, Mimi. 1993. "How to Tell the Players in 'The Joy Luck Club.' " *New York Times,* national ed., 5 Sept., 2: 14.

Azoulay, Katya Gibel. 1996. "Outside Our Parents' House: Race, Culture, and Identity." *Research in African Literatures* 27, no. 1 (spring): 129–42.

Bailey, Cameron. 1997. "Teens Go on a Tear in Reel Asian." *Toronto Now,* 20 Nov., n.p.

Baker, Kathryn. 1993. " 'Joy Luck Club' Roles Hit Actresses Close to Home." *USA Today,* 23 Sept., 10D.

Baker, Martha. 1992. "A View of the West through Chinese Eyes." Review of *Thousand Pieces of Gold. St. Louis Post-Dispatch,* 24 Jan., 3F.

Bakhtin, M. M. 1981. *The Dialogic Imagination.* Ed. Michael Holquist, trans. Caryl Emerson and Michael Holquist. Austin: University of Texas Press.

———. 1986. *Speech Genres and Other Late Essays.* Ed. Caryl Emerson and Michael Holquist, trans. Vern W. McGee. Austin: University of Texas Press.

Baldwin, James. 1990. *The Devil Finds Work.* 1976. New York: Laurel-Dell.

Baltake, Joe. 1997. "Indian-made *Fire* Burns with Passion and Change." *Sacramento Bee,* 31 Oct., TK20.

Bamyeh, Mohammed A. 1993. "Transnationalism." *Current Sociology* 41, no. 3 (winter).

Barrera, Mario. 1997. "Comparing Latino and Asian American Film Narrations." JSRI Occasional Paper 33, The Julian Samora Research Institute, Michigan State University, East Lansing.

Barsam, Richard M. 1992. *Nonfiction Film: A Critical History.* Revised ed. Bloomington: Indiana University Press.

Barthes, Roland. 1977. *Image, Music, Text.* Trans. Stephen Heath. New York: Farrar, Straus, and Giroux.

———. 1981. *Camera Lucida: Reflections on Photography.* Trans. Richard Howard. New York: Farrar, Straus and Giroux.

Baxter, Otis. 1993. *Weekly Journal* 74 (30 Sept.): 10.

Beechert, Edward D. 1985. *Working in Hawai'i: A Labor History.* Honolulu: University of Hawai'i Press.

Before Hollywood. 1987 New York: Hudson Hills Press.

Benjamin, Walter. 1968. "The Task of the Translator." Trans. Harry Zohn. In *Illuminations,* ed. Hannah Arendt. New York: Schocken Books, 69–82.

Berenstein, Rhona. 1990. "Remembering History: Films by Women at the 1989 Toronto Film Festival." *Camera Obscura* 22 (Jan.): 159–66.

Berg, Tina Desireé. 1996. "From Hollywood to Hanoi: Formerly a Femme '007,' Tiana Alexandra Directs for Oliver Stone." *Femme Fatales* 4, no. 6 (Jan.): 50–53.

Berry, Chris. 1996. "Sexual DisOrientations: Homosexual Rights, East Asian Films, and Postmodern Postnationalism." In *In Pursuit of Contemporary East Asian Culture,* ed. Xiabing Tang and Stephen Snyder. Boulder, CO: HarperCollins/Westview Press, 157–82.

———. 1998. "Introducing 'Mr. Monster': Kim Ki-young and the Critical Economy of the Globalized Art-House Cinema." In *Post-Colonial Classics of Korean Cinema,* ed. Chungmoo Choi. Irvine, CA: Korean Film Festival Committee.

Bhabha, Homi K. 1994. *The Location of Culture.* London: Routledge.

Biederman, Patricia Ward. 1995. "Film Combines Love Story and Tale of Chinese in the Old West." *Los Angeles Times,* 2 Nov., Valley ed., sec. Calendar: 1A.

Blaise, Clark, and Bharati Mukherjee. 1995. *Days and Nights in Calcutta.* St. Paul, MN: Hungry Mind Press.

Bluestone, George. 1957. *Novels into Film.* Berkeley: University of California Press.

Blumentritt, Mia. 1998. "*Bontoc Eulogy,* History, and the Craft of Memory: An Extended Conversation with Marlon E. Fuentes." *Amerasia Journal* 24, no. 3: 75–90.

Bordwell, David, Janet Staiger, and Kristin Thompson. 1985. *The Classical Hollywood Cinema: Film Style and Mode of Production to 1960.* New York: Columbia University Press.

Bowen, Peter. 1996. "Spontaneous Combustion." Review of *Fire.* http://sundancechannel.com/toronto/s92.html

Bowman, James. 1993. "The Fall of the Family." Review of *The Joy Luck Club. American Spectator,* Nov., 68.

Breitbart, Eric. 1997. *A World on Display: Photographs from the St. Louis World's Fair, 1904.* Albuquerque: University of New Mexico Press.

Brodie, John. 1994. "'Bride' Jilts Sundance Fest at the Altar." *Variety,* 10–16 Jan., 13–14.

Burr, Ty. 1993. "Asian Gracefully." Review of *The Joy Luck Club. Entertainment Weekly,* 17 Sept., n.p.

Butler, Judith. 1990a. *Gender Trouble: Feminism and the Subversion of Identity.* New York: Routledge.

———. 1990b. "Performative Acts and Gender Constitution: An Essay in Phenomenology and Feminist Theory." In *Performing Feminisms: Feminist Critical Theory and Theatre,* ed. Sue-Ellen Case. Baltimore: Johns Hopkins University Press, 270–82.

———. 1991. "Imitation and Gender Insubordination." In *Inside/Out: Lesbian Theories, Gay Theories,* ed. Diana Fuss. New York: Routledge, 13–31.

———. 1993. *Bodies That Matter: On the Discursive Limits of "Sex."* New York: Routledge.

Campbell, Bob. 1997. "Asian Film Festival Offers Eastern Exposures." *Star-Ledger,* 17 July, n.p.

Canby, Vincent. 1982. " 'Chan Is Missing' in Chinatown." *New York Times,* 24 Apr., 13.

Carr, Jay. 1997. " 'Fire' Adds Fuel to Feminism in India." *Boston Globe,* 3 Oct., D6.

Catr. 1987. Review of *Living On Tokyo Time. Variety,* 25 Feb.

"Caught at Filmex in L.A." 1982. Review of *Chan Is Missing. Variety* 31 Mar., 26.

Cha, Theresa Hak Kyung, ed. 1981. *Apparatus.* New York: Tanam Press.

———. 1995. *Dictee.* Berkeley, Third Woman Press.

Chambers, Veronica. 1993. "Surprised by Joy: Amy Tan and a Flock of Talented Actresses Hope 'The Joy Luck Club' Changes the Way Hollywood Treats Asian-Americans." *Premiere,* Oct., 80–84.

"*Chan Is Missing* Gets Rave Reviews in NY." 1982. *East/West,* 2 June, 8.

Chan, Maxine. 1982. "Wayne Wang, Finding Artistic Freedom." *International Examiner* 9, no. 16 (18 Aug.): 7.

Chan, Sucheng. 1991. *Asian Americans: An Interpretive History.* Boston: Twayne.

Chang, Lia. 1994. "Seen and Heard." *Asian New Yorker,* Nov.–Dec., 7.

Chatfield-Taylor, Joan. 1989. "Cosmo Talks to Amy Tan." *Cosmopolitan,* Nov., 178–80.

Chawla, Preeti. 1994a. "Head of the Club: A Talk with Tsai Chin." *A. Magazine* 3, no. 1 (Mar.): 32.

———. 1994b. "Wayne's World." *A. Magazine* 3, no. 1 (Mar.): 31–32.

Cheung, Kng-Kok. 1993. *Articulate Silences: Hisaye Yamamoto, Maxine Hong Kingston, Joy Kogawa.* Ithaca, NY: Cornell University Press.

Chiang, Mark. 1998. "Coming Out into the Global System: Postmodern Patriarchies and Transnational Sexualities in *The Wedding Banquet,*" in Eng and Hom, 374–95. Rpt. in Feng (2002), 273–92.

Chin, Charlie. 1993. "Extra! Read All About It!" *Asian New Yorker,* Apr., 5.

Chin, Frank. 1984. "The Most Popular Book in China." *Quilt* 4: 6–12.

———. 1991a. "Come All Ye Asian American Writers of the Real and the Fake." In *The Big Aiiieeeee! An Anthology of Chinese American and Japanese American Literature,* ed. Jeffery Paul Chan et al. New York: Meridian, 1–92.

———. 1991b. *Donald Duk.* Minneapolis: Coffee House Press.

Chin, Frank, and Jeffery Paul Chan. 1972. "Racist Love." In *Seeing through Shuck,* ed. Richard Kostelanetz. New York: Ballantine.

Chin, Frank et al., eds. 1991. *Aiiieeeee! An Anthology of Asian American Writers.* 1974. New York: Mentor-NAL.

Chin, Justin. 1999. *Mongrel: Essays, Diatribes, and Pranks.* New York: St. Martin's Press.

Chiu, Tony. 1982. "Wayne Wang: He Made the Year's Unlikeliest Hit." *New York Times,* 30 May, 17.

Cho, Sumi K. 1993. "Korean Americans vs. African Americans: Conflict and Construction," in Gooding-Williams, 196–211.

Chow, Rey. 1998. *Ethics after Idealism: Theory, Culture, Ethnicity, Reading.* Bloomington: Indiana University Press.

Chu, Janet H. 1996. "Film and Multiculturalism: Erasing Race in Nancy Kelly's *Thousand Pieces of Gold.*" In *Changing Representations of Minorities East and West.* Honolulu: University of Hawai'i Press, 75–97.

Chu, Louis. 1993. *Eat a Bowl of Tea.* 1961. New York: Carol Publishing Group.

Chua, Lawrence. 1995. "The Postmodern Ethnic Brunch: Devouring Difference." In *In a Different Light: Visual Culture, Sexual Identity, Queer Practice,* ed. Nayland Blake, Lawrence Rinder, and Amy Scholder. San Francisco: City Lights Books, 253–62.

Chua, Ling-Yen. 1999. "The Cinematic Representation of Asian Homosexuality in *The Wedding Banquet.*" *Journal of Homosexuality* 36, nos. 3–4: 99–112.

Chughtai, Ismat. 1990. *The Quilt and Other Stories.* Trans. Tahira Naqvi and Syeda S. Hameed. New Delhi: Kali for Women.

Citron, Michelle. 1999. *Home Movies and Other Necessary Fictions.* Minneapolis: University of Minnesota Press.

Clark, Mike. 1993. "With 'Joy Luck,' Disney Grows Up." *USA Today,* 8 Sept., D1.

Cohen, Anthony P. 1989. *The Symbolic Construction of Community.* 1985. London: Routledge.

Cook, David A. 1996. *A History of Narrative Film.* 3d ed. New York: Norton.

Corliss, Richard. 1993a. "All in the Families." Review of *The Joy Luck Club. Time,* 13 Sept., 68.

———. 1993b. "Pacific Overtures: In Movies and Music Videos, in Fiction and Fashion, Asian Chic Takes America." *Time,* 13 Sept., 68–70.

———. 1994. "The Gay Gauntlet: Now That *Philadelphia* Is a hit, Can Hollywood Still Shun Gay Themes?" *Time,* 7 Feb., 62.

Corrigan, Timothy. 1999. *Film and Literature: An Introduction and Reader.* Upper Saddle River, NJ: Prentice Hall.

Crane, David. 1989. "Trinh's 'Surname': Between 'Nam and a Hard Place." (Milwaukee) *Shepherd Express,* 26 Oct., 17.

Dare, Sheryl. 1995. "A Passage to Hawai'i: The Picture Brides' Tale." *New York Times,* 23 Apr., national ed., H13, 16.

Dariotis, Wei Ming, and Eileen Fung. 1997. "Breaking the Soy Sauce Jar: Diaspora and Displacement in the Films of Ang Lee." In *Transnational Chinese Cinemas: Identity, Nationhood, Gender,* ed. Sheldon Hsiao-peng Lu. Honolulu: University of Hawai'i Press, 187–220.

Dauphin, Gary. 1997. "Out of Asia: The 20th Asian American International Film Festival." *Village Voice,* 22 July, n.p.

Davis, Francis. 1986. "Introducing Sumi Tonooka." In *In the Moment: Jazz in the 1980s.* New York: Oxford University Press, 90–98.

de la Cruz, Enrique B., and Pearlie Rose S. Balayut, eds. 1998. *Confrontations, Crossings, and Convergence: Photographs of the Philippines and the United States, 1898–1998.* Los Angeles: UCLA Asian American Studies Center and UCLA Southeast Asia Program.

Del Mundo, Clodualdo A. 1998. *Native Resistance: Philippine Cinema and Colonialism, 1898–1941.* Manila: De La Salle University Press.

Denby, David. 1982. Review of *Chan Is Missing. New York,* 7 June, 72.

Denzin, Norman K. 1994. "*Chan Is Missing:* The Asian Eye Examines Cultural Studies." *Symbolic Interaction,* 17, no. 1: 63–89.

Desai, Jigna. 2000. "All the Rage: The Globalizing of Queerness and the Mobilizing of Sexuality through *Fire.*" Paper presented at Association for Asian American Studies, Scottsdale, AZ, 25 May.

"Dialogue on Film: Wayne Wang." 1986. *American Film,* July/Aug., 17–19.

Dirlik, Arif. 1996. "Asians on the Rim: Transnational Capital and Local Community in the Making of Contemporary Asian America." *Amerasia Journal* 22, no. 3: 1–24.

Dittmar, Linda, and Gene Machaud, eds. 1990. *From Hanoi to Hollywood.* New Brunswick, NJ: Rutgers University Press.

Dittus, Erick. 1983. "Chan Is Missing: An Interview with Wayne Wang." *Cineaste* 12, no. 3: 16–20.

Doane, Mary Ann. 1982. "Film and the Masquerade: Theorising the Female Spectator." *Screen* 23, no. 3–4: 74–88. Rpt. in Mast, Cohen, and Braudy, 758–72.

Dong, Lorraine. 1982. Review of *Thousand Pieces of Gold* by Ruthanne Lum McCunn. *Amerasia Journal* 9, no. 1: 113–14.

Downie, John. 1996. "Documents of Dispersed Identity." Review of *Bontoc Eulogy. Illusions* 25 (winter): 30–32.

Du Bois, W. E. B. 1989. *The Souls of Black Folk.* 1903. New York: Bantam Books.

Dyer, Richard. 1979. *Stars.* London: BFI Publishing.

Ebert, Roger. 1982a. " 'Chan Is Missing' Journeys through Real Chinatown." *Chicago Sun-Times,* 10 Sept., 47.

———. 1982b. " 'Chan Is Missing' Warm, Funny Look at Chinese in U.S." *Chicago Sun-Times,* 20 Apr., *Weekender,* 55.

———. 1991. "Angry and Romantic, 'Gold' Tells Powerful, Poignant Tale." *Chicago Sun-Times,* 8 Nov., n.p.

———. 1993. Review of *The Joy Luck Club. Chicago Sun-Times,* 17 Sept., n.p.

———. 1997. " 'Fire' Strikes at Indian Repression." *Chicago Sun-Times,* 17 Sept., 38.

Edelstein, David. 1987. "Passion on the Potomac." Review of *Living on Tokyo Time. Village Voice,* 18 Aug., 57.

Elley, Derek. 1992. Review of *From Hollywood to Hanoi.* (23 Nov.).
Elsensohn, Sister M. Alfreda. 1970. *Idaho Chinese Lore.* Cottonwood: Idaho Corporation of Benedictine Sisters.
———. 1979. *Idaho County's Most Romantic Character: Polly Bemis.* Cottonwood: Idaho Corporation of Benedictine Sisters.
Eng, David L. 1993. "*The Wedding Banquet:* You're Not Invited and Some Other Ancillary Thoughts." *Artspiral* 7: 8–10.
———. 1997. "Out Here and Over There: Queerness and Diaspora in Asian American Studies." *Social Text* 15, nos. 3–4 (fall–winter): 31–52.
Eng, David L., and Alice Y. Hom, eds. 1998. *Q&A: Queer in Asian America.* Philadelphia: Temple University Press.
Enloe, Cynthia. 1990. *Bananas, Beaches, and Bases: Making Feminist Sense of International Politics.* Berkeley: University of California Press.
Espiritu, Yen Le. 1992. *Asian American Panethnicity: Bridging Institutions and Identities.* Philadelphia: Temple University Press.
Everett, Marshall. 1904. *The Book of the Fair.* Philadelphia: P. W. Ziegler Co.
Fabian, Johannes. 1983. *Time and the Other: How Anthropology Makes Its Object.* New York: Columbia University Press.
Fanon, Frantz. 1967. *Black Skin, White Masks.* Trans. Charles Lam Markmann. New York: Grove Weidenfeld.
———. 1973. *The Wretched of the Earth.* Trans. Constance Farrington. New York: Ballantine Books.
Faris, William S. 1993. "*The Wedding Banquet* Looks at Love, Truth, and the Steps in Between." *Northwest Asian Weekly* 12, no. 30 (31 July): 4.
Felchlin, Marva R. 1996a. "A Classic Western with a Chinese Heroine." *Spur* 9, no. 1 (Apr.–June): 6+.
———. 1996b. "Thousand Pieces of Gold." *Cowboys & Indians* (spring): 105.
Feldman, Gayle, 1989. "The Joy Luck Club: Chinese Magic, American Blessings and a Publishing Fairy Tale." *Publishers Weekly* 236, no. 1 (7 July): 24–26.
Feng, Peter X. 1995. "In Search of Asian American Cinema." *Cineaste* 21, nos. 1–2: 32–36.
———. 1996a. "Being Chinese American, Becoming Asian American: *Chan Is Missing.*" *Cinema Journal* 35, no. 4: 88–118.
———. 1996b. "Redefining Asian American Masculinity: Steven Okazaki's *American Sons.*" *Cineaste* 22, no. 3: 27–29.
———. 2000. "Recuperating Suzie Wong: A Fan's Nancy Kwan-dary," in Hamamoto and Liu, (40–56).
———, ed. 2002. *Screening Asian Americans.* New Brunswick, NJ: Rutgers University Press.
———. "Romancing the Hybrid: The Texts 'of' Han Suyin." Unpublished ms.
"Filipinos Join Asian Film Fest." 1996. *Filipino Express* 10, no. 30 (28 July): 19.
Fischer, Michael M. J. 1986. "Ethnicity and the Post-Modern Arts of Memory." In *Writing Culture: The Poetics and Politics of Ethnography,* ed. James Clifford and George E. Marcus. Berkeley: University of California Press, 194–233.

Fong, Joe Chung. 1996. "Transnationalized Newspapers: The Making of the Post-1965 Globalized/Localized San Gabriel Valley Chinese Community." *Amerasia Journal* 22, no. 3: 65–77.

Foster, Gwendolyn Audrey. 1997. *Women Filmmakers of the African and Asian Diaspora: Decolonizing the Gaze, Locating Subjectivity.* Carbondale: Southern Illinois University Press.

Francia, Luis H. 1994. "The Painted Lady." *A. Magazine* 3, no. 1 (Mar.): 40–41.

———. 1995. Review of *Picture Bride. Village Voice* 2 May, 56.

Franke, Lizzie. 1995. "Yinshi Nan Nu." Review of *Eat Drink Man Woman. Sight and Sound* 5, no. 1 (Jan.): 83–84.

Friedman, Lester D., ed. 1991. *Unspeakable Images: Ethnicity and the American Cinema.* Urbana: University of Illinois Press.

Fuchs, Cynthia. 1993. Review of *From Hollywood to Hanoi. Vietnam Generation "Big Book"* 5, nos. 1–4: 407–8.

Fung, Lilia. 1993. "*The Joy Luck Club* Is a Hit." *Asian New Yorker,* Oct., Film-4.

Fung, Richard. 1990. "Multiculturalism Reconsidered." In *Yellow Peril Reconsidered,* ed. Paul Wong. Vancouver: On Edge, 17–20.

———. 1991. "Looking for My Penis: The Eroticized Asian in Gay Video Porn." In *How Do I Look? Queer Film and Video,* ed. Bad Object-Choices. Seattle: Bay Press.

———. 1993. "Shortcomings: Questions about Pornography as Pedagogy." In *Queer Looks: Perspectives on Lesbian and Gay Film and Video,* ed. Martha Gever, Pratihba Parmar, and John Greyson. New York: Routledge.

———. 1994. "Seeing Yellow: Asian Identities in Film and Video." In *The State of Asian America: Activism and Resistance in the 1990s,* ed. Karin Aguilar-San Juan. Boston: South End Press, 161–71.

Gabrenya, Frank. 1990. " 'Surname Viet' Is Intellectual Delight." *Columbus Dispatch* 25 May, 10H.

———. 1995. "Stories—and Audience—Carried along as Thoughtful 'Smoke' Drifts." Review of *Smoke. Columbus Dispatch,* 30 June, 12D.

Gach, Gary. 1994. "*Pushing Hands* Has a Sure Touch of Success." Review of *Pushing Hands. AsianWeek* 15, no. 55 (12 Aug.): 15.

Galperin, William. 1987. " 'Bad for the Glass': Representation and Filmic Deconstruction in *Chinatown* and *Chan Is Missing.*" *MLN* 102, no. 5 (Dec.): 1151–70.

Gates, Henry Louis, Jr., ed. 1986. *"Race," Writing and Difference.* Chicago: University of Chicago Press.

———. 1988. *The Signifying Monkey: A Theory of African-American Literary Criticism.* New York: Oxford University Press.

———. 1992. *Loose Canons: Notes on the Culture Wars.* New York: Oxford University Press.

Gee, Bill J. 1990. *Asian American Media Reference Guide.* 2d ed. New York: Asian Cinevision.

Gelmis, Joseph. 1987. "An Inconvenient Marriage of Convenience." Review of *Living on Tokyo Time. Newsday,* 14 Aug., II 5.

Gerstel, Judy. 1997. "Women Find Each Other in a House of Missing Men." Review of *Fire*. *Toronto Start*, 21 Sept., B6.

Gesensway, Deborah, and Mindy Roseman. 1987. *Beyond Words: Images from America's Concentration Camps*. Ithaca, NY: Cornell University Press.

Gleiberman, Owen. 1997. "Take My Wife: *Fire*, a Tale of Illicit Lesbian Love in Contemporary India, Evokes the Early Days of American Feminism." *Entertainment Weekly*, 12 Sept., 110.

Goellnicht, Donald C. 1997. "Blurring Boundaries: Asian American Literature as Theory." In *An Interethnic Companion to Asian American Literature*, ed. King-Kok Cheung. Cambridge, England: Cambridge University Press, 338–65.

Gold, Rich. 1989. Review of *Surname Viet Given Name Nam*. *Variety*, 27 Sept., 47.

Goldberg, David Theo, ed. 1990. *Anatomy of Racism*. Minneapolis: University of Minnesota Press.

Goldstein, Lynda. 1994. "Herself as History: Thi Thanh Nga's *From Hollywood to Hanoi*." Paper presented at Asian Cinema: Poetics and Politics, Ohio University, Athens, Ohio, 3 Nov.

Gooding-Williams, Robert, ed. 1993. *Reading Rodney King, Reading Urban Uprising*. New York: Routledge.

Goodman, Walter. 1987. Review of *Living on Toyko Time*. *New York Times*, 14 Aug., C20.

Gopinath, Gayatri. 1996. "Funny Boys and Girls: Notes on a Queer South Asian Planet." In *Asian American Sexualities: Dimensions of the Gay and Lesbian Experience*, ed. Russell Leong. New York: Routledge, 119–27.

———. 1997. "Nostalgia, Desire, Diaspora: South Asian Sexualities in Motion." *positions* 5, no. 2 (fall): 467–89.

———. 1998. "On *Fire*." *GLQ: A Journal of Lesbian and Gay Studies* 4, no. 4: 631–36. Rpt. in Feng (2002), 293–98.

Gotanda, Philip Kan. 1995. *Fish Head Soup and Other Plays*. Seattle: University of Washington Press.

Grant, Barry Keith, ed. 1995. *Film Genre Reader II*. Austin: University of Texas Press.

Green, Suzanne D. 1996. "Thematic Deviance or Poetic License? The Filming of *The Joy Luck Club*." In *Vision/Re-Vision: Adapting Contemporary American Fiction by Women to Film*, ed. Barbara Tepa Lupack. Bowling Green, KY: Bowling Green State University Popular Press, 211–25.

Grenier, Richard. 1994. "Enter the Chinese." Review of *The Joy Luck Club*. *Commentary*, May, 49–52.

Griffin, John. 1997. "*Fire* Is Fitting Festival Opener: Film Reflects Image & Nation's Less Hard-Core Approach." Montreal *Gazette*, 15 Oct., B4.

Gruner, Elliott. 1993. *Prisoners of Culture: Representing the Vietnam POW*. New Brunswick, NJ: Rutgers UP.

Gupta, Aruna Mallya. 1996. "Film Festivals Ignite: Deepa Mehta's Film 'Fire' Wins Awards in Toronto, Chicago." *India Currents* 10, no. 8 (30 Nov.): D8

Guthmann, Edward. 1982. "Goodbye Stereotypes." Review of *Chan Is Missing. San Francisco Bay Guardian,* 14 July, 14.

———. 1997. "Festival's 'Generasian X' of Young Filmmakers." *San Francisco Chronicle,* 5 Mar., E1+.

Haas, Lynda. 1995. " 'Eighty-Six the Mother': Murder, Matricide, and Good Mothers." In *From Mouse to Mermaid: The Politics of Film, Gender, and Culture,* ed. Elizabeth Bell, Lynda Haas, and Laura Sells. Bloomington: Indiana University Press, 193–211.

Hagedorn, Jessica, ed. 1993. *Charlie Chan Is Dead: An Anthology of Contemporary Asian American Fiction.* New York: Penguin.

———. 1994. "Asian Women in Film: No Joy, No Luck." *Ms.* 4, no. 4 (Jan.–Feb.): 74–79.

Hajari, Nisid. 1993. "Luck Is What You Make It." *Entertainment Weekly,* 24 Sept., n.p.

Hall, Doug, and Sally Jo Fifer. 1990. *Illuminating Video: An Essential Guide to Video Art.* New York: Aperture.

Hall, Stuart. 1994. "Cultural Identity and Diaspora," in Williams and Chrisman, 392–403.

Hamamoto, Darrell Y. 1994. *Monitored Peril: Asian Americans and the Politics of TV Representation.* Minneapolis: University of Minnesota Press.

———. 1996. "History and Memory: Social Voyeurism and Asian American Subjectivity." Paper presented at Society for Cinema Studies Conference, Dallas, Texas, 8 Mar.

———. 1998. "New Independence at the San Francisco International Asian American Film Festival." *Journal of Asian American Studies* 1, no. 2 (July): 204–9.

Hamamoto, Darrell, and Sandra Liu, eds. 2000. *Countervisions: Asian American Film Criticism.* Philadelphia: Temple University Press.

Han, Ji Hui Judy, with Marie K. Morohoshi. 1998. "Creating, Curating, and Consuming Queer Asian American Cinema: An Interview with Marie K. Morohoshi," in Eng and Hom, 81–94.

Hanley, JoAnn. 1993. *The First Generation: Women and Video, 1970–75.* New York: Independent Curators Incorporated.

Har. 1990. Review of *Thousand Pieces of Gold. Variety,* 9 May.

Harlan, Heather. 1997. "N.Y. Mayor Defends Immigration: Highlights Economic and Social Contributions of 'the Newest New Yorkers.' " *AsianWeek* 18, no. 22 (23 Jan.): 8.

Harper, Phillip Brian. 1994. *Framing the Margins: The Social Logic of Postmodern Culture.* New York: Oxford University Press.

Hastings, Tom. 1992. "Said's *Orientalism* and the Discourse of (Hetero)sexuality." *Canadian Review of American Studies* 23, no. 1 (fall): 127–47.

Hatch, Robert. 1982. "Films." Review of *Chan Is Missing. The Nation,* 3 July, 26–27.

"Here." 1996. *Filipinas Magazine* 5, no. 52 (31 Aug.): 42.

Hesford, Walter. 1996. "*Thousand Pieces of Gold:* Competing Fictions in the Representation of Chinese-American Experience." *Western American Literature* 31, no. 1 (May): 49–62.

Heung, Marina. 1990. "Haunting Film Probes Life and Art in Exile." Review of *Surname Viet Given Name Nam. New Directions for Women* 19, no. 1 (Jan.–Feb.): 11.

———. 1991. "Documentary Recovers Memories of Wartime Interment." Review of *History and Memory. New Directions for Women* 20, no. 6 (Nov.–Dec.): 12–13.

Higa, Karin M. 1992. "The View from Within." In *The View from Within: Japanese American Art from the Internment Camps, 1942–1945.* Los Angeles: Japanese American National Museum, 21–44.

———. 1999. "Bruce and Norman Yonemoto: A Survey." In *Bruce and Norman Yonemoto: Memory, Matter, and Modern Romance.* Los Angeles: Japanese American National Museum, 8–37.

Higashi, Sumiko. 1993. "Film Reviews: *History and Memory, Memories from the Department of Amnesia, Who's Going to Pay for These Donuts Anyway?, Days of Waiting.*" *American Historical Review,* Oct., 1181–84.

———. 1998. "Melodrama, Realism, and Race: World War II Newsreels and Propaganda Film." *Cinema Journal* 37, no. 3 (spring): 38–61.

Hinsch, Britt. 1990. *Passions of the Cut Sleeve: The Male Homosexual Tradition in China.* Berkeley: University of California Press.

Hinson, Hal. 1993. Review of *The Joy Luck Club. Washington Post,* 24 Sept., n.p.

Hoberman, J. 1989. "Mekong Delta Blues." Review of *Surname Viet Given Name Nam. Village Voice,* 11 Apr., 61.

Holden, Stephen. 1991. Review of *Thousand Pieces of Gold. New York Times* 27 Sept., C10.

Holt, Hamilton, ed. 1990. *The Life Stories of Undistinguished Americans As Told by Themselves.* 2d ed. New York: Routledge.

Hong, Minne Jung-Min. 1993a. "Janice Tanaka: A Personal Vision in the Public Eye [Part 1]." *Asian New Yorker,* July, 3+.

———. 1993b. "Janice Tanaka: A Personal Vision in the Public Eye [Part 2]." *Asian New Yorker,* Aug., 6.

———. 1995. "O Pioneers! Japanese Hawaiian History Unfolds in *Picture Bride.*" *Asian New Yorker,* Apr., 8.

hooks, bell. 1996. "The Cultural Mix: An Interview with Wayne Wang." In *Reel to Real: Race, Sex, and Class at the Movies.* New York: Routledge, 124–40.

Horkheimer, Max, and Theodor W. Adorno. 1991. *The Dialectic of Enlightenment.* Trans. John Cumming. New York: Continuum.

Hornaday, Ann. 1993. "A Director's Trip from Salad Days to a 'Banquet.'" *New York Times,* 1 Aug., sec. 2, p. 25.

Howe, Desson. 1987. Review of *Living on Tokyo Time. Washington Post,* 4 Sept., n.p.

———. 1993. Review of *The Joy Luck Club. Washington Post,* 24 Sept., n.p.

Hsiao, Andy. 1993. "The Man on a 'Joy Luck' Ride: Asian American Director Wayne Wang, at Home with Women and Tradition." *Washington Post,* 27 Sept., B1+.

Huang, Jack. 1994. "Ang Lee: Director Father Husband Son." *Northwest Asian Weekly* 13, no. 34 (27 Aug.): 17.

Hutcheon, Linda. 1989. *The Politics of Postmodernism.* London: Routledge.

———. 1994. *Irony's Edge: The Theory and Politics of Irony.* London: Routledge.

Huyn Sanh Thông, ed. and trans. 1979. *The Heritage of Vietnamese Poetry.* New Haven: Yale University Press.

Hwang, David Henry. 1990. *FOB and Other Plays.* New York: Plume.

Iezzi, Teressa. 1997. "Shopping for Fangs." *Playback,* 8 Sept., B11–12.

Im, Soyon. 1996. "Confucian-like Society in Jane Austen." Review of *Sense and Sensibility. International Exmainer* 22, no. 24 (2 Jan.): 12.

———. 1997. "The Second Generation's Payback: *Yellow,* Produced and Directed by Chris Chan Lee." *Korean American Historical Society Occasional Papers* 3, 111–15.

Ito, Robert. 1997. "From Taiwan to Tinseltown: With *The Ice Storm,* Ang Lee Directs a Likely Oscar Contender." *AsianWeek* 19, no. 12 (12 Nov.): 21.

Jaehne, Karen. 1989. "The 18th New Directors/New Films Festival." *Film Comment* 25, no. 3 (May–June): 68+.

James, Caryn. 1991. "Film as a Shaper of American Culture." Review of *History and Memory. New York Times,* 19 Apr., n.p.

James, David E. 1989. *Allegories of Cinema: American Film in the Sixties.* Princeton, NJ: Princeton University Press.

———. 1999. "Tradition and the Movies: The Asian American Avant-Garde in Los Angeles." *Journal of Asian American Studies* 2, no. 2 (June): 157–80.

Jameson, Fredric. 1981a. " 'In the Destructive Element Immerse': Hans-Jürgen Syberberg and Cultural Revolution." *October* 17 (summer): 99–118.

———. 1981b. *The Political Unconscious: Narrative as a Socially Symbolic Act.* Ithaca, NY: Cornell University Press.

Jameson, Fredric, and Masao Miyoshi, eds. 1998. *The Cultures of Globalization.* Durham, NC: Duke University Press.

Jeffords, Susan. 1989. *The Remasculinization of America: Gender and the Vietnam War.* Bloomington: Indiana University Press.

Johnson, Barbara. 1985. "Taking Fidelity Philosophically." In *Difference in Translation,* ed. Joseph F. Graham. Ithaca, NY: Cornell University Press, 142–48.

Johnson, Brian D. 1993. "Terms of Endearment." Review of *The Joy Luck Club. Maclean's,* 27 Sept., 70.

———. 1997. "Forbidden Flames." Review of *Fire. MacLean's,* 29 Sept., 86.

Jung, Soya. 1993a. "Tan Takes Her Tale to Hollywood." *International Examiner,* 15 Sept., 1+.

———. 1993b. "Wang Works Wonders in 'The Joy Luck Club.' " *International Examiner,* 15 Sept., 11.

Kakar, Sudhir. 1989. *Intimate Relations: Exploring Indian Sexuality.* Chicago: University of Chicago Press.

Kaliss, Jeff. 1989. "Vietnamese Film Maker's Unusual Work." Review of *Surname Viet Given Name Nam. San Francisco Chronicle,* 12 Feb., 28–30.

Kammen, Michael. 1993. *Mystic Chords of Memory: The Transformation of Tradition in American Culture.* New York: Vintage/Random House.

Kang, L. Hyun-Yi. 1993. "The Desiring of Asian Female Bodies: Interracial Romance and Cinematic Subjection." *Visual Anthropology Review* 9, no. 1 (spring): 5–21. Rpt. in Feng (2002), 71–98.

Kapke, Barry. 1989. Review of *Surname Viet Given Name Nam. High Performance,* summer, 74–75.

———. 1998. "Re-membering Home." In *Dangerous Women: Gender and Korean Nationalism,* ed. Elaine H. Kim and Chungmoo Choi. New York: Routledge, 249–90.

Kaplan, E. Ann. 1991. "Melodrama/Subjectivity/Ideology: Western Melodrama Theories and Their Relevance to Recent Chinese Cinema." *East-West Film Journal* 5, no. 1 (Jan.): 6–27.

Kapur, Ratna. 1998. "Fire Goes up in Smoke." *The Hindu,* 13 Dec., n.p.

Kauffmann, Stanley. 1982. "Mysteries, Comic and Otherwise." Review of *Chan Is Missing. The New Republic,* 16 June, 24–25.

———. 1993. Review of *The Wedding Banquet. The New Republic,* 16 Aug., 25.

Kehr, Dave. "A Feast from the East." (New York) *Daily News,* clipping file: n.d., n.p.

———. 1991a. "Pretty 'Paradise' Misplaces its Point of View." Review of *Come See the Paradise. Chicago Tribune,* 18 Jan 1991. Section 7, page B+.

———. 1991b. " 'Thousand Pieces of Gold' Is 24-karat Public Television." *Chicago Tribune,* 6 Nov., 7D.

Kempley, Rita. 1987. Review of *Living on Tokyo Time. Washington Post,* 4 Sept., n.p.

———. 1991. " 'Gold,' without Glitter." *Washington Post,* 17 June, C7.

Kessler, Lauren. 1993. *Stubborn Twig: Three Generations in the Life of a Japanese American Family.* New York: Random House.

Kim, Ben. 1998. "Fade to *Yellow.*" *KoreAm Journal,* May, 16–19.

Kim, David D. 1991. Review of *Thousand Pieces of Gold. Village Voice* 22 Oct., 70–71.

Kim, Elaine H. 1982. *Asian American Literature: An Introduction to the Writings and Their Social Context.* Philadelphia: Temple University Press.

———. 1990. " 'Such Opposite Creatures': Men and Women in Asian American Literature." *Michigan Quarterly Review* 29.1 (winter): 68–93.

———. 1992. Foreword to *Reading the Literatures of Asian America,* ed. Shirley Geok-lin Lim and Amy Ling. Philadelphia: Temple University Press.

———. 1993. "Home Is Where the *Han* Is: A Korean-American Perspective on the Los Angeles Upheavals," in Gooding-Williams, 215–345.

Kim, Elaine H., and Norma Alarcón, eds. 1994. *Writing Self, Writing Nation: A Collection of Essays on Dictée by Theresa Hak Kyung Cha.* Berkeley: Third Woman Press.

Kingston, Maxine Hong. 1989. *The Woman Warrior.* New York: Vintage/Random House.

———. 1990. *Tripmaster Monkey: His Fake Book.* New York: Vintage/Random House.

Kirkland, Bruce. 1997. "Film Lights a Fire under Tradition: Deepa Mehta Takes on the Customs of India in the First of Three Works." *Toronto Sun,* 24 Sept., 62.

Klawans, Stuart. 1989. Review of *Surname Viet Given Name Nam. The Nation,* 17 Apr., 529–31.

———. 1993. Review of *The Joy Luck Club. The Nation,* 4 Oct., 364–66.

Kort, Michelle. 1993. "To Love, Honor, and Dismay." *The Advocate,* 27 July, 71.

Koshy, Susan. 1996. "The Fiction of Asian American Literature." *Yale Journal of Criticism* 9: 315–46.

Kudaka, Geraldine, ed. 1995. *On a Bed of Rice: An Asian American Erotic Feast.* New York: Anchor-Doubleday.

Kureishi, Hanif. 1988. *Sammy and Rosie Get Laid: The Script and the Diary.* London: Faber and Faber.

Lacey, Liam. 1997. "When the East Meets the West: A New Festival Focuses on North American Filmmakers of Asian Ancestry." (Toronto) *Globe and Mail,* 20 Nov., n.p.

Lam, Michael. 1981. "Program Notes: *Chan Is Missing:* Hard-edged, Gutsy." *East/West,* 2 Dec., 11.

———. 1982. "Program Notes." *East/West,* 7 July, 13.

Lane, Jim. 1993. "Notes on Theory and the Autobiographical Documentary Film in America." *Wide Angle* 15, no. 3 (July): 21–36.

Lanning, Michael Lee. 1994. *Vietnam at the Movies.* New York: Fawcett Columbine/Ballantine.

Lasky, Julie. 1994. "A Jewish Writer Discovers the China Syndrome." *Forward* 98, no. 31 (18 Nov.): 9.

Lau, Alan Chong. 1982. "State of the Art." Review of *Chan Is Missing. International Examiner* 9, no. 14 (21 July): 4.

"L.A. Woman [Rosalind Chao]." 1990. *Transpacific* 5, no. 1 (Jan.–Feb.): 46–51.

Lawrence, Amy. 1992. "Women's Voices in Third World Cinema." In *Sound Theory/Sound Practice,* ed. Rick Altman. New York: Routledge, 178–90.

"Leaving Hollywood for Hanoi." 1993. *Asian New Yorker,* Aug., 2+.

Lee, C. Y. 1957. *The Flower Drum Song.* New York: Farrar, Straus, and Cudahy.

Lee, Chris Chan. 1996. "The Other Chris Lee in *My Yellow Life.*" *Yolk* 3, no. 3: 17.

Lee, Elisa. 1993. "Kayo Hatta Whips Up Some Hawaiian Movie Magic: *Picture Bride* Takes on Epic Proportions." *AsianWeek* 15, no. 3 (10 Sept.): 17.

Lee, Erica. 1994. "Breaking through the Chrysalis: Hanh Thi Pham." *Amerasia Journal* 20, no. 1: 129–35.

Lee, Helen. 1998. "A Peculiar Sensation: A Personal Genealogy of Korean American Women's Cinema." In *Dangerous Women: Gender and Korean Nation-*

alism, ed. Elaine H. Kim and Chungmoo Choi. New York: Routledge, 291–322.

Lee, JeeYeun. 1998. "Toward a Queer Korean American Diasporic History," in Eng and Hom, 185–209.

Lee, Joann Faung Jean. 2000. *Asian American Actors: Oral Histories from Stage, Screen, and Television.* Jefferson, NC: McFarland.

Lendon, Nigel. 1999. "The Trajectory of Agency in Hanh Nguyet Ngo's *Surname Viet, Given Name Kieu.*" *Third Text* 46 (spring): 73–82.

Leonard, Karen. 1997. "Finding One's Own Place: Asian Landscapes Revisioned in Rural California." In *Culture, Power, Place: Explorations in Critical Anthropology,* ed. Akhil Gupta and James Ferguson. Durham, NC: Duke University Press, 118–36.

Lesage, Julia. 1974. "The Human Subject: You, He, or Me? (Or, The Case of the Missing Penis)." *Jump Cut* 4 (Nov.–Dec.): 77–82.

Leventhal, Frances. 1989. "Trinh Minh-ha Breaks Convention in Film." *AsianWeek,* 17 Feb., 24.

Light, Ivan, and Edna Bonacich. 1988. *Immigrant Entrepreneurs: Koreans in Los Angeles, 1965–1982.* Berkeley: University of California Press.

Lin, Jeff J. 1993. "Lee Strikes Box Office Gold with Unlikely Subject Matter." *International Examiner* 20, no. 15 (17 Aug.): 17.

———. 1994. "Ang Lee: Pitting Chinese Tradition against Modern Freedoms: The Director of *Eat Drink Man Woman* Talks about Family, Society and Expectation." *International Examiner* 21, no. 16 (6 Sept.): 16.

Liu, Cynthia W. 1995. " 'To Love, Honor, and Dismay': Subverting the Feminine in Ang Lee's Trilogy of Resuscitated Patriarchs." *Hitting Critical Mass: A Journal of Asian American Cultural Criticism* 3, no. 1 (winter): 1–60.

Liu, Julie. 1996. "Rea Tajiri." *Tart Magazine,* winter, 43.

Loizos, Peter. 1993. *Innovation in Ethnographic Film: From Innocence to Self-Consciousness, 1955–1985.* Chicago: University of Chicago Press.

Lopate, Phillip. 1996. "In Search of the Centaur: The Essay-Film." In *Beyond Document: Essays on Nonfiction Film,* ed. Charles Warren. Hanover, NH: University Press of New England/Wesleyan University Press, 243–70.

Lowe, Lisa. 1991a. *Critical Terrains: French and British Orientalisms.* Ithaca, NY: Cornell University Press.

———. 1991b. "Heterogeneity, Hybridity, Multiplicity: Marking Asian American Differences." *Diaspora* 1, no. 1: 24–44.

———. 1996. *Immigrant Acts: On Asian American Cultural Politics.* Durham, NC: Duke University Press.

———. 1997. "Work, Immigration, Gender: New Subjects of Cultural Politics," in Lowe and Lloyd, 354–74.

Lowe, Lisa, and David Lloyd, eds. 1997. *The Politics of Culture in the Shadow of Capital.* Durham, NC: Duke University Press.

Lu, Sheldon Hsiao-peng, ed. 1997. *Transnational Chinese Cinemas: Identity, Nationhood, Gender.* Honolulu: University of Hawai'i Press.

Lum, Wing Tek. 1982. "*Chan Is Missing* Marks New Age of Asian American Film." *East/West,* 28 July, 9–10.

Lyons, Tom. 1997. "Asian Movies for Real." *Eye,* 20 Nov., 34.

Lyotard, Jean-François. 1984. *The Postmodern Condition: A Report on Knowledge.* Trans. Geoff Bennington and Brian Massumi. Minneapolis: University of Minnesota Press.

Ma, Sheng-mei. 1998. *Immigrant Subjectivities in Asian American and Asian Diaspora Literatures.* Albany: State University of New York Press.

Machida, Margo. 1994. "Out of Asia: Negotiating Asian Identities in America." In *Asia/America: Identities in Contemporary Asian American Art.* New York: Asia Society Galleries, 65–110.

Mackinnon, Ian. 1998. "Director Fights Back as Riots Halt Lesbian Film." *The Scotsman,* 8 Dec., 10.

Mai Thu Vân. 1983. *Viêtnam: Un peuple, des voix.* Paris: Pierre Horay.

Manalansan, Martin F., IV. 1994. "Searching for Community: Filipino Gay Men in New York City." *Amerasia Journal* 20, no. 1: 59–73.

———. 1997. "In the Shadows of Stonewell: Examining Gay Transnational Politics and the Diasporic Dilemma," in Lowe and Lloyd, 485–505.

Manuel, Susan. 1989. "Vietnamese Women Pulled from Obscurity." Review of *Surname Viet Given Name Nam. Honolulu Star-Bulletin,* 1 Dec., B1–2.

Marable, Manning. 1990. "The Rhetoric of Racial Harmony: What's Wrong with Integration?" *Sojourners,* Aug.–Sept., 14–18.

Marchetti, Gina. 1994. *Romance and the "Yellow Peril": Race, Sex, and Discursive Strategies in Hollywood Fiction.* Berkeley: University of California Press.

Marcus, Laura. 1994. *Auto/biographical Discourses: Theory, Criticism, Practice.* Manchester, England: Manchester University Press.

Margulies, Ivone. 1993. "Delaying the Cut: The Space of Performance in *Lightning over Water.*" *Screen* 34, no. 1 (spring): 54–68.

Marks, Laura U. 1994. "A Deleuzian Politics of Hybrid Cinema." *Screen* 35, no. 3 (Aug.): 244–64.

———. 1995. "Straight Women, Gay Porn, and the Scene of Erotic Looking." *Jump Cut* 40: 127–36.

———. 2000. *The Skin of the Film: Intercultural Cinema, Embodiment, and the Senses.* Durham, NC: Duke University Press.

Maslin, Janet. 1993. "Intimate Family Lessons, Available to All." Review of *The Joy Luck Club. New York Times,* 8 Sept., B1.

Mast, Gerald, Marshall Cohen, and Leo Braudy, eds. 1992. *Film Theory and Criticism: Introductory Readings.* 4th ed. New York: Oxford University Press.

Mayne, Judith. 1993. *Cinema and Spectatorship.* London: Routledge.

McCarthy, Todd. 1994. Review of *Picture Bride. Variety,* 23 May.

McCunn, Ruthanne Lum. 1988. *Thousand Pieces of Gold.* 1981. Boston: Beacon Press.

McGuire, Matt. 1990. "Filmmakers Kelly and Yamamoto Tap the Riches of History with *Thousand Pieces of Gold.*" *In Marin,* Nov., 16–19.

Mehta, Deepa. "Outlook." *http://www.tpl.com.sg/timesnet/data/ab/docs/ab1031.html*

Melwani, Lavina. 1993. "Ang Lee: Making the Movies That Matter." *AsianWeek* 14, no. 50 (6 Aug.): 1.

———. 1996. "Trial by Fire." *Little India* 6, no. 11 (30 Nov.): 59–61. [http://www.littleindia.com/india/Nov96/trial.htm]

Merrick, Hélène. 1990. "Septième Art: Une Affaire d'Argent." *La Revue du Cinéma* 465 (Nov.): 69–70.

Metz, Christian. 1974. *Film Language.* Trans. Michael Taylor. New York: Oxford University Press.

———. 1982. *The Imaginary Signifier: Psychoanalysis and the Cinema.* Trans. Celia Britton, Annwyl Williams, Ben Brewster, and Alfred Guzzetti. Bloomington: Indiana University Press.

Michaels, Lloyd. 1998. Review of James Griffith's *Adaptations as Imitations* and Brian McFarlane's *Novel to Film. Screen* 39, no. 4 (winter): 425–32.

Mielke, Robert. 1995. " 'American Translation': *The Joy Luck Club* as Film." *Paintbrush* 22 (autumn): 68–75.

Miller, D.A. 1990. "Anal *Rope.*" *Representations* 32 (fall): 114–33.

Miller, Ron. 1992a. "Actress Rosalind Chao Finds the Golden Role." *San Jose Mercury-News,* 1 May, 1D+.

———. 1992b. "Internment on TV: Talented Asian Actors Are Second-Class Citizens in the Land of Prime Time." *San Jose Mercury-News,* 1 May, 1D+.

Mimura, Glen Masato. 2000. "Antidote for Collective Amnesia? Rea Tajiri's Germinal Image," in Hamamoto and Liu.

Mitchell, Katharyne. 1996. "In Whose Interest? Transnational Capital and the Production of Multiculturalism in Canada." In *Global/Local: Cultural Production and the Transnational Imaginary,* ed. Rob Wilson and Wimal Dissanayake. Durham, NC: Duke University Press, 219–51.

Mitchell-Kernan, Claudia. 1973. "Signifying." In *Mother Wit from the Laughing Barrel: Readings in the Interpretation of Afro-American Folklore,* ed. Alan Dundes. Englewood Cliffs, NJ: Prentice-Hall, 310–28.

Mochizuki, Ken. 1997. "Filmmaker's Search for Missing Internment Past Leads to 'Strawberry Fields.' " *North American Post,* 30 May, 1+.

Morris, Meaghan. 1988. *The Pirate's Fiancée: Feminism, Reading, Postmodernism.* London: Verso.

Morrison, Toni. 1990. "The Site of Memory." In *Out There: Marginalization and Contemporary Culture,* ed. Russell Ferguson, Martha Gever, Trinh T. Minh-ha, and Cornel West. New York: New Museum of Contemporary Art, 299–305.

Morson, Gary Saul, and Caryl Emerson, eds. 1989. *Rethinking Bakhtin: Extensions and Challenges.* Evanston, IL: Northwestern University Press.

"A Mother and Daughter Rediscover China." 1993. *Parade Magazine,* 10 Oct., 20.

Muecke, D. C. 1982. *Irony and the Ironic.* 2d ed. London: Methuen.

Mullick, Swapan. 1998. "Explosive Power of the Woman." Review of *Fire. The Statesman,* 26 Nov., n.p.

Mulvey, Laura. 1975. "Visual Pleasure and Narrative Cinema." *Screen* 16, no. 3 (autumn): 6–18.

———. 1981. "Afterthoughts on 'Visual Pleasure and Narrative Cinema' Inspired by *Duel in the Sun.*" *Framework* 6, nos. 15–17: 12–15.

———. 1989. *Visual and Other Pleasures.* Bloomington: Indiana University Press.

Muñoz, José Esteban. 1999. *Disidentifications: Queers of Color and the Performance of Politics.* Minneapolis: University of Minnesota Press.

Muskat, Lisa, and Jesse Lerner. 1997. "On 'Bontoc Eulogy.'" *BLIMP Film Magazine* 36: 53–56.

Musser, Charles. 1991. *Before the Nickelodeon: Edwin S. Porter and the Edison Manufacturing Company.* Berkeley: University of California Press.

Nakanishi, Don T. 1993. "Surviving Democracy's 'Mistake': Japanese Americans and the Enduring Legacy of Executive Order 9066." *Amerasia Journal* 19, no. 1: 7–35.

Neale, Steve. 1980. *Genre.* London: BFI.

———. 1990. "Questions of Genre." *Screen* 31, no. 1 (spring): 45–66.

Nguyen Du. 1983. *The Tale of Kieu: A Bilingual Edition of* Truyen Kieu. Trans. Huynh Sanh Thong. New Haven: Yale University Press.

Nguyen Ngoc Bich, ed. 1975. *A Thousand Years of Vietnamese Poetry.* New York: Knopf.

Nguyen, Tri Q. 1993. "A Talk with the Man behind *The Wedding Banquet:* Ang Lee." *Northwest Asian Weekly* 12, no. 31 (7 Aug.): 1.

Nguyen, Viet. *Race and Resistance: Literature and Politics in Asian America.* New York: Oxford University Press, 2002.

Nichols, Bill. 1981. *Ideology and the Image.* Bloomington: Indiana University Press.

———, ed. 1985. *Movies and Methods, Vol. 2.* Berkeley: University of California Press.

———. 1996. "Historical Consciousness and the Viewer: *Who Killed Vincent Chin?*" In *The Persistence of History: Cinema, Television, and the Modern Event,* ed. Vivian Sobchak. New York: Routledge.

Niranjana, Tejaswini. 1992. *Siting Translation: History, Post-Structuralism, and the Colonial Context.* Berkeley: University of California Press.

Niu, Greta Ai-Yu. 1998. *People of the Pagus: Orientalized Bodies and Migration in an Asian Pacific Rim.* Ann Arbor: UMI, 1998.

Nornes, Abé Mark, and Fukushima Yukio, eds. 1994. *The Japan/America Film Wars: WWII Propaganda and Its Cultural Contexts.* Chur, Switzerland: Harwood Academic Publishers.

Okihiro, Gary Y. 1991. *Cane Fires: The Anti-Japanese Movement in Hawaii, 1865–1945.* Philadelphia: Temple University Press.

———. 1994. *Margins and Mainstreams: Asians in American History and Culture.* Seattle: University of Washington Press.

Omi, Michael, and Howard Winant. 1994. *Racial Formation in the United States: From the 1960s to the 1990s.* 2d ed. New York: Routledge.

Omori, Chizu. 1994. "Ang Lee's First Film a Touching, Marvelous Mix of Comedy and Pathos." Review of *Pushing Hands. International Examiner* 21, no. 8 (3 May): 3.

Ong, Aihwa. 1993. "On the Edge of Empires: Flexible Citizenship among Chinese in Diaspora." *positions* 1, no. 3: 745–78.

———. 1997. "Chinese Modernities: Narratives of Nation and Capitalism." In *Ungrounded Empires: The Cultural Politics of Modern Chinese Transnationalism,* ed. Aihwa Ong and Donald M. Nonini. New York: Routledge, 171–202.

Ong, Peter. 1995–1996. "Sense and Sensibility . . . Sensational!" *Asian New Yorker,* Dec.–Jan., 12+.

Ong, Walter. 1990. *Orality and Literacy: The Technologizing of the Word.* London: Routledge.

Ono, Kent A. 1993. *Representations of Resistance and Subjectivity in Japanese American Discourse.* Ann Arbor: UMI.

———. 1995. "Re/signing 'Asian American': Rhetorical Problematics of Nation." *Amerasia Journal* 21, nos. 1–2: 67–78.

———. 2000. "Re/membering Spectators: Meditations on Japanese American Cinema," in Hamamoto and Liu.

Onodera, Midi. 1990. "A Displaced View." In *Yellow Peril Reconsidered,* ed. Paul Wong. Vancouver: On Edge, 28–31.

———. 1995. "Locating the Displaced View." In *Feminisms in the Cinema,* ed. Laura Pietropaolo and Ada Testaferri. Bloomington: Indiana University Press, 20–27.

O'Toole, Lawrence. 1982. "Chinese Translations." Review of *Chan Is Missing. MacLean's* 95, no. 36 (6 Sept.): 54.

Owens, Craig. 1992. *Beyond Recognition: Representation, Power, and Culture.* Berkeley: University of California Press.

Pacheco, Patrick. 1993. "Cultural Provocateur: In 'The Wedding Banquet,' Ang Lee Stirs Up Custom." *Los Angeles Times,* 4 Aug., F1+.

Pang, Amy. 1993. "Janice Tanaka Finds the Present by Tracing Her Father's Past: *Who's Going to Pay for These Donuts, Anyway?* Debuts June 22." *AsianWeek* 14, no. 43 (18 June): 32.

Park, Aaron Han Joon. 1996. " 'Bride' Shows Harshness of Planned Marriage." Review of *Picture Bride. Daily Iowan,* 21 Feb., 6B.

Park, Jeannie. 1987. "The First Decade: The Asian American International Film Festival." *The Independent,* Nov., 25–27.

Parker, Andrew, Mary Russo, Doris Sommer, and Patricia Yaeger, eds. 1992. *Nationalism and Sexualities.* New York: Routledge.

Pateman, Carole. 1989. *The Disorder of Women.* Stanford: Stanford University Press.

Patterson, Richard. 1983. "Chan Is Missing, or How to Make a Successful Feature for $22,315.92." *American Cinematographer,* Feb., 32–39.

Payne, Robert M. 1997. "Visions of Silence [*History and Memory, Who's Going to Pay for These Donuts, Anyway?*]." *Jump Cut* 41: 67–76.

Pêcheux, Michel. 1982. *Language, Semantics, and Ideology.* New York: St. Martin's Press.

Peckham, Linda. 1989. "Surname Viet Given Name Nam: Spreading Rumors and Ex/Changing Histories." *Frame/Work* 2, no. 3: 31–35. Rpt. in Feng (2002), 235–42.

Penley, Constance, ed. 1988. *Feminism and Film Theory.* New York: Routledge.

Perrée, Rob. 1988. *Into Video Art: The Characteristics of a Medium.* Amsterdam: Idea Books.

Peterson, James. 1994. *Dreams of Chaos, Visions of Order: Understanding the American Avant-garde Cinema.* Detroit: Wayne State University Press.

Petrakis, John. 1997. "Asian American Filmmakers Focus on Themes of Transition." *Chicago Tribune,* 4 Apr., n.p.

Peyton, Patricia. 1979. *Reel Change: A Guide to Social Issue Films.* San Francisco: Film Fund.

Phelan, Peggy. 1993. *Unmarked: The Politics of Performance.* London: Routledge.

Picache, Beverly R. 1992. "Peter Wang's 'First Date': Growing Up in 1950s Taiwan." *AsianWeek* 14, no. 1 (21 Aug.): 22.

———. 1993. "*From Hollywood to Hanoi* Mixes Personal with Political." *AsianWeek* 14, no. 31 (26 Mar.): 28.

Pitman, Randy. 1990. "Video Movies." Review of *Chan Is Missing. Library Journal,* Jan., 164.

Porter, Dennis. 1994. "*Orientalism* and Its Problems," in P. Williams and Chrisman, 150–61.

Pui San Lok, Susan. 1999. "Staging/Translating: *Surname Viet Given Name Nam.*" *Third Text* 46 (spring): 61–72.

Rabinovitz, Lauren. 1991. *Points of Resistance: Women, Power and Politics in the New York Avant-garde Cinema, 1943–71.* Urbana: University of Illinois Press.

Reddy, Gita. n.d. "Culture Clash: Asian American Independents on the Edge." *A. Magazine* 2, no. 2: 33–35.

———. 1994a. Review of *From Hollywood to Hanoi. Cineaste* 20, no. 3: 45–46.

———. 1994b. "Saigon, Not Forgotten: Tiana Thi Thanh Nga's Journey Back Home." *A. Magazine* 3, no. 1 (Mar.): 38–39.

Renov, Michael. 1994. "Warring Images: Stereotype and American Representations of the Japanese, 1941–1991." In *The Japan/America Film Wars: WW II Propaganda and Its Cultural Contexts,* eds. Abé Mark Nornes and Fukushima Yukio. Chur, Switzerland: Harwood Academic Publishers.

Renov, Michael, and Erika Suderburg, eds. 1996. *Resolutions: Contemporary Video Practices.* Minneapolis: University of Minnesota Press.

Reynaud, Bérénice. 1994. "Picture Bride." *Cahiers du Cinéma* 479–80 (May): 34.

Review of *The Wedding Banquet.* 1994. *Migration World* 22, nos. 2–3: 44.

Rich, B. Ruby. 1995. "Mother of the *Bride.*" *Village Voice* 16 May, 58.

Rizal, José. 1997. *Noli me tángere.* Trans. Ma Saloedad Lacson-Locsin. Honolulu: University of Hawai'i Press.

Roan, Jeanette. 1994. "*The Wedding Banquet:* You Must Now Kiss the Bride." Paper presented at Ohio University Film Conference, Athens, OH, Nov.
———. 2001. *Fictions of Faraway Places: Travel, Exoticism, and Cinema from High Imperialism to Global Culture.* Ann Arbor: UMI, 2001.
Rodowick, D. N. 1982. "The Difficulty of Difference." *Wide Angle* 5, no. 1: 4–15.
Rony, Fatimah Tobing. 1996. *The Third Eye: Race, Cinema, and Ethnographic Spectacle.* Durham, NC: Duke University Press.
———. 1995. "Kayo Hatta." *The Independent* 18, no. 2 (Mar.): 1516.
Rosario, Carina A. del. 1993. "Family Duty Begets Comic Disaster in *The Wedding Banquet.*" *International Examiner* 20, no. 15 (17 Aug.): 16.
Rosenbaum, Jonathan. 1989. "Undermining Authority." Review of *Surname Viet Given Name Nam. Chicago Reader,* 23 June, 14+.
Rosenstone, Robert A., ed. 1995. *Revisioning History: Film and the Construction of a New Past.* Princeton, NJ: Princeton University Press.
Rothenbuhler, Eric W., and John D. Peters. "Defining Phonography: An Experiment in Theory." Unpublished ms.
Roy, Sandip. 1997. "Screen Sisters." *A. Magazine,* Aug.–Sept., 71–73.
Rydell, Robert W. 1984. *All the World's a Fair: Visions of Empire at American International Expositions, 1876–1916.* Chicago: University of Chicago Press.
Sachs, Ira. 1992. "Looking for Chan: Mapping Identity in Asian-American Cinema." *Off Hollywood Report* 7, no. 1 (spring): 24–27+.
Said, Edward W. 1979. *Orientalism.* New York: Vintage/Random House.
Schamus, James. 1994. Introduction to *Eat Drink Man Woman/The Wedding Banquet: Two Films by Ang Lee.* Woodstock, NY: Overlook Press, vii–xii.
Schatz, Thomas. 1981. *Hollywood Genres: Formulas, Filmmaking, and the Studio System.* Philadelphia: Temple University Press.
Schleitwiler, Vincent. 1991. "Truth Is Stranger than 'Paradise.'" Review of *Come See the Paradise. Chicago Tribune,* 18 Jan., n.p.
Sedgwick, Eve Kosofsky. 1990. *Epistemology of the Closet.* Berkeley: University of California Press.
Seidenadel, Carl Wilhelm. 1909. *The First Grammar of the Language Spoken by the Bontoc Igorot, with a Vocabulary and Texts.* Chicago: Open Court Publishing.
Seitz, Michael H. 1982. "The Unhyped." Review of *Chan Is Missing. The Progressive,* July, 50–51.
Selig, Michael. 1993. "Genre, Gender, and the Discourse of War: The A/Historical and Vietman [*sic*] Films." *Screen* 34, no. 1 (spring): 1–18.
Sengupta, Somini. 1997. "Asian-American Films Speak a New Language of Multicultural Variety." *New York Times,* 28 July, national ed., B4.
Shah, Nayan. 1993. "Sexuality, Identity, and the Uses of History." In *A Lotus of Another Color: An Unfolding of the South Asian Gay and Lesbian Experience,* ed. Rakesh Ratti. Boston: Alyson Publications, 113–32.
Shapiro, Laura. 1993. "The Generation Gap in Chinatown." Review of *The Joy Luck Club. Newsweek,* 27 Sept., 70.
Sharman, Leslie Felperin. 1994. Review of *The Joy Luck Club. Sight and Sound,* Apr., 44–45.

Sherman, Sharon R. 1998. *Documenting Ourselves: Film, Video, and Culture.* Lexington: University Press of Kentucky.

Shin, Paul H. B. 1997. "Asians Opening New Doors: 20th Film Fest Offers a Key to Unlocking H'wood Dreams." (New York) *Daily News,* 17 July, n.p.

Shint, David. 1994. "Cooking to Compensate: Director Ang Lee." *The Stranger,* 16 Aug., n.p.

Shumway, David R. 1995. "Screwball Comedies: Constructing Romance, Mystifying Marriage." In *Film Genre Reader II,* ed. Barry Keith Grant. Austin: University of Texas Press, 381–401.

———. 1998. "American Romance: *Casablanca* and *Gone with the Wind.*" Unpublished essay.

Simon, John. 1993. "Chinoiserie." Review of *The Joy Luck Club. National Review,* 15 Nov., 61–62.

Sinha, Reuben. 1996. "Deepa Mehta: Fire." *Masala* 11, no. 5 (31 Dec.): 38.

Siskel, Gene. 1982. " 'Chan' Reflects Life, Not Stereotypes." *Chicago Tribune,* 10 Sept., sec. 3, p. 1+.

Sklar, Robert. 1993. *Film: An International History of the Medium.* New York: Abrams.

Sklar, Robert, and Charles Musser, eds. 1990. *Resisting Images: Essays on Cinema and History.* Philadelphia: Temple University Press.

Smith, Craig R. 1992. "A Rare Shot at Screen Stardom for Asians." *Wall Street Journal,* 1 Sept., A12.

Smith, Valerie. 1992. "The Documentary Impulse in Contemporary U.S. African-American Film." In *Black Popular Culture: A Project by Michele Wallace,* ed. Gina Dent. Seattle: Bay Press.

Sondrup, Steven P. 1997. "Hanyu at the Joy Luck Club." In *Cultural Dialogue and Misreading,* eds. Mabel Lee and Meng Hua. Honolulu: University of Hawaii Press, 400–408.

Sollors, Werner. 1986. *Beyond Ethnicity: Consent and Descent in American Culture.* New York: Oxford University Press.

Spivak, Gayatri Chakravorty. 1994. "Can the Subaltern Speak?" in P. Williams and Chrisman, 66–111.

Stack, Peter. 1991. "Marin Film Maker Loves Her Success." *San Francisco Chronicle,* 20 June, E2.

Stam, Robert. 1989. *Subversive Pleasures: Bakhtin, Cultural Criticism, and Film.* Baltimore: Johns Hopkins University Press.

———. 1991. "Bakhtin, Polyphony, and Ethnic/Racial Representation," in Friedman, 251–76.

Stanley, John. 1991. "Journey of '1,000 Pieces' Began with One Step." *San Francisco Chronicle,* 19 May, *Datebook* 24–25+.

Sterritt, David. 1982. "Lively, Enriching Tale of the Chinese-American Experience." Review of *Chan Is Missing. Christian Science Monitor,* 1 July, 18.

———. 1989. "War's Impact Seen by Vietnamese Eyes." Review of *Surname Viet Given Name Nam. Christian Science Monitor,* 3 Apr., 11.

———. 1993. "'Joy Luck Club' Comes to Screen." *Christian Science Monitor,* 16 Sept., 11.

Stevens, Walter B. 1904. *The Forest City.* 30 vols. St. Louis: N.D. Thompson Publishing.

Stone, Albert E. 1982. *Autobiographical Occasions and Original Acts: Versions of American Identity from Henry Adams to Nate Shaw.* Philadelphia: University of Pennsylvania Press.

Stone, Jay. 1997. "*Fire* burns Beautifully Despite Obvious Agenda." *Ottawa Citizen,* 5 Dec., D3.

Stone, Judy. 1991. "A Woman's Journey from East to West." Review of *Thousand Pieces of Gold. San Francisco Chronicle,* 22 May, E2.

———. 1993. "Wayne Wang: Caught in Cross-Cultural Fire." (Toronto) *Globe and Mail,* 3 Sept., D1–2.

Stoos, Toni, and Thomas Kellein, eds. 1993. *Name June Paik: Video Time, Video Space.* New York: Abrams.

Straayer, Chris. 1990. "The She-man: Postmodern Bi-sexed Performance in Film and Video." *Screen* 31, no. 3 (summer): 262–80.

Studlar, Gaylyn. 1985. "Masochism and the Perverse Pleasures of Cinema," in Nichols 1985, 602–21.

Sturken, Marita. 1996. "The Politics of Video Memory: Electronic Erasures and Inscriptions." In Renov and Suderburg. Rpt. in Feng (2002), 173–84.

———. 1997. "Absent Images of Memory: Remembering and Reenacting the Japanese Internment." *Positions* 5, no. 3 (winter): 687–707.

Suderburg, Erika. 1996. "The Electronic Corpse: Notes for an Alternative Language of History and Amnesia." In Renov and Suderburg (1996).

Sun, Kevin. 1997a. "The Next Wave." *AsianWeek,* 28 Feb., 18.

———. 1997b. "Shooting from the Hip." *AsianWeek,* 24 Jan., 19–20.

———. 1997c. "Youngbloods: A Toast to Asian American Independents." *Release Print,* Mar., n.p.

"'Sunsets' Directors Tell It Like It Is." 1997. (Stanford) *Daily Intermission,* 27 Feb., 11.

Suyin, Han. 1976. *The Crippled Tree.* St. Albans, England: Panther.

Tajima, Renee E. 1989a. "Lotus Blossoms Don't Bleed: Images of Asian Women." In *Making Waves: An Anthology of Writings by and about Asian American Women,* ed. Asian Women United of California [Diane Yen-Mei Wong]. Boston: Beacon Press, 308–18.

———. 1989b. "War Booty." Review of *Eat a Bowl of Tea. The Village Voice,* 1 Aug., 67.

———. 1991. "Moving the Image: Asian American Independent Filmmaking 1970–1990," in UCLA Asian American Studies Center (1991), 10–33.

———. 1996. "Site-seeing through Asian America: On the Making of Fortune Cookies." In *Mapping Multiculturalism,* eds. Avery F. Gordon and Christopher Newfield. Minneapolis: University of Minnesota Press, 263–94.

Tajiri, Rea. 1991. "Rea Tajiri [Artist Page]." *Felix* 1, no. 1 (spring): 31–35.

———. 1999. "Director's Statement." http://www.strawberryfieldsfilm.com/sf-pages/sf-home.html (17 June).

Takahama, Valerie. 1998. "A Generational Shift: Asian-American Filmmakers Are Putting Their Own Spin on Independent Releases." *Orange County Register,* 24 May, *Show,* 8–9.

Takaki, Ronald. 1983. *Pau Hana: Plantation Life and Labor in Hawai'i, 1835–1920.* Honolulu: University of Hawai'i Press.

———. 1990. *Strangers from a Different Shore: A History of Asian Americans.* New York: Penguin.

Tamblyn, Christine. 1996. "Qualifying the Quotidian: Artist's Video and the Production of Social Space." In Renov and Suderburg (1996).

Tan, Amy. 1989a. *The Joy Luck Club.* New York: G. P. Putnam's Sons.

———. 1989b. "Watching China." *Glamour,* Sept., 302–3.

———. 1991a. "Lost Lives of Women." *Life* 14, no. 4 (Apr.): 90–91.

———. 1991b. "Mother Tongue." In *The Best American Essays: 1991,* ed. Joyce Carol Oates.

———. 1992. *The Moon Lady.* New York: Macmillan.

Tanaka, Janice. 1991. "Electrons and Reflective Shadows," in UCLA Asian American Studies Center, 206–7.

———. 1993. "Exchange: The Nature of Narrative." *Felix* 1, no. 3 (fall): 86–90.

Taylor, Diane. 1998. "Lesbian Sisters, Freaky In-laws and Pervy Men. This Is Indian Life as Deepa Mehta Knows It." (London) *Guardian,* 13 Nov., 10.

Terry, Patricia. 1994. "A Chinese Woman in the West: *Thousand Pieces of Gold* and the Revision of the Heroic Frontier." *Literature/Film Quarterly* 22, no. 4: 222–26.

———. 1995. "It's a Wrap: The 1995 Sundance Film Festival." *The Independent* 18, no. 3 (Apr.): 36–39.

"Thackeray's Terms for Screening of 'Fire.'" 1998. *The Hindu,* 14 Dec., n.p.

Thomas, Kevin. 1997. "'Fire' Is a Daring Tale of Love in India." *Los Angeles Times,* 27 Aug., F5.

Thompson, Kristin, and David Bordwell. 1994. *Film History: An Introduction.* New York: McGraw-Hill.

Thomson, David. 1985. "Chinese Takeout: Wayne Wang Interviewed." *Film Comment* 21, no. 5 (Sept.–Oct.): 23–28.

Thornham, Sue, ed. 1999. *Feminist Film Theory: A Reader.* New York: New York University Press.

Tiana (Thi Thanh Nga). 1995. "The Long March: From Wong to Woo: Asians in Hollywood." *Cineaste* 21, no. 4: 38–40.

Tibbetts, John C. 1994. "A Delicate Balance: An Interview with Wayne Wang about *The Joy Luck Club.*" *Literature/Film Quarterly* 22, no. 1: 2–6.

Titone, Julie. 1996. "Unraveler: Moscow Woman Digs for Facts about Legendary Chinese Woman." *Spokesman-Review* (Spokane, WA), 15 Dec., Washington ed., B6.

Tolentino, Roland B. 1997. "Identity and Different in 'Filipino/a American' Media Arts." *Amerasia Journal* 23, no. 2: 137–61.

Travers, Peter. 1990. Review of *Life Is Cheap . . . But Toilet Paper Is Expensive. Rolling Stone,* 20 Sept., 48.

Trinh T. Minh-ha. 1988. "Naked Spaces: Living Is Round." *Cinematograph* 3: 65–78.

———. 1989. *Woman, Native, Other: Writing Postcoloniality and Feminism.* Bloomington: Indiana University Press.

———. 1990. "Critical Reflections." *Artforum* 28, no. 10 (summer): 132–33.

———. 1991. *When the Moon Waxes Red: Representation, Gender, and Cultural Politics.* New York: Routledge.

———. 1992. *Framer Framed.* New York: Routledge.

———. 1999. *Cinema Interval.* New York: Routledge.

Tseo, George K. Y. 1996. "Joy Luck: The Perils of Transcultural 'Translation.'" *Literature/Film Quarterly* 24, no. 4: 338–43.

Turan, Kenneth. 1993. Review of *Fire. Los Angeles Times,* 4 Aug., F1.

Turner, Graeme. 1992. "'It Works for Me': British Cultural Studies, Australian Cultural Studies, Australian Film." In *Cultural Studies,* eds. Lawrence Grossberg, Cary Nelson, and Paula Treichler. New York: Routledge, 640–53.

Ty, Eleanor. 1996. "Exoticism Repositioned: Old and New World Pleasures in Wang's *Joy Luck Club* and Lee's *Eat Drink Man Woman.*" In *Changing Representations of Minorities East and West.* Honolulu: University of Hawai'i Press, 59–74.

"U of Penn Features Margaret Mead Festival." 1997. *Philadelphia Tribune,* 7 Mar., E11.

UCLA Asian American Studies Center and Visual Communications. 1991. *Moving the Image: Independent Asian Pacific American Media Arts,* ed. Russell Leong. Seattle: University of Washington Press.

Ungar, Steven. 1989. "Persistence of the Image: Barthes, Photography, and the Resistance to Film." In *Signs in Culture: Roland Barthes Today,* eds. Steven Ungar and Betty R. McGraw. Iowa City: University of Iowa Press, 139–56.

Van Buren, Cassandra. 1992. "Family Gathering: Release from Emotional Internment." *Jump Cut* 37 (July): 56–63.

Van Gelder, Lawrence. 1996. "Both Epic and Feminist, From India." Review of *Fire. New York Times,* 2 Oct., C16.

Viviano, Frank. 1987. "From Charlie Chan to Hyphenated Cinema." *Far Eastern Economic Review,* 30 July, 34–35.

Voedisch, Lynn. 1997. "Asian Artistry: Films with Bicultural Basis." *Chicago Sun-Times,* 4 Apr., *Weekend Plus,* 38.

Wallace, Michele. 1993. "Race, Gender, and Psychoanalysis in Forties Film: *Lost Boundaries, Home of the Brave,* and *The Quiet One.*" In *Black American Cinema,* ed. Manthia Diawara. New York: Routledge, 257–71.

Wang, L. Ling-chi. 1995. "The Structure of Dual Domination: Toward a Paradigm for the Study of the Chinese Diaspora in the United States." *Amerasia Journal* 21, nos. 1–2: 149–69.

Wang, Paul. 1991. Review of *Thousand Pieces of Gold. Asian New Yorker,* Nov., 4.

Wang, Wayne. 1984. *Chan Is Missing.* Ed. Diane Mei Lin Mark. Honolulu: Bamboo Ridge Press.

Warner, Michael. 1993. *Fear of a Queer Planet: Queer Politics and Social Theory.* Minneapolis: University of Minnesota Press.

Warren, Michael. 1995. "Ang Lee on a Roll: The Director of *The Wedding Banquet* and *Eat Drink Man Woman* Attempts an English Classic." *AsianWeek* 17, no. 5 (22 Sept.): 13.

Warshow, Robert. 1970. "Movie Chronicle: The Westerner." In *The Immediate Experience: Movies, Comics, Theatre and Other Aspects of Popular Culture.* New York: Antheneum, 135–54.

Waugh, Thomas. 1998. "Good Clean Fung." *Wide Angle* 20, no. 2: 164–75.

Wegars, Priscilla. 1993. *Hidden Heritage: Historical Archaeology of the Overseas Chinese.* Amityville, NY: Baywood Publishing Company.

Wei, William. 1993. *The Asian American Movement.* Philadelphia: Temple University Press.

Weinraub, Bernard. 1993. "'I Didn't Want to Do Another Chinese Movie.'" *New York Times,* 5 Sept., sec. 2, p. 7+.

White, Armond. 1989. "The 18th New Directors/New Films Festival." *Film Comment* 25, no. 3 (May–June): 69–72.

White, Jerry. 1995. "Spencer Nakasako and Sokly Ny: Documentarians." *The Independent,* Dec., 16–17.

Williams, Alan. 1984. "Is a Radical Genre Criticism Possible?" *Quarterly Review of Film Studies* 9, no. 2 (spring): 121–25.

Williams, Patrick, and Laura Chrisman, eds. 1994. *Colonial Discourse and Post-Colonial Theory.* New York: Columbia University Press.

Williams, Raymond. 1983. *Keywords: A Vocabulary of Culture and Society.* Revised ed. New York: Oxford University Press.

Williamson, Bruce. 1991. Review of *Thousand Pieces of Gold. Playboy,* Dec., n.p.

Wilmington, Michael. 1991. "Valuable Views of Old West in 'Gold.'" *Los Angeles Times,* 26 June, F8.

———. 1995. "Small Triumph." Review of *Smoke. Chicago Tribune,* 19 June, sec. 2, p. 5.

Wise, Kelly. 1983. "Marlon Fuentes Unites Icons with Earth Magic." *Boston Globe,* 15 Nov., 75.

Wolff, Kurt. 1989. "Local Filmmaker Questions Authority [Trinh T. Minh-ha]." *San Francisco Bay Guardian,* 15 Feb., 23.

Wong, Eugene Franklin. *On Visual Media Racism.* New York: Arno Press, 1978.

Wong, Paul, ed. 1990. *Yellow Peril Reconsidered.* Vancouver: On Edge.

Wong, Sau-Ling C. 1995a. "Denationalization Reconsidered: Asian American Cultural Criticism at a Theoretical Crossroads." *Amerasia Journal* 21, nos. 1–2: 1–27.

———. 1995b. "'Sugar Sisterhood': Situating the Amy Tan Phenomenon." In *The Ethnic Canon: Histories, Institutions, and Interventions,* ed. David Palumbo-Liu. Minneapolis: University of Minnesota Press, 174–210.

Wong, Wayman. 1981. "A Mystery Movie Is Actually Much More." Review of *Chan Is Missing. San Francisco Examiner,* 10 Dec., E10.

Woo, Elaine. 1982. "His Bargain-Basement Movie Is a Surprise Hit." *Los Angeles Herald Examiner,* 29 July, B1+.

Wynne, Robert Edward. 1978. *Reaction to the Chinese in the Pacific Northwest and British Columbia, 1850 to 1910*. New York: Arno Press.

Wynter, Leon E. 1993. "Business and Race: Joy Luck's Good Luck Bypassed Ethnicity." *Wall Street Journal,* 6 Dec., B1.

Xing, Jun. 1994. "Imagery, Counter Memory, and the Re-visioning of Asian American History: Rea Tajiri's History and Memory for Akiko and Takashige." In *A Gathering of Voices on the Asian American Experience,* ed. Annette White-Parks et al. Fort Atkinson, WI: Highsmith Press, 93–100.

———. 1998. *Asian America through the Lens.* Walnut Creek, CA: Altamira-Sage.

Xu, Ben. 1994. "Memory and the Ethnic Self: Reading Amy Tan's *The Joy Luck Club.*" *MELUS* 19, no. 1 (spring): 3–18.

Yamada, Mitsuye. 1992. *Camp Notes and Other Poems.* 1976. Latham, NY: Kitchen Table.

Yang, Jeff. 1992. "Shooting Back." *Village Voice,* 19 May, n.p.

Yeh Yueh-yu. 1998. "Defining 'Chinese.'" *Jump Cut* 42: 73–76.

Young, Donald, and Linda Li. 1998. "Distribution on a Shoestring Budget: The Inside Scoop from Quentin Lee and Chris Chan Lee." *Asian American Network* 15, no. 3 (fall): 6–8.

Yu, Jessica. 1993a. "I Was Drafted into the *Joy Luck Club.*" *Asian New Yorker,* Nov., 14.

———. 1993b. "Only Yu." *Los Angeles Times Magazine,* 24 Oct., n.p.

Zeitgeist. [Official Web site for *Fire.*] http://www.zeitgeistfilm.com/current/fire/

INDEX

Peter X Feng is Associate Professor of English and Women's Studies at the University of Delaware.

Library of Congress Cataloging-in-Publication Data

Feng, Peter X.
Identities in motion : Asian American film and video / Peter X Feng.
p. cm.
Includes bibliographical references and index. ISBN 0-8223-2983-2 (alk. paper) —
ISBN 0-8223-2996-4 (pbk. : alk. paper)
1. Asian Americans in motion pictures.
2. Asian Americans in the motion picture industry. I. Title.
PN1995.9.A77 F46 2002
791.43'6520395—dc21 2002003056